Quod scriptura, non iubet vetat

The Latin translates, "What is not commanded in scripture, is forbidden:'

On the Cover: Baptists rejoice to hold in common with other evangelicals the main principles of the orthodox Christian faith. However, there are points of difference and these differences are significant. In fact, because these differences arise out of God's revealed will, they are of vital importance. Hence, the barriers of separation between Baptists and others can hardly be considered a trifling matter. To suppose that Baptists are kept apart solely by their views on Baptism or the Lord's Supper is a regrettable misunderstanding. Baptists hold views which distinguish them from Catholics, Congregationalists, Episcopalians, Lutherans, Methodists, Pentecostals, and Presbyterians, and the differences are so great as not only to justify, but to demand, the separate denominational existence of Baptists. Some people think Baptists ought not teach and emphasize their differences but as E.J. Forrester stated in 1893, "Any denomination that has views which justify its separate existence, is bound to promulgate those views. If those views are of sufficient importance to justify a separate existence, they are important enough to create a duty for their promulgation ... the very same reasons which justify the separate existence of any denomination make it the duty of that denomination to teach the distinctive doctrines upon which its sepa- rate existence rests." If Baptists have a right to a separate denominational life, it is their duty to propagate their distinctive principles, without which their separate life cannot be justified or maintained.

Many among today's professing Baptists have an agenda to revise the Baptist distinctives and redefine what it means to be a Baptist. Others don't understand why it even matters. The books being reproduced in the *Baptist Distinctives Series* are republished in order that Baptists from the past may state, explain and defend the primary Baptist distinctives as they understood them. It is hoped that this Series will provide a more thorough historical perspective on what it means to be distinctively Baptist.

The Lord Jesus Christ asked, *"And why call ye me, Lord, Lord, and do not the things which I say?"* (Luke 6:46). The immediate context surrounding this question explains what it means to be a true disciple of Christ. Addressing the same issue, Christ's question is meant to show that a confession of discipleship to the Lord Jesus Christ is inconsistent and untrue if it is not accompanied with a corresponding submission to His authoritative commands. Christ's question teaches us that a true recognition of His authority as Lord inevitably includes a submission to the authority of His Word. Hence, with this question Christ has made it forever impossible to separate His authority as King from the authority of His Word. These two principles—the authority of Christ as King and the authority of His Word—are the two most fundamental Baptist distinctives. The first gives rise to the second and out of these two all the other Baptist distinctives emanate. As F.M. Iams wrote in 1894, "Loyalty to Christ as King, manifesting itself in a constant and unswerving obedience to His will as revealed in His written Word, is the real source of all the Baptist distinctives:' In the search for the *primary* Baptist distinctive many have settled on the Lordship of Christ as the most basic distinctive. Strangely, in doing this, some have attempted to separate Christ's Lordship from the authority of Scripture, as if you could embrace Christ's authority without submitting to what He commanded. However, while Christ's Lordship and Kingly authority can be isolated and considered essentially for discussion's sake, we see from Christ's own words in Luke 6:46 that His Lordship is really inseparable from His Word and, with regard to real Christian discipleship, there can be no practical submission to the one without a practical submission to the other.

In the symbol above the Kingly Crown and the Open Bible represent the inseparable truths of Christ's Kingly and Biblical authority. The Crown and Bible graphics are supplemented by three Bible verses (Ecclesiastes 8:4, Matthew 28:18-20, and Luke 6:46) that reiterate and reinforce the inextricable connection between the authority of Christ as King and the authority of His Word. The truths symbolized by these components are further emphasized by the Latin quotation - *quod scriptura, non iubet vetat*— i.e., "What is not commanded in scripture, is forbidden:' This Latin quote has been considered historically as a summary statement of the regulative principle of Scripture. Together these various symbolic components converge to exhibit the two most foundational Baptist Distinctives out of which all the other Baptist Distinctives arise. Consequently, we have chosen this composite symbol as a logo to represent the primary truths set forth in the *Baptist Distinctives Series.*

TRACTS

ON

LIBERTY OF CONSCIENCE

AND

PERSECUTION

TRACTS

ON

LIBERTY OF CONSCIENCE

AND

PERSECUTION.

1614 — 1661.

EDITED FOR

𝕿𝖍𝖊 𝕳𝖆𝖓𝖘𝖊𝖗𝖉 𝕶𝖓𝖔𝖑𝖑𝖞𝖘 𝕾𝖔𝖈𝖎𝖊𝖙𝖞,

WITH AN HISTORICAL INTRODUCTION,

BY

EDWARD BEAN UNDERHILL.

With a Biographical Sketch of the Author by John Franklin Jones

---

LONDON:
PRINTED FOR THE SOCIETY, BY
J. HADDON, CASTLE STREET, FINSBURY.
M.DCCC.XLVI.

he Baptist Standard Bearer, Inc.

NUMBER ONE IRON OAKS DRIVE • PARIS, ARKANSAS 72855

Thou hast given a *standard* to them that fear thee;
that it may be displayed because of the truth.
– *Psalm 60:4*

Reprinted 2006

by

THE BAPTIST STANDARD BEARER, INC.
No. 1 Iron Oaks Drive
Paris, Arkansas 72855
(479) 963-3831

THE WALDENSIAN EMBLEM
lux lucet in tenebris
"The Light Shineth in the Darkness"

ISBN# 157978996X

THE

HANSERD KNOLLYS SOCIETY,

FOR THE

PUBLICATION OF THE WORKS OF EARLY ENGLISH AND OTHER BAPTIST WRITERS.

It has been a matter of regret with many, that the writings of the early members and ministers of the Baptist churches of this country should be comparatively so little known. From various causes the present appears to be a favourable time to reprint such of them as may be deemed worthy of perpetuation, from their historical or theological importance.

These writings are confined to no peculiarity of sentiment, but embrace every topic of divine truth, which the word of God presents for the salvation of the believer, as well as for the regulation of the church of Christ.

To the Baptists, it will be seen, belongs the honour of first asserting in this land, and of establishing on the immutable basis of just argument and scripture rule, the right of every man to worship God as conscience dictates, in submission only to divine command. Through evil and through good report—" in cruel mockings and scourgings, yea, moreover in bonds and imprisonments,"-they held fast to the liberty of Christ.

Rejecting the authority of men in matters of faith, they wrote with great simplicity and directness of purpose. Scripture alone was their authority, and excepting some of their polemical works, their productions are remarkably free from that parade of learning which was the fault of their age.

They were not however destitute of learning. Most of the early Baptists had had a university education : and if this privilege was not enjoyed by their successors, it was because the national seats of learning denied it to them. The names of Bampfield, Canne, Cornwell, Danvers, Delaune, Du Veil, Denne, Grantham, Jessey, Knollys, Smyth, and Tombes, not to mention others, afford sufficient proof that the Baptist churches were not destitute of able and learned expounders of their sentiments, eminent for their attainments both in classical and divine knowledge.

The historical value of the works it is proposed to reproduce is very great. Their authors exercised no mean influence on the course of national affairs during the period of Cromwell's protectorate, and they became in subsequent reigns, as they had been in times preceding the Commonwealth, the especial objects of ecclesiastical and political persecution. These productions form therefore an important element in the study of that eventful and stirring time. But especially interesting do these works appear as the documents from which may be learnt the opinions and the bitter trials of those men to whom the Baptist body owes its existence in this country :—in whose stripes, and bonds, and death, was laid the foundation of that liberty we now enjoy.

As theological writers they are characterized by fervour of spirit; deep study of the word of God ; great facility of application of divine truths to passing events ; a holy attachment to " the truth as it is in Jesus ; " clear and pungent exhibitions of the word of life ; an uncompromising adherence to the scriptures as the rule of doctrine, practice, and ecclesiastical organization and discipline; and finally, a fearless following of their convictions, derived from the divine oracles.

There are also wanting for our congregational and family libraries works of this kind. It is to be feared that as a body we are too ignorant of our own history, and of the great and good men who lost all in the maintenance of our principles. Our young people especially need information on these points. Moreover they are needed for the libraries of our ministers. Even our collegiate institutions possess but very few, and such as still exist are daily becoming more scarce and inaccessible. The collection proposed would furnish at a very small cost a series of works peculiarly adapted to their use.

It is proposed therefore to reprint by an annual subscription of ten shillings and sixpence, all or such of the works of the early English, or other Baptists, as the Council shall decide.

The series will include the works of both General and Particular Baptists ; Records and Manuscripts relating to the rise and formation of the Baptist churches; Translations of such works as may illustrate the sufferings of the Baptists and the extension of their principles, together with such Documents as are to be found only in large historical collections, or may not yet have appeared in an accessible form. On the baptismal controversy only those treatises will be given which are of acknowledged worth or historic value. The whole will be accompanied with biographical notices of the authors, and with such notes and illustrations as may be essential to their completeness. The publications will consist of works produced before the close of the seventeenth century.

It is hoped that the cheapness of the works, combined with their intrinsic value, will ensure for them a wide circulation among every class of readers. With a body of three thousand subscribers, the Council will be enabled to issue *three* octavo volumes annually. It is obvious that the larger the number of members, the more frequent will be the publication of the works.

The following list comprises the names of some whose works are intended to form part of the series;—Bampfield, Blackwood, Bunyan, Canne, Collier, Collins, Cornwall, Danvers, Delaune, Denne, Du Veil, Drapes, Grantham, Griffith, Helwys, How, Jeffrey, Jessey, Keach, Kiffin, King, Knollys, Lawrence, Palmer, Powell, Pendarves, Smyth, Stennett, Tombes, Roger Williams, &c., &c.

The first volume of the Society's publications, containing "Tracts on Liberty of Conscience," edited by Mr. EDWARD BEAN UNDERHILL, is now in the hands of the subscribers. The second volume, consisting of the Unpublished Records of the Broadmead Church, Bristol, from 1640—1686, will be immediately sent to press, to complete the first year's subscription.

As considerable delay has unavoidably occurred in discovering and acquiring the exceedingly rare tracts it is proposed to reprint, the first subscription will be carried on to the end of the present year, by which time the volumes for the years 1845—6, will have been published.

On the 1st of January, 1847, the second subscription will be regarded as due. The immediate transmission of subscriptions, and the names of additional subscribers, are requested, that no disappointment may be experienced in obtaining the volumes, since only a limited number are printed beyond what are actually subscribed for.

Terms of Subscription.

1. Every subscriber of ten shillings and sixpence annually will be entitled to one copy of every work issued during the year of his subscription.
2. Subscriptions will be considered due, in advance, on the first of January of every year.
3. Ministers obtaining *ten* subscribers annually will be entitled to one copy of each work published in the year for which such subscriptions are paid.
4. Books will be delivered, free of expense, in London, Edinburgh, and Dublin, from which places they will be sent at the cost of the subscriber by any channel he may appoint.

Subscriptions will be received by the Treasurer, at Vassall Road, Kennington, by the Honorary Secretaries, DR. DAVIES, at Stepney College, and Mr. UNDERHILL, of Avening House, near Stroud, or by any member of the Council; also by Mr. G. OFFOR, jun., Secretary, Baptist Mission House, Moorgate Street, London, to whom all communications for the Society should be addressed.

J. Haddon, Castle Street, Finsbury.

ADVERTISEMENT.

In the prospectus of the Hanserd Knollys Society it was stated, that " to the baptists belongs the honour of first asserting in this land, and of establishing on the immutable basis of just argument and scripture rule, the right of every man to worship God as conscience dictates, in submission only to divine command."

The Council have now the pleasure of laying before the Subscribers the earliest writings extant in our language, on this deeply important subject.

They were the first articulations of infant liberty. The voice of truth and Christianity was heard in the mild and gentle entreaties of their despised and calumniated authors: unfortunately it was unheeded, and soon spake in the whirlwind and the storm of contending armies and national convulsion.

Happier times have succeeded, and it is permitted us to reap the fruits of the humble, but noble and self-denying labours of these pioneers of the soul's freedom. They fell martyrs " for conscience' sake ; " it were ingratitude to withhold a coronal of deserved commendation, wreathed from the bright leaves and blossoms of the tree they planted in sorrow, and watered with their blood ; but under whose shadow it is our happiness to live.

It is scarcely necessary to add, that the Council must not be held responsible for the sentiments contained in these pieces ; their duty is accomplished by laying before their brethren these memorials of our forefathers without alteration or abridgment.

The Editor is alone responsible for the notes and illustrations, which are uniformly placed in brackets. He has to regret that in one instance he was unable to discover a copy of the original edition.

The Historical Introduction closes with the reign of Mary, as the accession of much new and original matter relating to the baptists of Elizabeth's reign, would, if added, have unduly enlarged the size of the volume : it will however form a most appropriate introduction to the next.

EDWARD BEAN UNDERHILL.

Oxford, April 13, 1846.

CONTENTS.

HISTORICAL INTRODUCTION.

SECTION I.

HENRY VIII.

AMIDST the many eminent and remarkable events that signalized the rise and establishment of the Reformation in England—next after the introduction of the word of God, translated, and for the first time printed in the language of the people, in the year 1526, by the martyr Tyndale—there is not one of greater moment, nor so productive of large and continuing results, as the transference to the reigning sovereign of the ecclesiastical authority till then exercised by the pope. The exaltation of the royal prerogative above all ecclesiastical claims, and the imposition of a form of belief, accordant with the convictions or policy of the secular magistrate, were leading features of that great movement. To this, duty, based on a supposed right, sternly called him, even should it lead to the forfeiture of the life of a conscientious opponent. Thus in every country where the Reformation took root, and flourished, the church became subordinate to the civil power. The royalties of Jesus Christ were swallowed up in the *regale* of human potentates.

b

It is not within our object to relate the tortuous policy unremittingly pursued by noble, priest, and king, during the early part of the sixteenth century, by which the way was prepared for the bringing in of the reformed doctrines; nor to mark those preliminary steps, which, terminating in the fall of Cardinal Wolsey, who had exercised a more than papal authority over the land, ushered in a complete change in the religious policy of the state.

But taking up at this point our national history, we shall briefly sketch, from its rise to its settlement in 1603, that interference of the secular power in the things of God, which has proved itself to be alike fatal to liberty of conscience, and to the scriptural form and purity of the church of Christ.

It is not improbable that the ambitious cardinal, failing in all his efforts to obtain the triple crown, and foiled at his own weapons by the very parties he was endeavouring to cajole, had at last conceived the idea of erecting an ecclesiastical authority in England which should be free from papal control.[1] In the matter of the divorce of Henry from queen Katharine, he had sought to obtain unlimited powers. He wished that the sentence of his legantine court should be final, subject neither to the revision nor to the reversal of the pope.[2]

But "his last and highest office as vicar-general, had brought into this kingdom a species of authority, altogether unknown; and in doing this, he had put a cup to the lips of his royal master, and afforded him one taste, for the first time, of the sweetness of dominion over all the clergy of the kingdom."[3]

In the cardinal's service had been trained Thomas Cromwell. For some time his employment was that of secretary: but he had been particularly useful to his master, in the

[1] Tyndale's Practice of Prelates. Works, vol. i. p. 480. Russell's edit.
[2] Dodd's Church History, vol. i.
p. 103. Tierney's edition.
[3] Anderson's Annals of the English Bible, vol. i. p. 224.

suppression of certain monasteries, the revenues of which were devoted to the establishment of Wolsey's colleges at Oxford and Ipswich. By and by we shall find him acting as vicar-general also, and following, with no mean results, in the steps of his predecessor.

The authority exercised by the cardinal, as legate à *latere*, especially in the celebrated trial of queen Katharine, was the proximate cause of his fall. This power, having its existence in the arrogant claims of the papacy, had been often a matter of parliamentary interference, denunciation, and enactment; and was therefore exercised in defiance of the law. But those statutes were inoperative. " Several cardinals before Wolsey had procured, and executed with impunity, a legantine power which was clearly contrary to them;" and, in his case, with the full knowledge and approbation of the king, who had even granted letters patent to Wolsey, freeing him from the legal consequences of this breach of the nation's law.[4] This, however, mattered not; Wolsey must fall, and with him the papal supremacy. That fall made way for the elevation of his servant Cromwell, the instrument in the hand of God to overthrow the domination of Rome.

Many things also conspired to render the assumption of a regal sovereignty over the church, palatable to all classes of the community. The adherents of the *new* learning, a rapidly increasing section of the people, of course saw without regret the papal tiara trodden in the mire. To them such an event appeared as the " beginning of days," as " life from the dead." Their conviction of the religious errors of Rome, and their attachment to the life-giving truths of the scriptures, just put so providentially into their hands, led them to hail with joy the dethronement of antichrist. Experience

Burnet's Hist. of Reformation, vol. i. p. 204. 8vo. edit. Oxford.

had not taught them, as it has their posterity, how bitter are the streams that flow from the fountain of ecclesiastical authority and power, when diluted and measured out by regal hands.

Not much less desirable, though for other reasons, did this assumption appear to the adherents of the *old* learning. The nation had through long centuries sighed and groaned, uttering often inarticulate moanings, while suffering the intolerable exactions of the papal see. Its wealth was for ever flowing into the coffers of the church, enriching a gorgeous ceremonial, and gloating an idle priesthood. All classes were impoverished by the innumerable levies made upon them. Crowds of cowled monks, bare-footed friars, and Sir priests, of innumerable grades,[5] lined the avenues of heaven and hell, to tax earth's pilgrims, stumbling on their way, to those regions of joy and woe. And again, these publicans and tax-gatherers, were themselves taxed, and their merchandize of souls excised, to sustain the triple crown in its grandeur, and in its pride.[6] Good catholics mourned over this, and longed for some relief.

The papacy itself had lost much of its former power and dread. But a few years since, and Rome, the "holy of holies" of Christendom, had been pillaged, and the pope, its high priest, a prisoner. And now its bulls and its briefs, its anathemas and its blessings, were alike unheeded by the nations, except so far as policy dictated their observance, or desired their fragment of influence. Mightier than human words were being uttered with unwonted power, and souls were emancipated from the chains of error and superstition.

The king's cherished project of a divorce from Katharine

[5] " For there one sort are your grace, your holiness, your fatherhood: another my lord bishop, my lord abbot, my lord prior ; another master doctor, father, bachelor, master parson, master vicar, and at the last cometh in simple Sir John."—Tyndale's Pract. of Prelates. Works, vol. i. p. 396.

[6] Ibid, p. 433.

of Aragon, his queen, seemed also on the point of failing. The pope, now subject to the wishes of the emperor Charles the Fifth, the uncle of the queen, dared not pronounce a judgment in Henry's favour. Universities, English and foreign, had in vain determined from scripture and canon law, the unlawfulness of his marriage with his brother's wife, and the invalidity of the pope's dispensation to authorize the same; Rome was silent. That divorce was destined to pluck the fairest jewel of the papal tiara from its gorgeous setting, " *To the intent that the living may know that the* MOST HIGH *ruleth in the kingdom of men, and giveth it to whomsoever he will, and setteth up over it the* BASEST OF MEN." [7]

The House of Commons, after seven years repose, was summoned to meet in 1529. It evinced much determination to limit the extortions and immunities, so long, and so profitably to the papacy, submitted to. Their short session of about six weeks, was signalized by a bold and successful attack upon some of the leading sources of clerical wealth. Certain bills for the correction of the abuses of ecclesiastical power, were passed, and soon laid before the Lords; but they left not the hands of the Commons "without severe reflections on the vices and corruptions of the clergy of that time; which were believed to flow from men who favoured Luther's doctrine in their hearts." [8] It was not without much debate, and opposition from the clergy, the conservators of all profitable abuses, that the bills were suffered to pass; Fisher, bishop of Rochester, bitterly complaining, that "the charge of abuses on the hierarchy proceeded from disaffection, and that nothing would content the Commons, but pulling down the church."

This disaffection must have proceeded to some considerable extent, even to something like free-thinking, if a

[7] Dan. iv. 17.

[8] Burnet, History of Reformation, i.

149. Collier's Eccles. Hist. iv. 131. 8vo. edit.

notable speech, recorded by Herbert, may be taken as an indication of what was passing in thoughtful minds; "Because the chief business of man's life," says this unnamed member of the Commons, "is to inquire into the means of being happy for ever, it is fit he should not resign himself to chance, but carefully compute upon the qualities and conduct of his spiritual guides. . . . . Every man may collect the more essential and demonstrative parts of his own religion, and lay them by themselves. Neither ought he to be overruled in his freedom by the discountenance of any other persuasion. Having thus exerted his reason, and implored the assistance of the Supreme Being, his next business will be to find out what inward means Providence has furnished for a test of truth and falsehood. . . . Clear universal truths should be first ascertained; they will never check the progress of our faith, nor weaken the authority of the church. So that whether the eastern or the western Christians, whether my lord of Rochester or Luther, whether Eccius or Zuinglius, Erasmus or Melancthon, are in the right, we of the laity shall suffer nothing by the disagreement." [9] A sign truly, was such language as this, of a coming change. Superstitions were relaxing their grasp; a new era was about to dawn upon the prostrate religion and liberty of man. For once, the church was verily in danger; it was the distant flash of the approahing storm. Once more parliament prohibited all suits to the court of Rome for dispensations on non-residence and pluralities, and this time not without effect. It is the first successful blow at the papal supremacy in England.

The time is come for its overthrow. Another power, as much opposed to liberty of conscience, will gather up the fragments, and, having fashioned them anew, rule for centuries more in the temple of God. Cromwell's services to

[9] Collier, iv. 132—134.

Wolsey are nearly at an end, and he must seek another
master.   Not an unfaithful servant, nor wanting in diligence,
he had not failed to profit in the service of ambition, chi-
canery, and intrigue.   He has a secret of state-craft worth
communicating; to no one more valuable than to Henry,
now styled by papal grace, "Defender of the Faith." . . .
"And, forasmuch, as now his majesty had to do with the
pope, his great enemy, there was in all England none so apt
for the king's purpose, which could say or do more in that
matter, than could Thomas Cromwell."   The necessity of
the case puts the king's hatred of this "apt" man in abeyance; and an interview, the germ of many future things, is
had in the king's " garden at Westminster, which was about
the year of our Lord 1530."

After his "most loyal obeisance, doing duty to the king,"
Cromwell proceeds to make especially "manifest unto his
highness, how his princely authority was abused, within his
own realm, by the pope and his clergy; who, being sworn
unto him, were afterwards dispensed the same, and sworn
anew unto the pope, so that he was as but half king, and
they but half his subjects, in his own land; which was derogatory to his crown, and utterly prejudicial to the common
laws of his realm.   Declaring therefore how his majesty
might accumulate to himself great riches, so much as all the
clergy in his realm was worth, if it so pleased him to take
the occasion now offered."   Advice this, admirably adapted
to be " right well liked" by the royal listener; nor was the
occasion suffered to pass without its due and profitable improvement.[1]

With the parliament of 1531, just previous to which this
memorable interview took place, the clergy also assembled in
convocation.   The first subject laid before them was Henry's

---

[1] Fox's Acts and Monuments, ii. 1076.   edit. 1610.

divorce, which was quickly despatched, the clergy seeming satisfied that the marriage was unlawful. A far more weighty question, one that touched their spiritual gains and immunities, remained behind. At the close of the year preceding, an indictment had been brought into the king's bench against the clergy of England, for breaking the statutes against provisors. A little while before, and cardinal Wolsey had fallen beneath the penalties of a *premunire* for illegally exercising his legantine authority; now, all who had appeared in his courts, or who in any way had acknowledged his unconstitutional power, were involved in his guilt, and its consequent forfeitures.[2] The king is but "following the vein" of Cromwell's counsel; nor is he slow in availing himself of the aid of his counsellor.

By whom can the rising wrath of the astonished clergy, at this bold invasion of their time-sanctioned immunities and jurisdiction, be sooner calmed, than by the man whose suggestions threatened to evoke a storm of hierarchical indignation, before whose blast princes and potentates had often fled away? Shall ecclesiastical power and assumption again rise superior to royal and parliamentary control? Will the *new ropes* be again broken *like a thread* from off the arms [3] of this

" Giant of mighty bone, and bold emprise?"—Milton.

Nay, its hour is come! "Cromwell entering with the king's signet into the clergy-house, and then placing himself among the bishops, began to make his oration— Declaring unto them the authority of a king, and the office of subjects, and especially the obedience of bishops and churchmen under public laws, necessarily provided for the profit and quiet of the commonwealth. Which

---

[2] Burnet, i. 194.   [3] Judges xvi. 12.

laws, notwithstanding, they had all transgressed and highly offended, in derogation of the king's royal estate, falling in the law of *premunire*, in that not only they had consented to the power legantine of the cardinal, but also in that they had all sworn to the pope, contrary to the fealty of their sovereign lord and king; and therefore had forfeited to the king all their goods, chattels, lands, possessions, and whatsoever livings they had. The bishops hearing this, were not a little annoyed, and first began to excuse and deny the fact; but after that Cromwell had shown them the very copy of their oath, made to the pope at their consecration, and the matter was so plain that they could not deny it, they began to shrink and to fall to entreaty, desiring respite to pause upon the matter." [4]

Resistance was in vain—popular feeling was against them —old attachments, the very superstitions on which they had fattened, now availed them nothing—every compassionate emotion for their pitiable condition was swallowed up in the one absorbing idea of their rapacity and licentiousness;—by the one they had exasperated the people, by the other loosened all sense of moral and religious obligation. Submission was the only course open to them, and to save their lands and livings, a grant, by way of composition, was proposed of some hundred and eighteen thousand pounds. "But now a question rose, compared with which, the entire substance of the whole body, their goods and chattels, their lands and livings, were but like the drop of a bucket, or the small dust of the balance; a question which was to affect not England alone, but Great Britain and Ireland, with all their dependencies in other quarters of the world, for many generations. The anticipated moment had now arrived when it was convenient to divulge that no subsidy would be accepted, unless his

[4] Fox's Acts and Mon. ii. 1066.

majesty were acknowledged in the petition or address as
' Head of the Church.' " [5]

The immediate concurrence of the clergy could not be expected to this important and far-reaching measure. They
demurred as to the meaning of the words. Misunderstandings,
they said, might arise in future years, of a phrase so general,
and dangerous consequences would probably result. For
three days, in secret conclave, they debated the matter, with
hot words and strife. To hasten their decision, further
penalties were freely threatened by Lord Rochford, Cromwell,
and others of the king's council. The sense of the house was
at last called for by archbishop Warham—the last of catholic
archbishops. Most were silent. He told them, " Silence
implied consent." " Then we are all silent," was the reply.
A more explicit resolution was ultimately agreed upon, the
king was acknowledged to be " Supreme Lord and Protector,"
and also, as far as is consistent with the laws of the gospel,
" Supreme Head of the Church of England." [6]

Yet were they extremely unwilling to acknowledge, to
themselves or others, the true character of this fatal conces-
sion. They avoided all recognition of the compulsory nature
of the subsidy, so reluctantly granted to the king. It was
only a benevolence or gratuity, an evidence of their gratitude,
particularly for the king's book against Luther, his active
suppression of heresies, and his gracious interference in
checking the insults of the Lutheran party. As for their
submission, it was "not only penned with a salvo, but thrown
into a parenthesis, as if it came in only by the by." Any
reference to the premunire, or to the legantine authority of
Wolsey, their submission to which had prepared the way for
this sore humiliation, was most carefully eschewed. Nine
bishops, sixty-two abbots and priors, with eighty-four of the

[5] Anderson, Annals, &c. i. 292, 293.   [6] Collier, iv. 178.

clergy of the province of Canterbury, carried this obnoxious measure.[7]

The convocation at York, led by Tunstal, the bishop of Durham, the archbishopric being then vacant, yielded not so soon to the king's demand. This prelate protests against the measure. He intimates that some heretics had already questioned the jurisdiction of their ordinaries, and sought to escape the censures of the church, by appealing to the supposed higher authority of the king. The words should be therefore more precise. They might mean that the king was supreme head in his dominions, under Christ, only in temporal matters, which he would most willingly acknowledge; or they might be made to mean, that the king's lordship, by the laws of the gospel, related to both spirituals and temporals, than which nothing could be more contrary to the teaching of the catholic church. To the former he would most cheerfully subscribe, but against the latter he must protest, and would enter his protest on the journals of the convocation. These views of the bishop met with a no less distinguished opponent than the king himself. "The bishop," says the royal polemic, "had proved our Saviour the head of the church, that he lodged the branches of his spiritual and temporal jurisdiction in different subjects, that he made a grant of the latter to princes, and that bishops were commissioned for the other. But then the text cited, to prove obedience due to princes, comprehends all persons, both clergy and laity, and no order of the hierarchy is exempted. It is true, you restrain this submission to temporal matters, but the scripture expressions are general and without reserve. For you do not stick to confess, that whatever power is necessary for the peace of civil society, is included in the chief magistrates' commission. From hence we infer, that

[7] Collier, iv. 179.

the prince is authorized to animadvert upon those who outrage religion, and are guilty of the breach of the divine
precepts.   For certainly we are not bound to give our own
laws a preference over those of God Almighty, nor punish
the violation of the one, and connive at the other.   All spiritual things, therefore, in which liberty or property is concerned, are necessarily included in the prince's power.   Our
Saviour himself had a sacerdotal character, and yet submitted
to Pilate's jurisdiction.   And St. Paul, though a priest of
apostolical distinction, makes no scruple to say, 'I stand at
Cæsar's judgment-seat, where I ought to be judged.'" [8]

Such are the most important of the arguments advanced in
this valuable document; sufficient to evince the ignorance
of the high parties engaged, of the true nature of the church
of Christ.   It also exhibits their unacquaintance with the
Christian laws of liberty and of obedience; by the one of
which the church is free from secular control, and by the
other bound to the observance of the statutes of the King
of kings, to whom alone belongs the power and the right to
punish all breaches of his precepts, in that community of
which he is the rightful and only Head.   It is the priest and
the prince in conflict, for the exercise of an usurped power
over the consciences and souls of men.   But the star of
princely power was in the ascendant, and York, in spite of
some other similar protests, must bend, with Canterbury, to
the yoke.

The step thus successfully gained, did not however amount
to the entire rejection of the papal authority; it was not a
complete, nor an irrevocable separation of the kingdom from
the Roman obedience.   A series of minor measures were
necessary before the end could come.   All hope of compro-
mise with Rome was not yet abandoned, nor were the king's
projects yet ripe for the full assertion of the nation's eccle-

[a] Collier, iv. 183.

siastical independence. It was, however, a golden opportunity for the Commons to endeavour the destruction of the many oppressive burdens under which the people groaned—efforts which subserved the schemes of Henry, in his intercourse with the Romish see.

At an early period of the parliamentary session of 1532, which began upon the 15th of January, the Commons presented to the king an address, praying for reformation of the many grievances occasioned by the immunities and privileges of the clergy.[9] Though the supplication was well received, two years elapsed before these grievances were entirely redressed. The people were, however, gratified that their complaints were at length listened to, and the hierarchy, with the pope, kept in awe.

But the clergy deserved some recompence for their submission to the supreme head of the church, constrained as it was. The abolition of the payment of annates, or firstfruits, a year's value of ecclesiastical benefices, demanded by the see of Rome, was their reward. The convocation resolved upon an address to their head concerning the matter; to him not unwelcome. Was it not a practical acknowledgment of his supremacy? "May it please the king's most noble grace," say they, "having tender compassion to the wealth of this his realm, which hath been so greatly extenuate and hindered by the payments of the said annates, and by other exactions and slights, by which the thesaure of this land hath been carried

---

[9] Rapin, i. p. 795. "Unto the laymen, whom they have falsely robbed, and from which they have divided themselves, and made them a several kingdom of themselves, they leave the paying of toll, custom, tribute; for unto all the charges of the realm will they not pay one mite; and the finding of all the poor, the repairing of the highways and bridges, the building and reparations of their abbies and cathedral churches, chapels, colleges; for which they send out their pardons daily by heaps, and gather a thousand pounds for every hundred that they bestow truly." Tyndale, Pract. of Prel. Works, i. 423. Many curious particulars are to be found of the "practices" of the clergy, in this remarkable production.

and conveyed beyond the mountains to the court of Rome, that the subjects of this realm be brought to great penury, and by necessity be forced to make their most humble complaint for stopping and restraining the said annates, and other exactions and expilations, taking for indulgencies and dispensations, legacies and delegacies, and other feats, which were too long to remember; to cause the said unjust exactions of annates to cease, and to be foredoen for ever, by acts of this his grace's high court of parliament." [1]   It was calculated that upwards of two millions and a half had passed from the country since the second year of Henry VII.; on this account alone parliament was not backward to fulfil their desires.   It was also an uprooting of one great branch of papal prerogative. They accordingly resolved that annates should cease to be levied, and that if his holiness would not accept a composition of five per cent. for his trouble in drawing up bulls, sealing them in lead, &c. [2] he should be opposed altogether in his demands.   Should he attempt to enforce their payment by excommunications, interdict, or other censures, the clergy were to be at liberty to disregard them, and to perform the divine services "of holy church, or any other thing necessary for the health of the souls of mankind as heretofore." [3]

Anti-papal principles must have been widely held, and alienation of feeling from Rome very prevalent among all classes of the people, that this provision against the papal ban should be made at the clergy's own request!   For thus runs their prayer—"Forasmuch as all good Christian men be more bound to obey God than any man, it may please the king's most noble grace to ordain in this present parliament,

---

[1] Strype's Memorials, I. ii. 160, 8vo. edit.

[2] "And as bishops pay for their bulls, even so do an infinite number of abbats in Christendome.   And other abbats and priors send after the same ensample daily unto Rome, to purchase licence to wear a mitre and a cross, and gay ornaments, to be as glorious as the best." Tyndale, Works, i, 434.

[3] Dodd's Ch. Hist. i. 236.   Collier, iv. 187.

that then the obedience of him and the people be withdrawn
from the see of Rome."⁴ Such a check to Romish exactions
was too consonant with the desires of the king and nation to
allow any delay in granting their request; yet with a
provision, that the king might confirm, or disannul the statute, or any part of it, within two years. In the following
year, however, it became by the king's letters patent, the law
of the land. And thus another link, and that no unimportant
one, was broken, in the chain of the pope's supremacy.

Gratifying as was this affair to the avarice of the clergy, it
is manifestly but another step in furtherance of the king's
designs. He was not indifferent to the favourable opportunity presented to him by the temper of the Commons, to
proceed in his "advised" course. In all former periods, the
sovereign had encountered a clergy sustained by popular
religious feeling, but that had been outraged by their rapacity
and unrestrained licence through a long series of years. The
clergy now stood alone, to meet as they could the attack of a
monarch whom the people regarded as their friend and saviour.
For "the Commons, being resolutely bent to humble the
clergy to the very ground, remonstrated against them in
several articles, which all terminate in this;—that an independent power in the clergy to make laws, though entirely
spiritual, was prejudicial to the civil magistrate, and derogatory to the royal prerogative."⁵

In the formation and execution of ecclesiastical laws, exempt from secular control, lay the great strength of the papal
hierarchy. As between it and the state there was no difference of opinion upon the right of some party to impose forms
of belief, and to enjoin by a law, binding upon the conscience,
whether assenting or dissenting, the profession of some religious faith, then called the catholic faith. Thus the ground

⁴ Strype's Memor. I. ii. 161   ⁵ Dodd, i. 238.

of conflict was narrowed to the question, whether the privilege
of making laws to bind the conscience should vest in the
church, or in the chief magistrate.   This privilege the clergy
had most disgracefully abused, if indeed it can exist without
abuse, and the European mind had risen in revolt against it.
But such was the very partial prevalence of a purely religious
purpose among the secular authorities in the various stages
of the reformation, that it soon became evident that either
party must fail of attaining its object, or of preserving its
immunities, if left dependent on its own strength alone.
Hence, the universal fusion of the regal with the popular
power in every country where the reformation prevailed, the
conflicts which arose between Rome and its hitherto dependent
sovereigns, and the recognition by the reformers of the supremacy of the civil magistrate in matters of faith;—a supremacy as fatal to liberty of conscience as was that of Rome,
though perhaps, on the whole, not so liable to perversion.
Temporal interests, varying in character and power, may
clash or coalesce with the religious views of the secular
authority, to the production of a more moderate and vacil-
lating treatment of spiritual concerns.   But to the attainment of the one object of ecclesiastical rulers, the government of man's soul, all interests, of every kind, are made
subservient, and it is carried out with a singleness of aim
and purpose, not to be acquired by the state.   To the secular
arm, however, the reformers trusted for their superiority over
Rome.   That alone, they supposed, could or would assure the
final triumph of the gospel.   This union was fatal to their
object, and jeopardized very early the existence of the
reformed churches.   Less than half a century witnessed the
almost entire banishment of a pure and simple piety from the
communities thus allied.

The complaint of the Commons coincided with the views,
and met with the entire acquiescence of the king.   Full of

alarm, the bishops and abbots returned distinct answers to every part of the complaint. The time for defiance was passed. Their independent action, their canonical authority, their right to consecrate and administer the sacraments, to censure erroneous opinions, and issue precepts concerning faith and morals, were in peril; but they will not abandon them without a struggle.

Had not the king sufficiently humbled them? Had they not already submitted to a headship, questionable by scripture and canon law? What then will be their position, if they yield their prescript, and hitherto uncontrolled privileges, into the hands of the civil magistrate?

Has the inanity of age, or the darkening shadow of their coming fate, paralyzed the uplifted arm, at which nations and mighty monarchs have often trembled, that *words* of persuasion and entreaty must suffice to screen their feebleness?

Verily their glory has waned; it is ready to vanish away; the magic spell of centuries is broken.

Such pleas, however, as can be found, shall be employed. Humility, a stranger to these priestly men, and flattery, not unknown to them, are heard once more to speak, perhaps somewhat mechanically, from priestly lips; " After our most humble wise, with our most bounden duty of honour and reverence to your most excellent majesty, endued of God with most incomparable wisdom and goodness; pleaseth it the same to understand that we, your orators, and daily bounden bedesmen, the ordinaries, have read and perused a certain supplication, which the Commons of your grace's most honourable parliament now assembled, have offered unto your highness, and by your command delivered to us, to make thereunto answer." And what, if they have fallen foul of the constitution, and made canons contradictory to the laws of the realm; and passed ecclesiastical regulations without the assent of the laity or the crown; and trespassed somewhat

upon the royal prerogative ; and oppressed liberty and property, interdicting lands and estates; and menaced with
excommunication every breach of their spiritual injunctions.
Is not their authority founded upon the holy scripture, and
the resolutions of holy church?—on grounds and principles
unquestionable, proper to test and try the reasonableness
of all other laws, both temporal and spiritual? By this rule,
therefore, they profess themselves willing to amend all
that is amiss, and hope his highness will not be backward
to alter such laws of the state as deviate from the inspired
writings, or clash with the privileges of the church, so that
harmony may prevail between both societies.

Displeasure appears upon the brow of their supreme head.
Their humility and flattery are alike unavailing to move his
determination, or to repress his scornful refusal of their
prayer. Their scribe, Gardiner, of late made bishop of
Winchester, must even write a letter of excuse; " Did not
his highness's book against Luther concede the legislative
authority of the clergy in matters spiritual? But he hopes
his majesty will excuse his mistakes, and ignorance of the
strength of those proofs his majesty can produce. Still,
bishops have their authority by divine right, nor can it be
resigned to the secular magistrate ; such a surrender would
be dangerous both to giver and receiver." His wriggling
apology is offered in vain, the king is inexorable. A strange
and unusual sight is this. Since St. Ambrose bowed the stub-
bornness of an emperor, bishops and abbots have not been wont
to be thus treated by kings. Day after day, the upper house
of convocation is agitated, and in great commotion with the
anxious debate. "The defects and reservations in the answer,"
are at last thought too perplexing to be removed or amended
by episcopal acumen, and the lower house must now try its
hand.

The king's "most humble chaplains are sorry that the

answer of the clergy," does not please, nor satisfy "his highness;" and for his "better contentation in that behalf," they
do now more specially reply.

All Christian princes, say they, have hitherto recognized
themselves bound to suffer the prelates to exercise their
authority, in making laws in matters concerning faith and
good manners, necessary to the soul's health ; nor have they
required the prelates to seek their consent or license. The
spiritual jurisdiction of the clergy "proceeds immediately
from God, and from no power or consent authorizable of any
secular prince." Moreover, it "is right well founded, in
many places of holy scripture," as in his highness's book against
Luther, "with most vehement and inexpugnable reasons and
authorities," is proved. Notwithstanding, "we your most
humble chaplains and bedesmen, considering your high wisdom, great learning, and infinite goodness towards us and the
church, and having special trust in the same, and not minding
to fall into contention or disputations with your highness,—
promise—that in all laws we shall hereafter make by the
reason of our spiritual jurisdiction and judicial power, we
shall not publish, nor put them forth, except first we require
your highness to give your consent and authority unto them ;—
except such as shall concern the maintenance of the faith and
good manners in Christ's church, and such as shall be for the
reformation and correction of sin, after the commandments of
Almighty God, according unto such laws of the church, and
laudable customs as have been heretofore made." And for
the rest, such laws as are contrary to the prerogative and
statutes of the realm, shall be "right gladly" revoked.

Will not this pacify the king ? No. There is too much
ambiguity and subterfuge in it. Their fawning humility and
ill-disguised sense of weakness, excite his arrogance and
cupidity. His claims become more urgent and exorbitant.
They are required to sign a form of submission prepared by

himself, that not only shall all new laws have his approval
and royal assent previous to their promulgation, but also that
all the old constitutions shall be revised by a mixed commission of the laity and clergy, appointed by himself, and such
as they please be abrogated and annulled.   And now perplexities thicken around them.   They are in the hunter's toils,
and there is no escape.   Is there no experienced pilot at
hand, to steer them safely through the breakers, foaming on
every side?   Let that fast friend of the catholic faith, bishop
Fisher, of Rochester, advise them, and all may yet be well.
" And to wait for this prelate's resolution, they adjourn for
three days."[6]

Such a step bodes not well for the king's designs: it must
be prevented.   The speaker and twelve of the Commons'
house are sent for, and to them the sovereign thus addresses
himself: " Well, beloved subjects, we had thought the clergy
of our realm had been our subjects wholly ; but now we have
well perceived that they be but half our subjects.   For all
the prelates at their consecration, make an oath to the pope
clean contrary to the oath that they make unto us, so that they
seem to be his subjects and not ours."—" And so the king
delivering to them the copy of both the oaths, required them
to invent some order that he might not thus be deluded of his
spiritual subjects."[7]   The appearance of the plague alone
prevented some grave parliamentary censure ; for on this
account the house rose in three days after this message of the
king.   Yet it was not without its effect.   The first part of
the king's demands the clergy will now accede to, if the
promise might be binding for his life only ; but in the old
canons they can permit no change.

The king's determination is, however, unaltered; and a new
form of submission is sent them.   But to this the prelates

---

[6] Collier, iv. 189—199.   [7] Fox, Acts and Mon. ii. 961.   Burnet, i. 225.

object, and then venture upon a positive refusal. The lower house of convocation, more apprehensive of the royal wrath, at last submit; and the prelates also, with only one exception, finally agree, without any limitation whatever, not to enact, promulge, or put in use any new canons, without the royal permission.[8] If the king obtained not all that he desired, sufficient was gained to lay the whole body of the clergy at his feet. A little more time must pass, and all will be granted to the sovereign that his ambition or rapacity may instigate him to demand. Hitherto, no reformed doctrine had been admitted among the clergy. No change of religious faith had occurred. As catholics they had submitted to a catholic king, anxious only to preserve their livings, lands, and wealth; not dreaming that all would soon be in the grasp of the monarch, to whom they now yielded up their cherished independence, and for which act of spoliation they had themselves prepared the way.

The royal supremacy over the clergy was by no means suffered to sleep. One priest was imprisoned for upholding the papal authority. Another, charged with Lutheranism and thrown into prison by the archbishop of Canterbury, was immediately released on appealing to the king as supreme head. It now only remained to give these concessions of the clergy the force of public law, and for the commonalty to approve the exercise of this novel power. At present, it suited not with Henry's great cause at the court of Rome wholly to throw off the authority of that see; but every thing was gradually prepared to effect it. Early in 1533, the parliament passed an act against all appeals to Rome in testamentary and matrimonial causes, and on the rights of tithes and oblations. In the following language they set forth the reasons for this fresh inroad upon papal usages: "That the

---

[8] Collier, iv. 199.

kingdom of England is an empire provided with persons, both spiritual and temporal, well qualified to determine all controversies arising in it, without application to any foreign princes or potentates. And more particularly that part of the said body, called the spirituality, or the English church, have always been esteemed, and found upon trial, sufficiently furnished with skill and integrity to determine all such doubts, and to administer all such offices and duties," as appertain to their spiritual station.[9]

In the early part of this year, Cranmer was consecrated to the see of Canterbury, which had been vacant since August, 1532. For this purpose Henry procured bulls from Rome; and so anxious was Cranmer to exhibit his entire approval of the course adopted towards the clergy, that he refused to accept them but from the king's own hand. Nor would he take the usual oath to the pope, without first protesting against those parts of it which he conceived might be a bar to the performance of his duty to God, the king, and his country. By this expedient, unworthy of an honourable mind, he entered on his high functions as the first archbishop of Canterbury, recognizing in spirituals the supremacy of the king. The subserviency he here displayed marked his whole career; on all occasions he evinced a remarkable readiness to do and to say all that could be pleasing to his royal master. He was immediately instructed to declare the marriage of Henry with Katharine null and void, in conformity with the decision of convocation, and to pronounce on the legitimacy of the king's union with Anne Boleyn, some months after the nuptials had been solemnized.[1] Negotiations were kept up at Rome during the remainder of the year, until the decision of the pope (March 21st, 1534,) put an end to the entire procedure. An immediate separation from his new queen,

Burnet, i. 232. Collier, iv. 207.   [1] Strype's Cranmer, pp. 26, 29, 8vo. edit.

and the restoration of Katharine to all her conjugal rights, were the terms of the papal decree.[2]

It does not appear that these proceedings at Rome at all accelerated the complete establishment of the royal supremacy; although they may have conduced to that utter exclusion of the pope from every kind of influence in the internal spiritual affairs of the kingdom, which so quickly followed the settlement of this great question by the parliament then assembled. This exclusion was owing, for the most part, to the nature of those principles on which the king's ecclesiastical authority was based, rather than to any purpose of the sovereign, the clergy, or the nation, to bring it to pass.

But while the pope was thus busily engaged at Rome, in rendering irrevocable the humiliation of his power in this country, the houses of parliament, which assembled on the 15th of January, 1534, completed the work so auspiciously begun in former sessions. The king's council had in the previous month, but after the revocation of Cranmer's sentence of divorce by the pontiff, entered on the consideration of various questions relating to the pope's "usurped power," as it was called, "within the realm;" and measures were resolved upon for the support of the royal prerogative.[3]

The statutes relating to heresy, were the first to be singled out by the Commons for amendment. The inquisitorial power of the bishops' courts was destroyed; all proceedings were to take place in open court, and by witnesses. Those adjudged guilty were not to suffer death until the king's writ, *De heretico comburendo,* had been obtained; but none were to be troubled upon any of the pope's canons or laws.[4] They next proceeded to the submission of the clergy, who had acknowledged, " according to the truth," that their convocations

---

[2] Short, Ch. Hist. p. 92.   [3] Strype, Memor. I. i. 231.   [4] Burnet, i. 270.

ought to assemble only by the king's writ, and had promised never to attempt the promulgation or execution of any canons without the royal assent to the same.

This submission the parliament enacted for a law, and thus extinguished the independent power of the clergy for ever. All appeals to Rome were prohibited, and the monasteries put under the jurisdiction of the crown. The payment of annates was wholly forbidden; the procuring of bulls, briefs, or palls from the see of Rome denounced; every kind of payment formerly made under the names of pensions, censes, Peter-pence, dispensations, licenses, &c. &c. interdicted; the manner of the election of bishops determined to be thereafter by a *congé d'élire* from the king to the dean and chapter; and, lastly, the succession to the crown was settled on the issue of queen Anne.[5]

In the session at the close of the year all these acts were confirmed; the separation from Rome was completed, by the full recognition of the king, " as the supreme head in earth of the church in England," and to his spiritual jurisdiction all heresies and abuses were referred. It was made treason to deny the king this title, as also the once calling him heretic, schismatic, infidel, or usurper of the crown.[6]

In the interval of the two sessions, commissioners were sent through the land to offer the oath of submission to the clergy, in which was included a declaration that the king was head of the church; that the bishop of Rome had no more power than any other bishop; and that in their sermons they would not pervert the scripture, but preach Christ and his gospel sincerely, according to the scripture, and the tradition of orthodox and catholic doctors. Bishop Fisher and Sir Thomas More refused the oath, and forfeited their lives for resisting the royal power.[7]

[5] Collier, iv. 231—241.   [6] Burnet, i. 286.   [7] Burnet, i. 284.

Thus was consummated the abolition of the papal power in this country, and the formation of that regal prerogative in spirituals, as well as in temporals, which has continued to be an incubus upon the Anglican church to the present day. It is evident that in the procurement of this change, a sincere and profound conviction of the errors of Rome, and of the value of a scriptural faith and piety, had not the least share. The welfare of the church of Christ, the recognition of his claims as the King of saints, the emancipation of the human mind from the bondage of superstition, and the attainment of liberty of thought and freedom of conscience, formed no part of the object of the actors in this revolutionary drama.

" To this crisis the king of England had driven on...for with regard to the separation of this country from Rome, it has already been demonstrated, that Henry the Eighth had no credit whatever. At the moment 'he meant not so,' neither did he in his heart so intend. Could he only have moulded the pontiff to his will, no such event would have happened during his administration; and had Clement not been under the control of the emperor, Henry would have been an adherent still; as in opinion, if he had any opinions, he remained to the end of his life."[8]

The whole nation seems to have been content with the change. During the session of parliament in which it was effected, care was taken, that from Sunday to Sunday, at St. Paul's Cross, the usurpation of the pope in exercising jurisdiction within the realm, should be proclaimed to be as contrary to God's laws as it was to the rights of princes.

Divines were employed to write on the king's behalf; and books on the supremacy were plentifully distributed in the land. Gardiner, Tunstal, and Bonner, made their zeal in the king's cause eminently to appear by their writings and ser-

[8] Anderson's Annals, i. 406, 407.

mons. "If you think," says the bishop of Durham to
Reginald Pole, in 1536, "the hearts of the subjects of this
realm, greatly offended with abolishing of the bishop of Rome's
usurped authority in this realm, as if all the people, or most
part of them, took the matter as ye do....I do assure you, ye
be deceived. For the people perceive right well what profit
cometh to the realm thereby; and that all such money as
before issued that way, now is kept within the realm.....So that,
if at this day the king's grace would go about to renew in his
realm the said abolished authority of the bishop of Rome, I
think he should find much more difficulty to bring it about
in his parliament, and to induce his people to agree thereunto,
than any thing that ever he purposed in his parliament, since
his first reign."[9]

One tyranny was thus exchanged for another. A new
feature, likewise hostile to true Christian liberty, becomes
noticeable in the history of the church; and we now proceed
to trace its characteristics as embraced and moulded by the
teachers of reformation.

It was of necessity that Henry should call to his councils,
Cranmer, Cromwell, and Audley; men tinged, to say the
least, with the new learning. The position taken by the
sovereign, could not be maintained upon any principle recognised as catholic; nay, it was a position destructive of the
main pillar of *Roman orthodoxy*.

If the priestly order is by divine right the alone source and
executive of spiritual jurisdiction, then by no proper title can
it be claimed or exercised by any secular potentate; the
assumption of a controlling and legislative power over the
clergy, stands in direct antagonism with it.

The newly-acquired authority of Henry could find consistent supporters in the propagators of the new learning

---

[9] Burnet, Records, III. ii. No. 52.

alone. From the commencement of the Reformation they
had made the secular power their strength and shield. Nor
was it long before it became distinctly visible to those who
continued to adhere to the papacy, with all the fondness of old
and early associations, that submission to the king involved
an entire defection from the dogmas, as well as from the
power of Rome. The acquisition of the supreme headship
of the Anglican church, necessitated the introduction and partial toleration of the reformed doctrines, if only as a counter-
poise to the claims of the pope; and the king's reluctance to
entertain Lutheran views must give way to that necessity.
Gradually, but certainly, every consistent Romanist will be
obliged to place himself in opposition to the royal prerogative;
and as certainly will England, if determined to maintain that
exclusive privilege, be thrown into the bosom of the reformation. Cranmer, during his residence abroad, as ambassador,
had mingled much in the society of the leading continental
reformers, having, indeed, married the niece of Osiander.
From them he had imbibed the doctrine of secular interference
in religious affairs; and on his elevation to the archiepiscopal
see of Canterbury, he proceeded to introduce changes in the
doctrine and discipline of the Anglican church, so far as the
king's prejudices and policy would allow.

During the progress of the events already related, God's
word had been spreading, somewhat rapidly, among the
people. In 1526, the newly-translated Testament of Tyndale
was in general circulation, awakening the fears and fiery
wrath of Wolsey, Warham, and Tunstal. By the year 1534,
not less than twelve editions of the New Testament were
being perused throughout the land, besides some other portions of the lively oracles of truth.[1] The laws against heretics
were not, however, put into execution with any severity, until,

---

[1] Anderson's Annals, ii. Index.

on the disgrace of Wolsey, Sir Thomas More became lord
chancellor. It seems singular, that a man who in his Utopia
had allowed of no persecution for religious tenets, should be
thus blinded to " the partial advantage of that liberty," which
in theory he had advocated.[2] In conjunction with archbishop
Warham and Tunstal, this eminent man, and persecutor,
issued a warning against several heretical books in the English
tongue that had been lately introduced, especially informing
the people, that the king did well in *not* permitting the scriptures to be set out in the vulgar tongue.[3]

Great numbers of persons were brought before the bishops'
courts, and compelled to abjure; and were oftentimes condemned to a public penance of flogging, bearing fagots and
wax candles, in the white garb of penitents. It was their
crime, that they were " very expert in the gospels, and all
other things belonging to divine service;" that they refused
to go on pilgrimage, or to fast on saints' days, saying, that
salvation could not be obtained by good deeds; that " on
Sunday then last past, in sacring time, they held down their
heads and would not look upon the sacrament;" that they
were heard to say, that it booted not to pray to images; that
the " sacrament of the altar was not, as it was pretended, the
flesh, blood, and bone of Christ;" and especially, that they
possessed the gospels and the psalter in English, the sum of
scripture, and a variety of other books containing " pestilent
and other horrible heresies." A few were burnt, as Thomas
Hitton, for bringing in books from abroad; Thomas Bilney,
for preaching against images, pilgrimages, and prayers to
saints: Byfield and Tewksbury, as relapsed heretics. The
most eminent was John Frith, the friend and companion
of Tyndale. He combated successfully Sir Thomas More
on the real presence; his reply to his learned antagonist

[2] Burnet, i. 292.   Short, p. 95.   [3] Burnet, i. 294.

was written while in confinement and deprived of his books.[4]

These severities did not stay the progress of the truth, for the time was come, when, even in high places, the whole circle of Roman doctrines and ceremonies must be reviewed; and with the pope's supremacy, his dogmas, and discipline, be abandoned. The extirpation of the pontifical authority, and with it the rule of the canon law, threw the judgment of heresy upon its discordance with scripture; and by royal command, this became the standard of decision. Moreover, the necessities of the king's affairs abroad, constrained him to solicit the assistance of the foreign reformers, and of the princes by whom they were protected, in order to strengthen himself against the emperor, the nephew of his divorced queen, to whom was committed the execution of the pope's adverse decree.[5]

Now also, the encouragement shown by queen Anne, aided materially the extension of divine truth at home; and for a time, a greater liberty to preach and distribute the word of God prevailed. By her influence Latimer and Shaxton, both deeply imbued with the reformed doctrine, were advanced to bishoprics, and it is more than doubtful, whether Cranmer, without their help, would have dared to proceed in the path of reformation. The first use which had been made of his authority by this timid and obsequious prelate, was to issue, in conjunction with Gardiner, Stokesley, and Longland, an inhibition against preaching, unless permitted by a new license. To this was appended an order, " that no preachers for a year shall preach, neither with nor against purgatory, honouring of saints, that priests may have wives, *that faith only justifieth*, to go on pilgrimages, to forge miracles, considering these things have caused dissension."[6]

[4] Fox, Acts and Mon. 897, 898, 910, 934, 941.

[5] Burnet, i. 313.   Collier, iv. 290.

[6] Cranmer's Works, i. 98; iv. 253. Jenkyn's edit.

Under the fostering care of the royal prerogative, the year
1535 was chiefly occupied in preparing the way for the dissolution of the monasteries: the other portion of the "well-
liked" advice of Cromwell to his sovereign in 1529. For this
purpose Cromwell was named Vicegerent, the General Visitor
of all monasteries and privileged places, with authority also to
visit every archbishop and bishop of the kingdom. By the
year 1540, their suppression was complete, and the king and
his courtiers revelling in the spoils. Some few new bishoprics
were founded, the royal exchequer was replenished, and the
greatest hindrances to the advance of the Reformation were
moved out of the way.[7]

But the king's proceedings towards the bishops exhibited
the boldest exercise of his supremacy that had yet occurred.
On the 18th of September, he issued an order to the archbishops of Canterbury and York, suspending the ordinary
jurisdiction of the whole hierarchy, until the general visitation
of the clergy, he had recently set on foot, should be finished.
It appears that this novel exercise of the prerogative was
expected to call forth expressions of episcopal discontent; for
six days after we find Legh and Ap Rice, two of the
vicegerent's delegates, urging their master to persist in the
suspension. They say, that the bishops' jurisdiction is received, either by the law of God, by the bishop of Rome's
authority, or else by the king's grace's permission. If by the

---

[7] Collier, iv. 294. Burnet, i. 331,
346. " These means he (Cromwell)
used. He first found means to persuade
the king that it might lawfully be done ;
that for his crown and state in safety it
was necessary to be done, for that he
made appear to the king how by their
means the pope and clergy had so great
authority, revenue, alliance, and principally captivity of the souls, and obedience of subjects, that they were able to
put kings in hazard at their will ; that
for his revenue and maintenance of his
estate, wars, and affairs both in peace
and in war, at home and abroad, with
others, it was most profitable to dissolve
them for augmentation of his treasure."
Contemporary MS. in Letters relating
to the Suppression of the Monasteries,
Camden Society, p. 112.

first, let them bring forth scripture to prove it; if by the second, "let them exercise [it] still, *if they think it meet;*" or if by the last, wherefore should they be grieved if the king recall that which came from him? "It seems to us good that they should be driven by this means to agnize their author, spring, and fountain, as else they be too ingrate to enjoy it. Let them sue for it again by supplication, that they and all other may understand him to be the head-power within this realm under God; and that no jurisdiction proceedeth within the same, but from him."[8]

The suspension was not removed, until thus compelled they "sued with words of prayer" for the restoration of their episcopal functions. Their prayer was granted, to be enjoyed during the royal pleasure only, and attended with the following extraordinary declaration:—That as his vicegerent, Cromwell, was so fully occupied with the arduous duties committed to his charge, and fearing lest injury should accrue thereby to his subjects, the supreme head on earth of the Anglican church, therefore, empowered the bishops in his stead, to confer orders, to institute and to collate to benefices, and to exercise other branches of episcopal jurisdiction, "beside and beyond those things which are divinely committed to their charge by the holy scriptures."[9]

To this humiliation all the bishops quietly submitted, excepting only Gardiner who was abroad, apparently content to derive their office, as ministers of the gospel, from the civil magistrate; thereby virtually disclaiming the authority of the Lord Jesus Christ to set teachers in his church, and at the same time overthrowing the rights of the Christian community. The vicegerent's commissioners diligently carried out the instructions of their master, as is seen by the following letter to their employer:—" Right worshipful sir, my duty presup-

[8] Strype, Memor. I. ii. 216, 217.   [9] Collier, ix. 156.   Short, p. 104.

posed, this is to advertise you that Master Doctor Layton and
I, the 11th day of January (1536), were with the archbishop
of York, whom we, according to your pleasure, and precepts,
have visited, enjoining him to preach and teach the word of
God, according to his bound duty, to his cure committed unto
him; and to see others here in his jurisdiction, being indued
with good qualities, having any respect either to God, goodness, virtue, or godliness, to perform the same; enjoining,
moreover, to him, to bring up unto you his first, second,
and third foundations whereupon he enjoyeth his office and
prerogative power, with the grants, privileges, and concessions,
given to him, and to his see appertaining."[1]

The whole hierarchy was now at the king's command; a
despotic power was fully accorded him over body and soul.
His subjects await the next utterance of their sovereign with
anxiety and suspense; for he will immediately proceed to
determine what they must believe. Their consciences must
be for him a *tabula rasa;* a plastic, formless clay, ready to
receive whatever form of doctrine the royal potter may think
fit to frame. What is it to him that there is *one Lord and one
Lawgiver,* the Everlasting Word, whose voice alone can speak
into life, and illuminate the soul of man with the rays of
truth ? Is he not the only reflector of that bright image, and
by divine right the only promulgator of eternal verities, within
this his land ?

Is it not treason to believe otherwise than as the head of
the body politic? He deems it, therefore, to be his especial
duty to take into his care the well-being of the souls with the
bodies of his people.

The murder of Anne Boleyn was consummated; a spiritless
parliament and a time-serving prelate had sanctioned the
bloody deed; the one by reversing the law of succession, and

---

[1] Dr. Legh to Cromwell, Letters relating to Suppression, &c. p. 95.

Cranmer by annulling the marriage of his protectress and friend, as she stood in mockery of justice at his tribunal; when on Friday, the 9th of June, the new convocation assembled. "Therein the Lord Cromwell, prime secretary, sat in state above all the bishops as the king's vicar or viceregent-general in all spiritual matters."[2]

The convocation is opened with a Latin sermon from Latymer, in obedience to "the commandment of our primate." With great fidelity and boldness, the preacher sets before them their high duties as the stewards of Christ, though he fears many of them are children of darkness. He declaims, with pointed severity, against the general topics handled in their discourses to the people :—"Your care," he exclaims, "is not that all men may hear God's word, but all your care is, that no layman do read it; surely, being afraid lest they by their reading should understand it, and understanding, learn to rebuke our slothfulness. What have ye done hitherto, I pray you, these seven years and more? What one thing that the people of England hath been the better of a hair; or you yourselves, either more accepted before God, or better discharged toward the people committed to your care? Is it unknown, think you, how both ye and your curates, were, in a manner, by violence enforced to let books to be made, not by you, but by profane and lay persons; to let them, I say, be sold abroad, and read for the instruction of the people?" In a similar strain, he rebukes their cruel and persecuting spirit; their worldliness, their frauds, and deceptions practised on a foolish people, exhorting them to a reformation of their worship, to take away images, and relics, to purify the bishops' courts, and to reduce the number of holidays.[3]

This startling and ominous discourse gave note of that

[2] Fuller, Ch. Hist. Book v. Sect. 25.

[3] Latymer's Sermons, pp. 33—58. Parker Society edit.

d

which was about to follow. The first act of convocation, was to sign publicly an instrument, presented by Cromwell, relating to the nullity of the king's marriage with Anne Boleyn. " Oh! the operation of the purge of a premunire, so lately taken by the clergy, and a hundred thousand pounds paid thereupon! How did the remembrance thereof still work upon their spirits, and make them meek and mortified!—They knew the temper of the king, and had read the text, *The lion hath roared, who will not fear?* Amos iii. 8."[4]

And now the important object of their assembling was brought forward. On Friday, July 23rd, the prolocutor of the lower house laid before the prelates a collection of sixty-seven erroneous doctrines, which, to the great grief of the clergy, were publicly preached, printed, and professed, " and are either the tenets of the old Lollards, or the new reformers, together with the anabaptists' opinions."[5] Here are some of them. " That all ceremonies accustomed in the church, which are not clearly expressed in scripture, must be taken away, because they are men's inventions: the church is the congregation of good men only : that it is as lawful to christen a child in a tub of water at home, or in a ditch by the way, as in a font-stone in the church: it is sufficient for a man or woman to make their confession to God alone: that it is not necessary or profitable to have any church or chapel to pray in, or to do any divine service in : that saints are not to be invocated or honoured : that prayers, suffrages, fastings, or alms-deeds, do not help to take away sin : that by preaching the people have been brought in opinion and belief, that nothing is to be believed, except it can be proved expressly by scripture : that it is preached and taught, that, forasmuch as Christ hath shed his blood for us, and redeemed us, we need not to do any thing at all but to believe and repent, if we have

[4] Fuller, book v. sect 26.   [5] Burnet, i. 388.

offended: that no human constitutions, or laws, do bind any
Christian man, but such as be in the gospels, Paul's epistles,
or the New Testament, and that a man may break them without any offence at all." These opinions were the fruit of
freedom of thought, and of a sole regard to the testimony of
holy writ. We shall presently see that they did not in the
least harmonize with the views of either party, into which the
convocation was divided, nor with the determination of him,
by whom their faith is about to be settled—for the present. [6]

It is the king's study, says his noble representative, day
and night, to set a quietness in the church; nay, he cannot
rest till these controversies be fully debated and ended. A
very special desire moves him to " set a stay for the unlearned
people, whose consciences are in doubt what they may believe." But, well as the king is acquainted with these controversies, and able by his excellent learning to determine
upon them, yet his great love to the clergy prompts him to
lay the matter before them. He desires " you lovingly and
friendly to dispute among yourselves, and conclude all things
by the word of God, without all brawling and scolding."
But he will not suffer scripture to be wrested, nor defaced,
by any glosses, or papistical laws, or decrees of fathers and
councils. " And his majesty will give you high thanks, if
ye will sit and conclude a perfect unity."

After "this godly exhortation, of so worthy a prince,"
for which the bishops all rise up together to give thanks,
they proceed to disputation. The thorny questions of the
nature and number of the sacraments are their topics.
Rome and Wittenburg produce their arguments, in the
persons of opposing prelates. " Oh what tugging was
here," says Fuller, " betwixt these opposite sides, whilst
with all earnestness they thought to advance their several
designs." " Let us grant," submits the bishop of London,

[6] Fuller, book v. sect 28.

"that the sacraments may be gathered out of the word of God, yet are you far deceived, if you think there is none other word of God, but that which every sowter and cobler do read in their mother tongue. And if ye think, that nothing pertaineth unto the Christian faith, but that only which is written in the Bible, then err ye plainly with the Lutherans. . . . Now when the right noble Lord Cromwell, the archbishop, with the other bishops, which did defend the pure doctrine of the gospel, heard this, they smiled a little one upon another, forasmuch as they saw him flee, even in the very beginning of the disputation, into his old rusty sophistry and unwritten verities."[7] But what unity can be "set and concluded," when it is found, that seven against seven the antagonists stand, and each side immoveable? while a nation's faith, the obedience of myriads of consciences, must hang balanced in the scale—if it may.

A faith is however ready and at hand—at which these episcopal warriors will not venture to tilt. Unity *can* be "set and concluded," though bishops may fail to effect it; there is one, at least, bold enough to attempt it. "Articles concerning our faith, and laudable ceremonies in the church of Christ"—a "twilight religion"—may be framed, to which the consciences of the people, both cleric and lay, can and must obediently conform, and that by "Henry the Eighth, by the grace of God, King of England, and of France, Defender of the Faith, Lord of Ireland, and in Earth Supreme Head of the Church of England."[8] "For," saith he, "it most chiefly belongeth unto our charge, diligently to foresee, and cause that not only the most holy word and commandments of God should most sincerely be believed, and most reverently be observed, and kept of our subjects; but also that unity and concord in opinions, namely, in such things as

[7] Fox, p. 1080.
[8] Title to Book of Articles, then published. Fuller, book v. sect. 34, 35.

do concern our religion, may increase and go forward, and all occasion of dissent and discord touching the same be repressed and utterly extinguished." Such is the introduction to the articles, which after several disputations were assented to, and signed by the convocation, and then published for the souls' health of the community.

In the first, they are taught that the entire canon of the Bible, which, at that time, included the apocrypha, as also the Apostles', the Nicene, and Athanasian creeds, are "the most certain and infallible words of God," which ought and must be most reverently observed and religiously kept, else were they "infidels, heretics, and members of the devil, with whom they shall be perpetually damned." In the second, that of necessity they must and ought to believe, that baptism ordained by our Saviour, is to be given to all men, as also to infants, that thereby all sin, original and actual, may be washed away, and that "all the anabaptists' or Pelagians' opinions in this behalf, ought to be reputed for detestable heresies, and utterly to be condemned." In the third, that penance is a sacrament appointed by Christ, and that without it, and "such good works of the same," no one shall obtain everlasting life, neither remission nor mitigation of present pains and afflictions in this life. In the fourth, that in the sacrament of the altar, the very flesh and blood of Christ is really and substantially present. In the fifth, that sinners are justified "by contrition and faith, joined with charity:" not as deserving to attain the said justification, but through the merits of the blood and passion of Jesus Christ. Next follow articles concerning the ceremonies to be used. Images are to be employed as "representers of virtue and good example:" the images of Christ and our Lady to kindle, and stir men's minds to recollection and lamentation of their sins. Saints are to be honoured as the elect persons of Christ, who passed in godly life out of this transitory world, to whom we may

laudably pray, and their holy days observe, except so far as
they may be mitigated and moderated by the commandment
"of us the supreme head." Holy vestments, the giving of
holy bread, the sprinkling of holy water, bearing of candles
on Candlemas-day, giving ashes on Ash Wednesday, bearing
palms on Palm Sunday, creeping to the cross on Good Friday, and kissing it, setting up the sepulture of Christ, the
hallowing of the font, and other exorcisms, customs, and
benedictions, are not to be contemned, but used and continued. And lastly, prayers and masses are to be offered for
souls departed, though it " be to us uncertain by scripture,"
where they are.[9]

Such was the commencement of the doctrinal reformation
of the church of England, and the first example of the exercise of the royal prerogative in the imposition of dogmas of
faith on the consciences of people. " For good instruction
must they be taken " until such time as his majesty shall
change or abrogate any of them.[1] Neither priest, bishop,
nor king, seems to have thought of the impracticability of the
work they took in hand, or of the iniquitous presumption
of the endeavour to command and control the conscience.
Nay, with a condescension amounting to mockery, the people
are exhorted in "charitable unity and loving concord," to
observe the same, as thereby they will " not a little encourage
us to take farther travails, pains, and labours, for your com-
modities in all such other matters, as in time to come, may
happen to occur, and as it shall be most to the honour of
God, the profit, tranquillity, and quietness of all you, our
most loving subjects."

May we not fairly suspect that none of these parties knew
the power of true godliness to excite a most tender and sen-
sitive regard to every, even the least, commandment of Jesus

[9] Fuller, book v. sect. 34, 35. Burnet,   [1] Strype's Cranmer, p. 690.
I. ii. 457. Add. I. i. 390.

Christ? That such regard would lead its possessor through "floods and flames" to obey them? Surely their only conception of religion must have been that of a system of spiritual tyranny over the souls of men, as the source of wealth and power. The clergy, indeed, murmured at the authority assumed; but they knew the temper of Henry too well to offer any open resistance. Although their mass-money, their lucrative indulgencies, their shrined wealth, were at stake, a premunire might again pluck them of their gains, and the coffers of their sovereign be once more weighty with their gold, should they dare to oppose his will. The convocation completed its labours with a petition to the king, " that he would graciously indulge unto his subjects of the laity, the reading of the Bible in the English tongue,—and that a new translation might be forthwith made for that end and purpose." Their petition eighteen months before had not succeeded. Nor was this regarded; for although in the ensuing year a reprint of Tyndale's own translation, under another's name, was ushered into the world under royal auspices, it was *without* the consent of the clergy, and to their very great vexation.[2]

The people were by no means pleased with the freedom so boldly taken with their faith. A general discontent, breaking out into open rebellion, soon displayed itself, which was with difficulty quelled. Yet in marvellous blindness they acknowledged the sovereign to be their supreme head under God, for the settlement of their religious belief.[3] The articles alluded to above, were in the following year embodied in the book entitled, " The Institution of a Christian Man." Many additions were made to them, during the preparation of the work, by a number of bishops, and other learned men, who were appointed by the king to this weighty charge. It was not, however, easily achieved; so numerous

[2] Anderson, Annals, i. 548, 578. [3] Burnet, i. 413.

were the objections of the partisans of the old learning.
" Verily for my part," says Latymer, " I had lever be poor
parson of poor Kynton again, than to continue thus bishop of
Worcester." [4]   Here is the principle on which this reformed
faith was imposed on the people: " It appertains to Christian
kings and princes, in the discharge of their duty to God, to
reform and reduce again the laws to their old limits, and
pristine state of their power and jurisdiction, which was
given them by Christ, and used in the primitive church.
For it is out of all doubt that Christ's faith was then most
firm and pure, and the scriptures of God were then best
understood.   And therefore the customs and ordinances then
used and made, must needs be more conform, and agreeable
unto the true doctrine of Christ, and more conducing to the
edifying and benefit of the church of Christ, than any customs or laws used or made since that time." [5]   Thus another
rule of faith, one established by the prince and *his* church,
was introduced into the place of the word of God.

    For more than ten years, the sacred volume had found an
entrance into the land, although forbidden, and its suppression earnestly sought.   Until now, none in authority
cared for these things, when by the wonderful providence of
God the labours of the martyr of Vilvorde were crowned
with success.   Twenty-five editions of the New Testament
at least, and four of the whole Bible, had been distributed,
bearing fruit unto eternal life, ere it was allowed by the
king's grace to be bought and read in his realm.[6]   The law
of man and the law of God were now brought into conflict
for the sovereignty of the soul : not without an assured
victory to the latter, though it must win its way through
tears, imprisonment, and blood.   At the door of every man's
conscience the combatants stood, the wisdom of God and the

---

[4] Quoted in Cranmer's Works, i 186.   [6] Anderson's Annals, i. 579. ii. App.
[5] Strype's Cranmer, p. 77.

wisdom of man. A struggle was inevitable; it has been long and severe: our own day has yet to witness its close.

By royal permission and command, a Bible was ordered to be set up in every church, and none hindered in its perusal; for "it is the true lively word of God, which every Christian ought to believe, embrace, and follow, if he expects to be saved." But the people must beware of their own judgment. Let them not contest with each other the sense of difficult places, but refer themselves to men of better judgment, to the scribes and rabbis of the church.[7] Does the vicegerent, Cromwell, think, while he issues this injunction, that he can control the operations of the Spirit of God, whose living word he thus places before the eyes and understandings of the people? or that those consciences in which the Spirit of truth shall speak with power, are amenable to his judgment? It is to be feared, that he who thus opened the sealed waters of life to thirsty souls, was himself a stranger to the grace of God, and that nothing but a low and worldly policy, led him to an act so fertile in blessing to his country and the world.

But as if to illustrate the degree of liberty which the people were to be permitted to enjoy, the king himself engaged in the examination of Lambert for heresy. "A more miserable spectacle of a royal tyrant taunting and worrying his victim, Westminster Hall probably never witnessed, before nor since." At this sad scene, Cromwell and Cranmer assisted, in conjunction with Gardiner; the first of them delivering without repugnance, the sentence which consigned the martyr to the flames.[8] Other victims also were sought out to exhibit the fidelity of the sovereign to the catholic faith, but which he had unwittingly brought to the very verge of destruction. Cranmer again comes before us a persecutor. To him, with some others, including Robert

[7] Burnet, i. 453.   [8] Anderson's Annals, ii. 19. Collier, iv. 436.

Barnes, a martyr in the reign of Mary, was issued a commission signed by Cromwell, to seek out and try a certain people, "lurking secretly in divers corners and places," whose sentiments on baptism were not in harmony with the articles, recently set forth, to produce unity and contentation ; who, moreover, ventured "to contemn and despise, of their own private wills and appetites," the laudable rites and ceremonies of his grace's church.   They had committed treason in daring to think differently from the king, and for this they were to be pursued to death, *even, if need be, in a manner contrary to the due course of law !*   Three men and a woman, with fagots bound on their backs, did penance for the crime at St. Paul's Cross, and one man and a woman of the same sect, and country, were burnt in Smithfield.[9]

The leaders of the catholic party had been recovering their influence with Henry for some time past, "when Gardiner, Tunstal, and other bishops, zealous for the old religion,—put the king upon such methods, as dashed all the present hopes of the other party." [1]   The tide of Reformation began thus early to ebb.   The royal power which had hitherto opened channels for its flow, was now, and for the rest of Henry's days, to be employed in forming dykes against its further progress.   It was to be clearly manifest that *"it was not by might, nor by power, but by the Spirit of the Lord of hosts,"* that the flood of divine truth was to pour its salutary streams into the souls of the people.   Symptoms of the repaired strength of the old party had been shown in the prosecutions which had taken place in various parts of Kent, of "fautors of the new learning, as they call it," which the influence of Cranmer, even in his own diocese, and sustained by the vicegerent's power, could not prevent.[2]   But this change

9 Collier, ix. 161, iv. 436. Anderson,   1 Dodd's Ch. Hist. i. 305. Tierney's ed.
ii. 18.   Strype's Cranmer, p. 686.   2 Cranmer's Works, i. 242.

was most fully exhibited, when, in the parliament of 1539, the act of six articles was affirmed to be the law of belief to the king's subjects for the future.

The disagreement of the hierarchy on the doctrines to be enforced, afforded another opportunity for the royal polemic to exhibit his theological, as well as his regal power. For "in his own princely person," he vouchsafed "to descend and come into his said high court of parliament and council, and there like a prince of most high prudence, and no less learning, opened and declared many things of high learning and great knowledge, touching the said articles, matters, and questions, for our unity to be had in the same."[3] So the people must believe, or profess to believe, 1. That in the holy sacrament of the altar, under the form of bread and wine, is present really the natural body and blood of our Saviour. 2. That communion in both kinds is not necessary to salvation. 3. That priests may *not* marry. 4. That vows of chastity are according to the law of God. 5. As is also the mass. 6. And that auricular confession is necessary for the church of God.[4] The blessed effects of union, and the mischiefs of discord, could, however, be evinced and cured only by the fagot and the stake, to which the venturous being was to be consigned, who dared to deny the truth of the first article. He who denied the rest, was to be imprisoned during pleasure, and, if obstinate and hardy in his opposition, hanging should put an end to every conscientious scruple.

The bishops proceeded with alacrity to employ the powers intrusted to them. "Great perturbation," says our martyrologist, "followed in all parishes almost through London," and five hundred persons were soon immured in fetid dungeons for their faith. No wonder it was complained of as a

---

[3] Preamble to the Act, in Dodd. i. p. 444.   [4] Ibid.

great hardship against conscience. "Men do not love to be dragged into religion; to be under the necessity of being either a martyr, or an hypocrite, they thought singular usage." [5] But, "the godly study, pain, and travail of his majesty, was undergone for the conservation of the church and congregation, in a true, and sincere, and uniform doctrine of Christ's religion." Ought not therefore every loyal subject to accept the results of such self-imposed and disinterested toil? Could any motives but of the purest kind have influenced the sovereign in this kindly regard for the spiritual weal of his people? " This measure," we are told, "very much quieted the bigots, who were now persuaded that the king would not set up heresy, since he passed so severe an act against it, *and it made the total suppression of the monasteries go the more easily through.*" [6] The pocket and the conscience of the king were always nearly allied to each other; and probably he thought those of his subjects were so too.

The royal interference did not, however, reach to the prevention of the perusal of the word of God. Often were the church services interrupted by the loud voice of some reader, more lettered than his fellows, as, surrounded in the porch by listening crowds, he brake to the joyful and expecting throng the bread of life. Every where might be heard the eager conversation of minds, enlightened by the truth, speaking of those wonderful words which the Most High had spoken unto men; the street, the tavern, the ale-house, the church, and every company, were the scenes of earnest dispute, or holy zeal. Scripture was compared with scripture, and its sense closely scrutinized. The night of superstition retired before the morning dawn, and the "sacraments of holy church" were threatened with subversion and overthrow; some even had ventured to whisper thoughts which appeared

⁵ Collier, v. 48.   ⁶ Burnet, i. 471.

to destroy " *the power and authority of princes and magistrates.*'   It was time, therefore, that that power should vindicate its divine original, and remedy, by " most excellent wisdom," all irregularities and diversities of opinion, that by reducing the people to unity of judgment, there might be an increase of love and charity among them.   For this purpose, his majesty issued a proclamation at the commencement of the session.   His people must cease such disorderly practices. Nevertheless, his highness is content, " that such as can and will read in the English tongue, shall and may quietly and reverently read the Bible and New Testament by themselves secretly, at all times and places, convenient for their own instruction and edification, to increase thereby godliness and virtuous living."   Only let them not attempt to understand difficult places, without the assistance of the learned ; and moreover, " his majesty was not, nor is, compelled by God's word, to set forth the scripture in English to his lay subjects ; but, of his own liberality and goodness, was and is pleased that his said loving subjects should have, and read the same in convenient places and times, to the only intent to bring them from their old ignorance and blindness to virtuous living and godliness, to God's glory and honour, and not to make and take occasion of dissension and tumult, by reason of the same.   Wherefore his majesty chargeth and commandeth all his said subjects to use the holy scripture in English, according to his godly purpose and gracious intent, as they would avoid his most high displeasure and indignation." [7]

Thus did Henry strive to realize, in the omnipotency of his power, his supreme headship over the consciences of his subjects, and to restrain by his permission the all-conquering progress of the sacred word.   They had read, and would con-

[7] Dodd. i. 310, 451.

tinue to read, with or without his sanction, the holy page; notwithstanding that he may say by proclamations to the flood of heavenly truth, " *Hitherto shalt thou come; but no farther.*"

But few other events will require our notice in the present reign. The most important was the publication, in 1543, of "The Erudition of a Christian Man." The issue of this work closed the labours of a commission of bishops, appointed three years before by the king, to fix the rule of religious belief. The influence of the catholic party in this also prevailed, and put back still further the reformation of the national faith. The people were commanded to "order" their lives by this book, the doctrine of it "having been seen, and liked very well by both houses of parliament." It contained every thing needful for the attainment of everlasting life. They were no longer to busy "their heads and senses" about free-will, justification, good works, &c.; all these things were here fully and most certainly explained for their perfect contentation.

Moreover, they were instructed, "that the reading of the Old and New Testament is not so necessary for all those folks, that of duty they ought, and be bound to read it; but as the prince and the policy of the realm shall think convenient to be tolerated or taken from it." [8] This same parliament, which so well liked the new creed set forth by the king's authority, for the advancement of true religion, commanded that all Bibles and Testaments of Tyndale's translation, should be utterly extinguished and abolished, and all annotations and preambles be blotted out from all others. No women, except gentlewomen, no artificers, no journeymen, no husbandmen, nor labourers, were to read the Bible to themselves, nor to any other, privately or openly, on pain of a month's incarceration in prison.[9]

[8] Strype, Mem. I. i. 586.   [9] Burnet, i. 584.

Such were the fetters and restrictions under which the nation was to learn the divine truths of scripture. Nor must we be surprised that these were sanctioned and promoted by Cranmer, since he believed that all civil and ecclesiastical power had the same origin: that to the Christian prince was committed, immediately from God, not only the administration of things political, and civil governance, " but also the administration of God's word for the cure of souls." He thought that the election of the pastors of the church, should be " by the laws and orders of kings and princes."[1] Hence the simplest act of worship must be a matter of royal regulation; a prayer, in the people's tongue, may not rise from any lips in the public assemblies to the great Father and Fountain of mercy, until it shall please the sovereign to permit. The very matter of the preacher's sermon must be, and was determined for him: and every truth, even the most precious to the soul's salvation, must give way to the frequent inculcation of the profane dogma of the king's supremacy; *that* must never be forgotten.

If souls were awakened into life; if any found their way to the Lamb of God, through the thick mists of superstition which hid him from their view; if a gem of heavenly truth glimmered in the surrounding darkness, from the brow of one made free by the Spirit of God, it was not the fault of princes and bishops if the soul thus blessed did not ascend to the regions of bliss in the lurid glare of the martyr-pile, or from the filthy and pestilential dungeon. Guided by no conscientious motive, or true religious sense themselves, they could not understand, nor would they suffer any other to possess, that of which they were so painfully deficient. Soul, mind, thought, every thing which elevates man to his Creator, together with the secular interests of humanity, must be sub-

[1] Cranmer's Remains, ii. 101.

ject to a domination fatal to their welfare, their expansion,
their freedom, and their life.

We may close this portion of our sketch with the following
accurate picture of the state of this, so-called, reformation,
from the pen of an eye-witness. " Still remaineth their foul
masses, of all abominations the principal ; their prodigious
sacrifices, their censings of idols, their boyish processions,
their uncommanded worshippings, and their confessions in the
ear, of all traitory the fountain; with many other strange
observations, which the scripture of God knoweth not. Nothing is brought as yet to Christ's clear institution and
sincere ordinance, but all remaineth still as the antichrists
left it. Nothing is tried by God's word, but by the ancient
authority of fathers: now passeth all under their title. . . . .
If it were naught afore, I think it is now much worse; for
now are they become 'laudable ceremonies,' whereas before-
time they were but ceremonies alone. Now are they become
necessary rites, godly constitutions, seemly usages, and civil
ordinances, whereas before they had no such names; and he
that disobeyeth them, shall not only be judged a felon, and
worthy to be hanged, by their new forged laws, but also condemned for a traitor against the king. To put this, with
such like, in execution, the bishops have authority, every
month in the year if they list, to call a session, to hang and
burn at their pleasure. And this is ratified and confirmed by
act of parliament, to stand the more in effect." [2]

The king himself corroborates all this, though in more
courtly phrase, in his speech to his last parliament. The
close of his reign was at hand, though he knew it not; and
from the lips of the sovereign we receive a confession of the
utter futility of all his attempts to control the conscience, to
fix the faith of his liege subjects, or to establish that unity

[2] John Bale, quoted in Strype's Cranmer, p. 186.

and concord which had ever been pleaded, as the sufficient reason for his interference. "Behold, then," he says, "what love and charity is amongst you, when the one calleth the other heretic and anabaptist, and he calleth him again papist, hypocrite, and pharisee. . . . I see, and hear daily, that you of the clergy preach one against another, teach one contrary to another, inveigh one against another, without charity or discretion. Some be too stiff in their old mumpsimus, others be too busy and curious in their new sumpsimus. Thus all men almost be in variety, in discord, and few or none do preach, truly and sincerely, the word of God according as they ought to do. . . . You of the temporality be not clean and unspotted of malice and envy ; for you rail on bishops, speak slanderously of priests, and rebuke and taunt preachers. . . . . And although you be permitted to read holy scripture, and to have the word of God in your mother tongue, you must understand, that it is licensed you so to do, only to inform your own conscience, and to instruct your children and family, and not to dispute, and make scripture a railing and a vaunting-stock against priests and preachers, as many light persons do. I am very sorry to know and hear how unreverently that most precious jewel, the word of God, is disputed, rhymed, sung, and jangled, in every alehouse and tavern, contrary to the true meaning and doctrine of the same ; and yet I am even as much sorry, that the readers of the same follow it in doing so faintly and coldly. For of this I am sure, that charity was never so faint amongst you, and virtuous and godly living was never less used, nor was God himself amongst Christians never less reverenced, honoured, and served." [3]

His failure to rule the conscience was complete. Honours, wealth, and power, had induced many to applaud and follow

[3] Dodd. i. App. 454, 455.

their sovereign in his revolutionary proceedings, and multitudes with him had bowed in worship, and sacrificed their
souls, at the golden shrine of mammon; but others received
the reward of their fidelity to God in stripes, bonds, and
death. The soul eluded his grasp; it escaped his toils.
There were those whom the Son had made free indeed, who
dared to taste and handle the holy truths of the oracles of
God, apart from, and uncontaminated by, the doctrines of
men, however erudite and necessary to elucidate heaven's
laws they were proclaimed to be, by this usurper of Christ's
prerogative; of these we shall presently speak.

SECTION II.

EDWARD VI.

WHEN the youthful Edward ascended the throne, in 1547,
but little more had been effected in the way of reformation
than an entire separation of the English church from the
Roman obedience. Many corruptions and abuses had been
moderated, or destroyed, but the national faith and discipline
remained essentially catholic. It may be said, indeed, that
but one of the various doctrines which were regarded as peculiarly protestant, had obtained any ascendancy at all; a
doctrine too consonant to the pride and ambition of sovereigns,
to be allowed to remain in abeyance, by the tyrannical and
unscrupulous Henry. Every where among the reformers, the
right of the Christian magistrate to rule the conscience, as
well as the body of the subject, was asserted, and while themselves exercising their lately acquired liberty to the fullest

extent, they regarded with jealousy and bitter hatred, all who ventured, while copying their example, to depart from their standard of truth. " Whether the omnipotence of the state be or be not a Christian or protestant principle, this is at any rate the form that protestantism then assumed most distinctly in England. Political and worldly interests soon gained an entire preponderance over all questions of religion and of truth; with whatever sincerity the latter may have been pleaded at the beginning of the movement."[4] This vicious principle distorted the fairer features of the reformation from its very birth, and has been productive of untold mischiefs to the present hour. The doctrines, the ceremonies, the services of the Anglican church, were not founded on a conscientious conviction of their necessity to salvation, or of their harmony with the divine mind uttered in the oracles of truth. Neither were they the spring blossomings of an internal and renewed life, bursting forth into forms expressive of its vigour, its purity, and its heavenly origin. On the contrary, they were imposed upon an unwilling people, and but little, if any, improvement took place in the general character and religious feelings of the mass. Whatever of true piety was actually existent, was not the fruit of these changes; neither did it spring from the holy seed of the gospel sown and cherished by regal power. The unsanctioned, discountenanced, and persecuted efforts of men in lowly life, whose hearts the Lord had opened, alone issued in the planting of the tree of liberty and truth.

With the above principle as the basis of their proceedings, Somerset the protector, Cranmer, and others forming the influential portion of the young king's council, commenced their alterations in the national faith. They laboured to erect a church which should retain in mental slavery, and

---

[4] Heber's English Universities, edit. by F. W. Newman, i. 269.

under religious bondage, a people among whom the emanci-
pating truths of scripture were yet freely to circulate; thus
insuring a state of unceasing conflict. The Christian community was to be kept in a perpetual childhood, ever to
remain under the thraldom of tutors and governors. On the
day of the youthful sovereign's coronation, the archbishop
solemnly reminded him, " That being God's vicegerent, and
Christ's vicar in his own dominions, he was obliged to follow
the precedent of Josias, to take care the worship of God was
under due regulations, to suppress idolatry, remove images,
and discharge the tyranny of the bishop of Rome."[5] These
" due regulations" were quickly supplied by the primate's
zeal. A series of injunctions relating to every part of public
worship, pulpit instruction, and private devotion, were furnished to certain visitors appointed to proceed through the
length and breadth of the land, that idolatry and superstition
might be suppressed, the true religion planted, and all hypocrisy, enormities, and abuses extirpated.[6]

The publication of a volume of homilies, to be read to
their flocks by those ministers who could not preach, soon
followed, in which for the first time the important doctrine of
justification by faith alone, was clearly enunciated by state
authority. To Cranmer that part of the book is attributed.[7]
Latymer thus amusingly informs his sovereign how his homi-
letic instructions were received among his people: " Some
call them *homelies,* and indeed so they may be well called, for
they are homely handled. For though the priest read them
never so well, yet if the parish like them not, there is such a
talking and babbling in the church, that nothing can be
heard; and if the parish be good, and the priest naught, he
will so hack it, and chop it, that it were as good for them to
be without it, for any word that shall be understood. And

[5] Collier, v. 182.   [6] Documentary Annals, i. 4, &c.
[7] Cranmer's Remains, ii. 138.

yet (the more pity) this is suffered of your grace's bishops, in their dioceses, unpunished. But I will be a suitor to your grace, that ye will give your bishops charge ere they go home, upon their allegiance, to look better to their flock, and to see your majesty's injunctions better kept, and send your visitors in their tails, and if they be found negligent and faulty in their duties, out with them. I require it, in God's behalf, make them quondams, all the pack of them."[8] Such was the information and advice given by Latymer, himself a quondam bishop, to the youthful monarch, in the "preaching place," in the king's garden at Westminster, the very place where, thirteen years before, Cromwell had advised his sovereign to a course, of which the above was the fruit.

The mental activity of the people could not, however, be confined to the channels hewn out for it. Curious questions were passed about as to the nature of the mystery in the sacrament of the altar, which they were called upon to receive with an unreasoning faith. Even "unseemly and ungodly words" were uttered, by which "the holy body and blood of the Lord" were depraved and reviled. Was it indeed his "blessed body there, head, legs, arms, toes, and nails?" Could it be broken, or chewed in the mouths of the faithful, or was he always swallowed whole? Did they drink the very blood that flowed from his side, or that which remained in the lifeless, crucified form of the buried Saviour? And many other speeches, alike irreverent, were made on this profound mystery. "For reformation whereof, the king's highness, by the advice of the lord protector, and other his majesty's council, straitly willeth and commandeth, that no man, nor person, from henceforth, do in anywise contentiously and openly argue, dispute, reason, preach, or teach, than be expressly taught in the holy scripture;—until such

---

[8] Latymer's Sermons, pp. 121, 122. Parker Soc. edit.

time as the king's majesty shall declare, and set forth, an
open doctrine thereof, for he shall incur the king's high
indignation, and suffer imprisonment, or be otherwise grievously punished." [9]

The "private mind and fantasy" of many persons outran
the wishes of even Cranmer himself, though in some measure
sanctioned by him. The non-observance of many of the
laudable ceremonies of Henry's imposition, called forth, in
less than two months, another proclamation to restrain their
zeal. It was pronounced rash and seditious for any to
preach in any open and unlicensed place, without royal or
episcopal permission, especially since the people were persuaded by private curates, preachers, and other laymen, not
to observe the old and accustomed rites and formalities.[1]

The parliament also added its quota to the general progress. The statute of the six articles was repealed, which
opened the way for the return of many who had gone abroad,
fearing its cruel threatenings, among whom may be mentioned
John Hooper and Miles Coverdale. The communion was
commanded to be administered in both kinds, private masses
abolished, and bishops in future were to be appointed by the
royal letters patent alone. A further gift of all unsuppressed
chantries, and of legacies given for obits and lamps in
churches, was bestowed upon the king, to the profit of his
many hungry courtiers.[2]

Many of the old superstitions were by these means rooted
up, but without any general increase of true piety or even
morality. This "dissolution of life," says Becon, a reformer
and actor in these times, "this impiety of manners maketh
the gospel of our salvation to be evil spoken of. How can it
otherwise be ? For when they see an alteration in religion,
and no alteration in manners, but a continuance in the old, or

[9] Doc. Annals, Proclamation, Dec.   [1] Doc. Annals, i. 34.
27th, 1547, vol. i. 26.   [2] Neal, i. 33, 34.

else a practice of much more ungodliness than heretofore hath been used, the adversaries of God's truth take easily an occasion to blaspheme the Christian doctrine." [3] Churches did not escape profanation; frays, quarrels, blood-shedding, the passage of horses and mu es through them, were frightfully prevalent. " They were like a stable, or common inn, or rather a den and sink of all unchristness," says the proclamation by which these " evil demeanours " were forbidden. [4]

To this was added a prohibition of the exercise of the public ministry. The people had been fed with controversy, and with bitter disputes, it was said, instead of " the manna sent down from heaven."

But few, therefore, were permitted to exercise the calling of God, being those only who were licensed by the king's council. It appeared fitting to the rulers of the nation's conscience to send the clergy for a space into retirement, " to apply themselves to prayer to Almighty God." The loving subjects of the sovereign, could in the meantime occupy themselves with "due prayer in the church," although the service was still in Latin, "and in the patient hearing of the godly homilies," until one uniform order could be prepared for their use. [5] " What a system must that be, which recognizes in any human being a right to issue such an edict as this; an edict so fearfully impious as to involve a counteraction, and that on no limited scale, of God's wisest and most gracious designs! But such is the system which the Reformation perpetuated in this country, and which has subsequently been maintained by means in perfect harmony with its antichristian character." [6]

As the clergy were unable to instruct the people by an

[3] Becon's Jewel of Joy, p. 416. Works, Parker Soc. edit.

[4] Strype's Cranmer, p. 251.

[5] Fuller, book I. sect. i. c. 15, vol. ii. 314. edit. 1842.

[6] Price, Hist. of Nonconf. i. 76.

exhibition of divine truth, derived from a knowledge of God's word, and an experience of its power, so were they equally impotent and unqualified to pour forth at the throne of grace acceptable prayer.

With them, prayer could be nothing but a form, and that was now provided. Uniformity in divine worship was deemed a matter of the greatest moment. To effect this every holy emotion of the heart must be suppressed, every aspiration of the heaven-born spirit hindered in its flight, and all communion with the Father in heaven checked, but such as the book of Common Prayer now set forth allowed. True it is, that legends, responds, commemorations, synodals, and the uncertain stories of the Roman breviaries, had no place in this purgated edition of the missal; but yet there were prayers for the dead, Mariolatry was tacitly sanctioned, baptismal regeneration taught, and the exorcism of the unclean spirit from the infant to be baptized, was commanded to the officiating priest.[7]

"Here you have," say the compilers, in the preface, "an order for prayer (as touching the reading of holy scripture) much agreeable to the mind and purpose of the old fathers, and a great deal more profitable and commodious, than that which of late was used. It is more profitable, because there are left out many things whereof some be untrue, some uncertain, some vain and superstitious; and is ordained nothing to be read, but the very pure word of God, the holy

---

[7] " I command thee, unclean spirit, in the name, &c. that thou come out and depart from these infants, whom our Lord Jesus Christ hath vouchsafed to call to his holy baptism, to be made members of his body and of his holy congregation. Thou cursed spirit, remember thy sentence, remember thy judgment, remember the day to be at hand wherein thou shalt burn in fire everlasting, prepared for thee and thy angels. And presume not hereafter to exercise any tyranny towards these infants, whom Christ has bought with his precious blood, and by his holy baptism calleth to be of his flock." King Edward's Liturgies, pp. 108, 109 ; Parker Society's edit.

scriptures, or that which is evidently grounded upon the same." In this the Apocrypha was included.[8]

The ceremonies to be used were at the same time determined. In the exposition of their sentiments on this subject, it was declared by the compilers to be a great crime to neglect or break in upon the order of the church, and that private men ought not to presume to draw models or make such arrangements; it was the sole duty of the governors of the church. An exact uniformity of habits and ceremonies was insisted upon. The square cap and the surplice were so important, as to be retained at the risk of the reformation itself. Superstitious in their use, abused to idolatrous purposes as they had been, and conscientious as some were in the rejection of them, yet it was the pleasure of the rulers of the church to preserve them.

" Our reformers split upon this rock, sacrificing the peace of the church to a mistaken necessity of an exact uniformity of doctrine and worship, in which it was impossible for all men to agree." Nevertheless, in all this we are informed by the act of uniformity, which imposed the book upon the people, that the "archbishop of Canterbury, and certain of the most discreet and learned bishops, had as well an eye and respect to the most sincere and pure Christian religion taught by the scripture, as to the usages of the primitive church;" and thus had made " one convenient and meet order, rite, and fashion, of common and open prayer, and administration of the sacraments;....the which, at this time, *by aid of the Holy Ghost*, with one uniform agreement is of them concluded !"[9]

And now Cranmer and his associates in this work flatter themselves that the honour of God, and great quietness, will ensue by the compulsory use of a form thus divinely prepared;

[8] King Edward's Liturgies, p. 18. [9] Neal, i. 37, edit. 1837.

as if at their command life would breath its vital energy through this mechanism of piety. At all events, every other manifestation of spiritual life must be extinguished. He who ventures to "sing or say common prayer" after any other manner, or speak any thing that may derogate from the excellence of the book, shall forfeit a year's income from his benefice, and be imprisoned for six months. For a second offence, he shall be deprived altogether of his promotions, and be imprisoned for a year. A person having no preferment, shall be incarcerated; the first time for six months, the second during the remainder of his life. So solicitous indeed are they that due honour and respect should be paid to the work of their hands, that penalties are enacted for those who in "interludes, plays, songs, or rhymes, or by any other open words declare or speak" to the depravation or despising of the book.[1] Thus they enforced the motto so significantly adopted, and placed in "the border around the title page in black letter," *Let every soul submit himself unto the authority of the higher powers. For there is no power but of God. The powers that be are ordained of God. Whosoever, therefore, resisteth the power, resisteth the ordinance of God.*

Can it be supposed that a book, so imperfect as in three years to require revision, so full of erroneous sentiments, and imposed with such cruel conditions, was indeed according to the mind of the Spirit of God? Could this volume be the true exponent of the unutterable groanings which he oft raiseth in the hearts of God's children? Was this persecuting edict a fit accompaniment to the confessions of sin, of human frailty and corruption, marked down in its pages as the meet language of priest and people, of king and subject, when in His presence who willeth not the death of a sinner? Or must we think that the difference of the human and divine

---

[1] Dodd, ii. App. lxxii.

is such, that the work of man requires for its recommendation and defence, an artillery of power which the word of God in its plenitude of might rejects? Surely the claim of infallibility, involved in this assumption of sovereignty over conscience is alike odious and profane, whether exercised by a king or by a pope.

The reformation in this reign was completed by the promulgation of a series of forty-two articles, which were to constitute the doctrinal belief of the church of England. These vary but little from those afterwards adopted in the reign of Elizabeth, and which have ever since continued to be recognised as the standard of faith by the oaths and subscriptions of the Anglican clergy. Whether they have produced that unity in the faith, and rooted out "that discord of opinions," for which they were intended, we need not inquire. Those who subscribe either believe them to be true, or else they greatly prevaricate.[2] At all events, we know that their authoritative imposition has not quieted the scruples of tender consciences, nor silenced the utterances of some true-hearted men, whose faith has been drawn from another standard, which, in their weakness it may be, they have thought to be the only one—the volume of inspired truth.

That persecutions should result from these proceedings, was inevitable. Violent efforts to burst open the doors of conscience, and to sit enthroned on that seat of Deity, as his vicegerent, cannot fail to awaken resistance or produce hypocrisy; to advance true religion they were worse than useless. Therefore, "ambition and emulation among the nobility, presumption and disobedience among the common people, grew so extravagant and insolent, that England seemed to be in a downright frenzy. The wise and good among the papists grew confirmed in their persuasion, that a corrupt

---

[2] Burnet, ii. 313.

church was better than no church at all." The sermons of
the time give a frightful picture of the state of society. "All
men," says Hooper in one of his discourses, "confess that
sin never so abounded."[3] Gambling, prostitution, separations
of husbands from their wives, profane swearing, frauds in
every trade, impunity of murder and theft, owing to the
corruption of judges, and of every principle of justice, were
the frequent topics of denunciation from the pulpits of the
day.

While bishops and legislators were settling creeds, and
forms of worship, the people were running madly to destruction. The shackles of ancient superstitions were in part
broken, their spells were well-nigh gone. No new form of
spiritual belief had as yet taken their place, and bound the
partially freed spirit. Licentiousness even found a support
in a perverted view of gospel truth.

The martyr Ridley shall speak for us in a "Piteous Lamentation," when taking a retrospect of these times: "As for
Latymer, Lever, Bradford, and Knox, their tongues were so
sharp, they ripped in so deep in their galled backs, to have
purged them, no doubt, of that filthy matter that was festered
in their hearts, of insatiable covetousness, of filthy carnality
and voluptuousness, of intolerable ambition and pride, of
ungodly loathsomeness to hear poor men's causes, and to hear
God's word, that these men of all other, these magistrates
then could never abide. Other there were, very godly men,
and well learned, that went about by the wholesome plasters
of God's word, howbeit after a more soft manner of handling
the matter; but alas! all sped in like. For all that could be
done of all hands, their disease did not minish, but daily did
increase.....As for the common sort of other inferior magistrates, as judges of the laws, justices of the peace, serjeants,

[3] Haweis's Sketches of the Reformation, pp. 142, 143.

common lawyers, it may be truly said of them, as of the most part of the clergy, of curates, vicars, parsons, prebendaries, doctors of the law, archdeacons, deans, yea; and I may say, of bishops also, I fear me, for the most part, although I doubt not but God had and hath ever, whom he in every state knew and knoweth to be his; but for the most part, I say, they were never persuaded in their hearts, but from the teeth forward, and for the king's sake, in the truth of God's word; and yet all these did dissemble, and bear a copy of a countenance, as if they had been sound within."[4] Truly no very encouraging success for formularies of faith enjoined by royalty, for changes of religion supported by hope of gain, or fear of suffering.

The reformers were not backward in recognising, both in theory and in practice, the principle of persecution necessarily involved in the assumption of a regal right to determine the faith of the people. Persecution was not an accident of the system which the protestant divines sought to establish. It was as much involved in their idea of the might and majesty of kings, as rulers of the church and lawgivers to the consciences of their subjects, as in the pope's claim of supremacy over the soul, as the representative on earth of the Lord Jesus Christ. Both were hateful and blasphemous assumptions of a power belonging to the Highest alone; when exerted, it must persecute. For a hundred and fifty years the church of England became a persecuting church, and for another equal period she strenuously maintained the test and corporation laws; which, while in some measure they restrained her power, stamped with obloquy and degradation those whom she could no longer hurt nor destroy. The introduction to the pieces in this volume would not be complete, were we to fail to give prominence to this feature of the establishment, against which their authors were the earliest to reclaim and to condemn.

[4] Ridley's Works, p. 59 ; Parker Society's edit.

The act of parliament of 1534, by which the submission of the clergy to the royal supremacy was sanctioned, and enacted into law, provided that the various constitutions, canons, and synodical decrees, under which the church had been governed, should be revised by a commission of thirty-two persons, to be appointed by the king. Whatever canons they deemed worthy of preservation, were to be retained, the remainder abolished, "and made frustrate;" the royal consent being declared sufficient to give them the force of law. This act was renewed in 1536, and again in 1544. By the commissioners appointed under the last act, a body of ecclesiastical law was prepared, but the letter of ratification, though made out, never obtained the royal signature. Another ineffectual attempt to give it legal existence followed in 1550, when, under the immediate direction of Cranmer, assisted by Taylor, Haddon, and Peter Martyr, the compilation was perfected. Numerous corrections in the handwriting of Cranmer and Martyr, may still be seen in a manuscript copy of the code, preserved in the British Museum. The early death of Edward alone prevented it from having legal authority.[5] This code of ecclesiastical law punishes heresy with death.

We are told by the editor of Cranmer's Remains, that this book " may be safely referred to as an authentic record of the archbishop's opinions."[6] It threatens the penalty of death, and confiscation of goods, against a denial of the Trinity, and certain sentiments of the baptists. The unlawfulness of magistracy, a community of goods, the universal right of any to assume the pastoral office, the symbolical nature of the sacraments, and the unlawfulness of infant baptism, are particularly denounced as heretical. "In case excommunication was despised, and the discipline of the church made no impression, the culprits were then to be delivered into the hands

<hr/>

[5] Jenkyn's Cranmer, i. Pref. p. cx.   [6] Ibid, p. cxi.

of the secular magistrate, and they were to suffer death by the law."[7]

It has been questioned by some of our historians, as by Burnet, and more lately by Townsend, whether this deliverance to the secular power really implied the penalty of death. But no doubt can be left on this point, if we take into consideration the share that Cranmer had in the martyrdoms of Joan Boucher, and George Van Pare, and the expressed sentiments of others of the reformers.

Thus writes Thomas Becon, chaplain to archbishop Cranmer, and prebendary of Canterbury, in the reign of Edward the Sixth:—

" *Father.* And what sayest thou of heretics?

" *Son.* Even the same that I have said of idolaters, and false prophets.

" *Father.* May the magistrates also punish them?

" *Son.* Yea, and also take them out of this life, if they will not repent, amend, and come to the truth." Again—

" *Father.* Shall he be straightways put to death?

" *Son.* St. Paul saith, *The magistrate beareth not the sword in vain.* If he that beareth false witness against man be worthy of death by the commandment of God, is he worthy of less punishment that beareth false witness against God?..... Notwithstanding, it is to be wished, that.....the magistrate would first of all gently and lovingly deal with heretics, and see into what conformity he could bring them with his wisdom and counsel, and also suffer them to have access unto such as be godly learned, which may yet once again have conference with them."

It is somewhat sickening after this, to hear him exhorting the temporal rulers to " be no longer the pope's hangmen."

---

[7] Collier, v. 480, edit. 1840. Preb. Townsend's Prel. Dissertation to Fox's Acts and Mon. p. 181, last edit.

He adds, " these smeared pill-pates, I would say, prelates, first of all accused him, (the heretic), and afterwards pronounced the sentence of death upon him, and straightways delivered him to the temporal magistrate for to be put to execution, making the magistrate their hangman, and bondslave, to hang, to draw, to quarter, to burn, to drown, &c. as it pleased them to appoint. O slavery! O misery! O unnoble nobility !"[8] Is this mere blindness, or worthless hypocrisy? What appreciable difference is there between the reformer and the papist?

Even Latymer could speak complacently to his young sovereign of the cruel death that certain had suffered for their faith. " The anabaptists," says he, " that were burnt here in divers towns in England, (as I heard of credible men, I saw not them myself,) went to their death even *intrepide*, as ye will say, without any fear in the world, cheerfully.—Well, let them go !"[9]

To these let us add one more testimony; that of the ornament and boast of the English church, bishop Jewel. His adversary, Harding, taunted him with the brotherhood of certain heretics, whom the papists regarded as the spawn of the reformation. " There is Servetus," saith he, " the Arian, burnt at Geneva, and David George, whose bones were exhumed and burnt at Basil, were they not your brothers? And was not poor Joan of Kent also a sister of yours?" Thus replieth the " Bishop of Sarisburie. As for David George, and Servetus the Arian, and such other the like, they were yours, M. Harding, they were not of us. You brought them up, the one in Spain, the other in Flanders. We detected their heresies, and not you. We arraigned them; we condemned them. We put them to the execution

---

[8] Becon's Catechism, pp. 312—315.   [9] Fourth Sermon before Edward VI.
Parker Society's edit.   p. 160; Parker Society.

of the laws. It seemeth very much to call them our brothers, because we burnt them."[1] Alas! in Joan's condemnation many of the principal reformers had a hand, and countenanced her death. Cranmer, Latymer, Ridley, Lever, and Hutchinson, beside the members of the king's council, consented to imbrue their hands in the blood of this poor female, whose opinion it is more than probable they mistook on a point of the profoundest mystery. Our duty now calls us to refer to the history of the people to whom she belonged, and to view under these two reigns their struggle for truth and liberty.

SECTION III.

THE BAPTISTS.

"THE Reformation had scarcely boasted an existence of five years, when, from the midst of its adherents, men arose who declared it to be insufficient."[2] Their proceedings at once awakened the most virulent opposition and bitter complaint. The chief weapon of the reformers was most unexpectedly employed against themselves; their professed scriptural teaching came to be examined by the test they had so successfully applied to the dogmas of Rome; and scripture authority to be urged by men, whom universities had not nourished, nor academical honours graced, for practices and truths, to some extent destructive of the position which had been taken by the followers of Luther, Zuingle, and Calvin.

[1] Jewel's Works, Defence of Apology, pp. 27, 28, folio edit. 1611.

[2] Moehler's Symbolism, ii. 155, translated by Robertson.

f

The church of God must be a community of holy men.

Faith is the result of divine tuition alone, and cannot be compelled by fire or sword.

A rite which has neither the sanction nor command of the Lord Jesus Christ, or his apostles, must not be admitted among the ordinances of the Lord's house.

Secular potentates have neither place nor dominion in the kingdom of Him who is the *blessed and only Potentate, the King of kings and Lord of lords.* As there is but *one Lord,* so is there but *one lawgiver* in the church, Jesus Christ.[3]

Such were some of those principles, the enunciation of which called forth a torrent of abuse and persecution upon the heads of the baptists. They were regarded as the Pariah sect among religious communities, and no outrage upon truth or justice was left uncommitted to crush them.

One simple principle, now regarded as an axiom of a scriptural church policy, lay at the foundation of this internal movement in the bosom of the reformation. It shall be given in the words of the historian Mosheim: " The kingdom of Christ, or the visible church he had established on earth, was an assembly of true and real saints, and ought, therefore, to be inaccessible to the wicked and unrighteous, and also exempt from all those institutions which human prudence suggests to oppose the progress of iniquity, or to correct or reform transgressors."[4]

---

[3] Osiandri, Enchiridion, Controv. pp. 30,43,112,113. Tubingæ,1605. Credunt, Dominum nostrum et Salvatorem Jesum Christum, illud in regno suo spirituali, hoc est, in ecclesia Novi Testamenti, quæ non est de mundo, ideoque mundanum regnum maxime respicit, non instituisse, neque officiis suæ ecclesiæ adjunxisse,&c. Schyn, Hist. Mennonitarum Plenior Deductio, p. 50. Non

ensibus et corporalibus armis, sed spiritualibus solummodo, hoc est verbo Dei et Spiritu sancto pugnant. Ibid. p. 147. Populus Dei sese non armat carnalibus armis, sed solum armatura Dei, armisque justitiæ. Ibid, p. 214. Bullinger, adv. Catabaptist, fol. 108, 152, edit. 1535. Symbolism, ii. pp. 183—185.

[4] Eccles. Hist. pp. 517, 518 ; royal 8vo. edit.

All secular interference must therefore be excluded from this holy community. Its formation is the work of the divine Spirit operating through the word. Its laws are the precepts, holy and self-denying, of the Lord Jesus Christ. Its ceremonies are the simple emblems and memorials of a life imparted and sustained by the Spirit of God, through the death of the Son of God. Here, since no human laws can intervene, no human allegiance can be due. The conscience is God's seat, the church his temple; which no human legislator should dare to desecrate, no human power control.[5]

This primary and exalted idea of the church of Christ, cherished, and sought to be realized by the baptists, was adverse to the views of the reformers. From this difference naturally resulted the opposition, which, on the one side, led to the oppression of conscience, and on the other, to the maintenance of its freedom. The reformers, by inclosing in the fold of the church all of every degree, age, and character, were constrained to employ, and to rely upon external means to effect that internal change which was allowed to be an essential feature of the true Christian. The church with them was not the segregation of the good, in bonds of holy amity and alliance with each other and the Lord, from the mass of pollution reigning around them, but embraced in its maternal arms all who at any age had been sealed by baptism as the church's own, whether they were helpless infants, or strangers to the power of spiritual truth. It was sufficient that they bore the magic mark, which, it was asserted, made them children of God, and inheritors of the kingdom of heaven. Such a church might be constituted by human agencies; it was within human power to effect it; and accordingly, by the

---

[5] Nam quia Rex spiritualis est, ipsius regnum non de mundo, sed de cælo et spirituale, ipsius leges spirituales, ipsius subditi cælorum municipes, qui in hoc mundo non stabilem habent civitatem, sed futuram expectant. Schyn, Plenior Deduct, p. 53.

secular arm the reformers sought to frame it. The operations
of the divine Spirit were not absolutely essential to the
formation of such a community ; nor need they wait for living
stones to build the temple of the Lord. The materials were
at hand; the initiatory rite could be easily applied. Repentance towards God, and faith in the Lord Jesus Christ, could
be promised by surety, or supplied by an assent to creeds.

It was, moreover, the duty of the secular magistrate to
shape and fashion the church, so called, to that form which
his conscience, instructed by the word of God, or by the
interpretations of the church's teachers, should dictate.[6]
To kings was granted the high honour of being its nursing
fathers, to protect it from its foes, to maintain in physical
comfort its ministers, to root out the weeds of evil doctrine,
and to execute the decisions of the ecclesiastical body ; force
thus necessarily entered into this idea of the Christian community ; and, without exception, the reformers yielded to
the temporal powers the right of determining the form of the
church in their respective dominions.

The fundamental idea of the baptists was antagonistic
with all this. They thought and said that the temple could
not be built until God had provided the stones. Holy men
must be first produced by the power of the Spirit of God,
and then shall a building rise to the glory of Him who had
redeemed them by his blood. No human workman could be
of use but as the channel of blessing; it was the prerogative
of God to create anew in Christ Jesus. His word was the
only effectual instrument of divine energy : force and coercion
of every kind were inadmissible. *Faith is the gift of God.*

---

[6] Cur ego hodie tantam sibi potestatem
in rebus fidei sumit Christianus magistratus ?—Hoc agit non ut magistratus
sed ut Christianus magistratus, nec facit
hoc sine precepto et exemplo....Inspect-
emus exemplum Josaphat, Joiadæ,
Josiæ, Ezechiæ, Nabuchodonosoris, et
Darii, apud Danielem. Bullinger, adv.
Catabapt. fol. 108, 109.

Faith cometh by hearing, and hearing by the word of God; and no other weapon must the ministers of God's word employ.

Since then the church ought to be the aggregated result of an internal divine operation, exerted on every individual before he becomes a member of it, so in its formation no kind of outward compulsion can be permitted. The unconscious babe cannot be *made* a member of a community, where a hearty willing assent of the regenerated mind is an essential condition of membership, since intelligence is not there to give value and significance to the deed; nor may men be driven by force or fear, as foolish sheep, within the fortified barrier of the nation's church, since these cannot convert the soul. "Thus it was an ideal state of the Christian church, that floated before the imagination of the anabaptists,—the confused representation of a joyful kingdom of holy and blessed spirits, which inspired these sectaries with such deep enthusiasm, gave them such power and constancy of endurance, under all persecutions, and caused them to exert on all sides so contagious an influence."[7] In accordance with these views, they are represented by Justus Menius as thus introducing the novice into the sacred fold: "If thou wilt be saved, thou must truly renounce and give up all thy works, and all creatures, and lastly, thy own self, and must believe in God alone. But now I ask thee, dost thou renounce creatures? Yes. I ask thee again, dost thou renounce thy own self? Yes. Dost thou believe in God alone? Yes. Then I baptize thee in the name," &c.[8]

We may briefly state the opposite ideas of the reformers and the baptists on this important subject, as follows.

The former relied on the secular arm to build and maintain

[7] Moehler's Symbolism, ii. 157, 158.   [8] Quoted in Moehler's Symbolism, ii. 163.

the church; the latter, on the Spirit of God.   Hence arose on
the one side the civil changes, the congresses, the diets, the
wars, the conflicts of crowned heads, as they adhered to Rome
or Wittenberg.   On the other, the persecutions, oppressions,
sufferings, scourgings, the *noyades*, and fiery martyrdoms,
which attended and lit up the labours of these calumniated
men.   Oppression of conscience signalized the progress of
the first, liberty of conscience attended the teaching of the
last.

Nothing can be more plain on the surface of history than
the fact, that this people came every where into collision with
the civil magistrate.   Their existence was regarded as fatal to
the well-being of all society.   " They show themselves to be
the enemies of God and man," says Calvin.   " They wish,"
he continues, " to abrogate the power of the sword, the
administration of the public weal.   By a shorter cut, they plot
the ruin of the world, and the introduction of a greater license
for robbery, than can otherwise be found."[9]   But is this
heavy charge true?   Were they the enemies of all government, the sworn foes of all rule and magisterial authority?
Let the accuser himself reply; for it is thus he represents
their sentiments as from their own lips.   " We grant that the
sword is ordained of God, but it is without the fold or perfect
community of Christ.   For this reason the princes and powers
of this world are apppointed to punish offenders, even with
death.   But in the perfect church of Christ, excommunication
is the final punishment, and without corporal death."[1]   What
is this but to say that the sphere of the civil magistrate is
without the church, and not within it; that his laws bind man
in his social relations only, but that in the church there is
another Lawgiver, on whose prerogative he must not trench.
Obedience to the civil power they enjoined both as a civil and
religious duty, but resisted its exercise in things of God.

[9] Instruct. adv. Anab. in Tract. Theol. fol. 367. Amstel. 1667.   [1] Ibid. fol. 364.

A considerable number of the baptists, however, carried their views of the spirituality and purity of the church still further. It was thought to be opposed to the humility of the Christian, to seek for lordship over his brethren. Christians were to be subject only to the meek, gentle, and pure precepts of Jesus; their only power was that of separation from the evils that arose in their midst. Nor can we be surprised, that, witnessing as they did the perversion of the civil authority, and suffering inconceivable anguish from its cruel exercise, they came to deem it an office incompatible with their allegiance to their Lord, and thought it a forbidden thing to perform the functions of magistracy; that is, of such magistracy, since they saw it nowhere exercised in the mild and loving spirit of the gospel.[2] For, surely nothing could be more dreadful, or more unchristian, than the barbarous and excruciating tortures inflicted by magistrates in the name of law on these disciples of Christ; magistrates were their foes, their oppressors, their persecutors; inflicting punishment, not for sedition, treason, or crime, but for matters of opinion and faith.[3] Is it wonderful if in some few instances they became foes to magistrates? The coercion and force daily practised in both temporal and spiritual affairs, must have appeared to them inseparable from the magisterial office; which, however necessary for the civil rule of empires and kingdoms, are utterly inadmissible into the kingdom of Christ.

[2] Ipsis admodum difficile videtur, religioni Christianæ exacte obedire, et simul officio magistratus politici rite perfungi. Schyn, Plenior Deduct. p. 50. Some thought capital punishments altogether discordant with the spirit of the gospel, and desired their cessation.

[3] "Could the baptists," says Bayle, " only produce those who were put to death for attempts against the government, their bulky martyrology would make a ridiculous figure; but it is certain that several anabaptists, who suffered death courageously for their opinions, had never any intention of rebelling." Hist. and Critical Dict. Art. Anabaptists, Note F. edit. Lond. 1734. A specimen of the deeply interesting narratives, contained in the martyrology above referred to, will be presently given in the martyrdoms of Jan Peters and Hendrik Terwoort.

It is not within our purpose to examine or refute the common relations of the deeds at Munster. Various considerations might be suggested that would palliate or throw doubt on the narratives of those events. It is certain that the insurrection was clearly opposed to the doctrine, universally maintained among the baptists, of the divine institution of magistracy for the government of the world; [4] and it must be traced to that oppression which makes a wise man mad. Laden with chains, incarcerated in a noisome and pestilential dungeon, a cruel and merciless death before him, Knipper-dolling maintained to his examiners that magistracy was the ordinance of God, but that when the commands of the temporal were opposed to those of the heavenly superior, "we must obey God rather than man." We allow, said his interrogators, that we do not owe obedience to the magistrate when he would compel us contrary to the teaching of Christ; but it does not follow that it is lawful for a private person to repel force by force, he should rather observe the precept of Christ, who saith, *When men persecute you in one city, flee ye to another.* Most significant is the brevity and treacherous recollection of the examiner as he gives the prisoner's reply. " He answered, I know not what," says Corvinus, "concerning the tyranny of those who had been the cause of their revolt." The rapacity and cruelty of his employers must be touched with a gentle hand. The words of the " babbling " prisoner, might awaken, if repeated, unpleasant and perhaps fearful thoughts in the mind of the oppressor.[5]

---

[4] Credunt, eum esse Dei ordinationem, necessariam institutamque ad gubernationem communis societatis humanæ, &c. Schyn, Plen. Deduct. p. 49. Hist. Mennon. p. 214.

[5] Eadem inscitia de magistratu garriebat, quem, tametsi ordinationem Dei esse fatebatur, tamen rebellionem, si quid secus ac Christus docet, jubeat, approbavit, fretus petrina illa sententia, Oportet Deo magis obedire quam hominibus. Ubi quum nos fateremur obedientiam quidem magistratui non deberi, si nos a Christi doctrina transversos agere conetur, attamen hinc non sequi, idcirco vim vi repellere, privatis per-

It was the crime of these persecuted people, that they rejected secular interference in the church of God; it was the boast and aim of the reformers everywhere to employ it: the natural fruit of the one was persecution, of the other liberty. Among them, therefore, we must look for the germs of that religious freedom we now enjoy, though still imperfectly understood. Nor shall we be disappointed in our search; nor open to contradiction, when we say, that they alone clearly perceived its truth and value, and maintained it during the stormy and eventful period of the reformation. That they should hold it was the inevitable consequence of their idea of the church, and it was stamped upon them with a distinctness, which neither the flames nor floods of martyrdom could destroy. It is only thus can be explained the universal storm of execration and persecution that fell upon them. They were thought to deny one of the highest attributes of human government: it brought them into collision with the very mainspring and support of the reformation.

There is not a Confession of faith, nor a creed framed by any of the reformers, which does not give to the magistrate a coercive power in religion, and almost every one at the same time curses the resisting baptist. Thus, in the confession of Basle, it is written, " God hath assigned to the magistrate, who is his minister, the sword, and chief external power, for the defence of the good, and for the revenging and punishing of the evil, Rom. xiii. 4; 1 Peter ii. 14. Therefore every Christian magistrate doth direct all his strength to this, that among those which are committed to his charge, the word of God may be sanctified, his kingdom may be enlarged, and men may live according to his will, with an earnest rooting

---

sonis licere, Sed potius id faciendum esse, quod Christus docuerit, Si vos persecuti fuerint in hac civitate, migrate in aliam, respondit quid nescio de eorum Tyrannide, qui rebellandi ipsis occasionem præbuissent. De Miserabili Monast. Anabap. Epistola Ant. Corvini ad Spalatinum Viteb. 1536.

out of all naughtiness." Thus the confession of Bohemia,
" They do govern instead of God upon earth, and are his
deputies; it is meet that they frame themselves to the example of the superior Lord, by following and resembling him,
and by learning of him mercy and justice. . . . . He ought to
be a partaker, and, as it were, chiefly, a minister of the
power of the Lamb, Jesus Christ, ... by this authority of
his, to set forth the truth of the holy gospel, make way
for the truth wheresoever, be a defender of the ministers
and people of Christ, suffer not (so far as in him lieth)
idolatry, or the tyranny of antichrist, much less follow the
same." [6]

In these sentiments all the reformed communities agreed.
All committed themselves to a course fatal to the liberties of
man, and to the regal prerogatives of Jesus Christ.   Honour,
ease, and wealth, flowed in upon the supporters of thrones,
but tribulation unto death was the portion of those who ventured to oppose them.   Most affectingly does the eminent
Simon Menno refer to this contrast.   "For eighteen years
with my poor feeble wife and little children has it behoved
me to bear great and various anxieties, sufferings, griefs,
afflictions, miseries, and persecutions, and in every place to
find a bare existence, in fear and danger of my life.   While
some preachers are reclining on their soft beds and downy
pillows, we oft are hidden in the caves of the earth ;—while
they are celebrating the nuptial or natal days of their children,
with feasts and pipes, and rejoicing with the timbrel and the
harp, we are looking anxiously about, fearing the barking of
the dogs, lest persecutors should be suddenly at the door ;—
while they are saluted by all around as doctors, masters, lords,
we are compelled to hear ourselves called anabaptists, ale-
house preachers, seducers, heretics, and to be hailed in the
devil's name.   In a word, while they for their ministry are

[6] Harmony of Confessions, pp. 475—477.   Hall's edit. 1842.

remunerated with annual stipends, and prosperous days, our wages are the fire, the sword, the death." [7]

Were they inferior to their persecutors in godliness, or deserving of this fate for their crimes? Or was it but the fulfilment of the Saviour's word, *In the world ye shall have tribulation?* Let a catholic reply, the president of the famous council of Trent. "If you behold their cheerfulness in suffering persecutions, the anabaptists run before all their heretics. If you will have regard to the number, it is like that in multitude they would swarm above all others, if they were not grievously plagued and cut off with the knife of persecution. If you have an eye to the outward appearance of godliness, both the Lutherans and Zuinglians must needs grant that they far pass them.

"If you will be moved by the boasting of the word of God, these be no less bold than Calvin to preach, and their doctrine must stand aloft above all the glory of the world, must stand invincible above all power, because it is not their word, but the word of the living God. Neither do they cry with less boldness than Luther, that with their doctrine, which is the word of God, they shall judge the angels. And surely, how many soever have written against this heresy, whether they were catholics or heretics, [reformers] they were able to, overthrow it, not so much by the testimony of the scriptures as by the authority of the church." [8]

We cannot pass over one instance of their patience under suffering, and boldness in the face of death, illustrative as it is of their attachment to liberty of conscience, and of the views

---

[7] Schyn. Plenior Deduct. p. 133.

[8] The Hatchet of Heresies, translated by R. Shacklock, fol. 48, edit. 1565. After noticing the arguments of Guy de Bres, Bayle proceeds, "A proof how greatly prejudicial the sect of the ana-baptists has been to the protestants, who were obliged to refute it by arguments, which were turned against them by the papists." Bayle's Dict. Art. Anabaptists, note F.

of their character we have endeavoured to enforce.   The
scene is in Holland, the year 1551.   An old man of seventy-
five is brought before the bloody tribunal; his hair white,
his body lean with age, his manners irreproachable, springing
from a heart fearing God.   In his old age he had been baptized, and received into the community of the church.   And
now, as a sheep bound for the slaughter-house, and surrounded
by a number of the burghers, he sits calmly awaiting the
approach of the criminal magistrate to pronounce the sentence
of death.

An officer speaks to him; Good father, why do you continue thus obstinately in your cursed error, do you think there
is no such place as hell?

Old Man. Sir, I believe a hell most certainly, but I know
nothing of the errors you mention.

Another. Yes, you are in an error, and in so dreadful a
one, that if you die in it you will be damned for ever.

Old Man.   Are you sure of that?

Officer.   Yes, it as sure as any thing in the world.

Old Man.   If it is so, then are ye murderers of my soul.

There is silence in the multitude as the old man thus discourses; their attention is more earnest, and the officer, half
enraged, and ashamed, loudly continues.

Officer.   What do you say, you impertinent fellow?   Are
we the murderers of your soul?

Old Man.   Do not be angry, Sir, at the sound of truth.
You yourself know that faith is the gift of God, that neither
I nor any other can extort this saving gift out of God's
hands, that God bestows his gifts on one man early, on another late, just as he called the husbandmen into the vineyard.
Suppose now that I had not yet received this gift, as you
have, ought you to punish me for that misfortune?   Might
not God, in case you suffered me to live, might he not
impart to me as well as to you, this wholesome gift in a

week, a month, a year? If then you hinder me from sharing therein, by depriving me of this time of grace, what are you otherwise than murderers of my soul?

But the officer of justice hurries him away, amid the murmurs of the people, whose hearts are moved by his courage and his words. His condemnation does not linger, neither does the sun reach his meridian splendour, before the glory of the Lamb bursts upon the vision of his martyred servant. He was beheaded for his testimony to Christ.[9]

The reasoning of this old disciple cannot fail to strike the reader, as coincident with that employed by Busher in the pages of the first treatise in this volume.[1] They were taught in the same school, had received the "like precious faith," and they bare witness to the cruelty and wrong of persecution for conscience' sake.

No country afforded a refuge to this persecuted people, though everywhere identified with the beginnings of the reformation.[2] Under whatever phase the reformed doctrines appeared, the principle which governed their success or defeat met with strenuous opponents in the baptists. Others might lend their consciences to the yoke of the civil power, they must resist; it was not the easy yoke of Christ. Their appearance in England had been prepared by the publication of a book, entitled "The Sum of Scripture;" many extracts from which obtained the honour of a formal condemnation in an assembly of bishops and others, convened by Warham, the archbishop of Canterbury, at the command of king Henry VIII. in the year 1530. It does not appear whether this book was the production of a baptist, although

[9] Brandt's Hist. of the Reformation in the Low Countries, i. 92, edit. Lond. 1720.

[1] See pp. 22, 23.

[2] Nam ubicumque Christus emergit, mox adsunt catabaptistæ, ut ecclesias renatas et feliciter institutas vastent ac dissecent. Bullinger, adv. Catabapt. Epist. ad Lector.

the sentiments condemned were unquestionably held by them, and for aught that we can find, by them only. We pass by such as do not relate to our immediate subject, and produce the following:—

" There be two sorts of people in the world, one is the kingdom of God, to which belongeth all true Christian people, and in this kingdom Christ is king and lord, and it is impossible that in this kingdom, that is to say, among very true Christian men, that the sword of justice temporal should have aught to do."

" There is another sort of people belongeth to the world, and they be unrighteous; and they had need of the sword of temporal justice."

" Jesus Christ hath not ordained in his spiritual kingdom, which is all true Christian people, any sword, for he himself is the king and governor, without sword, and without any outward law."

" Christian men among themselves have nought to do with the sword, nor with the law, for that is to them neither needful nor profitable; the secular sword belongeth not to Christ's kingdom, for in it is none but good, and justice."

In another work, condemned at the same time, it was also asserted that, " No man ought to enforce, and compel men to fasting and prayer by laws, as they hitherto have done." [3]

Many other sentiments were with these pronounced ungodly and erroneous. Tyndale's New Testament was especially stigmatized, and the scriptures were declared to be unnecessary for the people. The source of these "damnable heresies " would seem to be indicated by the two proclamations for their suppression, which immediately followed the convention. They had been sown, it was declared, by the

---

[3] Wilkins, Concilia, iii. 732, 733, fol. ed. 1738.

disciples of Luther, *and other heretics*, perverters of Christ's religion. Severe punishments were threatened "against the malicious and wicked sects of heretics, who, by perversion of holy scripture, do induce erroneous opinions, *sow sedition among Christian people*, and finally disturb the peace and tranquillity of Christian realms, as lately happened in some parts of Germany, where, by the procurement and sedition of Martin Luther and other heretics, were slain an infinite number of Christian people." [4]

Reference is here evidently made to the tumults which sprang up in Germany in 1525, and with which it was supposed the doctrines of the baptists had much to do. To none other sect can the sentiments we have quoted, and the condemnation of them in the proclamation, be supposed to refer. Two years before, seven baptists from Holland had been imprisoned, and two of them burnt. [5] Thus clearly showing that such opinions had been broached in this country by members of that sect which was known to hold them.

The year in which Henry obtained the recognition of his claim as supreme head of the church, witnessed its exercise in two proclamations published against the baptists and sacramentaries, as the followers of Zuingle in his opinions on the eucharist, were called. Many of the king's "loving subjects had been induced and encouraged, arrogantly and superstitiously, to argue and dispute in open places, taverns, and ale-houses, not only upon baptism, but also upon the holy sacrament of the altar." The divine honour and glory required his immediate interference, and his grace's church must be defended from the inroads of these pestilent fellows. Of them, and his purposes towards them, he thus informs us:—
" Forasmuch as divers and sundry strangers of the sect and false opinion of the anabaptists and sacramentaries, being

---

[4] Ibid. iii. 737.   [5] Danvers, Treatise of Baptism, p. 307, edit. 1674.

lately come into this realm, where they lurk secretly in divers corners and places, minding craftily and subtilly to provoke and stir the king's loving subjects to their errors and opinions, whereof part of them, by the great travail and diligence of the king's highness and his council, be apprehended and taken, the king's most royal majesty declareth . . . . . like a godly and catholic prince, that he abhorreth and detesteth the same sects, and their wicked and abominable errors and opinions, and intendeth to proceed against such of them as be already apprehended, according to their merits, and the laws of the realm." And he further commands all such as have not been found, to depart in eight or ten days, with all celerity from the kingdom.[6]

The proclamation next following brings into yet closer juxtaposition the royal prerogative, and its persecuting character; it also shows, by its early publication after the above, the futility of all the despot's efforts to destroy the maintainers of these obnoxious opinions. Many strangers, we are informed, baptized in infancy, but who contemning that holy sacrament, had presumptuously re-baptized themselves, had entered the realm, spreading every where their pestilent heresies " against God and his holy scriptures, to the great unquietness of Christendom, and perdition of innumerable Christian souls." A great number had been judicially convicted, " and have and shall for the same suffer the pains of death." The king's most royal majesty, being " supreme head in earth, under God, of the church of England, alway intending to defend and maintain the faith of Christ, and daily studying and minding above all things to save his loving subjects from falling into any erroneous opinions," accordingly ordains the banishment of all such heretics in twelve days, "on pain to suffer death," if they abide, and be apprehended and taken.[7]

---

[6] Wilkins, iii. 777.   [7] Wilkins, iii. 779.

The royal pastor and vicar of Christ soon exhibited, in a somewhat sanguinary manner, his care and anxiety for the eternal well-being of his people. In the following year ten were put to death in sundry places of the realm, while ten others saved their lives by a timely recantation. Besides these, nineteen Hollanders were accused of heretical opinions, "denying Christ to be God and man, or that he took flesh and blood of the Virgin Mary, or that the sacraments had any effect on those that received them." Fourteen adhered to their convictions, and were burnt in pairs in several places. "It was complained," says the historian, "that all these drew their damnable errors from the indiscreet use of the scriptures." It was probably of these sufferers for conscience' sake that Latymer spake, in his sermon before king Edward in 1552, already referred to.[8]

The oppressive and persecuting nature of the royal supremacy was thus distinctly evinced. The political necessities of the king prevented its exercise on catholics or reformers; but it fell with crushing weight on a defenceless people, who dared not yield their religious convictions, as was done by others, to the dictation of an arrogant and impious trespasser upon the domain of the Highest.

The year 1538 is particularly noticeable for the zealous efforts made to eradicate the baptists from the land. The king had been for some time flattered with the hope of being placed at the head of the league, which was contemplated by the German Protestant princes for their defence, against the combined powers of the emperor, Charles the fifth, and the catholic states. It promised to be mutually advantageous, could it be effected. In 1535, therefore, the king sent bishops Fox and Heath, with Dr. Barnes, as ambassadors to Smalcalde, to treat upon the subject, and several divines were

ᵉ Crosby, i. 32. Burnet, i. 195. Page lxxii.

g

to be sent to England for the purpose of determining those points of a religious character to which the king hesitated to agree.

It was in this year (1538) that the ambassadors of the league appeared at Henry's court, headed by Burghardt, vice-chancellor of the elector of Saxony. Three points only remained for determination, the denial of the cup to the laity, the continuance of private masses, and the celibacy of the clergy. Henry would not give way. His mind was biassed by the bishops who still adhered to the old superstition.[9] In the month of October the king wrote to the elector, requesting the presence of Melancthon to assist him in promoting the "true glory of Christ, and the tranquillity and discipline of his religion." It might be that one so gentle could strike out a middle path, at once satisfactory to the royal conscience, and to the earnest desires of the reformers.

About this time one Peter Tasch, a baptist, was apprehended by the landgrave of Hesse. On him was found a correspondence with certain English baptists, some one of whom had recently published a book on the incarnation of Christ. Much benefit was expected to follow this publication, in the wider dissemination of their opinions in this country, whither Tasch himself purposed shortly to proceed, unless hindered, as he said, by the Spirit of God. Of these circumstances the elector informs Henry, when replying to his application for the assistance of Melancthon. A two-fold good was expected to follow this token of evident anxiety for the welfare of Henry's realm. The king would be flattered and pleased, and, at the same time, the elector would purge himself from all suspicion of harbouring these people in his own dominions; thus the main object of the ambassage, the union of Henry with the league, would be facilitated.   He

---

[9] Short's Hist. of Ch. of England, p. 132, edit. 1840.

therefore transmitted a copy of the correspondence, and described their heresies and practices. It was in Frisia and Westphalia, he tells the king, that the sect especially found its home. It fled those countries where the gospel shone with purest light. For this reason the churches of Germany were more tranquil than those of Belgia; still, through the whole of Germany these errorists, impostors, and fanatics, stealthily wandered. One feature, especially, marked them,—they condemned the baptism of infants. To this prime heresy they added many other errors. " And inasmuch as an appearance of great humility and patience is most efficacious in deceiving the souls of men, they teach a community of goods, disapprove of all punishment, deny the duty of a Christian to exercise magistracy or justice, refuse to take an oath, and lastly they take away the political administration which God hath appointed and approved." He further enumerates some other errors by which a superstitious people were led astray. " They wander," he says, "in secret places, and spread in privacy the virus of their doctrine. When seized, learned men attempt to save them, but if they pertinaciously defend their condemnation of baptism, or their other impieties, or their judgment of political duties, which itself is seditious, then they are punished." Thus did the elector, under the tuition of the reformers, and by the pen of Melancthon, exhibit his zeal and resolution to defend the "true and catholic doctrine of the church of Christ." [1]

Henry's zeal required but little to inflame it against these obnoxious oppugners of his supremacy over the church of God. On the 1st of October he issued a proclamation to Cranmer, and eight other bishops and clerics, to proceed inquisitorially against the baptists, to search for their books,

---

[1] Seckendorf, Hist. Lutheran, lib. III. sect. 66. Add. i. p. 181.

and particularly to scrutinize with all diligence their letters. They were to urge them to recant, confuting and judging them "by the dogmas of the catholic church, and by the scripture." But if they were obstinate, then were they to exterminate them from the congregation of the faithful, and finally at their pleasure commit them, with their writings, to the flames.[2] This cruel edict could not have much hindered the progress of the truth, since we find the king, on the 16th of November following, constrained to publish a proclamation commanding that no book should be imported or printed without a license, especially and again condemning to the flames the works of baptists and sacramentaries.[3]

Not that these proceedings were without their seal of blood and martyrdom. On the 24th of November some of these men, who, "whilst their hands were busied about their manufactures, their heads were also beating about points of divinity," bare fagots at Paul's Cross, and three days after a man and woman were burnt in Smithfield.[4] The violence of the king yet further appeared in the following month, while keeping Christmas at Hampton Court. Cruelty was pastime and festivity to him. A letter was issued to the justices of peace throughout the country "to set forth his good intentions for the wealth and happiness of his people!" Its burden was an increase of rigour against the unfortunate baptists.[5] Many of them fled. It was in the depth of winter when in secrecy and haste they sought refuge in Holland. But betrayed by envious men, they fell into the hands of tyrants there. After many trials of their faith, exhibiting throughout great patience and perseverance under their sufferings, they were sentenced to death. On the 7th of January, sixteen men were beheaded at Delft, and fifteen women drowned, for

[2] Wilkins, iii. 836, 837.   [4] Fuller, Bk. V. sect. iv. c. 11.
[3] Burnet, ii. 13", edit. 1715.   [5] Burnet, iii. 140.

their testimony to the truth of God. Twenty-seven other refugees had but a few months before passed through the great tribulation, and laid down their lives on the same spot.[6]

No crime was charged against them, but that of thinking differently from their persecutors. Whether their sentiments were true or false, they were martyrs for opinion. No pretence of rebellion, nor any disposition to resist lawful authority, could be substantiated. It was seditious in them merely to reject the exercise of royal or magisterial power in things of God. That this cruelty failed as it deserved, we have the king's own declaration; he found it needful to adopt milder measures, and to try what an act of grace could do. On February 25th, 1539, he accordingly issued his royal proclamation of mercy. The baptists were the particular objects of the sovereign's anxiety; many of his people had imbibed their doctrines, and this document is an unexpected and unquestionable testimony to their numbers and constancy.[7]

It is not conceivable that this degree of lenity should have been exhibited towards them, had they been guilty of rebellious or traitorous practices. Their religious sentiments alone exposed them to the stroke of the iron hand of the oppressor—

[6] Van Braght. Het Bloedig Toonel of Martelaers-Spiegel des Doopsgesinde, ii. 145.

[7] "And wherefore of late certain ana-baptists and sacramentaries, coming out of outward parts into this realm, have, by diverse and many perverse and crafty means, seduced many simple persons of the king's subjects, which, as his highness trusteth, now be sorry for their offences, and minding fully to return again to the catholic church.... the king's highness like a most loving parent much moved with pity, tendering the winning of them again to Christ's flock, and much lamenting also their simplicity, so by devilish craft circumscribed......of his inestimable goodness, pity, and clemency, is content to remit, pardon, and forgive......all and singular such persons, as well his grace's subjects as other all such faults as they have committed by falling into such wrong and perverse opinions, by word or writing." He concludes by announcing his determination that if any should in future "fall to any such detestable and damnable opinions," the laws should be strictly and without mercy enforced against them. Wilkins, iii. 843.

sentiments fatal to the high-handed and impious assumption
of the monarch.   But neither gentleness nor severity could
hinder the progress of the truth.   The king's care about
religion failed to prevent "divers great and real errors and
anabaptistical opinions from creeping about the realm."   In
1540 he again attempted what threats could do.   Resolved, if
possible, to exterminate them, the baptists were excluded from
the general pardon proclaimed at the rising of parliament in
July.   That none might mistake the objects of his indignation, he enumerated their errors.   "Infants ought not to be
baptized; it is not lawful for a Christian man to bear office
or rule in the commonwealth; every manner of death, with
the time and hour thereof, is so certainly prescribed, appointed,
and determined to every man by God, that neither any prince
by his word can alter it, nor any man by his wilfulness prevent or change it." [8]   Such were some of the opinions to be
answered with fiery wrath to those that maintained them.
Truly they imply the helplessness of sovereign authority to
turn back the purposes of God, or to change the ordinances
of his house.   But the oppressed, like the children of Israel
in Egypt, grew and multiplied.

Amid the fluctuating policy of this reign, an almost uniform
course of persecution was pursued.   And if both catholics
and protestants felt occasionally the severity of the royal
prerogative, they yet united to hunt down with loud howlings
of execration those who committed the unpardonable crime of
exercising liberty of judgment, and of uttering sentiments
destructive of the monstrous assumptions which make the
church the fold of every unclean beast, the prey of ravening
wolves wearing the garb of messengers of the living God.

The ascendancy of the reform party in the councils of
Edward, by no means improved the position of the baptists.

[8] Collier, v. 69.   Strype, Mem. I. i. 552.

Their presence was regarded as the reproach of the reformation, and doubtless in some measure retarded its progress. The reformers stigmatized their opinions as the depths of Satan—an artifice of the great enemy to support his tottering throne against the true followers of the Lamb. They attempted disputation by word and writing, inveighed strongly against their so-called sedition against the rightful power of princes, and urged its repression by force of arms. Not a reformer of any eminence can be named who did not take part in this crusade. Luther, Melancthon, Zuingle, Bucer, Bullinger, Calvin, and others abroad; at home, Cranmer, Latymer, Ridley, Barnes, Philpot, Becon, Turner, Veron, and many more. Whether the baptists were confounded in disputation or not, "the burden of the song is always, that at the last the magistrates exerted their authority." Penal laws, the *ratio ultima* of divines, were their most convincing arguments—their Achilles.[9]

It was natural that the reformers should highly laud the tranquillity which they enjoyed during the short reign of the youthful Edward. It was indeed to them "a breathing time." So far as they were concerned, the rage of persecution ceased: to try, as it were, their temper, and put to the proof their charity and magnanimity. But though the sword was wrested from their adversaries' hands, it was employed with unsparing severity on the obnoxious sect. Even in the first year of Edward's reign we find Ridley and Gardiner strangely united together in a commission to deal with two baptists of Kent. Gardiner had but lately been released from prison, into which he had been thrown for his bold remonstrances against the innovating purposes of the council. He must have been reluctant to act with his fellow bishop, though it were to persecute, since Ridley felt himself constrained

[9] Bayle's Dict. Art. Anabaptists, note B.

seriously to exhort his colleague, not only to receive the true
doctrine of justification, but also to be diligent in confounding
the numerous baptists of his diocese.[1]

Their numbers, however, still increased. Their opinions
were "believed by many honest meaning people."[2] It might
be that Robert Cook, or Cooch, was not one of this kind,
since through fear of loss of place he finally recanted, and
solaced himself for his retractation by retaining the office of
gentleman of the queen's chapel in Elizabeth's reign, which
his opinions had brought in jeopardy; at the period in
question, he was a man of some repute in the court of
Edward. He was of courteous, fair deportment, of some
learning, and well skilled in music; to which we may add,
the description of Dr. Turner, his antagonist a few years
later, that he wore a ring, was a curious musician, a tall man,
and lived single. He was in habits of intimacy with Park-
hurst, Coverdale, Jewel, Turner, and other learned men,
with whom he often disputed against the baptism of infants,
and on original sin, besides "dispersing divers odd things"[3]
about the Lord's supper. With them he went into exile
during the reign of Mary.

Dr. Turner seems to have been particularly incited to

[1] Strype's Memorials, II. i. 107.
" In very deed I was sent from the
council to my lord of Winchester, to
exhort him to receive also the true confession of justification. And because
he was very refractorious, I said to him,
Why, my lord, what make you so great
a matter herein ? You see many anabaptists rise up against the sacrament of
the altar ; I pray you, my lord, be diligent in confounding of them. For at
that time my lord of Winchester and I
had to do with two anabaptists in Kent."
Ridley's Examinations, Fox, Acts, &c.
iii. 489, ed. 1641.

[2] Strype, Mem. II. i. 110.

[3] Among the Zurich Letters, second
series, page 236, is a letter from him to
Rodolph Gualter, under the date of
August 13th, 1573. In this he in-
quires the opinion of Gualter on certain
circumstances attending the primitive
celebration of the Lord's supper, which
he thinks ought to be observed with a
plentiful supply of food and wine, after
the manner of the paschal feast, and the
Corinthian agapæ. In Edward's reign
he was keeper of the wine-cellar. Peter
Martyr wrote him a long letter in defence of infant baptism.

oppose him. "Because," says he, in the dedication of his book to Latymer, "I did perceive that divers began to be infected with the poison of Pelagius, I devised a lecture in Thistelworth against two of the opinions of Pelagius, namely, against that children have no original sin, and that they ought not to be baptized. But within a few weeks after, one of Pelagius' disciples, in the defence of his master's doctrine, wrote against my lecture, with all the learning and cunning that he had. But lest he should glory and crake among his disciples, that I could not answer him, and to the intent that the venomous seed of his sowing may be destroyed, and so hindered from bringing forth fruit, I have set out this book." [4]

The paucity of existing documents written by baptists of this age, renders any accession to our gains, however small, of great value. And though they may pass through the refracting medium of bitter enmity, they are of the more value from their unquestionable authenticity. We may then be permitted to quote a few passages from this rare work, the sentiments of which will be found singularly coincident with certain views propounded in the pages that follow, and place beyond dispute the historical identity of the doctrinal sentiments of the English baptists of the sixteenth century, with those of the authors of the early pamphlets in this volume.

[4] A Preservatiue, or Triacle agaynste the poyson of Pelagius lately renued and styrred up agayn by the furious secte of the Anabaptistes : deuysed by Wyllyam Turner, Doctor of Physick. Imprint, 30th Jan. 1551, not paged. In the reign of Henry, Turner was an active preacher of Lutheranism throughout the country, for which he was imprisoned. Being liberated, he went to Italy, and at Ferrara acquired the title of Doctor of Medicine. On Edward's accession he returned home, and was preferred to a prebend of York, and made canon of Windsor; he was ordained in 1552, after his preferment. He was also incorporated M.D. of Oxford, and made physician to the Duke of Somerset. After his exile under Mary, he regained all his preferments. Tanner, Biblioth. Script. &c. p. 726, ed. 1748.

The rejection of the reformers' practice of infant baptism might, on the principle of antagonism which so often rules in controversy, be expected to lead to some modification of the doctrine of original sin, on which it was professedly founded. It was held that baptism was necessary to salvation, that by it sins actual and original were remitted, and it was concluded that to refuse baptism to infants, involved either their final perdition, if so dying, or their freedom from that original depravity or guilt which brings death on all the posterity of Adam. It was in the following manner, Turner informs us, that the baptists met the former part of the assertion. " By baptism alone is no salvation, but by baptism and preaching; and certain it is that God is able to save his chosen church without these means. But this is his ordinary way to save and damn the whole world, namely, by offering remission of sins and baptism to all the world, that thereby the believers may be absolved from all conscience of sin, and the disobedient and unbelievers bound still either to amend or to be damned; for he that believeth not is already damned." In another place the baptist most plainly asserts, for Turner professes to quote from one of their writings, that a moral change must precede the rite; of this it is only the symbol, and without it is unprofitable. " For this, I say, the remission of sins is offered to all, but all receive it not; the church sanctified by faith in the blood of Christ only receiveth it, and unto them only baptism belongeth. Therefore none ought to receive it but such as have not only heard the good promises of God, but have also thereby received a singular consolation in their hearts, through remission of sin, which they by faith have received. For if any receive baptism without this persuasion, it profiteth them nothing. . . . . . . Sacraments do not profit them which hear not the promise, and know not what it meaneth."

But if so, the reformer would reply, how can the original

depravity of man be removed? The laver of baptism is the
fountain where the birth-sin is washed away; do you mean
to say that mankind did not fall in Adam, and become partaker of his guilt? "But now, I say," replies the baptist,
"that all the world hath sinned, and is defiled in Adam. How
now, will water scour away the filth of this corruption? No;
it is a wound received in the soul, and is washed away but
with the only faith in the blood of Christ. . . . . . Though sin
be common to all, yet baptism is not common to all." But
what of infants? Can they believe? Are they not defiled
with the leprosy of sin? How may they wash and be clean?
Thus then the baptist. "If Christ had counted infants so
defiled with Adam's sin as ye do, he would never have sent
his apostles and us unto children to be defiled of them. But
now he sendeth us thither for cleanness, to become such as
they are, if we would enter into the kingdom of God; washed
to the unwashed, christened to the unchristened, believers to
unbelievers: not to become leprous, but that we should be
full of innocency and simplicity; for it is written, *Except ye
convert, and become as these infants, ye shall not enter in the
kingdom of heaven.* (For they are pure virgins, and they have
made white their garments in the blood of the Lamb)." His
evident meaning is, that *the blood of Christ cleanseth from all
sin;* original, in those who cannot believe,—original and actual,
in those who can. Turner would seem most reluctantly to
quote the latter explanatory clause of this passage, (for he
places it in the margin,) important as it is to vindicate the baptists from the charge of denying with Pelagius all original
defilement; there was corruption, but not guilt; depravity,
but not sin. That ancient heretic held, "that baptism is
necessary for persons of all ages, in order that the baptized
person might be adopted as a son of God; not because he
derived from his parents any thing which could be expiated in

the laver of regeneration." [5]   An opinion sufficiently diverse
to have prevented the confounding the baptists with the
Pelagians.   But a point was gained, if ancient obloquy could
be attached to their supposed modern representatives.

Whether Dr. Turner felt himself unable to reply, or the
question too thorny for a clerical physician to handle, he was
not unwilling nor forgetful to remind his antagonist of the
peril in which he stood, while maintaining these obnoxious
views.   "For as much as ye are an open felon against the
king's laws, and have committed such felony, as ye are
excepted out of the pardon, whereof thieves and robbers
are partakers, Almighty God amend you, and bring you
into the high way again, and save you from it, that ye
have justly deserved."   Threats and bribes were well approved modes of conversion in those days, and Robert Cook
fell beneath their combined power.   Heresy had ceased to be
treated as an ecclesiastical offence among the reformers, inasmuch as it was felony and treason to oppose the will of the
magistrate in the imposition of religious belief.[6]   True martyrs
were thought to be found only amongst the protestants of
established churches, the upholders of national creeds.   All
other sufferers for conscience' sake, were execrable traitors
and felons, enduring that only which they had "justly deserved."   That life and death should hang on the profession
of such sentiments as the above, is truly a display of the most
hateful tyranny, to be abhorred by every one who receives
the words of Jesus, *I came not to destroy men's lives, but to
save them.*

[5] Davenant on Colossians, ii. 326.
Allport's translation.

[6] "Let it not make thee despair,
neither yet discourage thee, O reader,
that it is forbidden thee in pain of life
and goods, or that it is made breaking
of the king's peace, or treason unto his
highness to read the word of thy soul's
health." Tyndale, Pref. to Obedience
of a Christian Man. Works, i. 165.

The year 1548 witnessed several recantations of these sentiments. Many strenuous efforts were made to put down by force, opinions now freely broached in opposition to the views of the ruling party.[7] The absurdity of supposing that the civil magistrate has superior advantages for the discernment of truth, or that any thing short of infallibility can justify the presumption of dictating to the consciences of his subjects, may be well illustrated by a reference to the catechism now put forth by Cranmer for the guidance of the popular mind, and to preserve it from the heresies, and "naughty doctrine" taught by false and privy preachers. Could their doctrine be more heretical or "naughty" than the following?—"That if it had happened to us to be born of heathen parents, and to die without baptism, we should be damned everlastingly;" that the second birth is by the water of baptism, in which our sins are forgiven, and the Holy Ghost poured into us; that there are *three* holy seals or sacraments by which God's ministers do work, baptism, absolution, and the Lord's supper; that baptism makes us partakers of the remission of sins, of the Holy Ghost, and of the "whole righteousness of Christ;" and that when the minister absolves, we ought to believe that our sins are truly forgiven.[8] Was Cranmer indeed fitted to be the infallible instructor of the people, in pure doctrine, freed from the inventions of men?

At all events he will act as if it were so. For the next year (1547) becomes memorable for the establishment of a protestant inquisition, under the primate's especial direction, and by which two persons at least were doomed to a fiery purgation. This tribunal continued in active operation through the remainder of the reign. Upon the pretext that many strangers from abroad had appeared in the country, and were making many proselytes, a commission was issued on

[7] Strype's Cranmer, pp. 254—257. 183, 186—189, 197, 202. Oxford
[8] Cranmer's Catechism, pp. 51, 182, edition.

the 12th of April, granting the amplest powers to inquire
after heretical pravity.[9]   The inquisitors [1] were Cranmer,
the bishops of Ely, Worcester, Chichester, Lincoln, and
Rochester, with some of the king's counsellors ; his two
secretaries, with Cox, Latymer, Hales, and others. We must
give the opening portion of this document, as it will mark
distinctly the connection of the dogma of royal supremacy in
things of God, with its natural consequence—persecution.
" Although to all kings it belongeth to preserve intact the
Christian faith and church, by their royal authority, to us
especially it appertains, who are called by a certain title
DEFENDER OF THE FAITH, that we take care that the
noxious weeds of heresy, and the blemish of evil doctrine,
should not be privately sown among our people." The baptists are the peculiar objects of its provisions.   They are said
to have instilled into the ears of the king's subjects, and into
the minds of his "ignorant" people, their wicked opinions,
their impious and impure dogmas.   Therefore must they be
extirpated and repressed.   The commissioners are then
directed to inquire in every way for them, to examine witnesses upon oath, to proceed with secrecy, and even without
the forms of justice.[2] Salutary penances should be imposed
on the penitent, who might then be absolved, and re-admitted
to the church.   But the obstinate must be ejected from the
congregation of the faithful, and exterminated.   If the atro-
city of their deeds demands it, they must be delivered to the
secular power.   Prisons and chains might be freely employed
at the discretion of the tribunal.

  Joan Boucher, whose case now comes before us, must have
been at this time in the hands of her foes ; for on the 30th of
April, eighteen days only after the issue of the commission,

---

[9] Crosby, i. 47.

[1] Cognitores, inquisitores, judices, et
commissarios nostros, &c.   Rymer's

Fœdera Tom. vi. pars iii. ed. Hagæ 1741.

[2] Ac sine strepitu, et figura judicii.
Rymer Fœd. Tom. vi. pars iii.

she was arraigned for the crime of heresy before this protestant inquisition, and her sentence formally pronounced.
From Cranmer's own archiepiscopal Register we learn, that
he himself sat as principal judge on the occasion, assisted by
Sir Thomas Smith, W. Cooke, dean of arches, Hugh Latymer,
and Dr. Lyell, as the king's "proctors, inquisitors, judges,
and commissaries." [3]

Joan Boucher had been an active distributor of the proscribed
translation of the New Testament by Tyndale. The court
of Henry was the scene of her zealous labours, where she oft
introduced the sacred volumes unsuspected, tying the precious
books by strings to her apparel. [4] Although ready in the
scriptures, she could not read them; no uncommon defect
in that day, even in people of rank. Much of her time was
occupied in visiting the prisons, wherein were incarcerated
her companions in tribulation, whom it was her wont perpetually and bountifully to assist. [5]

But there was one error which was sufficient to expose her to
the poisonous breath of calumny, and to the burning flame. For
this she now appears before the inquisitors, " in the chapel of
the blessed Mary in St. Paul's." The examinations are long,
the judges learned, and apparently desirous to save her from
the stake. She cannot, she will not be convinced that she
holds any heresy derogatory to the truth. Neither entreaties
nor threats move her. A good conscience emboldens her. At
last she utters language grievous to hear, but which smites
the consciences of her judges with its telling truth. "It is
a goodly matter to consider your ignorance. It is not long
ago since you burned Anne Askew for a piece of bread, and
yet you came yourselves soon after to believe and profess the
same doctrine for which you burned her. And now forsooth
you will needs burn me for a piece of flesh, and in the end

---

[3] Wilkins, Concilia, iv. 42.
[4] Strype's Memor. II. i. 335.

[5] Fox Johan. Rerum in Ecclesiâ
Gestarum. Basil, fol. 202.

you will come to believe this also, when you have read the scriptures, and understood them." [6]

With the "fear of God before his eyes," and with invocacation of the name of Christ, the "reverend father in Christ, Thomas, archbishop of Canterbury," with the full approbation of his colleagues, now proceeds to pronounce her doom. The sentence contains her crime and its punishment. "You believe that the word was made flesh in the virgin's belly, but that Christ took flesh of the virgin you believe not; because the flesh of the virgin being the outward man, sinfully gotten, and born in sin, but the word by the consent of the inward man of the virgin was made flesh. This dogma, with obstinate, obdurate, and pertinacious mind, you affirm, and not without much haughtiness of mien. With wonderful blindness of heart, to this you hold; therefore, for your demerits, obstinacy, and contumacy, aggravated by a wicked and damnable pertinacity, being also unwilling to return to the unity of the church, you are adjudged a heretic, to be handed to the secular power, to suffer in due course of law, and finally the ban of the great excommunication is upon you." The inquisitors complete the labours of the day, by announcing to the youthful sovereign, through their president, that they had decreed her separation from the Lord's flock as a diseased sheep. "And since," say they, "our holy mother, the church, hath naught else that she can do on this behalf, we leave the said heretic to your royal highness, and to the secular arm, to suffer her deserved punishment." [7]

Considerable delay, however, occurred before the execution of the sentence. We may give the reformers credit for an earnest desire to lead Joan Boucher to more correct views, but must not withhold an expression of just abhorrence at the bloody deed, and at the hateful principle on which they acted.

---

[6] Strype, Mem. II. i. 335.   [7] Wilkins, Concilia, iv. 42, 43.

They had adopted an unsound basis for their reformation, and its necessary result was oppression of conscience; the exercise of freedom of thought and judgment, upon scripture truth was impossible. Ridley of London, and Goodrich of Ely, were especially active in their endeavours to reclaim her; to whom must be added, Cranmer, Latymer, Lever, Whitehead, and Hutchinson.[8]

A year within three days was passed in these unavailing efforts. Her constancy remained unshaken. On the 27th of April, the council issued their warrant to the lord chancellor to make out a writ for her execution; and Cranmer is said by Fox to have been most urgent with the young king to affix the sign manual to the cruel document. The youthful king hesitated. Cranmer argued from the law of Moses, by which blasphemers were to be stoned to death; this woman was guilty of an impiety in the sight of God, which a prince, as God's deputy, ought to punish. With tears, but unconvinced, the royal signature was appended.[9] Rogers, the proto-martyr of Mary's reign, also thought that she ought to be put to death, and when urged with the cruelty of the deed, replied, "that burning alive was no cruel death, but easy enough."[1] He was soon called, in the reign of Mary, to test the truth of his own remark.

The bishops had, however, resolved that she should die, and on the 2nd of May, 1550, she appeared at the stake in Smithfield. Here further efforts were made to shake her

[8] Hutchinson's Works, Biog. Notice, p. iii. Parker Society, edit.

[9] We do not attribute much importance to the attempt to vindicate Cranmer at the expense of Fox's veracity; since if he were not guilty of urging the king to sign the warrant of execution, nor present at the council when the issue of it was determined upon, he had mercilessly condemned her to death, and acted throughout as the chief inquisitor. Fox had too many reasons to withhold the statement were it not true, and it can add but little to Cranmer's guilt, that at his persuasion Edward committed her to the flames. See Hutchinson's Works, Biog. Notice, pp. 4, 5.

[1] Pierce's Vindication, p. 34.

confidence. To bishop Scory was allotted the duty of preaching
to the sufferer, and to the people, on the occasion. "He tried
to convert her; she scoffed, and said he lied like a rogue, and
bad him, 'Go read the scriptures.'" [2] It was doubtless an
indignant rejection of the shameful misrepresentations which
in that hour of trial were made of her faith. She clave to
those words of truth which were her joy and strength, in the
moments of her dying agony. She loved and adored the holy
and immaculate Lamb of God.

We must look for the rise of the opinion attributed to this
Christian female to the gross Mariolatry of the Romish church.
For more than two hundred years the pulpits of Christendom
had resounded with the conflicting asseverations of the followers of St. Dominic and St. Francis, the one maintaining,
the other denying, the immaculate purity and sinlessness of
the mother of God. [3] The grossest indecencies were uttered
in their intemperate harangues, and nature's secrets laid open
by vulgar hands to the vulgar gaze. Thus a subject wrapt
in profound mystery was forced upon thoughtful minds, and
it became heresy to doubt the common and gainful sentiment
of the holy virgin's untainted nature. Fox would seem to
refer to this when speaking of Boucher; he says, "that she
and others appeared to differ somewhat from the catholics;" [4]
and he then instances her views on this subject, as the alone
feature that marred her Christian excellence. At a much
later period, in 1620, a baptist distinctly avers that it was in
order to advance the high estimation in which Rome holds
the virgin, that the council of Trent declared her to be ex-

[2] Strype, Memor. II. i. 335.

[3] "And of what text the grave (grey?)
friar proveth that our lady was without
original sin, of the same shall the black
friar prove that she was conceived in
original sin." Tyndale's Obedience of
a Christian Man, Preface. Works, i.
195.

[4] A catholicis nonnihil dissentire vide-
bantur. Rerum in Eccles. Gest. fol.
202.

empt from all sin.[5] Were it not so, it was argued, how was
it possible for Jesus Christ to escape all contamination? Can
a clean thing come out of an unclean? So then must it be
that the mother and the son were alike sinless and undefiled.
It is easy to conceive that a simple mind, in rebutting this
view of the virgin's purity, might fall into a mode of stating
the mystery of the incarnation somewhat divergent from
the truth, if indeed the subject be susceptible of accurate
statement at all.[6]

But it is by no means clear that Boucher held a sentiment
every way so objectionable, as her persecutors would seem to
affirm. It was certainly stated by herself in a form, if not
perfectly intelligible, yet wanting in those offensive features
which are generally put prominently forth as her peculiar
demerit. "When I," says Mr. Roger Hutchinson, "and my
well-beloved friend, Thomas Lever, and others, alleged this
text against her opinions, *Semen mulieris conteret caput ser-
pentis, The seed of the woman shall grind, or break, the serpent's
head;* she answered, 'I deny not that Christ is Mary's seed,
or the woman's seed, nor I deny him not to be a man; but
Mary had two seeds, one seed of her faith, and another
seed of her flesh, and in her body. There is a natural and
a corporal seed, and there is a spiritual and an heavenly

[5] A Description of what God, &c. p. 121.

[6] St. Anselm taught in the eleventh century, Omnes in peccatis mortuos, demtâ solummodo matre Dei. He further says, Quemadmodum Deus ea substantiâ genuit eum, per quem cunctis originem dedit; ita beata virgo Maria de sua carne mundissimâ peperit illum. Magdeburg. Centuriatores, Cent. xi. tom. iii. 335, 34. The unspotted conception of the mother of Jesus, was taught in the twelfth century in France; Duns Scotus adhered to this opinion, and with him his followers, the Franciscans, and since that time, the Jesuits. It was opposed by Aquinas and the Dominicans, and led to a violent dispute in the church of Rome from the 15th to the 17th centuries. Knapp's Lectures on Christian Theol. p. 255. Ward's edit. Still Aquinas taught as follows: Beata virgo, in sui sanctificatione, fuit ab originali peccato purgata; in filii sui conceptione, totaliter à fomite mundata; in sui vero assumptione, ab omni miseriâ liberata. Magd. Centur. Cent. xiii. p. 117, tom. iii.

seed, as we may gather of St. John, where he saith, *The seed of God remaineth in him, and he cannot sin.* And Christ is her seed, but he is become man of the seed of her faith and belief, of spiritual seed, not of natural seed; for her seed and flesh was sinful, as the flesh and seed of others.' " [7] Had she been as "ready" in the fathers as in the scriptures, she might have added to her acute reply, and to the farther perplexity of her visitors, that Augustine also saith, " It behoved him to be born of a virgin, whom his mother's faith, and not natural desire, had conceived." [8]   At all events, Cranmer and his fellow-inquisitors, had no such special exemption from error on this point, as to entitle them to proceed as if infallibility was in their possession, and to attempt the exercise of a power over the body and the soul, to commit the one and the other to the blazing stake and to the flames of hell.

It would seem that a desire to intimidate a body daily increasing in numbers, hastened the end of this servant of God. More rugged methods than were agreeable to the principles of the gospel were determined upon.[9] The parliament which rose in February, especially exempted the baptists from the pardon granted to such as had been concerned in the late rebellion. Many were in prison. Their opinions on baptism, on oaths, and on magistracy, were declared inconsistent with the well-being of a Christian commonwealth.[1] Ridley, in the visitation of his diocese, received particular directions to inquire after the baptists. Their assemblies were to be sought out, and a report made, whether they separated from the rest of their fellow-parishioners for the private use of doctrine, and the administration of the sacraments.[2]

---

[7] Works, p. 145.

[8] De virgine nasci oportebat, quem fides matris, non libido, conceperat. Enchirid. ad Laurent. cap. xxxiv. p. 193. Tauchnitz edit.

[9] Strype, Memor. II. i. 335.

[1] Strype, Memor. II. i. 291.

[2] Cardwell's Doc. Annals, i. 79.

Complaints of the existence of some such congregations were made to the council from the counties of Essex and Kent. Secret assemblies were discovered at Bocking and Feversham, and in divers other towns and villages. These congregations were supported by the contributions of their members, mutual instruction was practised, and fellowship in the gospel regularly maintained. Four of their teachers, with a considerable number of the people, were accordingly seized. About sixty persons were met in a house at Bocking, when the sheriff interrupted their assembly. On appearing before the council, they confessed the purpose of their meeting to be "to talk of the scriptures," and that they had not gone to communion for two years. They were judged by their examiners to hold many evil opinions, and to be guilty of several superstitious and erroneous practices, and therefore worthy of great punishment. Some were at once committed to prison, and others bound in recognizances to the king in forty pounds each man, to appear when called upon.[3] For a while they were at liberty, but were soon brought into the ecclesiastical court, and examined on no less than forty-six articles. These articles related for the most part to the doctrines of original sin and predestination, which the baptists were supposed to deny. Their opinions on the former gained them the name of Pelagians.

Mr. Humphrey Middleton was the most eminent of the ministers thus summoned for conscience' sake before the ecclesiastical tribunal. He appears to have remained in prison, by the authority of Cranmer, until the last year of Edward's reign. To that prelate he is reported to have said, after his condemnation,—"Well, reverend sir, pass what sentence you think fit upon us, but that you may not say you were not forewarned, I testify that your own turn will be

[3] Strype's Cranmer, p. 335.

next." His release from prison took place at the king's death, but was of short duration ; for in the reign of Mary he was again the victim of intolerance, and with some others found in Smithfield a pathway of fire to heaven.[4]

Mr. Henry Hart was another of the teachers of this interesting community, and suffered with it the vicissitudes and dangers of persecution. In the next reign he was also imprisoned for heresy, when he made himself conspicuous, not only for his rejection of the predestinarian views of some of the martyrs, but also for the active controversy he maintained with them. We know not whether he too suffered at the stake. Greatly is it to be regretted that so little is known of a church, considerable for its numbers, yielding its proportion of confessors and martyrs to the Roman beast, and which, we are told, was the first that made a separation from the church of England, having gathered congregations of their own.[5]

Bold misrepresentations by professed ministers of peace, exciting the rulers of the land to an exterminating warfare against the baptists were not wanting. " Ye are placed in authority," writes John Veron to Sir John Gates, " for this our county of Essex, in the which, many of these libertines and anabaptists are running in, ' hoker moker,' among the simple and ignorant people, to impel and move them to tumult and insurrection against the magistrates and rulers of this realm. Whom I trust if ye once know them, ye will soon weed out of this country, to the great good and quiet of the king's subjects of the same county and shire."[6] It was their crime, that, sitting upon their ale-benches, wheresoever

[4] Pierce's Vindication, p. 35. Fox, Acts and Mon. p. 1519, edit. 1610.

[5] Strype, Memor. II. i. 369.

[6] A moste necessary and frutefull Dialogue betwene ye seditious Libertin or rebel Anabaptist, and the true obedient Christian, &c. Translated out of Latin into English, by Jhon Veron Senonys. Imprinted at Worcester, anno 1551.

they dare utter their poison, they taught the wrong of the attempt to unite things civil and divine. Men who held that magistracy was a civil ordinance of God, and to be obeyed in all civil affairs, were guilty of contention, sedition, and treason, when resisting its entrance into the church of God, seeing "it is neither profitable nor yet necessary to a Christian commonweal." "Which," continues Veron, "would God it were diligently weeded out by the magistrates and rulers, that these most pestiferous anabaptists and libertines, might once both feel and know, that they do not bear the sword delivered unto them of God in vain." [7]

The commission of 1549 was renewed, with a few changes in the commissioners, on the 18th of January, 1551, Cranmer still holding the place of chief-inquisitor. Under its provisions George van Pare surrendered his life at the stake. He was charged with a denial of the deity of our Lord, "that Christ is not very God." On the 6th of April he passed through the same forms of trial as Boucher, and was in like manner condemned. On the 25th he also was burnt in Smithfield. He was a man of exemplary life, passing much time in acts of devotion. He suffered with great constancy of mind, embracing the fagots and the stake that were about to consume him. [8]

These acts are an indelible blot on the memory of Cranmer, and have been referred to by the Romanists as a palliation of the enormities of the following reign. But it is said in reply, that no catholic suffered for religious opinions during the rule of the youthful and gentle Edward. It was a time of peaceful progress, when men might worship God as truth and scripture required. This however, if true, cannot excuse the persecutions that did occur, of which ample proof

[7] Grindal also appears as a persecutor of the Essex baptists. Ridley's Works, p. 331. Parker Society.

[8] Doc. Annals, i. 91. Wilkins, iv. 43. Neal, i. 42.

has been given; nor in the least exonerate Cranmer from the guilt of being its active and constant promoter. Other reasons, however, than the pacific disposition of the king, or the supposed unwillingness of Cranmer to resort to these cruel methods of propagating his faith, existed to render a catholic persecution at once impracticable and dangerous. No credit is due either to Edward or his council for their forbearance. It was a constrained lenity, and owed nothing of its propriety and worth to the generous or noble temper of the king's advisers; their principles were opposed to the existence of any faith but such a one as coincided with their own. The catholic party was too strong and too large to permit them to venture on the impolitic course of coercion. Reformed opinions had as yet but little hold upon that portion of the community in whose hands lay the wealth and power of the country. Romish practices were in many places used side by side with the new "laudable ceremonies." The nation did not feel itself reformed, and the leaders of the movement saw the impossibility of any other than a gradual submission to their imposed formularies of faith. Still there was no intention to bear the presence of Romanism beyond a certain point. If it ceased to be passive, it was at once met with stern threatening and reproof. Gardiner for his remonstrances was thrown into prison, and Bonner for his nonconformity deprived.

The insurrections in Devonshire and Norfolk, which had chiefly in view the re-establishment of the old religion, were put down with much loss of life and great severity; and a long and elaborate document, from the pen of Cranmer, was issued in reply to their articles, to justify the innovations that had been introduced. The omnipotence of the state in spiritual as in civil affairs, was the fertile parent of these sanguinary deeds, and Cranmer wielded it to that end, without shuddering or fear.

The same relentless rigour followed the baptists to the end. Towards the close of the last year of Edward's reign, the archbishop was again in motion to examine a number of persons who were said to have lately appeared in Kent. Of his researches we know nothing. We cannot suppose that the example of their probable friend and companion Joan Boucher, in any way repressed their zeal for the truth, or hindered its successful propagation.[9] It was not unnecessary that their testimony should be heard, since in the liturgy, now put forth, it was declared that he who refuseth the traditions of the church, hurteth the authority of the civil magistrate.[1] Against this pernicious principle the baptists nobly protested, and claimed for the church of God that liberty to receive laws from Christ alone which is its inalienable right.

The articles of religion, issued just previous to the king's death, are said to have been " principally designed to vindicate the English reformation from that slur and disgrace which the anabaptists' tenets had brought upon the reformation."[2] They could, therefore, have been neither few nor unimportant, to have merited this deference to their sentiments in the fundamental documents of the English church.

[9] Strype, Mem. II. ii. 19, 209.
[1] King Edward's Liturgies, p. 535.

[2] Lewis, Brief Hist. of the English Anabaptists, p. 54.

SECTION IV.

MARY.

THE reformed doctrines had not obtained such a predominance in the popular mind as to render long doubtful the succession of Mary to the crown. A nation's opinions cannot be changed in a few short years, much less its religious life. The protestant council of the late king failed therefore in their illegal attempt to place the amiable, but unfortunate, Lady Jane Grey upon the throne, and Mary, without bloodshed, entered upon the exercise of her regal functions.

Her fears had, however, forced from her the promise of permitting liberty of conscience. She assured the men of Suffolk, that there should be no alteration in the established worship. To the lord mayor and aldermen of London, on her arrival at the tower, she declared, that while her own conscience was stayed in matters of religion, she meant not to compel or strain her people's consciences.[3] But on the 18th of August, by proclamation, it was announced, that although she observed, and would maintain, the religion of her infancy, and be glad if it were received by her subjects, yet she did not intend to compel them to embrace it, "till public order should be taken in it, by common consent."[4] This proclamation was an advance upon her earlier promises, and darkly intimated the coming severities. She could, however, appeal to her brother's example, as a precedent for the suspension of all public preaching and scriptural exposition, which she proceeded to command: she therein only imitated the applauded policy of the reformers themselves. The first act of Mary's regal supremacy, was merely the exercise of a

---

[3] Neal, i. 59.   Price, Hist. of Nonconf. i. 99.   [4] Tierney's Dodd. ii. 57.

sovereignty over conscience, which they recognized, and had often employed.[5]

All the deprived catholic bishops, Gardiner, Bonner, Tunstall, Day, and Heath, were restored to their sees. Six other bishops, who had professed themselves protestants in the reign of Edward, conformed to the new order of things. The rest were deprived, either for being married, or for preaching doctrines unpleasing to the ruling party.[6] The catholics hastened to enjoy the public exercise of their worship. The mass was again restored, images and altars set up, the Latin service revived, and sermons, which irritated more than they convinced, were preached in maintenance of the old ceremonies.[7] The first session of parliament was opened with a high mass in Latin on the 5th of October, and it immediately proceeded to reverse the laws which obstructed the full establishment of popery.

Convocation went hand in hand with the houses of parliament. But few protestants were to be found in that assembly; only five, of whom archdeacon Philpot was the chief, appeared to defend the innovations of Edward, or to plead for their continuance. Great numbers of the more eminent of the reformers had withdrawn to various places abroad. From three to eight hundred are reckoned to have thus expatriated themselves from their native land.[8]

The change did not much affect the common people. They were ignorant and vicious; corruption of manners prevailed throughout the nation; the spreading light of the gospel had not penetrated the masses of society, nor wrought in them a purer morality. Unmoved by religious considerations, they had rejoiced only in the removal of the restraints and exactions to which, under the dominion of Rome, they had been

---

[5] Collier, vi. 12.
[6] Fuller, ii. 382, 383.

[7] Dodd, ii. 57.
[8] Ibid, pp. 56, 58.   Collier vi. 19.

subject.[9]   The transference from one faith to another, was to them an easy matter; neither class of religionists demanded the obedience of the heart; papist and protestant were both content with an outward observance of their respective rites. The upper classes had acquiesced in, nay coveted, the revolutions of former reigns, for they had brought to them an increase of wealth. This was the only obstacle to an immediate reconciliation with Rome; the spoliators of abbeys and monasteries feared a resumption of church property, an enforced restitution of their sacrilegious spoil. The houses of parliament therefore hesitated to acknowledge the supremacy of the pope, and it was not until Cardinal Pole, in the following year, by permission of the pope, surrendered this point, and gave secure possession to the holders of church lands, that the queen was allowed to lay down the title of supreme head of the church of England, although she regarded it as profane.[1]

It was on the 30th of November, 1554, St. Andrew's day, that the re-union of the nation to Rome was solemnly recognized, and its reconciliation effected. Cardinal Pole then appeared in parliament. His credentials, the briefs and bulls which authorized him, were read before the assembled Lords and Commons. He sought by moving words to confirm their resolution, to awaken repentance. England was a prodigal son, he said, who having wasted his spiritual substance, and destroyed all his ancestral monuments of piety, now returned to his father's house, to the centre of unity, the see of Rome. If heaven rejoiced over *one* repenting sinner, how much greater must be the angelic raptures, when a whole kingdom lay prostrate in their sight! Both houses knelt before the representative of the vicar of Christ; they besought God for mercy to themselves, and to the kingdom, by the hands of

<hr>

Strype's Cranmer, p. 447.   Short, p. 192.   [1] Dodd, ii. 65.

his servant; and, in the plenitude of his apostolic jurisdiction, the cardinal uttered the following absolution :—" Our Lord Jesus Christ, which with his most precious blood hath redeemed and washed us from all our sins and iniquities, that he might purchase unto himself a glorious spouse, without spot or wrinkle, and whom the Father hath appointed Head over all his church, he, by his mercy, absolve you: and we, by apostolic authority, given unto us by the most holy lord, Pope Julius III., his vicegerent in earth, do absolve and deliver you, and every one of you, with the whole realms and dominions thereof, from all heresy and schism, and from all and every judgment, censures, and pains, for that cause incurred; and also, we do restore you again unto the unity of our mother, the holy church, as in our letters more plainly it shall appear, in the name of the Father, and of the Son, and of the Holy Ghost." Both the houses of parliament answered aloud, " Amen!   Amen !"   Tears filled every eye ; many embraced each other in the gladness of their joy. Ambassadors were despatched to Rome to tender the obedience of the nation, and a jubilee over the whole church was proclaimed.[2]

It still remained to abrogate certain other laws relating to the supremacy. So soon as the houses of parliament were assured of the inviolability of the abbey and church lands, the acts passed since the twentieth year of Henry the Eighth, the year of schism, were summarily repealed. On that condition alone would they acknowledge the supreme jurisdiction of the Roman pontiff. Self-interest reigned paramount, and avarice again decided the national creed. Consideration must be shown towards the powerful and wealthy spoliators of the church's goods, the robbers of its plate and ornaments ; but none to those tender and scrupulous con-

---

[2] Dodd, ii. 62, 63.

sciences whose wealth lay in the possession of the truth. The laws against heretics were revived, the enormities of Lollardy were to be suppressed, and heretical preachers arrested. When delivered into the sheriffs' hands by their inquisitors, they were " then, on a high place, before the people, to be burnt." [3]

Thus the way was prepared for the exercise of those sanguinary cruelties which have rendered infamous the reign of Mary ; so great and numerous as to eclipse the feebler, but not less execrable severities of the parties who suffered them. " The system which had slowly grown out of the ignorance and superstition of mankind, was restored to its forfeited supremacy; and afforded another opportunity of developing its character, and of proving, more completely than ever it had yet done, its incompatibility with freedom of thought and the wide extension of knowledge." [4]

The feast of reconciliation being passed with joyful thanksgivings (Jan. 25th), the machinery of persecution was at once set in motion. On the 28th the cardinal issued a commission to search and examine all preachers of heresy, and commit them to prison. Commissioners and inquisitors went through the realm, and great numbers, from the counties of Kent, Essex, Norfolk, and Suffolk, were apprehended, sent to London, and immured in its pestilential dungeons, to await the fiery trial. [5]

The restored church of Rome proclaimed at the earliest moment her sanguinary purposes, and, without delay, sought by terror to repress rebellion against its spiritual authority. She chose for her ground of procedure a dogma repulsive to common sense, and therefore the better calculated to test the blind obedience she required. A simpler course could not have been selected to bring to the trial a man's faith in the

[3] Statutes at Large, 1 and 2 Phil. and Mariæ. c. vi. and viii.

[4] Price, i. 107.

[5] Fox, iii. 18. edit. 1641.

word of God, or in the dicta of the church.   Gardiner took
the lead in this warfare upon conscience, and on the 28th of
January, in the church of St. Mary Overies, in Southwark,
summoned the first of the martyrs before him.   Rogers and
Bradford, bishop Hooper and Dr. Taylor, appeared; they
were examined, excommunicated, and remanded to prison.[6]
On the 4th of February, Rogers was led to the stake, and
breathed his last triumphantly amid the suffocating flames.
Bradford was respited to the month of July.   Hooper laid
down his life with great firmness and joy, five days after
Rogers.   And, on the same day, Taylor passed through the
consuming flame at Hadley in Suffolk.[7]

These sanguinary measures had not been adopted without
considerable discussion among the councillors of the queen.
On the side of lenity, it is said, were the queen, king Philip,
and cardinal Pole; Gardiner and Bonner led the opposite
party.   Many things had occurred to irritate the ruling
ecclesiastics.   Actions at once indefensible and impolitic
proceeded from the reformers.   They had even gone so far as
to justify treason, and had looked with favour on Wyatt's insurrection.   The queen's preacher was shot at in the pulpit
at St. Paul's Cross; her chaplains mobbed, and pelted with
stones.   The ecclesiastical tonsure was made a mockery, a
dog's head being shaved in contempt; and a cat with a wafer
in her paws was hung upon a gallows at Cheapside, to ridi-
cule the sacrament.   One parson Rose publicly prayed,
"that God would either turn the queen's heart, or shorten
her days."[8]

Timely severities might also complete the work of re-union,
so auspiciously begun; cruelty to the few, might strike
terror in the many, and fix their wavering faith.   There was

[6] Collier, vi. 105.   [8] Collier, vi. 82, 93, 104.   Dodd,
[7] Macintosh, Mary, p. 290.   Collier,   ii. 97.
vi. 107.

much to countenance this idea. The leading reformers had fled, excepting only a very small number, whose death at Oxford and elsewhere was sufficient to mark the equity and sternness of the resolve. The professed adherents of the reformation were but a little band, and confined to a few localities. It would seem no difficult nor tedious employ, to extirpate a heresy whose roots had not yet struck deeply into the popular soil. It was, moreover, perfectly consonant with the maxims of a church, out of which there is no salvation, and had for centuries been sanctioned by success. Such or similar reasons weighed with the queen, when, on the intimation of her council that they had determined to resort to persecution, she replied, "Touching the punishment of heretics we thinketh it ought to be done without rashness, not leaving in the meanwhile to do justice to such, as, by learning, would seem to deceive the simple: and the rest so to be used, that the people might well perceive them not to be condemned without just occasion, whereby they shall both understand the truth, and beware to do the like. And especially within London, I would wish none to be burnt, without some of the council's presence, and both there and every where good sermons at the same."[1]

The first example awakened general disgust, which was so far effectual as to call forth the day following the death of Rogers, a disclaimer, on the part of the court, of any participation in the horrid transaction, by one Alphonso di Castro, a Spanish friar. He inveighed against the bishops for burning men, saying plainly that scripture taught them not to burn any for conscience; but on the contrary, that they should be permitted to live, in hopes of their conversion.[2] The spirit of intolerance seemed for a moment abashed, but was not quenched. The sermon was plainly a stratagem, to

---

[1] Collier, vi. 85.   [2] Fox, iii. 139.

remove the odium from the queen, and especially from Philip, who was extremely anxious to ingratiate himself with the people. In a few weeks the fires were again lighted up. The persecution continued until the end of the reign, when two hundred and seventy persons had perished in the flames of martyrdom.

The ravages of the persecutors were confined to a few districts of the country. At least two hundred were victims of the dark-minded and bloody Bonner. The northern dioceses were free from the fiery scourge, as were also some of the western. By far the largest number of martyrs was drawn from the dioceses of Canterbury, London, Norwich, Rochester, and Chichester. They were the foci of the reformed movement; from those places the sufferers of former times had come, and there it was that gospel-light penetrated farthest into the middle and lower ranks of society. The humblest conditions of life yielded a much more than proportionate number; " an instance of the power of conscience to elevate the lowest of human beings above themselves, and is a proof of the cold-blooded cruelty of the persecutors, who, in order to spread terror through every class, laboriously dug up victims from the darkest corners of society, whose errors might have hoped for indulgence from any passion less merciless than bigotry." [3]

[3] Fuller, ii. Macintosh, Mary, ch. xv.

SECTION V.

THE BAPTISTS.

By the aid of the historian Strype, we discover that not a few baptists were entangled in the meshes of the sanguinary foe. His information was chiefly gleaned from the papers of the English martyrologist, and it is much to be regretted that from a desire to please the ruling party, or a repugnance to acknowledge the merit of those who came not up to his standard of orthodoxy, Mr. Fox has either omitted altogether any reference to their sufferings, or when he has mentioned them, has suppressed those particulars which would enable us to identify them as belonging to this obnoxious sect. It will be remembered, that in the previous reign, a congregation of baptists had been discovered, assembling as they might find convenient, at various places in the counties of Kent and Essex, but especially at Feversham and Bocking. Many of its members were then immured in prison, with their two pastors, Mr. Henry Hart and Mr. Humphrey Middleton, but were probably released on the death of Edward. In 1554, those two preachers were again incarcerated with two other ministers of the same people.[4]

On the 12th of July, 1555, Mr. Middleton was burnt at Canterbury, with three others. His examinations were on the usual test-doctrine, transubstantiation. He averred that there was no real presence in the mass, that both the sacred emblems ought to be administered to the communicants, and in the English tongue. It was with difficulty that he was brought to answer the questions of his examiners, but he

---

[4] Strype's Cranmer, p. 502.

assured them, that he believed in his own God, saying, " My
living God, and no dead God." Bound to two stakes, he and
his fellow-sufferers passed into the presence of the Lamb
from amid the devouring flame. Like true soldiers of Jesus
Christ, they gave a constant testimony to the truth of his
holy gospel.[5]

Mr. Hart, with many others, was imprisoned in the King's
Bench, where also were confined several, who, under the
name of gospellers, adhered to the religion established by
Edward the Sixth. Among these prisoners of Jesus Christ
arose considerable contention and strife. The eternal predestination of the elect, and the ability of man to keep God's
commandments, were the topics which excited their unseemly
divisions. The baptists were distinguished by the epithets of
free-willers and Pelagians. The martyr Bradford entered
deeply into the subject with them, and more especially with
Hart. The latter wrote a piece in defence of his sentiments,
to which Bradford replied; in a letter to Cranmer, Ridley,
and Latymer, at Oxford, he communicates his fears, and
sends them both Hart's book and his own. He conceives
that these men confounded the effects of salvation with its
cause; on the matter of free-will he deems them plain papists,
yea, Pelagians. They also utterly contemned all learning.
Their holy life, for " they were men of strict and holy lives,"
commended them to the world, and rendered their sentiments
the more dangerous. To his letter were appended the names
of Bishop Ferrar, Taylor, and Philpot. Some yielded to his
persuasions; to the rest he showed uniform kindness, allevi-
ating the distresses of their imprisonment, from funds con-
fided to his care; for " that he was persuaded of them, that
they feared the Lord, and therefore he loved them." Others
dealt not so gently with their erring brethren. Archdeacon

[5] Fox, iii. 363, 373, 377.

Philpot was among their opponents. In a letter to John Careless, he calls them schismatics, arrogant and self-willed, blinded scatterers, contentious babblers, perverse and intractable.[6]

In a long letter to a friend in Newgate, Philpot endeavoured to establish the truth of infant baptism. Infants, he says, were included in the command of our Lord, *Go ye into all nations,* &c.; but especially had they the same covenant-right enjoyed by the posterity of Abraham. Evidently feeling these grounds somewhat unstable, he earnestly exhorts his correspondent " to submit to the judgment of the church, for the better understanding the articles of our faith, and of the doubtful sentences of scripture. Therefore." he continues, " let us believe as they have taught us of the scripture, and be at peace with them, according as the true catholic church is at this day."[7] To such a surrender of understanding and conscience, the baptists were and ever have been opposed, inasmuch as they conceive that the marks of infallibility have never yet been discovered, engraven by divine skill, either on the " holy Roman church," or on that constituted by the legislative enactments of king Edward and his successors on the British throne.

Singular, too, is the harmony of sentiment existing between our reformer and his cruel persecutor, Bonner, who this same year (1555) put forth his book of homilies. Their arrows are drawn from the same quiver, and winged on earth, not in heaven. Thus in the homily on the authority of the church, in almost the same language, doth this blood-stained hero of Rome's infallibility proceed to say : " I exhort and beseech all you, good Christian people, that in all doubts, opinions, and controversies, ye would resort to the holy church, and there learn what the same catholic church hath believed and

6 Strype's Cranmer, 502, 503, 907.   7 Fox, iii. pp. 606, 607.

taught, from time to time, concerning doubts or controversies." And in the exposition of the sacrament of baptism, he gives especial warning against the error of the baptists; for, says he, "certain heresies have risen up and sprung in our days, against the christening of infants;" which elsewhere he teaches, that "the most wholesome authority of the church doth command." [8]

While, then, our reformers endeavoured to reduce the catholic church to the standard of scripture, appealing to its doctrines, and honouring to some extent its commands; yet were they not free from a papal dread of too much light. They feared the perfect communication of the word of God to the laity, and dreaded the action of free minds on its contents. "To the unlearned and laity," says Roger Hutchinson, in 1552, "the publishing them without interpretation is a like matter as if a man would give to young children whole nuts; which, when they have tumbled long up and down in their mouths, and licked the hard shell, being not able to come to their sweetness, at last they spit out, and cast away both the shell and the kernel. The eternal God, to help the infirmity of man's capacity and understanding herein, hath ordained two honourable and most necessary offices in his church; the office of preaching, and the office of reading and interpreting." To these must the humble man resort; so great is the hardness and difficulty of holy writ, that without a teacher none can wade through it.[9]

Great therefore was the dismay of Ridley and others, when, as he says, these imprisoned baptists rejected an open, that is, an established ministry, as not necessary; when the sacraments were regarded as only "badges and tokens of Christian men's profession:" or, as Ridley puts it, they made

[8] A profitable and necessarye doctrine, with certayne homelyes adioyned thervnto, set forth by Edmunde, Byshop of London, &c. MDLV.

[9] Works, pp. 91, 94. Parker Society's edit.

no difference between the Lord's table and their own; yet more amazed was he, that they refused to attend the ministry, or submit to any Christian rite from the hands of any clergyman, however pure his succession, who was not known as a man of God by his holy life, and the fruits of piety. In such cases of schismatic folly, Ridley counselled a resort to coercion. Since conviction could not be produced by persuasion, force must be applied. To quote the more gentle Hutchinson: "If there be any suspected to be an anabaptist, I would to God well-learned preachers were authorized to compel and call such to render account of their faith—if it were found anabaptistical, that the preacher enter into disputation with him, and openly convict him by the scriptures and elder fathers; and if he remain obstinate, the same preacher to excommunicate him; and then to meddle no further with him, but give knowledge thereof to the temporal magistrate, which, for civil consideration, may punish him with imprisonment, death, or otherwise." [1] Hence the opprobrious epithets, the passionate language, the bitter invective, which marked the controversies of these fellow-sufferers for the truth.

Not the least among the opponents of the baptists was Mr. John Careless, an eminent martyr, and their fellow-prisoner in the King's Bench. He had much conference with them, but failed, to his great grief, in convincing them. In 1556, Careless wrote a confession of his faith, especially favouring absolute predestination against free-will. It was generally concurred in by the protestant prisoners in Newgate and the King's Bench, where he lay. A copy fell into Mr. Hart's hands, and on the back of it he wrote his sentiments. His colleague Mr. Chamberlain also wrote against it. Strype

---

[1] Works, p. 201. Ridley's Works, pp. 9, 264, 121, 129, 141, 142. Strype, Memor. III. ii. 454.

mentions only one article of this document, from which may be inferred the opposing sentiment of the baptists. "That the second book of Common Prayer, set forth in king Edward's days, was good and godly; but that the church of Christ hath authority to enlarge and diminish things in the same book, so far forth as it is agreeable to scripture." This reply of Hart fell into the hands of the catholic party, and gave rise to scoffs at the divisions and various opinions of the professors of the gospel. It ended in the disownment of the baptists by the gospellers, and a breach of all intercourse and unity between them.[2]

The friends of the prisoners sought to comfort and cheer them by letters. One of these is preserved. Strype thinks the writer was Mr. Hart; but it is evidently written from the country to those in London who were suffering for the truth; and, as Mr. Hart was one of them, it must have come from some other person. The writer prays that his imprisoned friends may be endued with all wisdom and spiritual understanding. He urges them to walk as the children of the light, and to be fruitful in all good works; to have no fellowship with unrighteousness, to walk circumspectly, to "use well the time, for it is a miserable time, yea, and such a time that if it were possible, the very chosen and elect should be brought into errors;" therefore, they must watch, search diligently the scriptures, and take gladly the yoke of Christ upon them. The writer then proceeds to argue from the precepts given by Christ to keep his commandments, and to love God with all the heart, soul, mind, and strength, that we are able to observe them; that God has given us understanding and reason for the purpose; and that life and death are set before men freely to choose. He concludes: "Wherefore, dearly beloved, let us look earnestly to the command-

---

[2] Strype's Cranmer, p. 505.

ments of the Lord, and let us go about to keep them, before
we say that we be not able to keep them.   Let us not play
the slothful servants, but let us be willing to go about to do
them, and then no doubt God shall assist and strengthen us,
that we shall bring them to conclusion.   And always, dearly
beloved, have the fear of the Lord before your eyes, for
whoso feareth the Lord walketh in the right path, . . . and at
the last God shall reward every man according to his deeds." [3]

How these followers of Jesus fared after this period, we
have no means of ascertaining.   The last mention of their
persecutions in this reign, is that of the sudden recall of
certain inquisitors, who in the year 1558 visited Essex, and
especially the district around Colchester, for the purpose of
feeding the languishing flames of the martyr's pile, with
fresh living fuel.   With regret the commissioners obeyed
the Council's commands.   " Would to God," they write, " the
honourable Council saw the face of Essex as we do see ; we
have such obstinate heretics, anabaptists, and other unruly
persons here, as never was heard of. . . . If we should give it
off in the midst, we should set the country in such a roar,
that my estimation, and the residue of the commissioners,
shall be for ever lost." [4]

The country began to groan over the ashes of the dead,
and to regard with horror the cruelties of bigotry and Rome.
On the 17th of November Mary died, and this darkest period
of our national annals, and of the reformed faith in this land,
yielded to a brighter day.

[3] Strype, Memor. III. ii. 321—329.   [4] Ibid. 125, 126.

RELIGION'S PEACE;

OR,

A PLEA

FOR

LIBERTY OF CONSCIENCE.

1614.

THis usefull Treatise (Entituled *Religions Peace*) long since Presented by a Citizen of *London* to King *J A M E S*, and the High Court of Parliament then sitting; I allow to be Reprinted.

Aprill 1.   *John Bachiler.*

RELIGIONS PEACE:

OR

A Plea for Liberty of Conscience.

Long since presented to King *James,* and the High
Court of Parliament then sitting, by *Leonard
Busher* Citizen of *London,* and Printed
in the Yeare 1614.

Wherein is contained certain Reasons against Persecution
for Religion; Also a designe for a peaceable reconciling of those that differ in opinion.

Rom. xiv. 5, 10. *One man esteemeth one day above another, another man esteemeth every day
alike, let every man be fully perswaded in his own minde.*
*But why dost thou judge thy brother, or why dost thou despise thy brother? for we shall all
appeare before the judgement seat of Christ.*

LONDON,

Printed for *John Sweeting* at the Angel in *Popes-head-alley,*

1646.

.

INTRODUCTORY NOTICE.

NOTHING whatever is known of the author of the ensuing treatise, beyond that which he himself has communicated in the course of his remarks. It is a mere conjecture, which has been hazarded, that he was a member of the church which, after the death of Mr. Smyth, chose Mr. Helwys to fill the pastoral office among them. He was a citizen of London, and had been an exile from his native land at some part of his life, when he probably became acquainted with the Brownists and Mr. Robinson, to whom he refers. From them he differed on several important subjects, especially on infant baptism, and liberty of conscience.

He speaks of himself as labouring for his subsistence, which with difficulty was obtained, owing to the persecutions he endured. "We that have most truth," he affectingly, and, however at the time doubted, yet, most correctly says, "are most persecuted, and therefore most poor." Still he laboured for the spiritual benefit of his fellow-countrymen. His poverty, arising from his sufferings, alone disabled him from printing two works that he had prepared. The one he calls, "A Scourge of small cords, wherewith Antichrist and his ministers might be driven out of the temple of God." The other, " A Declaration of certain False Translations in the New Testament;" he was zealous for the purity of the church and the truthful translation of the word of God. To his difficulties are doubtless to be attributed his unpolished style and occasional obscurity.

He appears to have been acquainted with the original Greek of the New Testament, and attentive to the criticism of the sacred text. His knowledge of the Syriac version, may perhaps be referred to the translation of it into Latin by Tremellius, which at the time was frequently printed in conjunction with Beza's Latin version of the Greek.

Though not the first of the noble band who manfully claimed liberty of private judgment in divine things for himself and for all others, Busher's work remains to us as the *earliest treatise known to be extant* on this great theme.

That his address to the king and parliament was not ill-timed, (although we may not say from want of evidence that it influenced the mind of his sovereign,) appears from the very liberal sentiments which fell from the royal orator on opening the parliament of 1614. " No state," says the monarch, " can evidence that any religion or heresy was ever extirpated by the sword, or by violence, nor have I ever judged it a way of planting the truth. An example of this I take where, when many rigorous counsels were propounded, Gamaliel stood up and advised, that ' if that religion were of God, it would prosper; if of man, it would finish of itself.' " [1] It is to be deeply regretted that the monarch's practic did not agree with his words.

All inquiries have failed in discovering an earlier edition than that from which the present is reprinted. Mr. Hanbury has supposed,[2] with much probability, that Mr. Henry Burton is the author of the address prefixed, " To the Presbyterian Reader." This courageous man and sufferer under Laud's tyranny, was among the earliest of the independents who claimed and allowed full liberty of conscience. This liberty was especially unpalatable to the presbyterians; and to them he saw fit to address his reprint. Their influence in the state was at the time predominant, and it was eagerly employed to repress all who differed from them.

Burton's edition is in 4to. His address occupies four pages, and Busher's treatise thirty-eight. No other work of our author is known to exist. An anonymous book referred to under his name in the catalogue of the Bodleian Library, is by another hand, in opposition to his views, and of much later date; though perhaps occasioned by this republication in 1646. Another copy may be found in the British Museum.

The Council is indebted to Mr. Read of Ipswich for the loan of the copy from which this edition is printed.

[1] Vaughan's Hist. of Eng. under the Stuarts, i. p. 89.

[2] Historical Memorials relating to the Independents, i. p. 224, note f.

PRESBYTERIAN READER.

THIS Treatise, which, as a supplication to King James and the parliament, was printed in the year 1614, is, for your good, now again reprinted. The author thereof, Leonard Busher, an honest and godly man, as I make no doubt will appear to you in the perusal of his book, intended two things therein.

First, to make it appear that the bishops were not true ministers, or successive from the apostles, but rather a scion or branch of the popish stock, descended from the Romish hierarchy, to whom they owed their instauration, ordination, and function. Had this advice been believed and embraced by the parliament then, the mischiefs they have since practised, much of the blood that hath been shed, and the miseries that by their means have been brought upon us, had in great measure been prevented; but his counsel was then slighted, though by the wisdom of this present parliament put in execution, whereby we are secured for the future from the domination, compulsion against conscience, and notorious cruelties of that sort of men.

BUSHER.]   B

Whence we may learn, that what to a people at one
time seems strange and absurd, and in no wise to be
admitted of, at another time appears an acceptable truth.
The reason is, because we are not masters of our own
understandings, but suffer them to be dulled and
corrupted, till misery and the sting of oppression open our
eyes, so that we embrace truth more out of necessity than
choice.

The second thing his discourse drives at, is to make it
appear by scriptures and sound arguments, that the only
way to make a nation happy, and preserve the people in
love, peace, and tranquillity, is to give liberty to all to
serve God according as they are persuaded is most agreeable to his word; to speak, write, print, peaceably and
without molestation, in behalf of their several tenets and
ways of worship, wholesome and pertinent laws being
made, upon penalties, to restrain all kinds of vice or
violence, all kinds of reproach, slander, or injury either by
word or deed.

And though this advice likewise seems not the best to
some, especially to you my brethren in the Presbyterian
way, yet am I well assured that this nation will never
be happy; but, as hitherto it hath been, so for the future
it will be, distracted with oppression and persecution, and
the faces of one sort of men set against another, till
liberty of conscience be allowed. Indeed a man would
think we had been schooled and whipt long enough to it
by our calamities, for want whereof this age, and that
age, and the other age, and every age hath been miserable.
For want whereof the apostles suffered martyrdom,

the saints and godly of all times have been hunted like partridges by birds of prey. And yet, good men, in the esteem of a great part of the world, especially of the rich and powerful, they have suffered as evil-doers, disturbers of the world, heretics, schismatics, seditious persons. And those that put them to death, have had the reputation of being maintainers of truth and sound doctrine. So apt in all ages have the people been to mistake good for evil, and evil for good.

The plea for liberty of conscience is no new doctrine; as old certainly as the blessed word of God itself, which gives us this immovable foundation thereof: That every man should be fully persuaded of the truth of that way, wherein he serves the Lord. And though there have been strugglings in all ages to make good this blessed birthright to all peaceful people; yet, through the potency and subtlety of popes, bishops, and ministers that preferred the advance of themselves, and their usurped and abused function, before the good and welfare of the people, we have been deprived of this blessing, next to the manifestation of God's love and goodness to us, the most excellent and desirable in this world. For want whereof, and by means of its contrary, persecution, this universe, especially the Christian part thereof, hath suffered a continual agony and earthquake.

War and its miseries have overspread all lands. States have been shaken and subverted. Love, meekness, gentleness, mercy, the truest badges of Christianity, have been damned and banished; and, in their room, cruelty, hardheartedness, respect of persons, prisons, tortures, &c.,

things that our blessed Lord and Master, and his apostles never proved, unless upon their own afflicted bodies, have had great sway for these many hundred years.   Hence is it, .that instead of peace, we have frequently had the sword; instead of sweet tranquillity, love, and affection, hatred, contention, disaffection, and the bitter fruits thereof, have reigned amongst us ; and, in all probability, will reign, till God shall put it into the heart of the parliament to make trial for the prevention thereof, of this God-like way, which, in the ensuing treatise, is held forth.

I hope, upon perusal thereof, you that are my brethren of the Presbyterian way, will abate much of your mis- guided eagerness in prosecuting your conscientious brethren.   Consider, I beseech you, St. Paul before his conversion.   He was as zealous, I make no question, Acts viii. 3. as any of you, when he persecuted the saints, and made havoc of the church, that is, of God's people congregated Verse 3. together, to worship and serve God; when he entered into every house, and drew out both men and women to put Acts ix. 1 them to prison; when he breathed out threatenings and Verse 2. slaughter against the disciples of the Lord; when he procured letters of the high priest to go to Damascus, where, if he found any of that way, then the heretical way in his account, he might bring them down to Jerusa- Acts viii. 1. lem ; when he consented to Stephen's death.

In all these violent motions he was zealous and hearty, and thought he did God good service in the suppres- sion of a rising sect, that was against the high priests, learned rabbis, and doctors of the law, ceremonies, strict injunctions and observations of the judaical and priestly law. You see how far mistaken zeal can go. Consider this, I beseech you. I know you are, especially you that are laymen, zealous as you think for God and his truth, as Paul was; but I hope there will a time come, and I wish it were now present, when in the midst of your heat and fervency, the glorious and shining brightness of love will appear in your hearts, like the light surrounding Paul going to Damascus; and the scales of ignorance and mistake will fall from your eyes. And then you will lament all the evil, which, through weakness, you have brought upon your brethren. You will then blame your own zeal and importunity, and apply yourselves more cordially and constantly to observe our Saviour's rule of equity, to do unto others what you would have others do unto you.

Peruse this treatise, I beseech you, with a single heart, and unprejudiced mind, and let it sway you: as the arguments thereof are efficacious, and the scriptures therein urged are pertinent and convincing.

So wisheth yours, and all other good

Men's true Friend,

H. B.

RELIGION'S PEACE,

ETC. ETC.

To the High and Mighty King JAMES, *by the grace of God
King of Great Britain, France, and Ireland, and to the
Princely and Right Honourable Parliament,* LEONARD
BUSHER *wisheth the wisdom of Solomon, the zeal of Josias,
and the mercy of Christ, with the salvation of your spirits* 1 Cor. v 5.
in the day of the Lord Jesus.

FORASMUCH as your majesty and parliament do
stand for the maintenance of the religion wherein
you are born, and for the same do most zealously persecute
with fire and sword; I have thought it good, and also my
duty, most royal sovereign, to inform your majesty and
parliament thereof. In all humility, therefore, I give you
to understand, that no prince or people can possibly attain
that one true religion of the gospel, which is acceptable to
God by Jesus Christ, merely by birth.

For Christ saith, *Except a man be born again, he cannot* John iii. 3.
see the kingdom of God. Also, the apostle James saith,
Of his own will he begat us by the word of truth. And the Jam. i. 18.
apostle Peter saith, *Being born anew, not of mortal seed, but* 1 Pet. i. 23.
*of immortal, by the word of God who liveth and endureth for
ever.* Therefore Christ commanded this word to be Matt. xxviii
preached to all nations, that thereby they may attain the Mark xvi.
new birth. By which your majesty and parliament may
[19, 20]; [15.]

perceive, that the one true religion of the gospel is not attained by natural birth; for then all princes and peoples, in all nations, should have that one true religion of the gospel, the which you see and grant they all have not. Yet many of them, also, will defend their religion wherein they are born, by fire and sword, as if it were their natural and earthly inheritances, or had with fire and sword been gotten, and therefore will with fire and sword maintain and defend it.

But your majesty and parliament may please to understand, that the scriptures do teach, that the one true religion is gotten by a new birth, even by the word and Spirit of God, and therewith also it is only maintained and defended. *For the word of God is lively, and mighty in operation, and* Heb. iv. 12; 2 Cor. x. 4; Eph. vi. 17. *sharper than any two-edged sword, and entereth through, even unto the dividing asunder of the soul and the spirit, and of the joints and of the marrow; and is a discerner of the thoughts and the intents of the heart.* Seeing, then, the one true religion of the gospel is thus gotten, and thus defended and maintained—namely, by the word preached only; let it please your majesty and parliament to be intreated to revoke and repeal those antichristian, Romish, and cruel laws, that force all in our land, both prince and people, to receive that religion wherein the king or queen were born, or that which is established by the law of man. And instead thereof, enact and publish that apostolic, Christian, Matt.xxviii. 19; Mark xvi. 16. gentle, and merciful law of Christ—viz. *Go, teach all nations, preach the gospel to every creature.* That is, Christ will have his ministers to preach and teach the people of all Acts ii. 41, viii. 12, 37; Luke xxiv. 47. nations, the things that concern the kingdom of God, and the name of Jesus Messiah, repentance and remission of sins, and to baptize in his name such as do believe.

And forasmuch, also, that the false and antichristian religion did come by the spirit of error and doctrine of devils, and not by fire and sword, therefore by the Spirit _{1 Tim. iv. 1 ;} Bev. xvi. 14. of Christ and doctrine of the word of God, must it be driven out of the hearts and consciences, both of prince and people; and not by fire and sword, as the false bishops and ministers have and do still persuade.

Therefore may it please your majesty and parliament to understand that, by fire and sword, to constrain princes and peoples to receive that one true religion of the gospel, is wholly against the mind and merciful law of Christ, dangerous both to king and state, a means to decrease the kingdom of Christ, and a means to increase the kingdom of antichrist; as these reasons following do manifest. The which, I humbly beseech your majesty and parliament carefully to consider, and that according to the word of God, which shall *judge every man according to his deeds.* And persecution is a work well pleasing to all false prophets and bishops, but it is contrary to the mind of Christ, *who came not to judge and destroy men's lives, but to save them.* And though some men and women believe not at the first hour, yet may they at the eleventh hour, if they be not persecuted to death before.

And no king nor bishop can, or is able to command faith; *That is the gift of God, who worketh in us both the will and the deed of his own good pleasure.* Set him not a day, therefore, in which, if his creature hear not and believe not, you will imprison and burn him. Paul was a blasphemer and also a persecutor, and could not be converted by the apostles and ministers of Christ; yet at last was received to mercy, and converted extraordinarily by Christ himself, *who is very pitiful and merciful, and would have no man to perish, but would that all men come to repentance.* But not by persecution, but by the word of reconciliation which he hath committed to his ministers. And as kings and bishops cannot command the wind, so they cannot command faith;

John iii. [8.] *and as the wind bloweth where it listeth, so is every man that is born of the Spirit.* You may force men to church against their consciences,[1] but they will believe as they did afore, when they come there; for God giveth a blessing only to 1 Sam. xv. his own ordinance, and abhorreth antichrist's.

15, 24.

    And kings are to think that they are men as well as kings, and that Christ hath ordained the same means of faith for kings, which he hath for subjects; and that sub-

Acts ix. 15;
1 Tim. ii. 1,
2.

jects are Christ's freemen, as well as kings' subjects; and

1 Cor. vii. 21, kings that believe are Christ's servants, even as subjects
22; Wisd.
vi. 1—8. are kings' servants, and both are bought with a price. Therefore both ought not to be the servants of men in matters of faith and religion. But kings shall give a greater account at the day of judgment than their subjects. And to judge men now for religion, is to judge afore the time, and also to sit in the judgment-seat of Christ, to Rom. ii. 16; whom only it belongeth, yet not before the day appointed.
Acts x. 42. How much less to kings and bishops?

    I read that Constantine the emperor, called the great, wrote to the bishop of Rome, that he would not force and constrain any man to the faith, but only admonish, and John xviii. commit the judgment to God.[2]   Christ's kingdom is not of
36, 10, 11. this world, therefore may it not be purchased nor defended

---

[1 By the act of uniformity, 1 Eliz. c. 2, a fine of 12*d.* was commanded to be levied on every absentee from the parish church, for each offence, and the offender to be corrected and punished by ecclesiastical censures. By the 23 Eliz. c. 1, every such offender being above sixteen years of age, was to forfeit 20*l.* for every month he should forbear frequenting the church; and threats of further penalties were added if he still continued obstinate. — Statutes at Large, vol. vi. pp. 123, 334.],

[2 [" And those that are led away with error, let them desire to live in peace and tranquillity with the faithful.   For friendly human society, and commerce with them, will be very much available to bring them to the right way.   Let no man molest another, but let every one follow the persuasion of their own conscience.— Let no man, in that which he is persuaded is right and good, give any offence to another; but rather he that hath knowledge and understanding, let him endeavour to instruct and con-

with the weapons of this world, but by his word and Spirit. Eph. vi. 10, 17.
No other weapons hath he given to his church, which is his
spiritual kingdom.   Therefore Christ saith, *He that will* Matt. xviii. 17.
*not hear the church, let him be to thee as a heathen and a pub-
lican.* He saith not, burn, banish, or imprison him ; that is
antichrist's ordinance.   And though a man be an heretic,
yet ought he not to be burnt, but to be rejected, *after once* Tit. iii. 10.
or twice admonition—that is, cast out of the church.

But as in the church of Rome, people of all sorts are by
persecution forced thereinto by the bishops and ministers
thereof; so it is in the church of England also.   Which
showeth that the bishops and ministers of Rome and England are of one spirit, in gathering people to their faith and
church, which is the spirit of Satan, who knoweth well
that his kingdom, the false church, would greatly decay, if
persecution were laid down.   Seeing himself cannot stand
before the word and Spirit of God, much less his bishops
and ministers ; therefore he will have them for a name and
show, to use the word of God.   But, indeed, if the false
interpretation and alleging of the scriptures will not help,
then, saith he, constrain them with fire and sword; or else
(if people have liberty of conscience) they will try the 1 John iv. 1.
spirits, which of them is of God, as the apostle John
teacheth : and then, saith he, the prince as well as people
will *try all things,* and *keep that which is good;* and will also [1 Thess. v. 21.]

vert his neighbour : but if he cannot,
let him give over.   For it is one thing
to embrace religion willingly, and another to be compelled through fear
of punishment." — Eusebius in Vit.
Constantin. l. ii. c. 55, 59, p. 32;
Saltonstall's Translation, 1659.—The
above extracts are from an edict of
Constantine.   The only letter extant
from him to a bishop of Rome, does not
contain any sentiments similar to those
referred to in the text.   See Du Pin,
Eccles. Hist. Cent. iv. p. 15, ed.
1697; and Eusebius, Hist. Eccles. l.
x. c. 5.   Constantine did not always
act on the tolerant principles here
avowed.—Eusebius in Vit. Constantin. l. ii. c. 63; Gibbon, Decline and
Fall, c. 21, p. 331, 8vo edit. London:
1830.]

2 Cor. xiii. 5. *prove themselves,* as the apostle Paul teacheth, *whether they are in the* apostolic *faith* or not.

And as the church of Rome provoketh the magistrates to persecute to death such as are excommunicated out of her, so doth the church of England provoke the magistrates to persecute to death such as she excommunicates.³ And as the bishops and ministers of Rome will persuade the prince and people to hear and read none but themselves, so do the bishops and ministers of England also.

But the bishops and ministers of the apostolic church do persuade all men, to prove and *try the spirits whether they are of God;* which they cannot do, except they hear and read other men's doctrines as well as the bishops' and their ministers'. Neither can they if they would, so long as the bishops have power from the king and state to silence and imprison, &c., all preachers, and to burn all books which teach not their doctrines.⁴

[1 John iv. 1.]

Your majesty and parliament shall understand, that all those *that confess,* freely, without compulsion, *that Jesus is the Messiah,* the Lord, *and that he came in flesh,* are to be esteemed the children of God and true Christians, seeing

1 John iv. 2.

---

³ [" Preachers may reprove and threaten, princes may seize the goods and chastise the bodies of such as offend: preachers may shut the gates of heaven against non-repentants, princes may root them from the face of the earth, and let them feel the just vengeance of their sins in this world. This is the power of princes which we say must be directed by bishops, but is not subjected to their wills or tribunals."—The True Difference between Christian Subjection and Unchristian Rebellion, by Thos. Bilson, Warden of Winchester, pp. 361, 362; edit. Oxford, 1585.]

⁴ [In 1562, we find the archbishops and bishops in convocation assembled, presenting the following bill for adoption, to the sovereign and parliament: — " Forasmuch as in these our days divers subjects of this realm, and others the queen's majesty's dominions, are grown into such license and contempt of the laws ecclesiastical and censures of the church, that unless it were for fear of the temporal sword and power, they would altogether despise and neglect the same: which temporal sword and power being oftentimes slowly and negligently executed, that the execution of justice thereby

such are *born of God;* and *no man can say that Jesus is the* ^{1 John v. 1;} ^{1 Cor. xii. 3.}
Lord, but by the Holy Ghost, therefore not to be persecuted.
And as Abel killed not Cain, but was killed himself; and
as Isaac and Jacob did not persecute Ishmael and Esau,
but were persecuted of Ishmael and Esau—who, and Cain, ^{Gal. iv. 29.}
were figures of all persecutors—so the believing do not
persecute the unbelieving, nor the true church the false;
but the believing and true church are, as they have been,
most often persecuted themselves. Of whom Abel, Isaac,
and Jacob, were figures, whose children are all believers
and freemen, that *stand fast in the liberty wherewith Christ* ^{Gal. v. i.}
hath made them free, and will *not be tangled with the yoke of
bondage.* No, not with circumcision, much less with the
discipline and doctrine of the church of Rome, whose bishops
are able ministers of the fire and sword, both to prince and
people, as many histories do lamentably witness, to their
utter infamy and overthrow.

Also, if the believing should persecute the unbelieving to
death, who should remain alive? Then none but the
believing should live in the world, and the unbelieving
should die in their unbelief, and so perish for ever. The
Lord will not that the believing should live to the destruction of the unbelieving, but unto their conversion, edification, and salvation. And by persecuting of prince and
people to death, because they will not hear and believe, is
no gaining of souls unto God, but unto the devil. And

---

is letted or delayed, and the party
excommunicated thereby encouraged
to continue and persist in wilful and
obstinate contumacy and disobedience:
May it therefore please your majesty,
that it be enacted, to attack and ap-
prehend the body of the person or persons excommunicated, and to carry
and convey the same unto the next
prison and gaol."—Strype's Annals I.
i. 460; Grindal, p. 431, 8vo edit.—It
was accordingly passed. The crimes
which exposed an individual to the
merciless severity of these ecclesiastics, were, "matters of heresy, or refusing to have a child baptized, or to
receive the holy communion, or to
come to divine service, or error in
matter of religion or doctrine now received in this church."—p. 467.]

whereas ignorant and wicked bishops may think to win souls, by killing prince and people for religion, they are deceived greatly; for thereby they lose many souls—viz., their own and the unbelieving. Their own they lose, because they wilfully break the Lord's commandment, that Luke xviii. saith, *Thou shalt not kill ;* meaning such as are not corporal malefactors. And the others which die in their unbelief, they themselves confess, are eternally lost ; except they, as some of their ministers, hold a redemption after this life.

And the bishops should know, that error and heresy cannot be killed by the fire and sword, but by the word and Spirit of God. These are the only weapons of Christ's bishops and ministers; and such only Christ's ministers do use. Whose lives and conversations are so harmless, holy, and gentle, that thereby, and by their deaths and sufferings, they win many souls unto God. Whereby they are known from all false bishops and ministers, who, like wolves and bears, not like sheep and lambs, make prey, and devour both prince and people, that are not of their kind, if they be able to master them.

Besides, may it please your majesty and parliament to understand, that the believing man that hath an unbeliev-ing wife, and the believing woman that hath an unbelieving husband, cannot live together as the scripture teaches, for the salvation of the unbelieving, if they be persecuted to death. Indeed, some thereby are forced to confess with the mouth, that which they believe not in heart, and so are made true dissemblers, instead of true Christians. Whereby many men and women are deceived with dissembling hus-bands and wives, as well as the king and state are deceived with dissembling servants and subjects. But the word of God, if permission of conscience might be granted, would procure upright, pure, and unfeigned husbands and wives, servants and subjects, so that thereby neither prince nor people should be deceived. For all good shepherds will divide and separate, and not force, slay, and persecute. For if men and women be found heretics, they shall be separated from the church; but if they be unbelievers, they shall not be joined unto it, until they be converted by the word of God, much less forced. Which conversion, for ought we know, may be at their death, if not afore, seeing the Lord calleth some at the eleventh hour, as well as at Matt. xx. 6, the first, and not at the king's and bishops' pleasures. 7.

Kings and magistrates are to rule temporal affairs by the swords of their temporal kingdoms, and bishops and ministers are to rule spiritual affairs by the word and Spirit of God, the sword of Christ's spiritual kingdom, and not to intermeddle one with another's authority, office, and function. And it is a great shame for the bishops and ministers not to be able to rule in their church, without the assistance of the king and magistrate; yea, it is a great sign they are none of Christ's bishops and ministers. If they were, they would not be afraid nor ashamed of their faith; nor yet would they persuade princes and people to persecute, and force one another to believe them; but would use only the assistance of God's word and Spirit, and therewith suffer their faith and doctrine to be examined, proved, and disputed, both by word and writing.

And he is a true bishop who is unreprovable, and that is Tit. i, 7, 9, able to stop the mouths of his adversaries by God's word 11. and Spirit only, and whose faith and discipline agree with the prophets, Christ, and his apostles, and maketh no contradiction. But all those bishops that force princes and peoples to receive their faith and discipline by persecution, do, with Judas, go against Christ, in his members, with swords, staves, and halberds; who, seeing God's word will not help them, betake themselves, with all haste and hazard, unto the authority of the king and magistrate.

I read that a bishop of Rome would have constrained a Turkish emperor to the Christian faith, unto whom the emperor answered, " I believe that Christ was an excellent prophet, but he did never, so far as I understand, command that men should, with the power of weapons, be constrained to believe his law; and verily I also do force no man to believe Mahomet's law." Also I read that Jews, Christians, and Turks, are tolerated[5] in Constantinople, and yet are peaceable, though so contrary the one to the other.

If this be so, how much more ought Christians not to force one another to religion? AND HOW MUCH MORE OUGHT CHRISTIANS TO TOLERATE CHRISTIANS, WHEN AS THE TURKS DO TOLERATE THEM? SHALL WE BE LESS MERCIFUL THAN THE TURKS? OR SHALL WE LEARN THE TURKS TO PERSECUTE CHRISTIANS? IT IS NOT ONLY UNMERCIFUL, BUT UNNATURAL AND ABOMINABLE; YEA, MONSTROUS FOR ONE CHRISTIAN TO VEX AND DESTROY ANOTHER FOR DIFFERENCE AND QUESTIONS OF RELIGION. And though tares have overgrown the wheat, yet Christ will have them let alone till harvest, *lest while you go about to pluck up the tares, you pluck up also the wheat with them;* as your predecessors have done, who thought they had gathered up the tares and burned them, but you see now that they have burned the wheat instead of tares. Wherefore in all humility and Christian modesty, I do affirm, that through the unlawful weed-hook of persecution, which your predecessors have used, and by your majesty and parliament is still continued, there is such a quantity of wheat plucked up, and such a multitude of tares

Matt. xiii. 29, 30, 38.

---

[5] [" The disciples of Abraham, of Moses, and of Jesus, were solemnly invited to accept the more perfect revelation of Mahomet; but if they preferred the payment of a moderate tribute, they were entitled to the freedom of conscience and religious worship."—Gibbon's Decline and Fall, &c., c. 51, p. 968, edit. 1830.]

left behind, that the wheat which remains cannot yet appear in any right visible congregation.

And now, beloved sovereign and parliament, I know that through ignorance you do persecute, as did also your predecessors. *Amend your lives, therefore, and turn, that your* Acts iii. 17, *sins may be put away, when the time of refreshing shall come* 18, 19. *from the presence of the Lord;* who *before hath showed by the mouth of* his holy servant John, that *the woman*—mean- Rev. xii. 14. ing the church—*should fly into the wilderness for a time, times, and half a time, from the presence* and persecution *of the serpent.* And that *the winepress should be trodden with-* Rev. xiv. 20. *out the city,* until *blood come out of the winepress unto the horse-bridles, by the space of a thousand and six hundred furlongs.* And thus he hath fulfilled it.

Now, therefore, I humbly beseech you, suffer not your bishops and ministers any longer to persuade [you] to force your subjects, or any others, to their faith and church by persecution; neither suffer them therewith to defend their faith and church against their adversaries. If they have not any thing from God's word against us, let them yield and submit themselves. If they think they have any thing against us, let them betake themselves only to God's word, both in word and writing. For *the whole scripture is given* 2 Tim. iii. *by inspiration of God* to that purpose, *and is profitable to* 16, [17.] *teach, to reprove, to correct, and to instruct in righteousness; that the man of God may be absolute,*[6] *being made perfect unto all good works.* With which scripture, and not with fire and sword, your majesty's bishops and ministers ought to be armed and weaponed. And whosoever shall not hear the words of such bishops and ministers, then such bishops

[6] [*Complete.* " Because the things that proceed from him are perfect without any manner of defect or maim; it cannot be, but that the words of his mouth are *absolute,* and lack nothing which they should have for performance of that thing whereunto they tend." — Hooker.]

BUSHER.]   C

and ministers are commanded by Christ, not to imprison,
Matt. x. 14, 15. burn, banish, and hang them; but *to shake the dust of their feet against them, for a witness, when they depart* from them:
Mark vi. 11. affirming, *that at the day of judgment, it shall be easier for Sodom and Gomorrah,* than for such persons. And this commandment of Christ did his bishops and ministers obey,
Acts xiii. 51. as you may read. By which, and by that which follows, your gracious majesty and princely and honourable parliament, may perceive the will and mind of our Lord and Saviour Christ: unto whose mercy I commend you, and to the word and wisdom of his grace, which is able to build further, and to give you an inheritance among all them which are sanctified. Amen.

Your faithful and loving subject,

LEONARD BUSHER.[7]

[7] Not Furbusher. There is one Furbusher, a preacher, in this land.

CERTAIN

REASONS AGAINST PERSECUTION.

FIRST—Because Christ hath not commanded any king, bishop, or minister to persecute the people for difference of judgment in matters of religion.

Secondly—Because Christ hath commanded his bishops and ministers to persuade prince and people to hear and believe the gospel, by his word and Spirit, and, as ambassadors for him, to beseech both prince and people to be reconciled unto God; and not, as tyrants, to force and constrain them by persecution. 2 Cor. v. 20.

Thirdly—Because through persecution it will come to pass, that the ambassadors of the only spiritual Lord and King, Jesus, may be persecuted and imprisoned, burned, hanged, or banished, for delivering the message of their gracious Lord, sincerely and often, both to prince and people. Which to do, is a more heinous fact, than to persecute the ambassadors of the greatest king and prince in the world. For instead of heretics, they shall, as they have already,[1] burn, banish, and hang the ambassadors of the Lord Jesus Christ, who doth choose out whom he pleaseth, to bear his name before kings and rulers, for a testimonial Mark xiii. 9. to them.

---

[1] Many thousand ambassadors and martyrs of Christ have bishops caused to be slain since Christ ascended.

Persecution
destroys
Christians,
but not er-
rors. Fourthly—Because then we cannot say we have the liberty of the gospel in our land; seeing where that is, there is no persecution for any difference in religion, nor [any] forcing of the conscience to believe the gospel, except by the word and Spirit of God only, the which do wound 2 Cor. x. 4. and kill the errors of men, and not their persons.

1 Tim i. 13, 15. Fifthly—Because *Christ came into the world to save sinners,* and not to destroy them, though they be blasphemers; seeing the Lord may convert them as he did Saul, after called Paul. And though they have difference in religion, Persecutors rebuked of Christ. or will not hear nor believe in Christ that they may be converted, yet ought you not to persecute them, seeing Luke ix. 53, 55. Christ rebuketh such; and his Father *sent him not into the* [John iii. 17] *world to condemn the world, but to save it.* Be ye, therefore, followers of Christ, and not of antichrist, in gathering people to the faith.

Col. iv. 5. Sixthly—Because then you shall not *walk wisely towards them that are without,* as the scripture teacheth; but shall 1 Cor. x. 32. offend also the Jews, and all other strangers, who account it tyranny to have their consciences forced to religion by persecution.

Seventhly—Because if persecution be not laid down, and liberty of conscience set up, then cannot the Jews, nor any strangers, nor others contrary-minded, be ever converted in our land. For so long as they know aforehand, that they shall be forced to believe against their consciences, they will never seek to inhabit there. By which means you keep them from the apostolic faith, if the apostolic faith be only taught where persecution is.

Eighthly—Because if freedom of conscience be not set up, and persecution laid down, then all the king's subjects, Persecution does make many stran- gers. and all strangers inhabiting the land, that shall believe the apostolic faith, must depart the land to some free country; or else abide the danger of burning, banishing, hanging, and imprisoning. The first will be a great impoverishing and weakening of our land, besides a loss of the faithfullest subjects and friends. The second will provoke the Lord to wrath, by spilling the blood of his faithful servants, ambassadors, and witnesses; and also open the mouths of all strangers, to speak yet more lamentably of the cruel and bloody persecution of our land.

Ninthly—Because if persecution continue, then the king and state shall have, against their will, many dissemblers in authority and office, both in court, city, and country. Yea, no man of any degree shall know, whether they are all faithful and true Christians that are about him, and with whom he hath to do : seeing most men will conform themselves for fear of persecution, although in their hearts they hate and detest the religion whereto they are forced by law.[2] The which is very dangerous and hurtful, both to

[2] [" A preacher, Mr. Smith, one of us, being called, and, upon their speeches and demands, answering that he marvelled, who being above eleven months prisoner, they should deal with men by imprisonment and other rigorous means, in matters of religion and conscience, rather than by more Christian and fit proceedings ; protesting unto them, that he should but dissemble with them, and play the hypocrite, if he should, to please them, or to avoid trouble, submit to go to church, and to join with the public ministry of those assemblies, as it now standeth; he being persuaded in conscience that it was utterly unlawful. The aforesaid commissioner said to him again, Come to the church, and obey the queen's laws, and be a dissembler, be a hypocrite, or a devil, if thou wilt."—Francis Johnson's Letter to the Lord Treasurer, Jan. 18th, 1593.   Strype, Annals, iv. 187.— " All know well enough, it is no matter how open and professed they be, so as they will be conformable to come to church once a month, and hear your divine service book. Did Mr. W. Smith, your great acquaintance, never tell you how Mr. Wroth, one of the commissioners themselves, when he was called before them, said unto him, Come to church, and be a devil if thou wilt ?"—F. Johnson's Answer to Maister H. Jacob, p. 200, printed in 1600. From this it appears that Mr. Brook is mistaken in presenting this scene as occurring in the life of Mr. John Smyth, who afterwards became a baptist. It must refer to a Mr. Wm. Smith, at that time in prison, and who frequently appeared before the commissioners.—Lives of the Puritans, ii. 194, 44.]

king and state, in time of temptation from beyond the seas, and in rebellion at home. For they that are not faithful to God in their religion, will never be faithful to the king and state in their allegiance; especially being tried by a great reward, or by a mighty rebel : but will, to increase their honours and revenues, conform themselves; and some to save their honours, lands, goods, and lives, will yield and submit, though against their will, even as they have done in case of religion. For through forcing men to church by persecution, the true-hearted subjects are forced out of the land, and out of the world. Some [are] banished, others burned, hanged, and imprisoned to death.

Persecution causes many religions in the church. Tenthly—Because if there be many religions in the land, as it is well known there are, then it will come to pass, through the continuance of persecution, that many religions will be continued in the church; seeing all are forced to church, who bring their religions with them as well as their bodies.[3] Whereby all their devotion is against their consciences, and all the church is a confused Babel, *full of* Rev. xviii. 2, 4 *every unclean and hateful bird,* even *a hold of foul spirits,* as the scripture speaketh; out of which the people of God are commanded to flee, lest, as of their sins, they be also partakers of their plague. And the bishops, the authors of persecution, are very ignorant to think that when they have gotten people to their church by persecution, that then they have gotten them to their faith and religion; the which is not so, for most people, though contrary-minded, to save life and goods will dissemble their religion. As, for example, the Jews in Spain and Portugal;[4] and the papists,

---

[3] Better were it to have many religions in the land, than in the church.

[4] [In the beginning of the seventh century, ninety thousand Jews were compelled to receive the sacrament of baptism, and the property of the obstinate confiscated. So rigorous were the proceedings of the Spanish sovereign, that the clergy sought to moderate his zeal. They " solemnly pronounced an inconsistent sentence —that the sacraments should not be

reformists, and others in England.[5] But when they come hither, or to some other free city or country, where (praised be God) is liberty of the gospel, then they show that before they dissembled, to avoid the cruel persecution of their land.

Moreover, the bishops bewray great ignorance, when they persuade the king and parliament to force prince and people to church by persecution. For if that be the means to come to the church of Christ, then Christ hath taught us to flee the means of salvation, seeing he hath taught us to flee   Matt. x. 23. persecution; the which the bishops and their ministers persuade to be a great means to bring men to the church. Indeed, I confess it is the only means to bring prince and people to the false church; and therefore Christ teacheth   Christ teacheth to flee us to flee that means, lest through persecution, which is a   persecution; ergo, it cannot possibly great temptation, we be constrained *to go the broad way,*   not possibly be good. which is the false church, *that leadeth to destruction, and many go in thereat.* And no marvel, for there men may be any   Matt. vii. 13.

forcibly imposed, but that the Jews who had been baptized should be constrained, for the honour of the church, to persevere in the external practice of a religion which they disbelieved and detested." Their frequent relapses led to the banishment of the entire nation, at an after period. —Gibbon, Decline, &c. c. 37, p. 617. —Their expulsion was ordered by an edict of Ferdinand and Isabella, in the year 1492, when it is computed that one hundred and seventy thousand families emigrated, comprising eight hundred thousand souls. " Persecution and intolerance compelled many of them to change their religion; and from these incidents, both Spain and Portugal became spread with secret Jews, in the guise of Christians, whose

hypocrisy, or the suspicion of it, chiefly upheld the inquisition." — Sharon Turner, Hist. of Edw. VI. vol. iii. p. 19.— The inquisition affected to have no jurisdiction over Jews until by baptism they had professed their adherence to the church. Any relapse, or suspicion of it, immediately exposed them to the fangs of this dreaded tribunal. — Limborch, Hist. Inquisitionis, pp. 238, 242; Amstel, 1692.]

[5 Great numbers of papists and puritans conformed to the services of the church, to avoid the pecuniary mulcts and imprisonments to which absence from church exposed them.—Neal, Hist. of the Puritans, i. 244, edit. 1837 ; Collier, Eccles. Hist. vi. 264, 8vo edit. 1840.]

Note.

thing, except good Christians. For besides Demas the worldling, and Hymeneus the blasphemer, and many other sorts of indifferent Christians, excommunicants, covetous,

See 2 Tim. iii. 3, 4.

and profane persons, there are notable rebels and traitors; yea, most cruel and desperate traitors and rebels, as Digby, Catesby, Percy, &c., whose unread and unheard-of treachery will never be forgotten. Which persons, if they had not been forced to church against their consciences, had never enterprised such horrible and hateful treason.[6]

And the bishops should understand, that it is preaching, and not persecuting, that getteth people to the church of

Rom. x. 17.

Christ. For the scripture saith, *Faith is by hearing, and hearing by the word of God;* and not by the sword of princes and magistrates, as they persuade and practise. And therefore the bishops of our land are truly called antichrists; for by their beastly and bloody persecution, as well as by their blasphemous titles, erroneous doctrines, and popish government, may they justly be termed antichrists.

Matt. xxiv. [24.]

Eleventhly—Because Christ foretold, that *many false Christs and false prophets should arise, and deceive many;*

2 Thess. ii. [3]; 1 Tim. iv. [1—3].

yea, if it were possible, the very elect. And the apostle Paul did prophesy a departure from the faith. And Peter said,

---

[6] [" The Roman catholics now utterly despairing, either by flattery to woo, or force to wrest, any free and public exercise of their religion, some of them entered into a damnable and devilish conspiracy, to blow up the parliament-house with gunpowder." Robert Catesby was the author of the plot, Thomas Percy, Sir Everard Digby, and ten others, with some Jesuits, uniting in it. " All of resolute spirits, most of ancient families, some of plentiful fortunes." — Fuller, Ch. Hist. bk. x. sect. ii. 24.— Their expectations of some relaxation of the penal laws were destroyed. Fines, confiscations even to two-thirds of their property, imprisonments, and death, fell upon them with increased rigour. The king, the parliament, and the bishops, united in enforcing attendance at church and conformity to ecclesiastical laws, repugnant alike to liberty and religion, with the severest penalties. Can we wonder that they should resent the intolerable oppression they suffered ? — See Dodd's Ch. Hist. vol. iv. p. 41, Tierney's edition, for a statement of these enactments.]

there should be false teachers now *among the people.*   And ^{2 Peter ii. 1.}
John said, the kings should *give their power and authority unto* ^{Rev.   xvii.
13, 17.}
the beast, until the words of God be fulfilled.   Therefore if
persecution be not laid down and liberty of the gospel set
up, you may persecute the true Christians instead of the
false, as your predecessors have done.   For they are now,
like as they were then, the smallest number; and the false
Christians are now, like as they were then, the greatest
number.   And persecution is a notable mark of the false
church and her bishops and ministers, and therefore Christ ^{Gal. ii. 3, 4,
v. 11, vi. 12.}
would have us flee from it; who overcame the devil and
his ministers by the word of God, and by a good, meek,
and gentle life; whose steps his bishops and ministers
ought to follow.

Twelfthly—Because persecution of such as do preach
and teach Christ, is a great hindrance to the liberty of the
gospel.   FOR THEREBY ARE THE JEWS, TURKS, AND
PAGANS OCCASIONED AND ENCOURAGED TO PERSECUTE ^{Note.
False bi-
shops teach}
LIKEWISE ALL SUCH AS PREACH AND TEACH CHRIST IN ^{Turks and
pagans to}
THEIR DOMINIONS.   For if Christian kings and magistrates ^{persecute
Christians.}
will not suffer Christians to preach, and preach the gospel of
Christ freely and peaceably, in their dominions: how should
you expect it of the infidels, unto whom bishops and Christian kings and magistrates ought to give a good example, and
not an evil [one], as to burn, banish, hang, and imprison,
peaceable and godly Christians, that are no traitors, nor
thieves, nor fighters, nor man-slayers, nor yet swearers, nor
drunkards, nor whoremasters, nor such like.

And the king and parliament may please to permit all
sorts of Christians; yea, Jews, Turks, and pagans, so long
as they are peaceable, and no malefactors, as is above mentioned; which, if they be found to be, under two or three
witnesses, let them be punished according to God's word.
Also, if any be found to be willing liars, false accusers, false

allegers and quoters of the scriptures, or other men's writings—as some men willingly do—let them be punished according to right and justice; it is due desert, and no persecution. But let God's word have its full and free passage among them all, even to the end of their lives, in all bountifulness, long-sufferance, and patience; knowing that it is ordained of God's rich mercy, to lead the infidels and such as err unto repentance and amendment, out of the snare of

Rom. ii. 4;
2 Tim. ii. 25. the devil, of whom they are taken and deceived.

Thirteenthly—Because persecution for religion is to force the conscience; and to force and constrain men and women's consciences to a religion against their wills, is to tyrannize over the soul, as well as over the body. And herein the bishops commit a greater sin, than if they force the bodies

2 Cor. xi. 2. of women and maids against their wills. Yea, herein they

False bi-
shops worse
than Turks
and pagans. are more cruel and greater tyrants than the Turks, who, though they force the bodies of strangers to slavery and bondage, yet they let the consciences go free, yea, to Christians that are so contrary to them in religion.[7]

But these idol-bishops will force the consciences of Christians, their own natural countrymen, even unto

Note.
False bi-
shops spiri-
tual fornica-
tors. spiritual bondage and slavery. And herein they commit fornication both with prince and people, and *have made all, both small and great, to receive a mark in their right hand, or*

[Rev. xviii.
9, xiii. 16,
17.] *in their foreheads, so that no man may buy or sell,* save he that will go to church, and submit to the bishop's ordinances, and name and mark of their beastly and bloody persecution; through which, as God, they sit in and reign over the con-

---

[7] [" Indeed, the Turk within his dominions compelleth no man to alter his religion; by reason whereof he is the more able peaceably to enjoy so large an empire. But if he thought he might bring all men to Mahomet's law, as he seeth the contrary, he would use that rigour in religion that he doth in other things."—A third political discourse made by Wm. Thomas, Esq., for the king's study. Strype's Memorials, II. ii. p. 381, 8vo edit.]

sciences, both of prince and people, which are the spiritual seat and temple of God, bought at a dear price, even with the precious blood of their only spiritual Lord, Jesus Messiah, the true shepherd and bishop of their souls. 2 Thess. ii. 4 ; 1 Cor. vi. 19,   20 ; 2 Cor. vi. 16, 17,   with Rev. xviii. 4 ; 2 Peter ii. 1 ; 1 Peter i. 19.

And the bishops in forcing men and women's consciences do therein play the antichrist, as well as the popes. And, indeed, there is never a bishop in the land but is a pope ; for pope in Latin is *papa,* and *papa* signifies father in English. All the bishops in our land are called reverend fathers, therefore all the bishops in our land are called reverend popes. So many lord bishops, so many reverend fathers, so many reverend popes. And these are all so many antichrists, so many idols, and so many false gods of England. How many are thy gods, whom thou dost serve! For whose spiritual adoration, the knee of every man and woman must bow,[8] or else they shall be persecuted.[9] Unto whom the king ought not any longer to give his authority and power, lest he fulfil the scripture, which saith, that kings should *give their power and authority unto the beast.* Rev. xvii. 13.

Fourteenthly—Because the burning, banishing, hanging, and imprisoning of men and women by protestants, for difference of religion, do justify the burning, banishing, and imprisoning of men and women, by the papists, for difference of religion; even as the papists do justify the Turks

---

[8] If idolaters ought to be slain, then ought all those that submit and yield spiritual obedience and reverence unto these bishops to be slain. Who then should remain in [the] land alive ?

[9] [In the " Reformatio Legum," compiled chiefly by Archbishop Cranmer, edited and published by John Fox, the martyrologist, under the direction of Archbishop Parker, and which body of ecclesiastical law, to the great regret of the hierarchy, but happily for the puritans, never received the approbation of parliament, it is provided, that so long as an excommunicated person " continued unrelenting, nobody was to pray, to eat, or drink with him, to salute him, or invite him to their houses."—Collier, Eccles. Hist. v. p. 494, 8vo edit. 1840; Fox's Acts and Mon., Preb. Townsend's Preliminary Dissertation, vol. i. p. 179, 8vo edit. 1841.]

and pagans in such like cruelty and tyranny. Wherein now are the protestants more merciful than the papists, or the papists than the Turks? Therefore as the papists, when they complain of the Turks and pagans, for their bloody persecution, do therein condemn themselves; because they are found to do the same, yea, worse—for it is greater tyranny for one Christian to force and kill another, than for Turks and pagans to kill a Christian. For that is no such great wonder, seeing it is a paganish part, who have no better knowledge. But Christians should have better knowledge and more mercy, than to play the pagans against

Note. Christians. So also the protestants, when they complain of the papists for their bloody and beastly persecution, do therein condemn themselves, seeing they do the same for which they blame others; and so are rebuked of the scrip-

Rom. ii 1,3. ture, which saith, *Therefore thou art inexcusable, O thou man, whosoever thou art, that blamest another: for in that thou judgest another, thou condemnest thyself; for thou that judgest doest the same things. And thinkest thou this, O thou man, that judgest them that do such things, and thou doest the same, that thou shalt escape the judgment of God?*

Fifteenthly—Because his majesty and parliament would not willingly themselves be forced against their consciences, by the persecution of the bishop of Rome and his princes.

Luke vi. 31. So, I beseech them, according to the law Christ hath enjoined Christians, not by persecution to force other men's consciences against their wills, by the irritation[1] of the bishops of our land.

Sixteenthly—Because persecutions do cause men and women to make shipwreck of faith and good consciences, by forcing a religion upon them even against their minds and consciences: and also do send them quick to the devil in

---

[1] Or provocation.

their errors, if that be heresy for which they are hanged and burned. Which to do, is a most unchristian, unnatural, cruel, and tyrannous deed; and I am sure you would not be content to be so dealt withal yourselves.

But, indeed, the popish and idol-bishops are the authors hereof against the people, as well as of other persecutions against the princes. For antichristian bishops do draw Rev. xvi. 14. kings and princes hereto against their minds, as may appear by Edward the Sixth, that godly king of famous memory, who being urged by his bloody bishops to subscribe to the burning of a woman called Joan Boucher, he answered, The Christian answer "Will you have me to send her quick to the devil in her of King Edward. error?" But when his blood-thirsty bishops would have no nay, he said again to Archbishop Cranmer, " I lay all the charge thereof on you before God." And Cranmer said, " He had never so much to do in all his life" as to procure it.[2]

Whereby I do perceive that godly kings are drawn to battle against the saints, by antichristian bishops and false prophets, who otherwise would rule and reign more agreeable to the mind of Christ. Also, hereby may all men perceive, that the council and bishops could not satisfy the king's conscience by their persuasion. If they could have showed him the word of God for burning that Christian, it would have prevailed with that godly king, and he might then of faith have consented. But his answer showeth that he was not of their mind, for all that they had said. And therefore now, if it please you to require of your bishops,

---

[2] King Edward was an enemy to persecution.—Acts and Mon. p. 1179, [edit. 1610. " He always spared and favoured the life of men; as in a certain dissertation of his once appeared, had with Master Cheke in favouring the life of heretics: inso- much that when Joan Boucher should be burned, all the council could not move him to put to his hand, but were fain to get Doctor Cranmer to persuade with him, and yet neither could he, with much labour, induce the king so to do, saying," &c.]

warrant from the word of God for the persecuting of Christians, or for forcing prince and people to church, you shall find not one bishop, yea, not all of them together, though assisted with their ministers, will be able to show warrant from God's word, whereby to persuade your consciences Rom.xiv.23. thereunto. And *whatsoever is not of faith is sin,* and whatsoever is not from God's word cannot be of faith.

Seventeenthly—Because persecutions of Christians by Christians, do not only justify papists, and teach the Jews and pagans to persecute Christians; but also do teach the papists and others, that know not the mind of Christ and once get the upperhand, to persecute those that persecuted them. Yea, it is a means, as we have had lamentable experience,[3] to set such as are forced to church against their consciences, at deadly hatred against the king and state; and urgeth all them to treason and rebellion, that have not truly learned Christ, who himself was persecuted to death; Matt. xi.29; whose harmless cross all true Christians must take up, and Luke xiv. 27. whose gentle and humble steps they must follow and walk in, or else they cannot be his disciples, nor sheep of his pasture.

And neither can the papists be persuaded that persecution is a sin, so long as they, and other Christians also, are persecuted by the protestants; seeing the papists do build their persecution on the same ground with the protestants. But both sorts of bishops do err grossly, as shall be showed, God willing, when they make their defence: except, herewith, their consciences be convinced to yield, as I wish they may, for the salvation of their own souls, the peace both of prince and people, and the safety of the king and state.

In the meanwhile it is to be observed, that those bishops and ministers which persuade the king and parliament to burn, banish, hang, and imprison, for difference of religion,

[3] By Digby, Catesby, &c.

are bloodsuckers and manslayers. And such, it cannot be denied, caused kings and magistrates to be their executioners and tormentors, in burning the martyrs in former times, even in the days of king Henry the Eighth and queen Mary, as the books of Acts and Monuments will witness, if they be not burned. And I ask the bishops and their ministers, if the martyrs should have obeyed the king Acts iv. 19. and queen, rather than have suffered death?

And now I must humbly, and, with all reverence, do beseech his majesty and parliament advisedly to consider among themselves, whether the prince or princess, differing with the church now in matter of conscience and religion, established by law in our land, as the right noble princess Elizabeth did in queen Mary's days, do not incur the danger and cruelty of the law now, as that worthy princess did then?[4] Seeing that popish and cruel law standeth still in force in most points of religion; and who dare trust the bishops and their adherents in such a case, the matter lying Note well. in their hands?[5]

Let it be supposed that the prince's heart should be moved by the Lord to embrace the apostolic faith and discipline; shall he be forced to believe as the bishops do, against his conscience? Shall he be constrained to submit

---

[4] [" Elizabeth, like Mary, preferred the religion of her mother; and she had the same claims to urge which Mary had so justly made, to be allowed to worship her Creator as she had been educated to do. But what had been permitted to the queen by her brother Edward she now refused to her only sister."—Sharon Turner, Hist. of Edw. VI. iii. 416. Elizabeth was shortly after committed to the Tower, and great efforts were made to connect her treasonably with the rebellion of Wyat. The Bishop of Winchester appears to have been her chief enemy. " For this is credible to be supposed, that the said wicked Gardiner of Winchester had long laboured his wits, and to this only most principal mark bent all his devices to bring this our happy and dear sovereign out of the way, as by his words and doings may sufficiently appear."— Fox, Acts and Mon. iii. 1900, ed. 1610.]

[5] The bishops, as the high priests, force men to obey man rather than God

to their government and discipline, against his conscience?
Shall he live in vexation and persecution, and in danger of
his life, by the bishops and law established, as the princess
Elizabeth did? Yea, it must be thus with our right noble
prince,[6] except there be partiality. Yea, it will be thus
with his princely person, except those popish and cruel laws
be repealed and extinguished.

Better to-
day, than
tarry till to-
morrow. Wherefore I meekly entreat, seeing death is most certain,
though most uncertain when, that those antichristian and
popish laws may be disannulled and made void in time, lest
we all lament and bewail it, when it will be too late. And
I pray your majesty and honours to consider, that *kings'*
[Prov. xxi.
1.] *and princes' hearts are in the hands of the Lord, as the rivers
of waters; to turn as he will.* And the scripture saith,
Rev. xvii.
16. *the ten horns,* by which I understand ten kings, *shall hate
the whore, and make her desolate and naked.* Likewise the
scripture saith to Abraham, the father of believing princes
Gen. xvii. 6;
Rom. iv. 17. as well as believing people, *Also I will make thee exceeding
fruitful, and will make nations of thee; yea, kings shall pro-
ceed of thee.*

Which scripture doth also overthrow the judgment of
those men, that hold a Christian may not be a king nor
magistrate. Let such consider, that the Lord here speaketh
of Abraham's spiritual seed, and not of his natural seed.
Because if it be understood of his natural seed, then cannot
Abraham be the father of many nations, seeing all Abraham's natural seed are called Jews, and are but one nation
of the Jews.[7] So that the covenant of God could not be
performed, that said, *I will make nations of thee; yea, kings
shall proceed of thee.* Therefore it must be understood of
his spiritual seed, of which may be kings and princes that
are not naturally descended of him, as well as people that

---

[6] [Prince Charles, afterwards king.]   Gen. xvii. 8, with xv. 13, 18, and
[7] Ishmael and Edom excepted,   xvi. 10, xvii. 18, 20, xxvi. 3, xxi. 13.

are naturally descended of him. Therefore believing kings may safely walk in the steps of their father Abraham, and Gen. xiv. 14. with their swords defend their subjects against their adversaries, and redeem their brethren out of the jaws of all devouring beasts and bloody persecutors, for they bear not Rom. xiii. 4. the sword for nought.

And now, also, I desire those subjects, of what degree soever, that would destroy their kings and governors for difference in religion, to consider, that therein they justify their kings and governors, which destroy their subjects for difference of religion. For as it is sin for kings and governors to destroy their subjects for difference of religion, at the persuasion of their bishops: so is it sin, but in a higher degree, for subjects to destroy their kings and governors for difference of religion, at the persuasion of their bishops and ministers.

Therefore persecution for difference in religion is a monstrous and cruel beast, that destroyeth both prince and people, hindereth the gospel of Christ, and scattereth his disciples that witness and profess his name. But permission of conscience in difference of religion, saveth both prince and people; for it is a meek and gentle lamb, which not only furthereth and advanceth the gospel, but also fostereth and cherisheth those that profess it: as may be seen by the permission of the Princess Elizabeth,[7] and others that were permitted and fostered in Dutchland at that time.[8]

Permission of conscience a furtherance to the gospel, and a safety both to prince and people.

---

[7] ["After the death of this Gardiner, followed the death also and dropping away of other her enemies, whereby by little and little her jeopardy decreased, fear diminished, hope of comfort began to appear as out of a dark cloud." Philip of Spain, the husband of Queen Mary, interfered on behalf of the princess, and she shortly obtained her release, although for a time she partially conformed to some of the external observances of the papal church.—Fox, Acts and Mon. iii. 1900; Rapin, ii. 40, fol. 1733.]

[8] [By the influence of William, Prince of Orange, their liberator, various edicts were issued by the

Also permission of conscience is a great and sure band and benefit to the king and state, as may likewise be seen in the same Princess Elizabeth; who, if she had not been permitted, but had suffered death, as the bloody bishops earnestly desired, then had not the kingdom been so surely, nor yet so purely, kept and preserved for his majesty and his royal issue, as now it is. The Lord be praised therefore.

Further, I beseech his right excellent majesty and parliament to observe, that persecution was the occasion that the apostolic church was at first scattered and driven into the wilderness, that is, desert places of the world; whither she fled to save herself from the rage and tyranny of antichrist, and his apostles and ministers, the first authors of persecution under the gospel. Therefore his majesty and parliament may please to consider, that so long as persecution continue, so long will the apostolic church continue scattered and persecuted into the secret places of this world. And no marvel, for her faith and discipline is as offensive, as odious, and as unwelcome unto antichrist and his bishops and ministers now, as it was then; as their burning, banishing, hanging, and imprisoning do witness even unto this day.

And it is to be noted, that as the apostolic faith and discipline—in the apostles' days, when through them true signs and wonders were wrought by the extraordinary gift and power of the Holy Ghost—did let and hinder the mystery of iniquity, wrought by antichrist, his apostles and

Rev. xii. 6, 14, xiii. 1, 7; 2 Cor. xi. 13.

States of Holland, granting liberty of conscience to all in their dominions. Such an edict was published in Antwerp in 1579, after a noble declaration from him, that "nothing could, in his opinion, be more unreasonable than to force conscience, and to refuse that liberty to others which even we ourselves desire to enjoy."—Brandt's Hist. of Reformation in the Low Countries, i. 359. Lond. edit. 1720.]

ministers, by whom the lying signs and wonders were done, 2 Thess. ii. 6, 7, 9; 1 Tim. iv. 1, 2, 3 ; 2 Tim. iii. 1, 4, 5; 2 Peter ii. 1, 3 ; 1 John iv. 1 ; 2 John 7 ; Jude 4, 11, 16, 18. through the extraordinary spirit of Satan; so now the catholic or antichristian faith and discipline, having gotten the upper hand by her lying signs and wonders, and by persecution, do by the same let and hinder the mystery of godliness, wrought by Christ, his apostles and ministers, by whom the true signs and wonders were done without persecution.

And it is well worthy to be observed, both of king, Note well, prince, and people, that the bishops [and] ministers of antichrist cannot abide nor endure the faith and discipline of the apostolic church; because it will be the overthrow of their blasphemous and spiritual lordships, and of their antichristian and bloody kingdom; and therefore are they so fiery hot and zealous for the catholic, or antichristian faith and discipline. For by their faith they show plainly, that they are succeeded and descended from antichrist, who confessed not that the Messiah came in flesh. And by 1 John iv. 3. their discipline or government they plainly show, [that] they are antichrist's bishops and ministers, who persecute with fire and sword all degrees, both king, prince, and people, that will not confess their faith and obey their discipline. And it is very plain and easy, both for king, prince, and people—if they will not take up religion on credit, and content them with the religion they were born and brought up in, as do the papists—to discern who they be that teach the apostolic faith and discipline ; and who they be that teach the antichrist's faith and discipline.

For the holy apostle showeth it to all men that will give heed thereto; for he saith, *Dearly beloved, believe not every* [1 John iv. 1, 2, 3. *spirit, but try the spirits whether they are of God; for many false prophets are gone out into the world,* which confess not that Jesus Messiah came in flesh. *Hereby shall you know the Spirit of God : Every spirit that confesseth that Jesus*

Messiah came in flesh[9] *is of God ; and every spirit that con-*
fesseth not that Jesus Messiah came in flesh is not of God:
but this is the spirit of antichrist, [*of*] *whom ye have heard how*
that he should come ; and now already is he in the world.
1 John ii. *The same is the antichrist that denieth the Father and the*
22, 23.
Son. Whosoever denieth the Son, the same hath not the
Father. The apostle meaneth, such as deny Jesus to be
John xvii. 3, Messiah, *the Lord that came down from heaven,* as Christ
5, 8 ; 1 Cor.
xv. 47 ; John and the apostles have taught, such have not the Father,
vi. 38, 42, 62,
vii. 26, 27. but do deny him also as they have taught him. And therefore Christ saith, *The times shall come, that whosoever killeth*
John xvi. 2, *you will think that he doth God good service ; but these things*
3, 27, 31.
they will do unto you, because they have not known the Father
nor me. The Father loveth such as believe that I came out
from God. Thus saith Christ. But antichrist and his
ministers believe not this doctrine, neither do they thus
teach Christ Jesus the Messiah.

And you may please to understand, that of this antichrist, or rather as the Syriac, of this false Christ,[1] came
the church of Rome, whose bishops and ministers teach not
this doctrine; and as the mother, so the daughter also,
teacheth not this doctrine, but will likewise persecute both
prince and people, that shall *confess that Jesus Messiah came*
1 John iv. 2. *in flesh,* as John teacheth; or *that the Son of man ascended*
John vi. 62, *up where he was before;* or *that he was glorified with his Father*
iii. 13, xvii.
5. *before the world was,* as himself saith; or that he was *the*
second man, the Lord from heaven; or that he had, and hath
1 Cor. xv. 47, a heavenly body, as Paul teacheth. For these and such
49.
like doctrines, do the church of Rome and her daughters
persecute with fire and sword, being endued with the spirit

---

[9] The Syriac saith, *came in flesh.*
[" Christus venit in carnem."—Tremellius ex vers. Syriac. edit. Lond.
1585.]

[1] [" Hic est *pseudochristus.*"—Tremellius ex vers. Syriac. " Hic est
antichristus." — Beza. edit. Lond.
1585.]

of antichrist. By which antichrist, his apostles and minis- 1 John iv. 3.
ters, the apostolic church was scattered and driven into the 2 Cor. xi. 13.
wilderness, that is, desert and secret places of this world, 15 ; Rev. xii. 6, 14.
even by their bloody persecution. The which still they
continue and raise against the members and witnesses
thereof, who were and are the martyrs which in all ages
have and do suffer death, imprisonment, and banishment,
since the first persecution ; and we never read, nor ever
shall read, that the apostolic church, or such as have
derived their faith and discipline of her, did ever persecute.

Therefore I humbly desire his majesty and parliament,
with all godly carefulness, to consider that it is not possible
that the church of Rome, called catholic, or those that are
descended of her, and have received their ministry and
ordination from her, ever was, or could be, the apostolic
church, called primitive church; or she that is descended
from her. Seeing the scripture saith, that the apostolic
church, called in scripture the woman, hath a place prepared Rev. xii. 6, 13, 14.
of God in the wilderness, a thousand two hundred and sixty
days from the presence of such as did persecute her. How,
then, I beseech you consider, may it be possible that the
church of Rome—called in scripture, a *mystery, great* [Rev. xvii. 3
Babylon, the mother of whoredoms and abominations of the —6.]
earth.   The woman that sitteth upon a scarlet coloured beast,
full of names of blasphemy.   The woman arrayed in purple
and scarlet, and gilded with gold and precious stones and pearls,
having a cup of gold in her hand, full of abominations and
filthiness of her fornication. The woman that is *drunken*
with the blood of saints, and with the blood of the martyrs, or
witnesses *of Jesus* by her beastly persecution—was, or
could be, ever the apostolic church, or those that are descended from her ; seeing the scripture saith, *she hath a* Rev. xii. 6, 13, 14.
place in the wilderness prepared of God, where she should be

fed a thousand two hundred and sixty days from the presence
of her persecutors.

Note.

If so be, you will have the church of Rome, and those
that are descended from her, to be the true apostolic church,[2]
then it will follow, that the church, called the woman, and
did fly into the wilderness from her persecutors, was and is
the false antichristian church; and also it will follow, that
those which we account to be the martyrs and witnesses of
Jesus, were not of the true apostolic church, but were
obstinate persons and heretics, even as their adversaries in
Rome, Spain, England, and elsewhere, did persecute,
adjudge, and execute them for.

But if you will have the prophecies of the apostles to be

2 Thess. ii. true, and will believe their holy writings, and also will
3, 6, 8; 1
Tim. iv. 1– have the martyrs that have been burned, banished, hanged,
3.
imprisoned, to be of the true apostolic church; then it will
follow, and that justly, according and agreeable to the

Rev. xii. 6, scriptures, that the church of Rome, and those that did and
11, 14, xvii.
2, [5,] 6, 17 ; do persecute, are descended from the false, antichristian
2 Tim. iii. 1,
5, iv. 3–5 ; church, called a *mystery, great Babylon, the mother of whore-*
2 Peter ii. 1,
3 ; 1 John ii. *doms and abominations of the earth, &c.,* which was and is
18, 19, iv. 1 ;
2 John 7 ; drunken with *the blood of saints and martyrs of Jesus.* See-
Jude 4, 11,
16. ing they have her antichristian faith and lordly discipline,

---

[2] [Thus King James : " I acknowledge the Roman church to be our
mother church, although defiled with
some infirmities and corruptions, as
the Jews were when they crucified
Christ." — Speech, 1603; Works,
p. 491. Hooker before him had said,
that the church of Rome was " to be
held and reputed a part of the house
of God, a limb of the visible church
of Christ."—Book v. §. 68, vol. ii.
p. 307, Hanbury's edition. The con-
trariety of this view of Rome to the
opinion of the reformers is well seen
in the Christian letter, quoted vol. i.
p. 202. King James was more than
suspected of approximating to Rome
in some other points of no little importance. He was willing to recognize
the episcopal supremacy of the bishop
of Rome, as the patriarch of the west;
the observance of festivals; the honour
due to saints; and a reverence for the
Virgin Mary.—Tierney's Dodd. Ch.
Hist. note, vol. iv. p. 36.]

and for the defence and maintenance thereof, will also burn, Like mother
like daugh-
banish, hang, and imprison; so hot and fiery zealous, that ter.
thereby they show plainly that they walk so just and even
in the steps and paths of the *mystical woman, great Babylon* [Rev. xvii.
5.]
their bloody parent and mother.   So even, I say, as if they
studied her lying and hypocritical doctrine; her deep and
devilish divinity; her blasphemous, princely, and danger-
ous dignity; and her beastly, bloody, and deadly discipline. 1 Tim. iv. 2;
Rev. ii. 24.

Through the continuance whereof, not only the apostolic
church is continued still in the wilderness and desert of this
world; but also the Jews and others, both in Great Britain
and all over the world, are kept back from the knowledge
of God's holy word, the only order and ordinance Christ
hath appointed for the gathering of his church together,
out of all places of the world.   And so long as persecutions
continue, you cannot try the spirits of the *many false pro-* 1 John iv. 1.
phets that are gone out into the world, as the holy apostle
doth lovingly advise and admonish you.   But like the
papists, [you] must be tied only to the spirits of your
lordly bishops and their ministers, who will have all, both
king, prince, and people, to receive their spirits, and therefore will not have any others to preach and print within
the land, lest their lying doctrine and lordly discipline be
discovered and disclaimed.[3]   And instead of disputing and
writing by the word and Spirit of Christ against their

---

[3] [" A Christian king must take direction not from the pope's person or pleasure, but from the laws and commandments of Christ, to whom alone he oweth subjection. *And as for the bishops and pastors of his realm, those he should and must consult, in respect they be God's messengers sent to him and his people,* but with great care to try them and free liberty to refuse them, if they be found not faithful. *And when the prince, learning by their instruction what is acceptable to God in doctrine and discipline, shall receive and publish the same,* the bishops themselves are bound to obey."—True Difference between Christian Subjection and Unchristian Rebellion, by Thos. Bilson, p. 358, edit. 1585.]

adversaries, they will cruelly persecute and fight against them by fire and sword,[4] and spirit of antichrist, from whom

Mystically. they are descended and succeeded, both lineally and of great antiquity.

Wherefore I humbly beseech the king and parliament, that you will betimes listen unto the Holy Spirit in the

Ps. ii. 10, [11, 12.] mouth of the prophet, which saith, *Be wise now therefore, ye kings; be learned,* or instructed, *ye judges of the earth. Serve the Lord in fear, and rejoice in trembling. Kiss the Son,* of God, *lest he be angry, and ye perish in the way,* of persecution, *when his wrath shall suddenly burn.*[5] Let not, therefore, *the kings of the earth band themselves* with the

Ps. ii. 2, 3; 1 John ii. 18; Rev. xvii. 14. bishops and ministers of antichrist, *nor princes assemble themselves together, against the Lord, and against his anointed,* that is, against Christ and his church. Seeing both he and she break your bands, and cast your cords from them; yea,

Rev. xii. 11. her seed *overcometh you by the blood of the Lamb, and by the word of their testimony,* for *they love not their lives unto death.*

Beware then in time, lest you offend any more of these little ones that believe in Christ, seeing Christ saith, *it*

Matt. xviii. 6, 10. *were better to have a millstone hanged about the neck, and drowned in the depth of the sea,* than so to do. He meaneth,

Matt. x. 38, 39. that it were better for you to lose your lives, than any way to consent to the offence of such little ones that believe in Christ. See then, I pray, that they be not despised, burned, banished, hanged, and imprisoned; for *their angels always behold the face of Christ's Father in heaven.* And

Matt. xii. 33, 35, 36. remember he saith, *the tree is known by his fruit;* but persecuting of Christians is an evil fruit. And, that *a good man out of the good treasure of his heart, bringeth forth good things;* but persecuting of Christians is no good thing. And,

---

[4] Fire and sword no equal weapons to the Spirit and word.

[5] ["Etenim ira ejus brevi exar- descet."— Dathe in Bibl. Cabinet, vol. 32, p. 392.]

*that for every idle word [that] men shall speak, they shall give
account at the last day of judgment.* How much more for
every wicked and cruel deed of persecution, as burning,
banishing, hanging, and imprisoning of those that *confess
with the mouth and believe with the heart the Lord Jesus,* and Rom. x. 9.
that God raised him from the dead; whose laws and ordinances they are careful to keep and obey! Christ saith
that such shall be saved; and yet you fear not to burn,
banish, hang, and imprison such. But if you believe that
God will avenge his elect, beware of persecuting his servants Luke xviii.
that call on his name, especially such as witness his truth 7.
against the abominations of antichrist.

Suffer not your bishops to destroy those men and women
that strive to serve God, according to his will in his word.
Be not your bishops' executioners in burning, banishing,
hanging, and imprisoning of harmless and peaceable Christians; but let them enjoy freedom of the gospel and liberty
of conscience: that so the apostolic church, which is scattered and driven into the wilderness and desert of this
world, may be again gathered together, both Jews and
Gentiles, into visible and established congregations. And
that the catholic and universal church of antichrist may be
consumed and abolished, by his word and Spirit, as the holy 2 Thess. ii. 8.
apostle hath foretold;' even the uttermost of his arrival,
which is the imperial and triple crown, through the triple
sea of Rome.[6]

And again, I humbly entreat the king and parliament to
vouchsafe to hear me with patience yet a little further. If
freedom of the gospel and permission of conscience might
be granted, then would not papists, nor any others, dissemble their religion, to the dishonour of God, the destruction
of their souls, and to the great danger both of king and

---

[6] I pray the Lord to give such grace,
The sea [see] of Rome may ebb apace.

state, seeing they are forced to church against their consciences. And may not popish priests and Jesuits, unawares
to the bishops, become the bishops' ministers, seeing the
change of their religion and religious habit differ so little ;[7]
and so by degrees infect the people with more popish doctrine, as occasion shall be? And such men will readily
embrace the bishops' orders, and so they shall readily have
the bishops' favours.[8] By which means they may more
easily and speedily have access unto the court, and presence
of the king and prince, which indeed is very dangerous,
howsoever not regarded. Therefore I do, according to my
duty, humbly advise his majesty not to beautify his court
and presence with any popish stones, not with one, though
it be of alabaster.

But permission of conscience, and freedom and liberty of
the gospel, will no way be dangerous to the king or state,
if such like rules as these be observed :—

1. That no people tainted with treason do bear any office.

2. That all sorts of people tainted with treason do, at all
times from home, wear a black hat with two white signs,
the one before, the other behind, in open sight.

---

[7] [The use of papal arguments by the bishops in their conflict with the puritans, led the latter to suspect that their opponents availed themselves of the assistance of Jesuits, and other partisans of the papacy. In a curious dialogue, written about 1580, a bishop is represented as saying, that if he had not had a papist for an assistant, he " could never have looked to have prevailed. Because our dignities and government cometh wholly and every part thereof from the pope, and is ruled and defended by the same canons, whereby his popedom is sup- ported. So that if 1 had wanted their helps, I had had none authority, either from God and man, no help either by reason or learning, whereby I could have been furthered." And the dia- logue closes with the papist recom- mending a variety of measures for the repression of the puritans, which, if executed, would open the way for the return of the catholics to place and power.—A Parte of a Register, &c., pp. 342, 354. Udal, an eminent puritan, is supposed to be the author of this dialogue.—Brook's Lives of the Puritans, ii. 23.]

[8] From popes' submission
There is great suspicion.

3. That no people tainted with treason approach within 1 Kings ii. 36, 41, 42. ten miles of the court without licence.

4. That no people tainted with treason do inhabit the Rom. xiii. 1 —5. city of London, nor yet within ten miles thereof.

5. That none tainted with treason do make any assembly or congregation.

6. That no person or persons, in whatsoever difference by reasoning or disputing, do draw any weapon, nor give any blow, stroke, or push, in pain and penalty, as his majesty and parliament think meet.

7. That for the more peace and quietness, and for the satisfying of the weak and simple, among so many persons differing in religion, it be lawful for every person or persons, yea, Jews and papists, to write, dispute, confer and reason, print and publish any matter touching religion, either for or against whomsoever; always provided they allege no fathers for proof of any point of religion, but only the holy scriptures.

Neither yet to reproach or slander one another, nor any other person or persons, but with all love, gentleness, and peaceableness, inform one another, to the glory of God, 2 Tim. ii. 24, 25; Jas. iii. honour of the king and state, and to their own good and 17. credit.

By which means, both few errors and few books will be written and printed, seeing all false ministers, and most A Note. true sign people, have little or nothing else, besides the fathers, to of false bi- shops and build their religion and doctrine upon. Or if it be once ministers. established by law, that none shall confirm their religion and doctrine by the fathers, and by prisons, burning, and banishing, &c., but by the holy scriptures; then error will not be written nor disputed, except by obstinate persons and seared consciences, seeing the word of God will be no shelter for any error.

Yea, I know by experience among the people called

Brownists, that a man shall not draw them to write, though they be desired; for one of their preachers, called Master Rob[inson], hath had a writing of mine in his hands above six months,[9] and as yet I can get no answer. It seems he knoweth not how better to hide his errors, than by silence. And this will be the case of all false bishops and ministers, who had rather be mute and dumb, than to be drawn into the light with their errors.

John iii. 10, 20.

Therefore permission of conscience, and liberty of the gospel, in our land of Great Britain, will mightily further the advancement of the apostolic faith, and chiefly their books, whereout sufficient matter will be drawn for the convincing of every particular religion which is against the religion established by Christ and his apostles: who by all means lawful, sought the conversion and salvation both of Jews and Gentiles. And they are inconstant and faithless men, or at least very ignorant, that think error will overcome and prevail against the truth.

1 Cor. ix. 20, 21 ; Acts xvi. 3.

For the abolishing of such thoughts, I desire such men to consider the mighty victory and prevailing‾of the truth, in the time of Christ and his apostles; which, notwithstanding resisted and disputed against by the most part of the priests and learned men, both of Jews and Gentiles, yet overcame and prevailed against all the errors of the high priests and great learned men, both of the Jews and Gentiles. And the apostle saith, *We cannot do any thing against the truth, but for the truth.* And seeing it is the same truth which all good men would embrace, why should we not hope the same victory by it? Did not king Darius and all the people, both Jews and Gentiles, cry out and say, that truth is great and strongest? Why, then, should those that have the truth, and those that would have the truth,

2 Cor. xiii. 8.

1 Esdras iv. 38, 41.

---

[9] Now above twelve months.

be afraid of error? Seeing truth discovereth dark and
dangerous ways of error, though abroad in open books,
even as light discovereth dark and dangerous places, though
abroad in open highways. And as the more dark and
dangerous the ways be, the more necessary and needful
will light be found of all that travel; so the more dark and
dangerous the errors be, the more needful and profitable
will truth be found of all that would travel to heaven.

But some may object and say, 'Let all this be granted,
yet it is no wisdom, we think, to bring dangerous errors
into the light, that so many men may stumble at them;
which being not brought to light, would not be so much as
known to some.'

I answer, no more than a rock that lieth hid under water, Answer.
which, for want of bringing into the light, many men may
make shipwreck thereon, and so stumble or fall, nevertheless, though it be not so much as known to them before.
Therefore, as a rock in the seas, though not so much as
known to some, yet, for want of being made known, many
men stumble and fall thereon, and so perish, both men and
goods: so an error, though not so much as known to some,
yet, for want of being made known, many men may stumble and fall thereon, and so perish, both bodies and souls,
the which is more lamentable. And as rocks in the seas,
the more they manifest themselves, so errors in the world,
the more they manifest themselves, the more furtherance
in the way to heaven. And you shall understand, that
errors being brought to the light of the word of God, will
vanish as darkness before the light of a torch. Even as the
chaff before the wind cannot stand, so error before truth
cannot abide. Therefore it is no hindrance, but a great
furtherance, to have all erroneous rocks in the haven to
heaven, made known and published.

And a great and sure argument it is, that those bishops

Another true sign of false ministers.

and ministers have not the truth, that publicly dare not dispute or write against error; as may be seen in the bishops and ministers in Queen Mary's days, which could not abide to have books written and printed of that which they called error and heresy;[1] but caused, that if any such were written, both them and the authors to be burned, if they could come by them.

Therefore, if permission of conscience and liberty of the gospel be not granted, and burning laws repealed, then the bishops and ministers now, may persuade and cause to be burned, both the books and the authors that have the truth, instead of heresy and heretics, even as their predecessors have done already; and so shed more innocent blood, and also provoke the Lord to further wrath against the king

The word of God the only defender of the faith of Christ.

and state. It is not the gallows, nor the prisons, nor burning, nor banishing, that can defend the apostolic faith. Indeed, the king and state may defend religion's peace by their sword and civil power, but not the faith, otherwise than by the word and Spirit of God. The Dutch princes and peers say, " that force, sword, and gallows, in matter of religion, is a good means to spill blood and make an uproar in the land; but not to bring any man from one faith to another."[2] The pagans will not persecute one another for religion, though, as I read, there be above three thousand sorts among them.[3] And you know, both King

[1] [In the convocation of 1554, it was proposed, That all books, both Latin and English, concerning any heretical, erroneous, or slanderous doctrines, might be destroyed and burnt, throughout the realm." And also that all statutes " against heresy, Lollards, and false preachers," might be enforced.—Strype's Cranmer, p. 500; Oxford edit. These cruel laws were still in force and executed in the reign of King James, as in the instances of Legate and Wightman.]

[2] [Brandt, Hist. of Ref. in Low Countries, i. 149, 150; edit. Lond. 1720.]

[3] [" Among the ancient heathens, all whose deities were local and tutelary, diversity of sentiment concerning the object or rites of religious worship, seems to have been no source of animosity, because the acknowledging

Henry and Queen Mary, thought themselves defenders of the faith: and thought they burned heretics and heresy when they burned men and their books. But now you see, and must acknowledge, that they were persecutors of the faith, instead of defenders thereof; and also that they, through the instigation of their bloody bishops, burned the word of God, and those that professed and wrought it, instead of heresy and heretics. Idol bishops and false ministers, authors of persecution.

And thus it will be now, if the bishops and their ministers may have their will; and therein they, as their predecessors, fulfil the word of God, in *gathering kings of the earth to the battle of the great day of God Almighty.* For they persuade kings to force their subjects to receive the faith, and to be of the church. Whereas the word of God teacheth otherwise, saying, *Faith cometh by hearing and hearing by the word of God,* and not by the king's sword. And Christ saith, *Teach all nations,* and not, force all nations. And this teaching is to be understood, by the word and writings of the prophets and apostles of our Lord and Saviour Christ, which is the word of God. For they that will be of the true faith and church, must be called thereunto out of the world, by the word of God, in every nation; and not forced and constrained in every nation, as the bishop of Rome, and all other false bishops and ministers, have and do persuade kings, emperors, and magistrates.[4] Rev. xvi. 14. Rom. x. 14, 17. [Matt. xxviii. 19.]

---

veneration to be due to any one god, did not imply denial of the existence or the power of any other god: nor were the modes and rites of worship established in one country, incompatible with those which other nations approved and observed. Thus the errors in their system of theology, were of such a nature as to be productive of concord; and notwithstanding the amazing number of their deities, as well as the infinite variety of their ceremonies, a sociable and tolerating spirit subsisted almost universally in the pagan world." — Robertson's Charles the 5th, iv. 129, tenth edition. Gibbon, Decline and Fall, chap. 2.]

[4] [By the canon law, " the bishop

And his majesty and parliament may please to understand, that so to do, is to quench the Spirit of God in Christ's bishops and ministers; and also to frustrate the *precept* of Christ which saith, *Preach the gospel to every* *creature.* Besides it maketh their one office and function void. They ought to preach and *instruct with all meekness* *them that are contrary-minded ; proving if God at any time* *will give them repentanee, that they may know the truth :* for the ministers of the Lord *must not strive, but be apt to teach,* *gentle towards all men,* suffering evil men patiently ; telling kings and princes, that the *weapons* of Christ's bishops and ministers, *are not carnal,* as the weapons of all false and antichristian bishops and ministers are, *but spiritual, and* *mighty through God to cast down holds ; casting down every* *high thing that is exalted against the knowledge of God, and* *bringing into captivity every thought to the obedience of Christ.*

Also, if all within the land be forced to be of the church, as the bishops and their ministers would still have it, then there would be no world in the land, but all the land would be the church, which is absurd and contrary to the scriptures. And great ignorance do the bishops and their ministers show, when they think the whole nation of people is the church of Christ : for then it cannot be said, out of Great Britain, *the Lord added to the church, from day to* *day, such as should be saved;* seeing, within the land there would be none without to be added.

Also, within that land there would be no persecution, seeing the church of Christ doth not persecute at all, much less itself. But the ministers and members of that church do persecute one another ; and therefore it cannot be the

Marginal notes:
Mark xvi. 16 ; 1 Thess. v. 19.
2 Tim. ii. 24, 25.
2 Cor. x. 4, 5.
Rev. xi. 2.
Note. Acts ii. 41, 47.
A true church will not persecute.

of Rome may compel, by an oath, all rulers and other people to observe and caused to be observed, whatever the see of Rome shall ordain concerning heresy, and the factors thereof ; and who will not obey, he may deprive them of their dignities."—Cranmer's Works, by Jenkins, ii. 8.]

spiritual kingdom and church of Christ, but of antichrist,
seeing it is divided against itself, and persecuteth one Matt.xii.25.
another; and will, with her mother, great Babylon, be consumed and condemned, seeing, as she, they burn, banish, Rev. xviii.
hang, and imprison one another.   Which is no Christian, 2, 8.
but antichristian, monstrous, cruel, wolfish, and tyrannous
part and practice; for Christ sent his ministers as lambs
among wolves, and not as wolves among lambs. 1 Cor. viii.
11, 12 ; Luke
   Again, I humbly, and with all reverence, do beseech his x. 3.
right excellent majesty to give me leave to put him in
mind of those things that do concern the glory of God, the
assurance of his own salvation, the establishment of his
throne, and the benefit both of the church of Christ and
the commonwealth of all his dominions.   And though, as
Josiah, he find, by reading in the book of the New Testament, a great alteration of the apostolic faith, and change
of the laws and ordinances of Christ, within his dominions;
yet not to be dismayed, as Henry le Grand,[5] but be
encouraged, as Josiah, to labour and endeavour the redress
thereof, according to the mind of Christ, in his New Testament.   And I doubt not, but as Jacob the patriarch pre- Gen. xxxii.
vailed with God and men, so shall Jacob the king prevail xiii. 4.
both with God and men, especially being his chief steward,
by his New Testament.
   Through the zealous reading whereof, it will be found

---

[5] [Henry the 4th, king of France,
"sacrificed the dictates of conscience
to the suggestions of policy; and, ima-
gining that his government could have
no stable nor solid foundation as long
as he persisted in disowning the authority and jurisdiction of Rome, he re-
nounced the reformed religion and
made a solemn and public profession
of popery.   Perceiving, however, that
BUSHER.]

it was not possible either to extirpate
or suppress entirely the protestant religion, he granted to its professors, by
the famous edict drawn up at Nantes,
in the year 1598, the liberty of serving
God according to their consciences,
and a full security for the enjoyment
of their civil rights and privileges."—
Mosheim, Eccles. Hist., Cent. xvi.
pt. 2, c. 2, sect. 15.]

E

that antichrist, the king of the catholic faith and discipline, called the mystery of iniquity, *doth sit in the temple of God,* even as the scripture hath foretold.   But it is to be noted, that the scripture hath also foretold the consummation and abolition of this antichrist, the man of sin, and his mystery of iniquity, with the utmost of his arrival, or highest top of dignity he is come unto.   And this shall be done by the Spirit of the Lord in the mouth of his servants.   For when the words of God be fulfilled, then shall the servants of the Lord prevail, by his word and Spirit, with ten kings that shall hate and make the whore desolate, which sitteth in the hearts and consciences of peoples,[6] multitudes, and nations. And this whore is the woman called the great city, which reigneth over the kings of the earth, meaning the church of Rome, by her false faith and discipline; which is so fast settled in the hearts and consciences of the kings of the earth, that they think they do God good service, in killing and burning his servants that do speak against her faith and discipline, and that will not buy any of her wares — that is, her antichristian doctrines and ordinances.

But as she hath had her exaltation, and arrival to the height and dignity of the *sea* empire of Rome, by the love of kings, who have given their power and authority unto her, and have fought for her against the saints and servants of Jesus : so she shall have her consummation and abolition from that height and dignity, by the hatred of kings, who again shall take their power and authority from her, and therewith defend the peace and persons of the saints and servants of Jesus; and now for religion's peace, will use their power and authority against the bloody persecution of antichrist and all his bloody bishops and ministers, and so become nursing fathers unto the church of Christ.

Marginal references:
2 Tim. iii. [1 — 5] ; 1 Tim. iv. [1 — 3]; Rev. xvii. 15, 16, 17 ; 2 Thess. ii. 8.

Rev. xvii. 1. 13, 14, 15, 18.

John xvi. 2.

---

[6] Called the temple of God, 2 Thess. ii. 4.

And as it hath pleased God to give his majesty peace round about, as he did unto king Cyrus, in whose days the material temple began to be repaired—which was a figure $^{\text{Isaiah ii. 4;}}_{\text{Ezra iv. 7;}}$ of the spiritual temple—so, I pray, it may please him also, $^{\text{Hag. ii. 4, 9.}}$ in the peaceable days of king James, to begin to repair the spiritual temple, the apostolic church, scattered and driven abroad into the wilderness of this world; whose calling and gathering together, must be by the preaching of the word of God, both to Jews and Gentiles, and not by the sword of the kings of the earth, as antichrist and his ministers have now a long time persuaded and prevailed. Whereby not only the Jews and infidels, but also papists and other false Christians, are hindered and deprived from the knowledge of the apostolic faith. And it is to be noted, that David $^{\text{1 Chron.}}_{\text{xxviii. 3.}}$ might not build God's temple, because he had spilt much blood; which showeth no blood ought to be spilt for the building of the spiritual temple. *Ergo*, peace in religion is a good means to make a unity of religion among so many Christian sects.

And it is well worthy consideration, that as in the time of the Old Testament, the Lord would not have his offer- $^{\text{Exod. xxv.}}_{\text{2, xxxv. 5.}}$ ings by constraint, but of every man whose heart gave it freely; so now in the time of the gospel, he will not have the people constrained, but as many as receive the word gladly, they are to be added to the church by baptism. And therefore Christ commanded his disciples to *teach all* $^{\text{Acts ii. 41;}}_{\text{Matt.xxviii.}}$ *nations, and baptize them;* that is, to preach the word of $^{[19];\ \text{Mark}}_{\text{xvi. 16;}}$ salvation to every creature of all sorts of nations, that are $^{\text{Matt. x. 11,}}_{14.}$ worthy and willing to receive it. And such as shall willingly and gladly receive it, he hath commanded to be baptized in the water; that is, dipped for dead in the water. And therefore the apostle saith, *Else what shall they do,* $_{\text{1 Cor. xv. 19}}$ *who are baptized for dead, if the dead be not raised, why are they baptized for dead?* And therefore he saith, *We are* $_{\text{Rom. vi. 4.}}$

E 2

Col. ii. 12. *buried then with him by baptism, &c.*   And it is to be well
observed, that when Christ would have preached the word
Luke viii.37. of salvation to the Gadarenes, he did not compel them
when they refused; but finding them unwilling to receive
him and his word, he turned from them without hurting
them.   Also, when James and John saw that some of the
Samaritans refused Christ, they would have commanded
fire from heaven to consume them, as Elias did; but Christ
Luke ix. 54, rebuked them and said, *Ye know not of what spirit ye are,*
55. *for the Son of man is not come to destroy men's lives, but to
save them.*

By all which it may please his majesty and parliament
to take knowledge, that Christ will have none consumed
with fire and sword, for not hearing and not receiving his
word.   And that, howsoever it hath been the mind of
antichrist to destroy men's lives for religion, and therein
hath not spared either prince or people; yet it is not the
mind of Christ that princes should destroy their subjects,
nor yet that subjects should destroy their princes, for difference in religion.

And, therefore, why should bishops persuade princes and
people, and why should king, prince, and people be persuaded by their bishops and ministers, to be contrary-
minded to Christ?   Verily it is a notorious and plain token
of a false faith and discipline, that is defended by fire and
sword, the power and authority of princes.   And they
cannot be Christ's bishops and preachers[8] that persuade
princes and people to such antichristian tyranny and cruelty;
and it is very evident that those bishops and ministers
which give over men and women to the magistrate to be
persuaded by persecution, do show clearly that their
doctrine is not good, and that they want the word and

---

[8] Christ's bishops will not be lords over the conscience.

Spirit of God, and therefore flee to the magistrate's sword for the forcing of them to their faith and discipline. And as the wine is not good which we are forced to drink, so those doctrines are not good which we are forced to believe.

But it may be by this time, [that] all those bishops who unfeignedly fear God and truly love the king, will haste and make speed to come unto his majesty for pardon; acknowledging the truth of this book; confessing their ignorance and arrogance in the knowledge of God's word; and in compelling the people to hear the word preached; and for imprisoning, burning, banishing, and hanging for religion, contrary to the mind of Christ; and also for stopping the mouths of men, and burning their books, that preach and write contrary to their minds and wills.

Yea, it may be, they will also confess and say, 'Oh! most ' gracious king! We beseech your majesty to show us mercy, ' and to forgive us our spiritual pride and ambition, in that ' we have thus long usurped the blasphemous titles of ' spiritual lords and lord graces; the which titles we now, ' to the glory of God and honour of the king, do with ' unfeigned hearts confess to be due and belong only to ' Christ himself. And that the name and title of spiritual ' lord cannot belong to any earthly creature; no, not to the ' king or emperor, because it is an heavenly name and title.[9] ' How much less can it belong or be due unto us, your ' majesty's unworthy subjects and scholars.

'And for so much as we now understand, the Lord be ' praised therefore, that the holy and heavenly name and ' divine title of spiritual Lord, is as much, yea, as high and ' great as the name and title of a spiritual God; and also, ' that it is a name above every name, which God the Father Phil. ii. 9, ' hath given unto Christ only, to the end that every knee 10, 11.

---

[9] The bishops do know in their consciences that this is true. Job. xxxii. 22.

' should bow unto that only and heavenly name, and that
' every tongue should confess that Jesus is the Messiah, the
' Lord, unto the glory of God the Father, that in all things

Col i. 18. ' Christ might have the pre-eminence. For he alone is the
' head of the church, which is his body ; the which cannot
' be, so long as we, or any other bishops, do hold and retain
' that divine, high, and super-excellent name and title of
' spiritual lord. Because then it cannot be said that God
' hath so highly exalted him, as to give him a name above

The bishops
in titles
equal to the
Son of God. ' every name, seeing our names and titles are also spiritual,
' and [we] are called spiritual lords, as well as the Son of
' God, Jesus the Messiah. The remembrance hereof, most
' gracious sovereign, doth make us to tremble before God
' and the king ; and therefore we most earnestly desire
' your sacred majesty and the whole parliament, to discharge
' and release us of these fearful names and titles, that do
' only belong to the Son of God, Jesus, the only spiritual
' Lord that God hath given unto his church.

  ' Moreover, we do, according to the truth, acknowledge
' that if we should any longer retain these divine and high
' names of spiritual lords and lord graces, we should therein
' be entitled, not only with a name equal to our Lord Jesus,
' the only begotten Son of God, but also we should be
' entitled with a name and title above your right excellent
' majesty; yea, above all emperors, kings, and princes of
' the earth. The which alone we do acknowledge to be a
' sufficient cause to put us down, and to deprive us of these
' usurped names and blasphemous titles.[1]

  ' Also we do confess, that our pomp and state wherein
' we now live, is more like the bishops of the catholic
' church of antichrist, than any way like the bishops of the

---

[1] *Note.* God's blessings ill expected, unless these idols be rejected, who are
exalted above all earthly gods.

' apostolic church of Christ; unto whom we acknowledge
' we ought to be made like, and also to be qualified with
' the like gifts and graces of the Spirit; or else in no case
' can we be meet bishops for the church of Christ, as the
' apostle plainly teacheth both to Timothy and Titus, &c.   1 Tim. iii. [1—7]; Tit. i. 6—9.
    ' And we must further acknowledge and confess, that our
' houses, households, and revenues, are more fit and meet
' for princes, dukes, and earls, than for the bishops of Christ.
' Wherefore, being moved and stirred up hereto by the fear
' of God, we earnestly beseech your majesty and parliament
' also to disburden us of this great pomp and state, and of
' our great and prince-like houses, households, and revenues,
' that so we may be made equal and conformable to the
' ministers of Christ; and then we shall have both hope and
' comfort of the world to come, although but little in this,
' except your majesty and parliament do grant free liberty
' of conscience.
    ' The which we now do also, with the poor distressed
' Christians, most humbly intreat and desire; and that for
' these four reasons:—First, because thereby the gospel of
' Christ will be set free and at liberty, whereby all people,
' both Jews and Gentiles, will be gathered to the apostolic
' faith, church, and discipline.
    ' Secondly, because many of your majesty's subjects, both
' men and women, who now are forced to dissemble their
' religion, for fear of our persecution, will be released and
' set free from their spiritual bondage and slavery, wherein
' we now do hold them, against their consciences; and so
' they will become more faithful Christians to God, and
' more loyal subjects to your majesty, than ever they were
' before, to the salvation of their souls and the safety of the
' crown and state.
    ' Thirdly, because the poor distressed Christians now
' banished and dispersed out of their fatherland over the

' face of the earth, will be redeemed from great misery and
' bondage, wherein now, no doubt, they live and abide,
' because they will not be in bondage to any other spiritual
' lord or head, than the Lord Jesus Messiah alone; whose
' faith and discipline they desire only to learn and obey.

' Fourthly, because thereby great benefit and commodity,
' will redound both to your majesty and to all your subjects,
' within your highness's dominions, by the great commerce,
' in trade and traffic, both of Jews and all people: which
' now, for want of liberty of conscience, are forced and
' driven elsewhere.

' And also from the revenues and livings which we and
' our clergy do possess, and from the courts and offices we
' hold and keep, great profit and commodity will redound
' both to your highness and to all your kingdom. We say,
' more profit and commodity than we or any man is able to
' express.

' And therefore, we also desire all his majesty's subjects
' both great and small, in all love and fear of God, not to
' be offended, or any way moved or grieved, when they
' shall see such a reformation of us as that famous king,
' Henry the Eighth, did make of our lordly brethren, the
' abbots and their clergy. For, indeed, such a reformation
' ought to come among us and our clergy; seeing we are
' no way agreeable to the New Testament of the only
' spiritual Lord Jesus Messiah,[2] but are limbs and fellow-
' members of that antichristian and Romish church, which
' in the scripture is prophesied to be abolished and destroyed.
' Now therefore, we pray you all, let not king David say
' the sons of Zeruiah are too strong for him, for that will
' be unprofitable for you all.

' And for conclusion, we intreat his majesty and parlia-

---

[2] Too great are the odds, to use the sword against God's word.

' ment, to enact that as our adversaries come against us
' only with the word of God, so we go against them only
' with the word of God; and not as we have done, by civil
' authority, for so ourselves may be forced to dissemble.'

Thus it may be, the Lord will persuade and work in the
hearts of some of the bishops, who will willingly resign
their antichristian titles and popish pomp and state, with
their prince-like houses and livings, into the hands of
the king, without any compulsion or constraint. But if
they do not, yet if it please God to open the king's heart to
see their antichristian and idol estate, and the danger and
damage they cause, both to the king, prince, and people,
they will be compelled thereto, even as their lordly brethren,
the abbots, in king Henry's days, were. And howsoever
it be not regarded, or perhaps not discerned, yet in the
sight of God and his people, they are greater idols than
their lordly brethren the abbots; yea, greater idols than
the images of wood and stone, which that famous and godly
king Edward did pull down and destroy.[3] For they did
not imprison, nor burn, nor hang, nor yet cause to be
banished, any of the king's subjects that would not worship
them, as these idol-bishops do. And out of doubt, these
bishops are greater idols than the golden calf Aaron made,
and offered unto; for the calf did not persecute, nor vex

The bishops greater idols than the abbots' images, or golden calf.

[3] [" Images in churches had been so grossly abused, and such idolatry and superstition committed by means of them, that it was in the King's Injunctions commanded to the visitors to remove them every where, wheresoever they had been abused by pilgrimages, censings, and offerings."—Strype, Memor. II. i. 124. " Consider then howe godlye an acte is this to take away so manye ymages, not made by Goddes commandementes, wherunto contrary to Goddes commandementes and his honor wer so manye idolatries committed. For vnto Christen princes office and cure appertayneth the defence of Goddes true word and Christen religion, and to take away all those thinges, which hynder or let true godlynes and religion, or make trouble and contention, within their realmes." Cranmer's Catechism set forth in 1548, p. 29. Oxford. edit. 1839.]

such as did not acknowledge it for their lord, as the bishops do: neither did the calf reign and rule by force over the consciences of the people, as these idol-bishops do.

Exod. xxxii. 1, 7. Besides, the calf was set up instead of Moses, who brought the people out of Egypt, and showed them the will of God. But these bishops are set up instead of Christ, who hath brought us out of the bondage of hell, and who showeth us his Father's will in his New Testament. The which these idol-bishops will not suffer us to obey; but instead thereof, will force us to fall down, worship, and obey their father antichrist's will and old testament,[4] which stinks in the nostrils of all reformed strangers that hear thereof, as well as in ours that have taken our flight from it. Therefore these spiritual lords and idol-bishops, ought to be pulled down and suppressed like the abbots, their lordly brethren; though not sacrificed unto the Lord in Smithfield, as the godly king Josiah sacrificed the idol-2 Kings xxiii. 20. priests of the high places on the altars thereof.

And I do verily believe, that if free liberty of conscience be granted, that the spiritual kingdom of these idol-bishops, will in time fall to the ground of itself as the idol Dagon 1 Sam v. 3. fell before the ark. For through the knowledge of God's word, all godly people will withdraw themselves, in all peaceable and godly wise, from the spiritual obedience of these spiritual lords and idol-bishops, and quietly betake themselves unto the obedience of the only spiritual Lord, Jesus Messiah. But howsoever it be, I shall be contented therewith, and so I wish all others; for we all ought to be content if we obtain liberty of conscience: and therefore to give God praise continually, that hath wrought so blessed a work in the hearts of the king and parliament. For

---

[4] What greater idolatry, than to obey other spiritual lords than the Lord Jesus?

whom, as the scripture teacheth, we ought to *make suppli-* 1 Tim. ii. 1,
cations, prayers, and intercessions, that they may come to the ²·
knowledge of the truth, and *that we may lead a peaceable
and quiet life, in all godliness and honesty.* And unto whom
we ought to give, by the laws of God, all earthly honour,
fear, and reverence ; and willingly to pay tribute and custom, tax and toll, so much and so often as it shall please his
majesty and parliament to appoint and gather, by any
officer or officers whatsoever. For whom also, and for the Rom. xiii.
whole commonwealth of all his kingdoms, we ought to be ¹⁻⁷·
diligent, and ready to hazard and lay down not only our
goods, but also our lives, at all times and occasions.

For Christ hath only set us free from all ecclesiastical
laws and ordinances, which himself hath not commanded in
his last will and testament. Yea, from the ecclesiastical
laws and commandments of the Old Testament. How
much more hath he set us free from the ecclesiastical laws
and ordinances of antichrist? But he hath not set us free Col. ii. 14;
from the moral and judicial law of God ; for that the king Heb. viii.13.
is bound to execute, and we are bound to obey : and for
want of the execution thereof, there are in our land many Deut. xvii.
whores and whore-keepers, and many children murdered ; 18, 20.
besides the death and undoing of many persons about
whores. Wherefore, I humbly desire, that the moral and
judicial law of God, may be practised and executed on all
degrees, both high and low, without respect of persons,
according to the mind of Christ. For the Lord will have
that every man shall love him above all, and his neighbour
as himself. And Christ saith, *As ye would that men should* Luke vi. 31.
*do to you, so do ye to them likewise.*⁵

---

⁵ [The profligacy and debauchery
of the court of James the First descended and defiled every grade of
society. Foreigners were astonished
at the gross manners of the court, and
of both sexes of the higher classes.
And although the taverns were " dens
of filth, roaring songs, and roysters,"

Therefore as the king would not have his subjects to take away his life, because he is contrary to them in religion; so let not the king take away his subjects' lives, because they are contrary to the king in religion. And as you would not that men should force you to a religion against your consciences, so do not you force men to a religion against their consciences. And as it is the duty of subjects to seek the conversion of their king and state by the word of God, and not his and their destruction by fire and sword; so it is the duty of the king and state to seek the conversion of their subjects by the word of God, and

Note.   not their destruction by fire and sword, as the pope and his prelates do teach; whose vassals therein, both emperors and kings, as well as people, have been a long time, both to the destruction of themselves and their subjects.

For who knoweth not that prelates and priests, have persuaded subjects to destroy their kings and princes, as well as kings and princes to destroy their subjects. But I pray them both to take notice that the scripture saith, *He that*

1 Cor. iii. 17, *destroyeth the temple of God, him will God destroy.* Let not
vi. 19, 20. therefore kings, princes, nor subjects, be any longer persuaded to destroy one another, through the subtlety of bishops and their ministers, who most of them seek only the security of their own pomp and glory, and the esta-

yet women of rank allowed themselves to be entertained in such places. The number of the poor daily increased. They were turned forth from the towns "to beg, filch, and steal for their maintenance." A police order, issued a few years later, prohibits all persons from harbouring rogues in their barns, and authorizes constables to demand of persons wandering about with women and children, where they were married, and where their chil- dren were christened. " For these people live like savages, neither marry, nor bury, nor christen ; which licentious liberty makes so many delight to be rogues and wanderers." Harris's Life of James I. pp. 65—78. Pict. Hist. of England, iii. 633. 660. The dark picture of national vice presented by our author in a future page, is a too true description of the facts, as corroborated by historical documents.]

blishment of their spiritual thrones therein. For so long as they may confirm that, they pass[6] not who perish, whether king, prince, or people.

Again, therefore, I humbly pray his majesty and parliament, to repeal and make void all popish laws and canons, and to see the moral and judicial law of God both firmly enacted and carefully practised, after the mind of Christ. And then shall Christ's spiritual throne, be established in the hearts and consciences both of king, prince, and people, so as the church, Christ's spiritual kingdom, shall increase in the knowledge of faith, and obedience thereof, with all love, peace, and charity one towards another;[7] and the commonwealth of his majesty's kingdoms will flourish and prosper, and also his throne be constantly established, both to him and his heirs, throughout all his dominions, in a sure land[8] of peace and love the one with and towards another, to the glory of God, and the comfort of his majesty and of all his subjects; and also to a famous and excellent glorious pattern of government to all kingdoms, nations, and countries round about, as in the days of Solomon, king of Israel.

For if the holy laws of God's word be practised and executed after Christ's will, then shall neither king, prince, nor people be destroyed for difference in religion. Then

[6] [*Pass*, to heed.

" As for these silken-coated slaves, I
pass not ;
It is to you good people that I speak."
Shakspeare.]

[7] Frederic and John Palsgrave said, that under pretext of the Holy Ghost's office of correction, little else was sought than to reign over the consciences of the magistrate and subjects, like as in the accursed popedom is come to pass, &c. [Brandt, Hist.

of Reform. i. 330. Lond. 1720. Frederic the Third, the Elector Palatine, was a prince of eminent virtue, and since his death has been honoured with the epithet godly. He was much engaged in supporting the affairs of the protestants, employing his sons, Christopher and John Casimir, the Palsgrave, to whom the above was addressed in his last will. Strype, Annals, II. ii. 161.]

[8] [Dan. iv. 26. Thy kingdom shall be *sure* unto thee.]

treason and rebellion, as well as burning, banishing, hanging, or imprisoning, for difference in religion, will cease and
be laid down. Then shall not men, women, and youth be
hanged for theft. Then shall not the poor, lame, sick, and
weak ones, be stocked and whipped ; neither shall the poor,
stranger, fatherless, and widows, be driven to beg from
place to place; neither shall the lame, sick, and weak persons, suffer such misery and be forsaken of their kindred,
as now they be. Then shall not murder, whoredom, and
adultery, be bought out for money. Then shall not the
great defraud and wrong the small ; neither the rich oppress the poor by usury and little wages. Then shall not
men bring up and inherit other's children, instead of their
own : neither shall an honest man be forced to live with
a whore instead of an honest wife : nor yet an honest
woman be forced to live with a whorekeeper instead of an
honest husband. Then shall not servants be forced from
marriage by bonds, nor yet be bound to servitude longer
than six years : neither shall they be brought up contrary
to covenant, nor posted from one quarter or one year to
another, for their freedom, and in the end be forced to buy
it of their masters, or else to go without it too.

Note well.   Then shall neither prince nor people be disinherited, for
not being of the church : neither shall they be held lawless
persons, though excommunicated : neither shall any man
dare kill them, as now they may, and be quit by law :
neither shall any man fear to have his mouth stopped, for
preaching the truth. Then shall no man need to flee out
of his native country and fatherland, for persecution' sake.
Then shall all men live in peace under their own vine,
lauding and praising God, honouring and obeying the
king. Then also will no blood be eaten among Christians,
Acts xv. 28,   whereby the Jews should have just cause to stumble or be
29, & xxi.   offended ; neither should any relics of the ceremonial law,
25.

as tithes and offerings, &c., be any longer in use, whereby Jews kept back from the faith by persecution.
the Jews should be hardened in their unbelief, and kept
from the faith of the Messiah.   Then shall the Jews inhabit and dwell under his majesty's dominion, to the great
profit of his realms, and to their furtherance in the faith;
the which we are bound to seek in all love and peace, so
well as others, to our utmost endeavour: for Christ hath
commanded, to *teach all nations*, &c., and they are the
first.[9]

Lastly, then shall not so many men and women be deceived by false ministers, neither by their sermons, nor yet
by their books, which are full freighted with false doctrines, and confirmed and countenanced, not only by the
king's authority and power,[1] but also by wresting and

[9] [Previous to the reign of Edward I. Jews in considerable numbers resided in England, and flourished, though often plundered and slain. At length the fanaticism of this monarch got the better of his avarice, and by the parliament of 1290, they were finally and for ever banished the realm. Upwards of 16,000 are said to have left the kingdom. On their voyage many were robbed by the seamen, their throats cut, and the bodies cast into the sea. From this time no Jews were to be found resident in England until, by the tolerant spirit of Cromwell, they were again permitted to exercise their various callings; though *he* failed, through the persecuting spirit of the presbyterian divines and others, to obtain for them a full and impartial liberty. Under various disabilities they have continued until the present day. At a subsequent period to the plea made by Busher above, we find the Baptists honourably distinguished for their li-

berality to this oppressed people; and while themselves labouring under the weight of persecution, extending to them the hand of sympathy. Mr. Thos. Collier dedicated to the Protector the following work, " A Brief Answer to some of the Objections and Demurs made against the coming in and inhabiting of the Jews in this Commonwealth.   With a plea on their behalf, or, Some arguments to prove it not only lawful, but the duty of those whom it concerns, to give them their liberty and protection (they living peaceably) in this nation."—4to. Lond. 1656.]

[1] [" The king, having given the reins of the church into the hands of the prelates and their dependants, these in return became zealous champions for the prerogative, both in the pulpit and from the press. Two books were published this year (1607), which maintained the most extravagant maxims of arbitrary power, one written by Cowell, LL.D., the other by

false interpreting of the scriptures, and by alleging of popish fathers, which, through the great ignorance of the people, do greatly prevail: but then shall be abolished, Rev. xi. 3, through the word and Spirit of God, his two witnesses, in & xix. 10. the mouth of his servants, who by word and writing shall breed such knowledge that none of wisdom's children shall be deceived.

Another reason, why so many good people are now deceived, is, because we that have most truth, are most persecuted; and therefore most poor. Whereby, we are unable to write and print, as we would, against the ad-
2 Pet. ii. 2. versaries of the truth. It is hard to get our daily food with the labours of our weak bodies and feeble hands. How then should we have to defray other charges, and to write and print? I have, through the help of God out of his word, made a scourge of small cords, wherewith anti-christ and his ministers might be driven out of the temple of God. Also a declaration of certain false translations in the New Testament. But I want wherewith to print and publish it. Therefore it must rest till the Lord seeth good to supply it.

In the mean while, I humbly intreat his majesty² and parliament to give me leave to prove the bishops with one question, by which you may perceive the ignorance of your bishops. It is this, how will they be able to prove a
Exod. iii. 6. resurrection from these words, *I am the God of Abraham, the God of Isaac, and the God of Jacob.* Only from these words will they prove the resurrection, if they be the
Luke xx. 17. bishops of Christ; for he proved the resurrection from

---

Dr. Blackwood, a clergyman, who maintained that the English were all slaves from the Norman conquest. The parliament would have brought the authors to justice, but the king protected them by proroguing the houses in displeasure." Neal, Hist. of Puritans, i. 441. edit. 1837.]

² " It is the king's honour to search out a thing." Prov. xxv. [2.]

hence. The question is hard, I grant, but if their lordships be not able to interpret it according to the meaning
of Christ, as I am sure they are not, then it will be
another cause, very sufficient, for their deprivation from
their lordly and idol offices, and princely livings.

But because most men do wrest and misinterpret the
scriptures, some of wickedness, and some of ignorance, for
the utterance of their doctrines, and so deceive both prince
and people, I will show how you shall perceive it, lest
thereby you be still deceived.

Every scripture, therefore, misinterpreted, doth make a
contradiction. As for example, Mr. Johnson, one of the
preachers called Brownists, to prove Rome a true church,
allegeth 2 Thess. ii. 4,[3] where the apostle showeth, that

[3] [" God hath his people in the Romish Babylon ; and when he calleth
them out from thence, doth not enjoin
them to leave whatsoever is there had,
but requireth of them that they have
no communion with her sins......Now
baptism is not of her idolatries, but of
Christ's ordinances; it is not a thresh-
old or post which she hath brought
into the *temple of God*, but was set
therein of old by the Lord himself,
2 Thess. ii. 2—8." A Brief Treatise
against two errors of the Anabaptists,
by F. Johnson. London. 1645, p.
12, 13 ; first printed about 1608. In
a subsequent publication he appears
to refer to these remarks of Busher,
and replies as follows : " How can we
soundly defend and retain the visible
baptism received in the church of
Rome, if we do not accordingly acknowledge the church of Rome to be
a visible church and the people of
God ? A visible church, I say, though
miserably corrupted, adulterate, and
apostate; having antichrist set therein, &c......Where, for further manifestation of the point, note, and remember still, to put difference between
' the man that sitteth,' and ' the
temple of God, wherein he sitteth.'
Which not being observed aright—
besides many unsound speeches and
assertions that have passed such as
are otherwise good writers — much
error hath arisen hereabout, and great
confusion of things that differ." " My
words were these, speaking of the
apostle's speech, where he saith antichrist should sit in the temple of
God, 2 Thess. ii. 4, that here, by the
temple of God, understanding the
church of God, it will follow that
antichrist should sit in the church of
God; and is there to be sought and
found, and not among the Jews,
Turks, Pagans, &c. Where first mark
that I spake not of the temple only,
but of the temple of God, as the
apostle also doth. Secondly, I do
indeed here derive the reason from
this exposition thereof; that by the

BUSHER.]   F

the man of sin, and *son of perdition, sitteth in the temple of God.* Which words, *temple of God,* he interpreteth to be the church of God; whereby he doth greatly err. For then such interpretation will contradict this scripture,

1 Tim. iii. 15. which saith, *The church of God is the pillar and ground of truth.* But if the *man of sin sitteth* there, then it is a

Rev xviii. 2. *hold of foul spirits, a cage of every unclean and hateful bird,* as the scripture speaketh; yea, *the pillar and ground* of falsehood, and not *of truth.* Neither would the Lord call

Rev. xviii. 4. his people out of her, as he doth, if it were the true church. Also, if the temple of God in that place be interpreted the church of God, this foul absurdity and contradiction will follow, viz., that the church, called the woman, to whom was given two wings of a great eagle, that she might fly into the wilderness from her persecu-tors, for a time, times, and half a time, was not perse-

Rev. xii. 13, 14. cuted; neither yet did fly into the wilderness so long a time. Neither yet was the church, (called both woman

Rev. xvii. 1, 5, [6.] and whore, also *great Babylon, the mother of whoredoms and abominations of the earth,) drunken with the blood of the saints and of the martyrs of Jesus,* as the scripture testifieth.

Again, if that be the church of God where the man of sin sitteth, then the winepress was not trodden without, but within the church. And so it also crosseth this scrip-

Rev. xiv. 20. ture, which saith, *The winepress was trodden without the city,* so that *blood came out unto the horses' bridles, by the space of a thousand and six hundred furlongs. Ergo,* a false interpretation.

Moreover, we are not to understand the word temple at

[John ii. 19.] all times to mean the church; for when Christ said, *De-stroy this temple, and in three days I will raise it up again,*

temple of God is understood the   See also Hanbury's Memorials, vol.
church of God." Johnson's Christian   i. p. 311.]
Plea, ed. 1617. pp. 123, 125, 146.

[he] did not mean the church, nor yet the material temple wherein he was, but meant his body. Yet the Jews understood the word temple otherwise. Even as Mr. Johnson, &c., do here understand the word temple otherwise, than the bodies of peoples, multitudes, nations, and tongues, which they ought not to do.[4]

Likewise Paul, when he said, *If any man destroy the temple of God, him will God destroy,* [he] did not mean the church, but the members of the church. So when he said, *The man of sin sitteth in the temple of God,* he did not mean so much as the members of the church, much less the church. [1 Cor. iii. 17.]

Therefore it must be understood, that all those in whom the man of sin sitteth, are called *the temple of God,* only in respect that the *Lord hath bought them,* for the Lord hath bought all men, even the *false teachers* that deny him. Therefore no man is his own in that respect, but the Lord's. 2 Pet. ii. 1; 1 John ii. 2. 1 Cor. vi. 19, 20, vii. 23.

Also the bishops themselves, to prove brothers' and sisters' children may marry, allege Lev. xviii. [6.] But that scripture doth not prove such marriages, but the full contrary. For it saith, *none shall come near to any of his kindred, to uncover shame.* But brothers' and sisters' chil-

---

[4] Rev. xvii. 15. [These views of our author are identical with those of the martyr Penry. " Antichrist, I grant, should sit as God in the temple of God, but it was never the temple of God since he planted his pestilent chair therein. Popery indeed hath invaded the seats and possessions of true religion, and began first where the truth was professed. For the mystery of iniquity first appeared within the church, and not elsewhere; where true religion flourished, and not among the heathen; neither could he be that adversary, whose beginning should be in paganism. But although popery took root in the soil where the true church was planted, yet it so grew there, that it still continued to be the synagogue of Satan, and could never as yet be the church of God : however it hath overgrown the possession thereof." A Godly Treatise by Robert Some, D.D. p. 164. London. 1588.]

dren are kinsfolks, therefore they may not come near to
uncover shame, for that were wickedness. This they
must confess, or else prove that brothers' and sisters' children are not kinsfolks, which they cannot, seeing, then,
brothers' and sisters' children cannot call cousin. And
so all cousinship is blotted out, by their doctrine, for
uncles and aunts call their brothers' and sisters' child,
nephew and niece.

Thus many bishops and preachers do deceive kings,
princes, and peoples, by wresting and misinterpreting the
scripture. Therefore I earnestly desire your majesty and
parliament, to *beware, lest there be any man that spoil you
through philosophy and vain deceit, through the traditions of
men, according to the rudiments of the world, and not after
Christ.* And to *avoid profane and vain babblings, and* anti-
theses, or *oppositions, falsely called learning, which, while
some profess, they have erred concerning the faith.*

And now, O king, prince, and parliament, open your
eyes, and listen[5] your ears, unto compassion and mercy.
Fear God and be like unto him, for he causeth his sun to
shine, both on just and unjust. Think at last you must
give an account of your works: many at the day of judgment will be ever burned, for killing and burning innocent
Christians; but no man shall be damned for saving their
lives. Lean then, I humbly beseech you, on the right
side of mercy, rather than yield unto such as persuade
[you] to persecute innocent Christians. For they cannot
help you, when you must give account thereof unto
Christ, who adviseth you otherwise, although they be such

Lev. xviii. 17.

Col. ii. 8.

1 Tim. vi. 20, 21.

2 Cor. v. 10; Matt. v. 21, 22, 45; Lu. xviii. 7, 8; 2 Thess. i. 4, 8; Jas. i. 5, 6; Matt. xii. 36.

---

[5] *Listen your ears,* let your ears be attentive.
" Listeneth, lordinges, in good intent,
And I will tell you verament
Of mirthe and of solas."
Chaucer's Rime of Sir Thopas.

as err, how much more such as do but seem to err, and
for difference in religion ought you to save their lives?

And I do in all humility affirm, that those who advise
you to pluck up and burn the tares, which Christ com- Matt. xiii.
mands to be let alone till the end, do advise you to pluck 29, 30, 39;
up and burn the commandment of Christ, unto whom Actsxvii.31.
assuredly, except [there is] amendment, you shall give
account at the day appointed. Therefore believe not such
as counsel you to shed blood for [differences of] judgment
in religion; for if themselves should suffer the pain, they
would verily give you other counsel. Be not then their
executioners any longer, for *all that will live godly in* 2Tim.iii.12.
Christ shall suffer persecution, though you do your best
to hinder it.

And I pray [you] to remember, that to preach the
gospel, after the mind of Christ, is to bring glad tidings Luke ii.10;
unto the people. But to burn, banish, hang, and imprison Rom. i.16.
for religion, is not to bring glad, but woful, tidings unto
the people. Let it not therefore be any longer preached
in your majesty's dominions, I meekly intreat. *Though* 1 Cor. iii.6.
*Paul plant, and Apollos water, yet it is God that giveth the
increase.* But your bishops and ministers will have an
increase whether God will or not, or else they will burn,
banish, hang, and imprison. Kings and magistrates are
God's ministers, and not the bishops'. Therefore, I
humbly beseech you to withstand the bloody minds of
your bishops, that there be no more innocent Christians
persecuted to death for religion. A crying sin.

I read that in the Netherlands above a hundred thousand persons have been put to death for religion.[6] But

---

[6] [Under the government of the notorious Duke of Alva, countless numbers were destroyed, for their attachment to liberty and pure religion, by
the direction of the no less cruel
Philip, king of Spain. On Alva's
departure from the Netherlands, " he
lodged one night on the borders of

now, praised be God, we have no such woful tidings preached among us. The Lord work as much in our land, I beseech him! that so you may no longer burn and

John xvi. 3. banish the servants of Christ. For he saith, *They that do these things have not known the Father nor me.*

Yet, I confess, you have the zeal of God, for you think you do God good service in burning Christians that differ from your religion. But I also confess [that] your zeal is

Rom. x. 2, 3. not according to knowledge. For your bishops and ministers being endued with university and high school learning, divinity, and doctrine, but being ignorant of the lowly learning, heavenly divinity, and doctrine of Christ, have and do still go about to establish their own, and have not yet submitted themselves to the lowly learning, divinity, and doctrine of Christ. And therefore, like their predecessors, will persuade you to burn, banish, &c., such Christians as they hold to be in error about doctrines and questions of faith and religion; right[7] as if they had the power to rule, govern, and dispose the hearts and spirits of kings, princes, and people, even as they list; and also to make them good and righteous when they will, and to cause them to understand and believe the gospel, even by a day and hour appointed; which to do, belongeth to God

---

Germany with Count Lewis Von Königstein, to whom he boasted, as a noble achievement, 'That he had caused above eighteen thousand heretics and rebels to pass through the hands of the executioner, without counting any of those whose blood had been shed in the war.' " This he did in the space of less than six years. Some write that in fifteen years there were 100,000 souls massacred, only on account of religion, within the bounds of the Low Countries. Koornhert tells us that he heard from the mouth of a great person, that he had procured an account from two provinces, and from some other registers, in the year 1566, before the troubles were at their height, the names of more than 36,000 persons that were put to death for religion. Brandt, i. 306, and Annot. p. 20.]

[7] [*Right*, truly. Chaucer.]

alone. And therefore Christ saith, *No man can come to* John vi. 44.
me, except the Father draw him.

And Christ will have his ministers to preach to such as
are worthy and willing, and not as your ministers, who Matt. x. 11,
14.
come to them whom they hold unworthy, and find unwilling, and say, "Will ye not come to church and hear,
and will ye not believe our doctrine? but we will make
you, or else we will burn you for heretics." Thus will
they taunt meek and holy Christians, who are torn like
sheep among the wolves. But Christ's ministers will *with* 2 Tim. ii. 25;
Joh. xiii. 25.
meekness instruct such as are contrary minded, tolerating the
evil men patiently; proving if God will at any time give
them repentance, that they may know the truth. Whereby
they show plainly that they are Christ's disciples, and
have that true faith which worketh by love, even as the
apostle saith. The which I pray you to consider, that so
you may both know and obey the will of Christ. *Now,* 1 Cor. xlii.
saith he, *abideth faith, hope, and love; but the chiefest of*
these is love. For where love is, there is no disdain; it
seeketh not her own things; it is not provoked to anger; it
suffereth all things: it hopeth all things: it endureth all
things. Yea, the love of Christ so loveth, that it will not
vex, nor persecute any that call on his name.

Therefore, I humbly pray you to *remember them that are* Heb. xiii. 3.
in bonds, as though ye were bound with them; and them that
are in affliction, as if ye were also afflicted in the body. And
to show them mercy, for *mercy rejoiceth against judgment,* Jas. ii. 13.
but judgment merciless shall be to them that show no mercy.
If ye be friendly to your brethren only, what singular Lu. vi. 32—
37.
thing do you? Do not the sinners the same? Be not like
unto them, but unto your heavenly Father. Whose wisdom, love, and mercy, I beseech him to grant you, that so
you may come to the knowledge of the truth, and be
saved: and that we, your majesty's faithful subjects, *may*

1 Tim. ii.
[2.]

lead a quiet and peaceable life, even in our own nation, *in all godliness and honesty.* Amen.

Now, them that are persecuted, I exhort with the words

1 Pet. iv.
12—16.

of the apostle Peter, *Dearly beloved, think it not strange concerning the fiery trial that is among you to prove you, as though some strange thing were come unto you: but rejoice, inasmuch as ye are partakers of Christ's sufferings; that when his glory shall appear, ye may be glad and rejoice. If ye be railed upon for the name of Christ, blessed are ye; for the spirit of glory and of God resteth upon you: which on their parts is evil spoken of, but on your part is glorified. But let no man suffer as an evildoer, or as a murderer, or as a busy body in others' matters. But if one suffer as a Christian, let him not be ashamed: but let him glorify God in that*

Acts xxiv.
14.
[1 Pet. iv.
17—19.]

behalf. For all the martyrs of the apostolic church have suffered as evildoers and as heretics. *For the time is, that judgment must begin at the house of God: and if it first begin at us,* saith the apostle, *what shall the end be of them that obey not the gospel of God? And if the righteous scarcely be saved, where shall the ungodly and [the] sinner appear? Wherefore let them that suffer according to the will of God, commit their souls unto him in welldoing, as unto a faithful Creator.*

Antichrist
and his
persecution
shall be
made low.
2 Thess. ii. 4,
8.

Read Isaiah ii. 2, 4, 11, [12,] 16. *He shall judge among the nations, and rebuke many people: they shall break their swords into mattocks, and their spears into scythes: nations shall not lift up a sword against nations, neither shall they learn to fight any more. The high looks of man shall be humbled, and the loftiness of man shall be abased, and the Lord only shall be exalted in that day. For the day of the Lord of hosts is upon all the proud and haughty, and upon all that is exalted, and it shall be made low.*

Little David overcame great Goliath, yet not brought up in war. Unlearned Peter confuted the learned priests, yet by calling a fisherman.   Attend and help, and you shall see the wonderful works of God.   For *the foolishness of God is wiser than men, and the weakness of God is stronger than men.   And God hath chosen the foolish things of the world to confound the wise ; and things that are despised hath God chosen, to bring to nought things that are.*

Gal. vi. 6;
1 Cor. ix. 7.

1 Cor. i. 25, 28.

LEONARD BUSHER.

FINIS.

PERSECUTION

FOR

RELIGION

JUDGED AND CONDEMNED.

1615.

OBIECTIONS:

Answered by way of Dialogue, wherein is proved

By the Law of God:
By the law of our Land:
And by his Maiesties many testimonies

That no man ought to be persecuted for his religion, so he testifie his allegeance by the Oath, appointed by Law.

Esa 2.4. He shal judg amonge the Nations, & rebuke many people: they shal breake their swords also into mattocks, & their speares into sithes, Nation shall not lift vp a sword against Nation, neither shall they learne to feight any more.

Esa. 11.9. Then shall none hurt nor destroy in all my Holy mountaine.

2. Cor. 10.4 For the weapons of our warrfare, are not carnall, but mighty through God to cast downe holds.

Printed 1615.

Persecution for Religion

JUDG'D and CONDEMN'D:

In a DISCOURSE, between an

ANTICHRISTIAN and a CHRISTIAN.

PROVING

By the Law of God and of the Land, And
By King *James* his many Testimonies,

That no man ought to be *Persecuted* for his *Religion*, so he
Testifie his Allegiance by the Oath appointed by Law.

Proving also, That the Spiritual Power in *England*, is the Image of
the Spiritual Cruel Power of *Rome*, or that Beast mentioned,
Rev. 13. Manifesting the fearful Estate of those who subject to
such Powers, that Tyrannize over the Conscience: And
shewing the Unlawfulness of Flying, because of the
Trouble men see or fear is coming upon them.

To which is added,

An humble SUPPLICATION to the Kings Majesty;

Wherein (among other things) is proved,

1. That the Learned usually Erre and resist the Truth. 2. That
Persecution is against the Law of Jesus Christ. 3. Against the Profession and Practice of famous Princes. 4. Condemned by ancient
and later Writers. 5. Freedom in Religion not hurtful to any
Common-wealth, and it depriveth not *Kings* of any Power given
them of God.

---

2 Cor. 10. 4. *For the Weapons of our Warfare are not carnal, but
mighty through God, to the pulling down of strong holds.*

Printed in the years, 1615. and 1620. And now Reprinted
for the Establishing some, and Convincing others, 1662.

INTRODUCTORY NOTICE.

THERE can be but little doubt that we owe the two following pieces to the same pen; or that the author was a member of the church, which under Mr. Helwys's pastorate returned to England, manfully to breast the waves of persecution, that they might seek the "salvation of thousands of ignorant souls in their own nation." That church had been formed about the year 1609, at Amsterdam, in Holland, partly by separation from the Brownists on the question of baptism, and partly by the successful labours of their first pastor, Mr. John Smyth, "a man of able gifts and a good preacher."[1] His adoption of baptist sentiments exposed him to great and unmerited reproach, and, so far as we have examined his writings, to charges of maintaining opinions the reverse in some cases of those he held. The common artifices of controversy were freely used against him; and the conclusions of his opponents attributed to him as his own.

Mr. Helwys, his successor, was probably the author of the Confession of Faith published in 1611, to silence, if possible, the calumnies, widely circulated, against the opinions and practices of his people. He refers to it in a

---

[1] Crosby's Hist. of Engl. Baptists, i. 90—94. Hanbury's Hist. Memorials, i. 459.

work with the following title, and dated the same year:
" A Proof that God's Decree is not the Cause of any
Man's Condemnation, and that all Men are redeemed by
Christ, and that no Infants are condemned," 12mo. pp.
111. This work agrees in sentiment with the Confession.
In the same year he also published " An Advertisement or
Admonition unto the Congregation which men call New
Fryelers in the Low Countries," &c. 16mo. pp. 94. His
topics are, the true humanity of Christ, the sabbath, on
succession in the ministry, and that magistracy doth not
debar any from the church of Christ. On the latter subject he says, " For proof that it is an holy ordinance or
office pleasing unto God, it is showed that we are commanded to obey of conscience, and that it is only in that
which is holy and good. For God forbid, that his children
should be tied of conscience to obey in any thing that is
unholy and not good. The apostle shows that the Holy
Ghost intends no such thing, when he saith, *Magistrates
are not to be feared for good works;* and *Fear God; honour
the king.* And therefore if magistrates shall command any
things against God or godliness, the people of God are not
bound to obey."[2]

As this last work was " written in Dutch and printed in
English:" and as in the following year, 1612, we find Mr.
Helwys defending himself and his people, against the
reproaches cast upon them on their return from exile ; we
are able to fix pretty accurately the date of their return
home, at the close of the year 1611, or early in 1612.
His defence is found in " A Short Declaration of the
Mystery of Iniquity," 16mo. pp. 212. The larger portion
of the work is an application of prophecy to the times ;
but it is especially directed against the evils of prelacy
and persecution. He expresses an earnest anxiety for the

[2] Page 58.

king's salvation, and nobly determines to suffer persecution, if needs be, for conscience' sake.

It was from the bosom of a community thus well instructed in the principles of liberty, came forth the following "enlarged and accurate views" on religious freedom.[3] It is a question whether Mr. Helwys was living at the time of their publication in the form following, as nothing is known of his history after the year 1612, the date of the last writing which bears his name: yet he must have been living in 1614, when Mr. Robinson assailed him, in a work to be presently noticed.

Though Mr. Helwys was not the author of the ensuing treatise, in its sentiments he heartily and deeply sympathized, as his extant writings testify. A book several times quoted in the notes of the following pages under the title of "A Description of what God hath predestinated concerning Man," is attributed by Mr. John Robinson, to "John Murton and his associates."[4] These extracts bear undeniable evidence of the same authorship as the dialogue, and would seem to fix it upon that gentleman, or one of his friends.

The closing paragraph of the dialogue traces the origin of the work to a "late book of Mr. John Robinson," and to the objections the baptists had met with to their views on persecution. The form of expression, "any of us," seems to imply that another than Mr. Helwys had on this occasion appeared in defence. Mr. Robinson's book was published in 1614, under the title "Of Religious Communion, Private and Public. With the silencing of the Clamours raised by Mr. Thomas Helwisse against our

[3] Price, Hist. of Nonconformity, i. 522.

[4] "A Defence of the Doctrine propounded by the Synode at Dort; against John Murton and his associates, in a Treatise intituled, A Description what God, &c., printed 1624." 4to.

PERSECUTION, &c.]   G

retaining the Baptism received in England; and administering of Baptism unto Infants. As also, a Survey of the
Confession of Faith, published in certain Conclusions, by
the remainders of Mr. Smyth's Company," 4to. pp. 131.[5]

Whether Mr. Robinson has either " confuted" Mr.
Helwys, or silenced his " clamours," it would be beside
our purpose to inquire. The warmth and personal invective displayed in his remarks, would do but little, at all
events, to conciliate his opponent. Mr. Robinson's insi-
nuation of " headiness and indiscreet courses,"—the only
part of his remarks to justify flight from persecution,
given by Mr. Hanbury—will not prevent us from regard-
ing Mr. Helwys and his brethren as actuated by motives
at once pure and exalted, in daring " to challenge king
and state to their faces, and not give way to them, no, not
a foot."[6] That daring challenge is now in the hands of
the reader; and for its admirable sentiments, its clear
and powerful reasoning, and its accurate discrimination of
the magistrate's office in religious and civil affairs, claims
" a due meed of praise" from an impartial posterity.[7]

It is in the latter part of his work that Mr. Robinson
proceeds to examine the conclusions embraced in the Confession of Faith, and in this case with a mildness of
manner, which contrasts most favourably with that assumed in his attack on Mr. Helwys. To many of the
conclusions he demurs; some stand in need of explanation;
some come " short of the truth, though there be no
untruth in " them; some are doubtfully set down, and in
part untrue; others are unsound in sundry ways. These
relate chiefly to the doctrines of God's decrees, original

---

[5] Hanbury's Hist. Memor. i. 256.
The title is given from Mr. Hanbury's
work, as the copy we have examined
has lost the title-page.

[6] Of Religious Communion, &c.,
p. 41.

[7] Price, Hist. of Nonconformity, i.
522.

sin, free-will, and universal redemption.[8] But the following we quote as being the passages to which the ensuing
pages are a reply.

"In Conclusion 83, 'where the office of the magistrate,'
is called a 'permissive ordinance of God,' is both a contradiction, and evil speaking of them in authority. Where it
is called 'an ordinance of God,' it is confessed good, for
every creature of God is good, and all his ordinances are his
creatures. And so, many things are ascribed to the office
of magistrates in this, and the other conclusions about it,
which prove it to be good, and lawful in itself; but where
it is made 'permissive,' it is condemned as evil: since only
evil is permitted, or suffered of God."

"And where it is objected, Prop. 85, 'that Christ's
disciples must love their enemies, and not kill them; pray
for them, and not punish them, &c.': I answer, that the
godly magistrate may do both. Doth not God punish
with temporary death those that he loveth? And why
may not God's deputies, the gods upon earth, be minded
as God herein? When the godly kings and governors in
Israel were commanded to execute judgment and justice
upon the people for their transgressions, were they commanded not to love them, and pray for them?—

"They add, 'that the magistrate is not to meddle with
religion, or matters of conscience, nor compel men to this
or that form of religion, because Christ is the King and
Lawgiver of the church and conscience, Jam. iv. 12.' I
answer, that this indeed proves that he may alter, devise,
or establish nothing in religion otherwise than Christ hath
appointed, but proves not, that he may not use his lawful
power lawfully for the furtherance of Christ's kingdom
and laws. The prophet Isaiah, speaking of the church of

[8] Many of these conclusions may be seen in the Appendix to the first volume of Crosby's History of the English Baptists.

Christ, foretells *that kings shall be her nursing fathers, and queens her nursing mothers;* which, if they meddle not with her, how can they be? And where these men make this the magistrate's only work, ' that justice and civility may be preserved amongst men,' the apostle teaches another end, which is, *that we may lead a peaceable life under them in all godliness.* It is true they have no power against the laws, doctrine, and religion of Christ; but for the same, if their power be of God, they may use it lawfully, and against the contrary. And so it was in special foretold by John, *that the kings of the earth should make the whore desolate, and naked, and eat her flesh and burn her with fire.*

" This Mr. Helwisse frivolously interprets ' of their spiritual weapons;' which are no other than the spiritual weapons of all other Christians. Besides that, it is contrary to the clear meaning of the Holy Ghost, which is, that these kings should first use their civil power for the *beast and whore,* and after against them to their destruction.

" To conclude this point then : both these men, and Mr. Helwisse especially, in his whole discourse about this matter, labour of the common disease of all ignorant men, in pleading against the use of the ordinance by the abuse: which stands either in prohibiting any thing which God hath commanded, or in commanding any thing which he hath forbidden; as indeed he hath whatsoever he hath not commanded, either expressly, or by consequence, in his religion and worship."[9]

Such were the views of Mr. Robinson on the duties of

[9] Of Religious Communion, &c., pp. 128—130. Mr. Hanbury has omitted to quote these passages in his long account of this work, important as they are to the illustration of the views of the "father of independency," on liberty of conscience. See Hist. Mem. i. p. 270.

the civil magistrate towards religion; to which the following pages are an ample and satisfactory reply. The
enforcement of God's laws by a godly magistrate, with
penalties for disobedience, is just as subversive of the
gospel and of liberty of conscience, as when the laws
enforced are mere human inventions in the worship of
the Supreme, and the power that coerces is that of the
ungodly.

The other conclusions, being but briefly touched upon,
received a more enlarged discussion in the work already
referred to: " A Description of what God hath predestinated concerning Man, &c.: printed in 1620," 12mo.
pp. 176.

The present edition is reprinted from a collated copy
of the original one of 1615. It appears to have been
printed in Holland, and is without name or place. The
persecutions to which the author and his friends were
exposed, doubtless rendered this expedient.

By the kindness of Dr. Bandinel, librarian of the Bodleian Library, we are enabled to present a fac-simile of the
title page. Two copies of the work exist in that large
collection; no others are known to be extant. The book
is in 16mo., in black letter, except the remarks of Antichristian, which are in roman; the whole consists of
eighty-seven pages.

As in the previous treatise, the quotations from scripture are retained in the language of the author; he appears
to have quoted from the originals, and not from any
English translation of the Bible with which we have
been able to compare his references.

An edition appeared in 1662, in 4to., of which the title
is annexed. To this was added a petition presented to
King James and his parliament in 1620. From this reprint the passages on original sin in infants, free-will, and

predestination, as also the last paragraph, are altogether omitted. The most important of these differences are marked in the notes.

Another reprint was published in the same year, leaving out all those parts which identify the work as the production of a baptist. Its title is, " The Judgment of the Old-Nonconformists against Conformity to the Church of England, being the Testimony they bore against it, in the beginning of King James's reign. Reprinted in the year 1662," 4to. pp. 40. This seems to have been printed from the same forms of type as the preceding, up to the point where the omissions rendered it necessary to set up the type anew. These omissions amount to eight pages.

An edition in 8vo. was also published in the year 1827, with a preface by the late Rev. Joseph Ivimey. This is a literal reprint of the edition of 1662.

THE EPISTLE.

To all that truly wish Jerusalem's prosperity and Babylon's destruction; wisdom and understanding be multiplied upon you.

IN these days, if ever, that is true which the wise man said, *There is no end in making many books, and much reading is a weariness to the flesh:* yet considering how heinous it is in the sight of the Lord to force men and women by cruel persecutions, to bring their bodies, to a worship whereunto they cannot bring their spirits; we thought it our duty, for God's glory, and the reformation thereof in this our own nation, to publish this little writing following, wherein is manifestly proved by the law of God, the law of our land, and his Majesty's own divers testimonies, that no man ought to be persecuted for his religion, be it true or false, so they[1] testify their[2] faithful allegiance to the king.

Eccles. xii. 12.

What shall men do striving about matters of religion till this be ended? For, if this be a truth, that the kings of the earth have power from God to compel by persecution all their subjects to believe as they believe, then wicked is it to resist, and the persecutions of such are justly upon them, and the magistrates that execute the same are

---

[1] [he ; 1662.]   [2] [his ; 1662.]

clear from their blood, and it is upon their own heads: but if the kings of the earth have not power from God, to compel by persecution any of their subjects to believe as they believe, seeing faith is the work of God, then no less wicked is it in the sight of God to disobey, and the persecutions of such are upon the magistrates, and the blood of the persecuted crieth unto the Lord, and will be required at the magistrates' hands.

Wherefore in all humility, reverence, and loyalty, we do humbly desire of our sovereign lord the king, and all God's ministers under him, as judges, justices of peace, &c., by whom this persecution is executed, themselves to consider, not whether herein they please lord bishops, but whether they please the Lord Jesus Christ, who after a little while shall judge all judges according to their works, without respect of persons, and therefore are commanded to *kiss the Son lest he be angry, and they perish in the way.* Our humble desire is, that they would consider what is testified in the scriptures ; that the kings of the earth shall *give their power unto the beast, till the words of God be fulfilled ;* then shall they take their power from her.

Ps. ii. [12.]

Rev.xvii. 13, 17.

If it be granted, as it is, that the kings of this nation formerly have given their power unto that Romish beast, it shall evidently appear that our lord the king, and all magistrates under him, do give their power to the same beast, though the beast be in another shape : for, as that spiritual power or beast of Rome sets up a worship, as they pretend, for God, and force all thereto by cruel persecutions, the kings of the earth giving their power thereunto ; so this spiritual power or beast of England, sets up a worship, as they pretend, for God, and force all thereto by cruel persecutions, the king's majesty giving his power hereunto.

Oh! that all that are in authority, would but consider by the word of God, which shall judge them at the last day, what they do, when they force men against their souls and consciences to dissemble to believe as they believe, or as the king and state believe: they would withdraw their hands and hearts therefrom, and never do as they have done, partly through inconsideration, and partly to please lord bishops being in favour with the king.

It cannot but with high thankfulness to God, and to the king, be acknowledged of all, that the king's majesty is no blood-thirsty man; for if he were, bodily destruction should be the portion of all that fear God, and endeavour to walk in his ways; as may be seen in the primitive time of this spiritual power, or beast of England, after that King Henry the Eighth had cast off the Romish beast; and since, so far as leave hath been granted them, by hanging, burning, banishing, imprisoning, and what not, as the particulars might be named. Yet our most humble desire of our lord the king is, that he would not give his power to force his faithful subjects to dissemble to believe as he believes, in the least measure of persecution; though it is no small persecution to lie many years in filthy prisons, in hunger, cold, idleness, divided from wife, family, calling, left in continual miseries and temptations, so as death would be to many less persecution; seeing his majesty confesseth, that to change the mind must be the work of God.[3]

---

[3] [" Now must I turn me—to you, my lords the bishops, and even exhort you earnestly, to be more careful than you have been, that your officers may more duly present recusants, than heretofore they have done, without exception of persons; that al- though *it must be the work of God that must make their minds to be altered*, yet at least by this course they may be stayed from increasing, or insulting upon us." King James's Works, p. 545, fol. ed. 1616. Speech at Whitehall, anno 1609.]

And of the lord bishops we desire, that they would a
little leave off persecuting those that cannot believe as
they, till they have proved that God is well-pleased
therewith, and the souls of such as submit [are][4] in safety
from condemnation. Let them prove this, and we protest
we will for ever submit unto them, and so will thousands :
and therefore if there be any spark of grace in them, let
them set themselves to give satisfaction, either by word or
writing, or both. But if they will not, but continue their
cruel courses as they have done, let them yet remember
that they must come to judgment, and have their abominations set in order before them, and be torn in pieces when
none shall deliver them.

And whereas they have no other colour of ground out
of the scriptures, than that they have canonized a law,
viz. "That whosoever shall affirm that the king's majesty
hath not the same power over the church that the godly
kings of Israel had under the law, let him be excommunicate *ipso facto*."[5] The unsoundness of which ground is
manifested in this dialogue following, wherein is showed
their palpable ignorance, in that they know not the mystery of God ; and therefore have they made this canon in
flattery to the king, only to support their pride and cruelty. For, if the kingdom or land of Israel, or Canaan,
now under the gospel, be an earthly kingdom or land, or

[4] [Edit. 1662.]

[5] [" Whosoever shall hereafter affirm that the king's majesty hath not
the same authority in causes ecclesiastical that the godly kings had among
the Jews, and Christian emperors in
the primitive church, or impeach in
any part his regal supremacy in the
said causes restored to the crown, and
by the laws of this realm therein established, let him be excommunicated
ipso facto, and not restored but only
by the archbishop after his repentance
and public revocation of those his
wicked errors." Canon ii. of Constitutions and Canons Ecclesiastical,
agreed upon in the Synod begun at
London, anno Dom. 1603. Now published for the due observation of them
by his Majesty's authority. Printed
by John Norton, 1633.]

Israel now a worldly or fleshly Israel, as both were under the law, then we would confess there should be an earthly king thereof. But if the kingdom of Israel now be not earthly, but heavenly, and the Israelites now not of this world, then the king thereof is not of this world, as they are not of this world. And if these spiritual lords confess that Christ is king now of the land and people of Israel, but yet he hath left our lord the king his deputy, to make such laws and lords over the church as pleaseth him, the word of the Lord is against them: *There is but one Lord,* and *one Lawgiver,* over his church.

John xviii. 36.

John xv. 19.

John xvii. 16.

Eph. iv. 5.

James iv. 12.

Nay, his majesty himself is against them, who saith, "There is no earthly monarch over the church, whose word must be a law." And saith further, "Christ is his church's monarch, and the Holy Ghost his deputy," alleging, Luke xxii. 25, *The kings of the gentiles bear rule one over another, &c.,* but *it shall not be so among you.* Saying further, "Christ when he ascended, left not Peter with them to direct them in all truth, but promised to 'send the Holy Ghost to them for that end, &c."[6] If any will be rebellious against the word of the Lord herein, yet let them not be rebellious against the word of the king.

Oh! that any thing would prevail with them, to make them leave off these cruel courses, of persecuting poor souls that desire truly to fear God, and are most faithful subjects to the king, and desire also the salvation of the souls of these their cruel persecutors, who do seek their utter undoing by all the forenamed persecutions, only because they cannot of faith offer up such worship to God, as these spiritual lords command; and the rather let them leave off persecuting, seeing the king's majesty acknow-

---

[6] [Works. Premonition to all Christian Monarchs, p. 306.]

ledgeth, it is a sure rule in divinity, that God loves not to plant his church by violence and bloodshed.[7] And if it be a law for all Christians, that in indifferent things one must not offend another, but the strong [to][8] forbear rather than

1 Cor. viii.
[12.]

offend his weak brother, otherwise he *wounds the weak conscience, and sins against Christ;* then how much less hath any man power to be lord over the weak conscience,

Rom. xiv.
[23.]

forcing it to practise that it hath not faith in, bringing it thereby unto sin, and unto condemnation.

We do unfeignedly acknowledge the authority of earthly magistrates, God's blessed ordinance, and that all earthly authority and command appertains unto them; let them command what they will, we must obey, either to do or suffer upon pain of God's displeasure, besides their punishment: but all men must let God alone with his right, which is to be lord and lawgiver to the soul, and not command obedience for God where he commandeth none. And this is only that which we dare not but maintain upon the peril of our souls, which is greater than bodily affliction. And only for the maintenance of Christ's right herein, do false prophets and deceivers (who by that craft are clothed in fine apparel, and fare deliciously every day) labour to make us odious in the ears and eyes of prince and people, knowing well that if they had not power by persecution to force men to dissemble to believe as they, their kingdom and gain would soon come to nought; the wickedness of which course is discovered in this writing following.

For the manner, being dialogue-wise, we thought it the fittest in two respects: first, for the understanding of the simple, to whom especially God's mysteries appertain, more than to the wise and prudent of the world. Se-

---

[7] [Works. Speech at Whitehall,   [8] [but; 1615.]
anno 1609, p. 544.]

condly, because all the objections that we have met with, might be set down, and the plainlier answered. And because we have faith and assurance that many will see and acknowledge the unlawfulness of tyrannizing over the conscience, by persecuting the bodies of such as cannot be subject, we have also thought it meet to manifest the fearful estate of such subjection, that they may deliver their souls, if they will be saved : and also have set down the beginning of that old and good way, that John Baptist, Christ Jesus, and his apostles, have left unto all that will be saved unto the end of the world. Beseeching that Almighty Worker, that he would work in the hearts and consciences of men, that they may inquire for it, and that out of the scriptures, and walk therein; then shall they find rest unto their souls, although afflictions to their bodies. Oh! it is time for the Lord to work, for they have destroyed his law, and have set up in many nations such worship for God as best pleaseth them that are in authority, and have power to persecute the contrary-minded. Let all God's people cry, "How long, Lord? when wilt thou come to destroy antichrist's cruel kingdom, and establish Christ's meek and peaceable kingdom? As thou hast begun, even come, Lord Jesus, by the spirit of thy mouth, and the brightness of thy coming; even come quickly." Amen.

By Christ's unworthy Witnesses,
His Majesty's faithful Subjects:
Commonly (but most falsely) called
ANA-BAPTISTS.

A DIALOGUE,

Antichristian. Why come you not to church?

Christian. What should I do there?

A. Worship God.

C. I must worship God as he requireth, and not as any mortal man requireth.

A. True, but the worship that we require you to offer up, is the worship God requireth.

C. If it be so, I will with all willingness assent unto it; but my conscience must be satisfied thereof by the word of truth, that I may have faith in it, otherwise it is Rom. xiv.23. my grievous sin. For I may not believe it so to be, because you affirm it.

A. Well, you must go to church, otherwise you are disobedient to the law, and will fall under punishment.

C. But still, remember that you would have me worship God, as you pretend, therefore let us agree what worship God requireth. Christ saith, *God is a Spirit, and* John iv 24. *they that worship him must worship him in spirit and truth.* Here we see what worship God requireth, viz., that we worship him with our souls and spirits, and also that we worship him according to the truth of his word: and therefore for your book-worship, if it were according to truth, from the which it is as far as light is from darkness,

yet if I cannot offer it up with my spirit, it is not acceptable to God, but most abominable.

A. Well, you must come to church.

C. I pray let me ask you a question, Do you seek the
glory of God, and the salvation of my soul herein, or your
own obedience?

A. I seek the glory of God, and the salvation of your
soul, and not my own obedience.

C. Then manifest it not by words only, but by deeds
and truth; which if you do, you will not threaten me
[with]¹ punishment to cause me to come, but with meekness
and patience satisfy my conscience by the word of truth,
for this is the duty of the minister of Christ, that I may
come with a willing mind: so shall I be accepted. For if
by threatening me [with]² punishment, as imprisonment,
banishment, or death, you cause me to bring my body,
and not my spirit or soul: so shall I come near to the Lord
with my lips, when my heart shall be far from him, which
he accounteth vain worship and hypocrisy.

A. I perceive what you aim at; you would have
none brought to church, but such as come willingly of
themselves, so should every man worship God as himself
pleaseth.

C. Your conclusion I aim not at; for I acknowledge,
that as there is but *one* God, so there is but *one* way of
worshipping him, out of the which way, whosoever is, and
repenteth not thereof, shall pay a dear price; and therefore it standeth all men upon, not to please themselves in
worshipping of him. But you perceive aright that I aim
at this, that none should be compelled to worship God but
such as come willingly; for I will, by God's assistance,
prove most evidently by the scriptures, that none ought,

2 Tim. ii. 24.
2 Cor. viii.
12; Ps. cx. 3.

Matt. xv. [7,
8]

¹ [Edit. 1662.]   ² [Edit. 1662.]

nor can be compelled to worship God to acceptance, by any worldly means whatsoever.

A. Prove that.

C. Well, I prove that[3] I have affirmed, thus: first, Heb. xi. 6, *Without faith it is impossible to please God;* and, Rom. xiv. 23, *Whatsoever is not of faith, is sin.* These two scriptures prove most evidently, that whatsoever I have not faith in, in worshipping God, although it were undoubtedly true, I may not offer it up unto God, for it is displeasing to him, and it is sin against him. As also it appeareth plainly by him that came in to the king's sup- Matt. xxii. per, and wanted his wedding garment. [11.]

A. It is the king's law that you must go to church, and therefore you must be obedient.

C. The intent of the king's law is not so, as appeareth both by the statute for the oath of allegiance, and also by his majesty's own words, manifested in his 'Apology for the Oath of Allegiance,' as hereafter is more fully declared. For, if the intent of the law were to make me come to church to worship God, and not of faith, the intent of the law were to compel me to sin, which his majesty requireth not.

A. I deny not but whatsoever is not of faith is sin; but we would have you come to church to worship God of[4] faith.

C. It is not so: you regard not whether I have faith or no; for if you did, you would not urge the king's law against me, which is but a carnal weapon, and cannot beget faith, and therefore is no sure ground of faith. For, in my obedience to God, I must not presume *above that* 1 Cor. iv. 6. *that is written.* For the word of God is the only ground Rom. x. 17. of faith; and therefore, if you would have me come of[4]

---

faith, you would only urge the law of the King of kings against me.

A. Hath[5] not all the learned of the land considered of these things, and set them down? Are such simple men as you likely to see more than all these?

C. I demand of you whether they be not all subject to err, as all men are; and therefore I must *try their spirits*, whether they err or no. For I may not hold, either that they cannot err, or that, if I find them to err, I must obey them notwithstanding. Do you not herein teach me that popish and accursed doctrine, that you inveigh so much against in the papists, that I must believe as the learned of the land believe?

A. I do not hold that they cannot err.

C. Yes, you hold either that they cannot err, or, if they do err, I must obey them; for, if I do not obey them, you threaten me[6] punishment.

A. Nay, but I hold, that they being learned do not err, and therefore you must obey them.

C. Then this is your argument: the learned do not err, and therefore must be obeyed. The bishops and the rest of that rank are learned, and do not err, and therefore they must be obeyed. Another argument as vain as this, may be collected from this ground, the learned do not err, and therefore must be obeyed. The pope and the rest of that rank are learned (yea, as learned as yours), and do not err, and therefore they must be obeyed. The one is as true as the other; but both abominable. If you prove, that they that want this learning must not meddle with the ways of God but as these learned men teach them, then indeed you said[7] something; but if you cannot, as most certain it is you cannot, for the word of

Marginal note: 1 John iv. 1.

God is against you herein, then for shame to God and men leave off your cruel persecuting. For why do you persecute men that cannot of[8] faith submit to your direction concerning the ways of God, upon which consisteth their salvation, if they walk in the true way of faith with love thereof, and their condemnation if they walk in a bye-path?

A. Then I perceive, if a man can plead that he hath not faith in any thing which the king commands, he need not to be obedient.

C. Would God all men could see your dealing herein! This is your usual course when your mouth is stopped by the power of God's word that you know not what to answer, then you run to the king's command, and so make your matters good. Like unto your predecessors, the wicked scribes and pharisees, who when our Lord and Master had stopped their mouths that they had no word of answer, then they sought to make him a trespasser against Cæsar. But I have learned in some weak measure, that as there is a Cæsar unto whom of[8] conscience I must be obedient: so there is another king, one Jesus, that is King of kings, unto whom if you will not be obedient, in giving *unto God that which is God's, he will tear you in* [Luk. xx. 25; Ps. l. 22; *pieces, when there shall be none that can deliver you, and cast* Rev. xx. 10, 15; xiv. 11; *you into the lake that burneth with fire and brimstone for* Matt. v. 25.] *evermore, where there shall be no rest day nor night;* and therefore *agree with this your adversary quickly, whilst you are in the way with him.*

The power and authority of the king is earthly, and God hath commanded me to *submit to all ordinances[9] of man;* [1 Pet ii. 13, 14.] and therefore I have faith to submit to what ordinance of man soever the king commands, if it be a human ordi-

---

[8] [in; 1662.]   [9] [every ordinance; 1662.]

H 2

nance, and not against the manifest word of God; let him require what he will, I must of conscience obey him, with my body, goods, and all that I have. But my soul, wherewith I am to worship God, that belongeth to another King, *whose kingdom is not of this world*; whose people must come willingly; whose weapons *are not carnal, but spiritual.*

John xviii. 36.

Ps. cx. 3. 2 Cor. x. 4, &c.

A. Is this all the authority that you will give to the king?

C. What authority can any mortal man require more, than of body, goods, life, and all that appertaineth to the outward man? The heart God requireth. He commanded *to give unto Cæsar [the]*[1] *things that are Cæsar's, and to himself the things that are his.* Now if all the outward man be Cæsar's, and the inward man too, so that he must be obeyed in his own matters, and in God's matters also, then tell us what shall be given to God? If you, or any man, will give him more power or authority than I give him, then you give him more than his majesty requireth, as shall be shown.

Prov. xxiii. 26.

Luke xx. 25.

A. We do not say that the king can compel the soul; but only the outward man.

C. If he cannot compel my soul, he cannot compel me to worship God, for God cannot be worshipped without the soul. If you say he may compel me to offer up a worship only with my body, for the spirit you confess he cannot compel, to whom is that worship? Not to God. Then consider you whom they worship, that are thus compelled, say you, by the king. Let it be here well observed, that you make the king a commander of such worship as is not to God, contrary to his majesty's own mind, manifest in his writings. But this you do, not to advance God's glory, nor the king's honour, but your own cursed kingdom of

John iv. 24

[1] [Edit. 1662.]

darkness, which you hold by flattery and falsehood. For if this compelled worship, which is not to God, were taken away, then your kingdom would fall to hell, from whence it came; and therefore all men may here see it is supported only by wickedness.

A. I confess the king's authority is earthly, but he is head over the church under Christ.

C. God forbid that any mortal man should so equalize himself with Christ, who alone is head of his church, as the husband is of the wife, and hath left no vicegerent in that his office, for he is never absent from his church. All that any mortal man can be, is to be a subject of his kingdom; for there is but *one Lord,* and *one lawgiver.* And that this is so, his majesty confirmeth by his own testimony, in his 'Apology for the Oath of Allegiance.'[2] "But as I well allow of the hierarchy of the church for distinction of orders, for so I understand it, so I utterly deny that there is an earthly monarch thereof, whose word must be a law, and who cannot err in his sentence by an infallibility of spirit: because earthly kingdoms must have earthly monarchs, it doth not follow that the church must have a visible monarch too: for the world hath not one earthly temporal monarch; Christ is his church's monarch, and the Holy Ghost his deputy. *The kings of the Gentiles reign over them; but ye shall not be so,* Luke xxii. 25.[3] Christ did not promise before his ascension to leave Peter with them, to direct and instruct them in all things; but he promised to send the Holy Ghost unto them for that end." These are his highness's own words, whereby it evidently appeareth his majesty challengeth no supremacy over the church, but laboureth to overthrow that abomi-

Eph. v. 23.
Matt. xviii. 20, xxviii. 20.
1 Cor. xii. 5.
James iv. 12.

[2] [Works. Premonition to all Christian Monarchs, p. 306.]
[3] [" Reges gentium dominantur eorum, vos autem non sic."]

nable exaltation of that man of sin in the Romish profession ; for Christ hath given no supremacy in nor over his
church to any mortal man, but expressly commanded the
contrary, as the place of Luke, mentioned by his majesty,
plainly declareth. His highness is supreme head and governor over all his subjects' bodies and goods within his
dominions, and therein I detest and abhor all foreign
powers whatsoever.

But now for the thing in controversy betwixt you and
me, of compelling men by persecutions to do service to
God, as is pretended, wherein they have not faith; it shall
be manifest not to be of God, in that Christ Jesus himself,
the only Lord and law-giver to the soul, neither had any
such power and authority, neither taught any such thing
to his disciples, but the contrary.   First, Matt. xxviii. 18,
19, *All power is given me in heaven and in earth ; go, there-*
fore, and teach all nations. · And 2 Cor. x. 4, *The weapons*
of our warfare are not carnal, but mighty through God, to
cast down holds,[4] *&c.*   Here we see Christ hath no worldly
power, nor worldly weapons.   Secondly, he practised and
taught the contrary.   When the Samaritans would not
Luke ix. [51
—56.] receive him going to Jerusalem, his disciples would have had
fire come down from heaven, and devoured them.   Christ[5]
rebuked them, and said, *Ye know not of what spirit ye are:*[6]
the Son of man is not come to destroy men's lives, but to save
2 Tim. ii. 24,
[25, 26.] *them.*   And the apostle, by the Spirit of Christ, commandeth the servants of the Lord, *not to strive , but to be*
gentle towards all men, apt to teach, suffering the evil men
patiently, instructing them with meekness that are contrary-
minded ; proving, if God at any time will give them repentance,
that they may know the truth, and come to amendment out of

---

[4] [strong holds ; 1662.]   [6] [are of: for, 1662.]

[5] [But Christ ; 1662.]

the devil's snare, &c. These scriptures need no explanation
for this most evident truth.

A. Well, yet notwithstanding all this, it is manifest in
the scriptures, by the example of the apostle Peter smiting
Ananias and Sapphira to death, and of the apostle Paul Act.v.[5,10.]
striking Elymas the sorcerer blind, and also by delivering Act. xiii. 11.
Hymeneus and Alexander unto Satan for the destruction
of the flesh; that punishment upon the body may be used, [1 Tim. i. 20; 1 Cor. v. 5.]
and the flesh destroyed. For if it were lawful for them
to smite to death, and the like, though by extraordinary
means, then it must be lawful for us by ordinary means,
since extraordinary means now fail. If you say it be not
lawful for us, then you must say it was not lawful for
them; and that were to accuse them of laying a false foundation, which none fearing God will affirm.

C. I dare not once admit of such a thought, as to dis-
allow the truth of that foundation which the apostles, as
skilful master-builders, have laid; but for your argument
of Peter's extraordinary smiting of Ananias and Sapphira,
he neither laid hand upon them, nor threatened them by
word, only declared what should befall them from God,
and therefore serveth nothing to your purpose. Also that
of Paul to Elymas, he laid no hands upon him, but only
declared the Lord's hand upon him, and the judgment that
should follow. If you can so pronounce, and it so come to
pass upon any, do it, and then it may be you may be
accounted master-builders, and layers of a new foundation,
or another gospel.

And for the apostle Paul his delivering Hymeneus and
Alexander unto Satan, it was not by any temporal sword 1 Tim. i. 20.
or power, but even *by the power of our Lord Jesus Christ,*
in his name, *by the sword of the Spirit.* And this was not 1 Cor. v. 4; [Eph. vi.17.]
extraordinary, but ordinary, to continue in all churches to
the end; and not to destroy the outward man, as you teach

and practice, but to destroy those lustful affections which
dwell in the flesh, that so the flesh being mortified, the
spirit may be quickened, and the soul saved in the day of
the Lord Jesus. And whereas you say, that as they did
it by extraordinary means, so you may do it by ordinary
means : if you would use only those weapons which Christ
commanded his disciples to use in this business, which are
not carnal, we would agree with you herein ; but if your
ordinary means be such as Christ never had, nor any of
his disciples, then it is a means of your own devising, for
Christ hath all means whatsoever for bringing men to the
obedience of the truth.

A. Doth not Christ in the parable teach, that he com-
[Luke xiv. pelled all to come in ?
23.]

C. I demand of you, wherewith doth he compel them?
He hath no carnal weapons. Doth he not compel them by
Heb. iv. 12; his word, which is his two-edged sword ? Doth he smite
Rev. ii. 12.
Isa. xi. 4. the earth with any other weapons than by the breath of
his lips ?

A. Well then, you see then compulsion may be used.

C. Yes, I confess to you, such compulsion as much as
you will, if when you have done you will walk in his
[Luke viii. steps, who when the Gaderenes prayed him to depart, he
37.]
left them, and taught his disciples where they should
preach the word of God, if they would not receive them,
Mark vi. 11. that they should *shake off the dust of their feet for a*
Act. xiii. 51, *witness against them;* which accordingly they practised.
and xviii. 6,
&c. He never taught them to pull the contrary-minded out of
their houses, and put them in prisons, to the undoing of
them, their wives and children. This was Saul's course
Acts ix. 1, when he was a blasphemer and persecutor, &c. Christ
&c.
taught his disciples *to wait if at any time God would give
the contrary-minded repentance,* and not to prevent their
repentance by seeking their blood.

Indifferent Man. I have heard you all this while, and by that I have heard, I see evidently that none ought to be compelled by any worldly means to worship God, neither can any be accepted in such worship, in that it is spiritual worship that he accepteth.

C. Blessed be the Lord that you see it; I would not you only, but all men did see that the sword of the magistrate, and all afflictions proceeding therefrom, are only upon the outward man, and cannot convert a soul from going astray, nor beget faith. It comes by hearing the word of God, and therefore is no instrument in this work. All that a magistrate can do is to compel me to bring my body; for, except there be a willing mind, which no man can see, there is no acceptance with God; and, therefore, it is not God's glory, nor my acceptance with him they seek by forcing me, but merely their own obedience, to God's great dishonour, and the destruction of my soul, if I should so do. But if it would suffice them to bring my body to that they call their church, and require of me no worship, I will go when they will, only not when their false worship is performed. For I abhor the accursed doctrine of the familists herein.[7]

Rom. x. 17.

I. It is a lamentable thing to consider how many thousands in this nation there be, that, for fear of trouble, submit to things in religion which they disapprove of.

C. Oh! whose eye doth not gush out with tears in the consideration thereof? seeing in all that God is highly displeased, and all those are under the judgments of God everlasting[8] if they repent not.

A. If it were as you would have it, that all religions should be suffered, how dangerous would it be to the king's person and state. What treacheries and treasons would be plotted!

[7] [See Addenda, A.]   [8] [everlastingly; edit. 1662.]

I. Indeed that is a thing greatly to be suspected, but if permission of all religions should be cleared of that,[9] there is no question but it might prevail with the king and state.

C. If it be not cleared of that, then let all men abhor it. First, it is the commandment of him who is the God, not of confusion, but of peace and order, and therefore to be obeyed. *Let the good and bad grow together unto the end of the world: suffering the contrary-minded patiently, proving, if God at any time will give them repentance, that they may acknowledge the truth, &c.* Secondly, if the just laws in that behalf made be but duly executed, which is, that all his subjects should protest their faithful allegiance to his majesty's person, crown, and dignity, all that will not be obedient, let them be disposed of at his majesty's pleasure, and you shall see no such treacheries and treasons practised as hath been.[1] First, for all those that seek and practise in themselves reformation in religion, Satan himself cannot tax them with the least jot of treachery. And for the papists, may it not justly be suspected that one chief cause of all their treasons, hath been because of all the compulsions that have been used against their consciences, in compelling them to the worship practised in public, according to the law of this land; which, being taken away, there is no doubt but they would be much more peaceable; as we see it verified in divers other nations, where no such compulsion is used; for if they might have freedom in their religion unto their faithful allegiance to the king, the fear of the king's laws, and their own prosperity and peace, would make them live more inoffensively in that respect.

I. Only the papists are dangerous, in that some of them

Marginal notes:
Matt. xiii. 30.
2 Tim. ii. 24.

[9] [could be cleared in that; 1662.]   [1] [This sentence is omitted in edit: 1662.]

hold, that kings and princes that be excommunicate by the pope, may be deposed or murdered by their subjects, or any other.[2]

C. For that damnable and accursed doctrine, as we abhor it with our souls, so we desire all others may ; and, therefore, all the laws that can be made for the prevention of such execrable practices are most necessary. But now I desire all men to see that the bishops and we justly cry out, against this accursed doctrine and practice in the pope and his associates, that princes should be murdered by their subjects for contrary-mindedness in religion ; yet they teach the king to murder his subjects for the self-same thing, viz. for being contrary-minded to them in their

---

[2] [By the canon law it is expressly declared, "that subjects owe no allegiance to an excommunicated lord, if after admonition he is not reconciled to the church." (Hallam, Europe during the Middle Ages, ii. 288.) The best commentary on this papal usurpation is found in the bulls of deposition, published by pope Paul the third against Henry the eighth, and by pope Pius the fifth against Elizabeth. " We, out of the plenitude of our apostolical authority," says the latter pope, " declare the aforesaid Elizabeth an heretic, and an encourager of heretics. We declare the said Elizabeth deprived of the pretended right to the kingdom above-mentioned, and of all dominion, dignity, and privilege whatsoever; and that all the nobility and subjects of the said realm, who have sworn to her in any manner whatsoever, are for ever absolved from any such oath, and from all obligation of fidelity and allegiance." (Collier vi. 474. The original Latin is in Doc. Annals i. 330.) That the catholics acted on this doctrine in the plots of Elizabeth's reign there can be no doubt, several of them "by their owne confessions" acknowledging its truth. (Tierney's Dodd. iii. 13, 14, and App. No. 3.) The Jesuits have ever been the chief maintainers of the pope's supremacy and deposing power. A collection of testimonies, from their writings on this subject, may be seen in "The Principles of the Jesuits," pp. 216—261. " We are not," says one of them, Gretser, " so timid and faint-hearted that we fear to affirm openly that the Roman pontiff can, if occasion require, absolve catholic subjects from their oath of allegiance, if the prince should use them tyrannically, and destroy the true religion." (p. 256.) See also Barrow's Treatise on the Pope's Supremacy, pp. 3—19, ed. 1839. This claim has never yet been disallowed by any succeeding pope or council.]

religion.[3] So, likewise, as that accursed doctrine is to be
abhorred in the papists, who teach subjects not to be
obedient to their princes that are excommunicate by the
pope; even so is that accursed doctrine of the bishops to
be abhorred, who teach princes not to protect their subjects that are excommunicate by them, in not affording
them either law or justice, not to bear testimony in any
court. Do not the bishops herein justify this accursed
doctrine and practice in the papists?

A. There is great difference in the persons, for the one
are princes, the other subjects ; and subjects must be
obedient.

C. Most true it is, but is it not also true that princes
must afford all their subjects justice and equity, although
they be as heathens and publicans? For, if princes be freed
from doing right and justice, and protecting their subjects
that be excommunicate, why are not subjects also freed
from subjection and allegiance to their princes, being excommunicate, if excommunication be Christ's law to all
alike that will be saved, without respect of persons? And
also, is not that law of Christ herein to be observed, that
Matt. vii. 12. *whatsoever ye would men should do to you, even so do you
to them?*[4] And therefore, as princes would that all their
subjects should be faithful and obedient unto them, so
ought princes to be just and equal to all their subjects, in

---

[3] [" The first point of kingly service unto God is to purge and cleanse
his church. It appertaineth to princes, to magistrates, to them which are
now assembled in this honourable
court of parliament, by all good
means and laws, to see God's house
made clean ; that it may be the house
of prayer, and not a den of thieves."
— (Archbishop Sandys' Sermon before Parliament, 1585, p. 42. Parker

Society's edit.) " Their duty is not
to suffer God's enemies to invade or
hurt, slander or blaspheme, those that
they have charge over, but to draw
the sword, if need be, to drive away
such wolves, and punish such wicked
tongues." (Bishop Pilkington's Exposition on Nehemiah, 1585, p. 360.
Parker Society's edit.)]

[4] [unto you, even so do ye unto,
1662.]

maintaining them in every just and equal cause between man and man ; for, *for this cause,* not for religion, saith the apostle, the saints at Rome *paid their tribute* to Cæsar, [Rom. xiii. 6.] their heathen prince, who was against them in religion. Shall they escape damnation for this accursed doctrine and practice, and think you you shall ? *Thou that judgest* [Rom ii. 1.] *another, judgest thou not thyself?* By this it may appear, as also by exceeding many other doctrines and practices, how near you are to that bloody spiritual power, what pretences to the contrary soever you make.

A. It were a lamentable thing if that bloody religion should be practised again in this nation.

C. I acknowledge it a bloody religion, but God hath cast down the power thereof in this kingdom, blessed be his name. But I would you could see your own cruel bloody religion ; but that God of his mercy hath restrained it by the king's majesty, who thirsteth not after blood. How many, only for seeking reformation in religion, have been put to death by your power in the days of queen Elizabeth ?[5] and how many, both then and since, have been consumed to death in prisons ? Yea, since that cruel spiritual power hath been set up, hath no hanging, burning, exile, imprisonments, and all manner of contempt been used, and all for religion, although some for grievous errors? And yet you see not this to be a bloody religion.

---

[5] [" These towers on Zion, the painful pastors and ministers of the word, by what malice we know not, are now of late at every assizes brought to the bar, marshalled with the worst malefactors, indicted, arraigned, and condemned for matters, as we presume, of very slender moment ; some for leaving holy days unbidden—some for singing the hymn *nunc dimittis* in the morning—some for turning the question in baptism, concerning faith, from the infants to the godfathers, which is but *you* for *thou*—some for leaving out the cross in baptism— some for leaving out the ring in marriage. Now, a most pityful thing to see, the back of this law turned to the adversary, and the edge, with all the sharpness, laid upon the friend and the true-hearted subject." (Parte of a Register, &c. The Complaint to the

Further, you cry out of their bloody cruelty; the reason is, because you will not be of their religion. And when you have done, [yourselves]⁶ are most bloody and cruel, so far as is in your power, because we and all men will not be of your religion.

A. If men hold errors, and will not obey the truth, do they not sin against God, and deserve punishment?

C. Yes, such deserve punishment, but God hath appointed their punishment, and the time thereof. Their punishment: *To them that are contentious, and disobey the truth, and obey unrighteousness, shall be indignation and wrath, tribulation and anguish shall be upon the soul of every one that doeth evil. He that will not believe, shall be damned. In flaming fire, rendering vengeance unto them that know not God, and obey not the gospel of our Lord Jesus Christ, which shall be punished with everlasting perdition from the presence of the Lord, and the glory of his power.* The time thereof, the last place recited. *When the Lord Jesus shall show himself from heaven with his mighty angels.* And, *the day of wrath. At that day when God shall judge the secrets of men by Jesus Christ. At the end of this world the Son of man shall send forth his angels, and they shall gather out of his kingdom all things that offend, and them that do iniquity, and shall cast them into a furnace of fire, &c.* Here is showed the punisher, the punishment, and the time thereof. This

Rom. ii. 8. 9.

Mark xvi. 16.

2 Thess. i. 8.

Verse 7.

Rom. ii. 5.

Ver. 16.

And Matt. xiii. 40, 41, [42.]

Privy Council, p. 128) "It would be endless to relate the sufferings of the puritans in this reign. Silencings, deprivations, and imprisonments, and not unfrequently the gibbet and the stake, were the merciful lot of those who could not digest the nauseating drugs imported from Rome. The wit of man could not invent any thing more terrible than the ecclesiastical courts. Papists and protestants partook alike of the queen's severity, and she dipt her hands in the blood of both parties. Under the dreadful pretence of heresy, eleven Dutchmen [baptists] were condemned to be burnt alive, and two of them were made to expiate their supposed crime in Smithfield." (Wilson's Hist. of Dissent. Churches, iv. 507.)]

⁶ [Edit. 1662.]

Punisher hath commanded you to wait for their repentance, by his own example, which is in his hands to give them; and not to cut them off and send them to hell as you teach and practise, which is contrary to God, who is patient towards mockers, which *walk after their lusts.* Because he would have *no man to perish, but would that all* men whatsoever *should come to repentance.* But you, contrary to him, use all the means you can to cut men off that they might perish, in that you seek to destroy their bodies whilst they remain in their errors. 2 Peter iii. 3. [Verse 9.]

A. I confess that God commandeth that the good and bad must grow together unto the end of the world, but that is in the church. Matt. xiii. [30.]

C. Well, if that be the true exposition, I pray you why do you then excommunicate any out of your church, contrary to your own acknowledgment? And here let all men take notice, that by this exposition you overthrow your own excommunication quite, and accuse Christ for giving a rule, and the apostle Paul, and the church of Corinth, for practising that rule, in casting out of the church. For you say all must grow together to the end in the church; but the exposition of the Law-giver himself is against you, that *the field is the world.* Yet in that you confess that the wicked and the godly must be let alone in the church unto the end, much more in the world unto the end. For, if the wicked pollute not the church, sure it is they pollute not the world. This then you are commanded unto: *Nay, gather them not, let them grow together unto the end of the world.* Matt. xviii. [17.] 1 Cor. v. [5.] Verse 38. Verse 29, 30.

A. Let them come to church, and they shall grow together unto the end.

C. Indeed I think so. Hereby you manifest you regard not how wicked and ungodly men be; so they come to your church, you will not destroy them, though they remain in their abominable lusts; but if they will not come to your church, let them be wheat or tares, you will gather them, and, as much as in you is, send them to burning.   Herein all men may see, as I said before, that you seek your own glory and obedience, and not God's, and so exalt yourselves above God.

2 Thess. ii.
[4.]

I. Well, I bless God, I see this as clearly as the sun shining in his brightness, that it is to fight against God to compel any, contrary to their consciences, to perform any service unto him, in that there are so many places of scripture commanding the contrary.

C. The whole New Testament throughout, in all the doctrines and practices of Christ and his disciples, teach no such thing as compelling men by persecutions and afflictions to obey the gospel, but the direct contrary, viz. to suffer at the hands of the wicked; when they were persecuted for righteousness' sake, to suffer it; when the unbelievers and wicked curse them, to bless, and pray for their repentance, and that God would forgive them, and never lay these sins to their charge, as our Saviour, Stephen, and the rest did.   And for a conclusion of this point, that your faith may be full herein, consider that we are to wait for the Jews' conversion, and not to destroy them.

[1 Pet. iii. 14.]
[Matt. v. 44.]
Luke xxiii. 34.
Act. vii. 60.

I. It is true, that might give all men satisfaction in these things.

C. Oh yes, if men had any regard of God or his word, they would never deal more in this thing; the Lord, we see, hath promised, that when the fulness of the Gentiles is come in, the Jews shall be converted.   Now if the Jews, who are such fearful blasphemers of Christ and his gospel, that contemn him and his testament with all despite, if their conversion must be waited for, and that they may not be destroyed from the face of the earth; then who may not see (if they shut not their eyes) that the conver-

Rom. xi. [25, 26.]

sion of all is to be waited for? and, that no man for blaspheming Christ and his gospel may be destroyed, or afflicted
by imprisonments, death, or any calamity whatsoever.

I. It is not be gainsaid with any show of truth. I would
God the king's majesty would consider of this point, seeing
that the cruel bishops, by using his power, commit such
sin against God in this thing, both in persecuting them
that cannot of faith yield, and also in forcing them that do
yield contrary to their consciences, to sin against God, and
to perish, if they repent not.

C. I am persuaded that if his highness did but once
well weigh and consider it, he would never suffer such
high iniquity to be committed against God, contrary to
his express commandment, and all to be done by the king's
power, for nothing have they else to bear them out. The
Lord persuade the hearts of his majesty and his posterity
unto it, seeing his throne is established by him, that he
and his posterity may sit and reign over these nations and
kingdoms, till Jesus Christ, the commander of these things,
come in his glory to recompense every man according to
his works, without respect of persons.

A. If wicked malefactors should be let alone to the end
of the world, then where is the magistrate's sword? It is
of no force if evil men may not be cut off.

C. I acknowledge unfeignedly, that God hath given to
magistrates a sword to cut off wicked men, and to reward
the well-doers. But this ministry is a worldly ministry, Rom. xiii.
their sword is a worldly sword, their punishments can extend [3, 4.]
no further than the outward man, they can but *kill the body*. Luke xii. 4.
And therefore this ministry and sword is appointed only
to punish the breach of worldly ordinances, which is all
that God hath given to any mortal man to punish. The
king may make laws for the safety and good of his person,
state, and subjects, against the which, whosoever is dis-

PERSECUTION, &c.] I

loyal, or disobedient, he may dispose of at his pleasure. The Lord hath given him this sword and authority, foreseeing in his eternal wisdom, that if this his ordinance of magistracy were not, there would be no living for men in the world, and especially for the godly; and therefore the godly have particular cause to glorify God for this his blessed ordinance of magistracy, and to regard it with all reverence.

But now, the breach of Christ's laws, of the which we all this while speak, which is the thing only I stand upon; his kingdom is spiritual, his laws spiritual, the transgressions spiritual, the punishment spiritual, everlasting death of soul, his sword spiritual, no carnal or worldly weapon is given to the supportation of his kingdom. The Law-giver himself hath commanded that the transgressors of these [Matt. xiii. laws should be *let alone until the harvest,* because he knows, 30.] they that are now tares may hereafter come to repentance, and become wheat; they that are now blasphemers, per- [1 Tim.i.13.] secutors, and oppressors, as Paul was, may, by the power of God's word, become faithful, and a faithful witness, as he was: they that are now fornicators, &c., as some of the 1 Cor. vi. 9. Corinthians once were, may hereafter become washed, cleansed, and sanctified, as they were: they that are now Pet. ii. 10. no people, nor under mercy, as the saints sometimes were, may hereafter become the people of God, and obtain mercy, as they did. All come not at the first hour, some come not till the eleventh hour; if those that come not till the last hour should be destroyed, because they came not at the first hour, then should they never come, but be prevented.

Lev. xxiv. *A.* Were not blasphemers put to death in time of the law? 11, &c.

C. Yes, an Israelite blaspheming the Lord, or doing Num. xv. 30. any thing presumptuously, which was blasphemy, no sacrifice [was] to be offered for him. But would you from hence have the king's majesty put all his subjects to death that contemn the truth of Christ? If yea, see what will follow: all papists ought to be put to death, who are direct blasphemers; when the vial of God's wrath was poured Rev. xvi. 10, upon the throne of the beast, which all England confess is meant the popish power, they *blasphemed the God of heaven*, &c. All the Jews that speak many things blasphemously against Christ, ought to be put to death. Yea, of what profession soever he be, doing any thing presumptuously against Christ, ought to be put to death by your affirmation; no sacrifice to be offered, no repentance to be admitted, die he must under two or three witnesses. But that this is most false, Christ and his apostles in his testament do manifestly declare, as is before shown. Was not Paul, a blasphemer, yet received to mercy? But this the Holy Ghost teacheth from blasphemy under the law. *He* Heb. x. 28. *that despiseth Moses' law, dieth without mercy, under two or three witnesses. Of how much sorer punishment suppose ye, shall he be worthy, that treadeth under foot the Son of God, and counteth the blood of the testament as an unholy thing, wherewith he was sanctified, and doth despite to the Spirit of grace?* Speaking of such as had received and acknowledged the truth. Ver. 26.

This is now the due proportion: an Israelite according to the flesh, in the time of the law, presumptuously sinning against God's commandment, by his command must die by the worldly sword, no sacrifice to be offered for him. So in the new testament, or time of the gospel, a spiritual Israelite according to the faith, contemptuously or despitefully sinning against Christ's commands [which][7] he hath formerly acknowledged, despiting and contemning them, by his command must die by the spiritual sword, no repentance to be admitted, seeing *he crucifieth again to* Heb. vi. 6. *himself the Son of God, and makes a mock of him.* David

[7] [Edit. 1662.]

and Peter came not within this compass; though they sinned of knowledge, yet they did it not contemptuously nor despitefully, but through frailty. If an Israelite under the law did aught through ignorance, or through frailty, there was sacrifice for him : so under the gospel, an Israelite doing aught through ignorance, or through frailty, as Peter and Barnabas, with the rest of the Jews, mentioned Gal. ii. [13,] or the incestuous person, 1 Cor. v. [1,] there is repentance for him.

As Num. xv. [24.]

As Lev. vi. [2.]

This is it that confounds all true religion. That because it was so in the time of the law, therefore it may be so in the time of the gospel, by which reason men might set up as truly the whole law, as some part, and utterly abolish Christ. I pray you seriously consider what is here said.

A. Hath not the king the same power that the kings of Israel had, who compelled men to the observation of the law of God?

C. First, I answer you, that the kings of Israel had never power from God to set up any thing in, or for the service of God, but that only which was commanded by God, no, not so much as the manner of any law; and therefore this will not serve your purpose, that kings may set up within their dominions such spiritual lords and laws for the serving of God; no, nor the manner thereof, as may best please themselves, under what pretence soever, thereby making God for his worship subject to their pleasures. And his majesty acknowledgeth, that Christ's church after the establishing of it by miracles in the primitive time, was ever after to be governed "within the limits of his revealed will."—Speech at parliament, anno 1609.[8]

Deut. iv. 1, 2, xii. 32.

Num. xv. 16, and ix. 14.

[8] [Works, p. 531. "God, during the time of the old testament, spake by oracles, and wrought by miracles, yet how soon it pleased him to settle a church which was bought and redeemed by the blood of his only Son Christ, then was there a cessation of both ; he ever after governing his peo-

Secondly, the kings of Israel might compel men to the sacrifices and ordinances of the old testament, all which were carnal, and purged not the conscience, as circum- Heb. ix. 9, 10. cision, the passover, &c. But no mortal man, whatsoever he be, can compel any man to offer the sacrifices of the new testament, which are spiritual, and purge the conscience, except he can beget faith in him, and convert his soul. The ordinances of the old testament were to be performed by the posterity of Abraham according to the flesh, that thereby they might be taught Christ; but the ordinances of the new testament are to be performed only by the posterity of Abraham according to the faith, that have learned Christ, and have put on Christ, and so having [Gal. iii. 7, 29.] him, all things else appertaineth to them. But one thing I demand of you, Who now is king of Israel?

A. I confess Christ is king of Israel.

C. Yes, Christ alone is king of Israel, that sits upon David's throne, and therefore mark the true proportion: in the time of the old testament, the kings of Israel had power from God to compel all to the ordinances of God, or to cut them off by their sword from the earthly land of Canaan, and the promises thereof; so in the new testament, the king of Israel, Christ Jesus, hath power from the Father to compel all to the ordinances of God, or to cut them off by the sword from the heavenly land of Canaan, and the promises thereof. The kings of Israel only had this power under the law, and the king of Israel only hath this power under the gospel. And therefore, whosoever will challenge this power under the gospel, he must be the king of Israel in the time of the gospel, which is particular [9] only to Jesus Christ, unto whom all power in heaven and earth is given.

ple and church within the limits of his revealed will."]   [2] [peculiar, 1669.]

And let it be here well observed, that by this opinion of yours, you make the kingdom and ordinances of Israel under the law, and the kingdom and ordinances of Israel under the gospel, all one, directly contrary to the whole scripture; for the kingdom and ordinances of Israel under the law were of this world, but the kingdom and ordinances of Israel under the gospel are not of this world, as Christ the king thereof himself testifieth, John xviii. [36.] And therefore, you, setting up a worldly king over this heavenly kingdom and ordinances, you and all of your profession, declare yourselves to be of that worldly kingdom, and so to look for that heavenly and spiritual king, yet to come in the flesh, being of the number of those that deny him to be come in the flesh, and so are deceivers and antichrists, whatsoever you say to the contrary.

A. Well, yet I cannot see, but that as the kings of Israel hath power from God to compel all their subjects to the worship then appointed, so the king, being a Christian king, hath power to compel his subjects to the worship now appointed.

C. You may see, if you shut not your eyes, that what power the kings of Israel had under the law in matters of religion, Christ Jesus, the king of Israel, hath under the gospel. But I pray you let me ask you this question; you say, the king's majesty hath this power as he is a Christian king; my question is, whether it appertain unto him as he is a king, or as he is a Christian?

A. Neither simply as he is a king, nor as he is a Christian, but jointly as he is complete in them both; for I grant that no heathen king hath power to compel in matters of religion, but a Christian king hath.

C. Then you confess, that if a Christian king may be deprived of his Christianity, for of his kingdom or kingly power, or any part thereof, I affirm he may not be deprived, he hath lost this power you plead for, in compelling men in matters of religion. What say you to this?

A. I confess, if he may be deprived of his Christianity, he hath not this power I plead for.

C. Then I demand this question, Whether every Christian, without respect of persons, ought not to be subject to Christ's laws for his salvation?

A. Yes, it cannot be denied.

C. Christ hath given his censure, excommunication, for the salvation of every Christian, that *he that will not hear* the church *is to be as a heathen and a publican;* that is, hath lost all right and title in Christ and in his church, till he repent. Now I know it cannot be denied but every Christian whatsover is subject to sin, and so to excommunication, to be as a heathen, &c. If you say that kings either are not subject to sin, and to impenitency therein, and so [not]¹ to this censure of Christ, of excommunication for their impenitent sin, then consider what you make them, and God you make a liar. [Or] if you grant, as you cannot deny, that kings as well as others, are subject to impenitent sin, and so to excommunication for the same; then, they being deprived of their Christianity, by your own confession they are deprived of power to compel in matters of religion, the which, if it were any part of their kingly power, they might be deprived of a part of their kingly power by being excommunicate. Consider what a wicked doctrine you teach herein.

A. Doth not the prophet say, that *kings shall be nursing fathers, and queens nursing mothers* to the church? And also it is said, that kings *shall hate the whore, make her desolate, eat her flesh, and burn her with fire.* Where we see, that kings that have power and authority, shall destroy

Matt. xviii. 17.

[Is. xlix 23.]

[Rev. xvii. 16.]

---

¹ [Edit. 1662.]

antichrist's kingdom, and nourish and cherish Christ's kingdom.

C. Most true it is: the Lord hath spoken it, and there-fore it ought to be a great comfort to God's people. But what is this to the purpose in hand, namely, that kings may persecute the contrary-minded. The words of the prophet Isaiah prove, that kings and queens that have formerly persecuted and destroyed the church, their hearts shall be turned, by the power of God's word, to be lovers and preservers of the church. And the other place proves, Rev. xvii.16. that kings shall make that whore desolate, &c., not by their temporal authority or sword—as some say, that make more show of religion than you do, although themselves be now persecuted, yet, if kings were of their minds, would 2 Thess. ii. 8. be as cruel as you, for they maintain the same thing—*but by the spirit of the Lord's mouth, and the brightness of his* Dan. viii. 25. *coming.* For this kingdom of antichrist shall be destroyed without hand, only by the everlasting gospel, the true armour indeed wherewith the witnesses fight against the antichrist: as the king's majesty acknowledgeth.[2]

A. You are so stiff against using of outward weapons in church matters. Did not our Saviour make a whip of

---

[2] Apology. [Works, pp. 316, 317. " By these two witnesses should (pro-bably) be meant the old and new testament: for as the antichrist can-not choose but be an adversary to the word of God above all things; so will he omit no endeavour to disgrace, corrupt, suppress, and destroy the same.

" And yet, praised be God, we be-gin now with our eyes, as our prede-cessors have done in some ages before, to see these *witnesses* rise again, and shine in their former glory : God, as it were, *setting them up again upon*

their feet, and *raising them to the heavens* in a triumphal cloud of glory, like *Elias* his fiery chariot. Which exalting of the gospel again, hath bred such *an earthquake* and alteration amongst many nations; as *a tenth part,* or a good portion of these that were in subjection to *that great city,* to wit, *Babylon,* are fallen from her ; *seven thousand,* that is, many thousands, *having been killed* upon the occasion of that great alter-ation; and many other converted to the fear of God, *and giving glory to the God of heaven.*"]

small cords, and whip the buyers and sellers out of the [John ii. 15.]
temple? And why may not we follow his example?

C. In this and many other actions of Christ our Saviour,
we are to consider him as the fulfiller and ender of the
law; as in the action of the passover, and sending him [Luke v. 14.]
that was cleansed of his leprosy to offer to the priest the
gift that Moses commanded: in which things we are not
to imitate him; for by him the ceremonies are fulfilled
and abolished, and the everlasting gospel established, in
the which we are to walk: and it were more than foolish
to reason thus: Christ whipped wicked men out of God's
temple made with hands, with whips made of cord, therefore we may whip wicked men out of God's temple made
without hands, with whips made of cord. There is a
wholesome doctrine to be collected from the type to the
truth, as thus: Christ drove out wicked men out of the
temple made with hands, by a carnal or worldly whip; so
Christ, by his people, must drive wicked men out of the
temple made without hands, by a spiritual whip, even his
word, which is called a whip or rod, Rev. ii. 27, and Ps.
ii. 9. So is excommunication, 1 Cor. iv. 21.

A. If freedom of religion should be granted, there would
be such divisions as would breed sedition and innovation in
the state.

C. Thus when your shows out of the scripture are
answered, then you run to conceits, and imaginations of
sedition, innovation, and the like, thinking thereby to dis-
suade princes and all that are in authority therefrom,
knowing else your kingdom of iniquity would fall. But
that it may appear to all that you deal deceitfully herein,
let us consider, first, the scriptures; secondly, behold the
success of suffering of religion free in other countries.
And first, Christ our Saviour, who is that *Prince of peace*, Is. ix. 6.
not of sedition, hath taught that he *came not to send peace* Matt. x. [34, —36.] Luke xii. [51, 53.]

*on the earth, but debate ; to divide five in one house, two
against three, and three against two ; the father against the
son, &c.   And a man's enemies shall be they of his own household.*   And his desire is that the fire of such sedition
should be kindled.   Where we see, this Prince of peace
putteth difference in religion by preaching his gospel,
which some receive as the savour of life unto them; others
refuse it, and so become enemies unto the truth, and witnesses thereof, as they did to Christ Jesus himself and his
disciples, and as you do to me and others.   Secondly, behold the nations where freedom of religion is permitted,
and you may see there are not more flourishing and prosperous nations under the heavens than they are.

1. The convocation of bishops, and the rest, have made
a canon, that whosoever shall affirm that the king's majesty
hath not the same power in causes ecclesiastical under the
gospel that the godly kings of Israel had under the law,
let him be excommunicate, *ipso facto*.[3]

[3] [In 1532 the bishops and clergy
assembled in convocation, formally
" obliged themselves, neither to make
nor execute any canons or constitutions ecclesiastical, but as they
were thereto enabled by the king's
authority." Various attempts were
made by archbishops Cranmer, Parker, and Whitgift, to enact a body of
ecclesiastical laws obligatory on both
the clergy and laity. In the convocation of 1603—4, by the king's
licence, a book of canons was at last
compiled, from the " queen's articles,
orders of her commissioners, adver-
tisements, canons of 1571 and 1597,"
which with many others added at the
same time are the " Constitutions and
Canons Ecclesiastical," by which the
church of England is professedly governed. The number is one hundred
and forty one, of which the canon
referred to in the text is the second.
Although sanctioned by king James,
yet not having been confirmed by
parliament, the laity are not bound
by them, " except where they are explanatory of the ancient canon law."
Touching their damnatory and persecuting character, it *is* " said amiss
of such ecclesiastical canons," by the
learned Hooker, " That by 'instinct
of the Holy Ghost they have been
made, and consecrated by the reverend acceptation of all the world.' "
Godolphin's Abridgment, p. 584.
Fuller's Church History, iii. 203, ed.
1843. Price's Hist. of Nonconformity, i. 475. Conder's View of all
Religions, p. 355. Hanbury's Hooker,
i. 231.]

C. Yes; they have so. In the beginning of his majesty's reign, when they had got him sure unto them—of the which they so much doubted, as with my own ears I heard some of their chief followers say, when his highness was coming into England:[4] "Now must steeples down, and we shall have no more high commission!" (with lamentation they spake it)—then they made this canon; because their consciences are convinced that they stand only by his power; and if his hand be turned, their spiritual power of darkness falleth to the pit of darkness, from whence it

---

[4] [It was with language like the following that James had raised the hopes of the Puritans, and depressed those of the prelates. In the eighth session of the General Assembly of 1590, "to please the Assembly, he praised God that he was born in such a time, as in the time of the light of the gospel; to such a place, as to be king of such a kirk, the sincerest kirk of the world. The kirk of Geneva," said he, "keeped Pasch and Yule, what have they for them? They have no institution. As for our neighbour kirk in England, their service is an evil said mass in English, they want nothing of the mass, but the liftings." (Calderwood, Hist. of Ch. of Scotland, p. 256.) "And now it was strange with what assiduity and diligence the two potent parties, ,the defenders of episcopacy and presbytery, with equal hopes of success, made, beside private and particular addresses, public and visible applications to king James,—the first to continue, the latter to restore, or rather set up their government; so that whilst each side was jealous his rival should get the start by early stirring, and rise first in the king's favour, such was their vigilance, that neither may seem to go to bed, incessantly diligent both before and since ₘthe queen's death, in despatching posts and messages into Scotland to advance their several designs. . . . . . . Dr. Thomas Nevill . . . being solemnly employed by Archbishop Whitgift . . . brought back a welcome answer, to such as sent him, of his highness's purpose, which was to uphold and maintain the government of the late queen, as she left it settled." (Fuller, Ch. Hist. iii. p. 168, 169.) James thus speaks of his reception by these anxious and conflicting parties, in his first speech to the parliament :—" Shall I ever, nay, can I ever be able, or rather so unable in memory, as to forget your unexpected readiness and alacrity, your ever memorable resolutions, and your most wonderful conjunction and harmony of your hearts in declaring and embracing me as your undoubted and lawful king and governor? Or shall it be ever blotted out of my mind, how at my first entry into this kingdom, the people of all sorts rid and ran, nay rather flew to meet me? their eyes flaming nothing but sparkles of affection, their mouths and tongues

came, and whither it must go, there being[5] never so much
Rev. xviii. means used for the supporting of it; for the strong Lord
hath spoken it. As for their sending men to hell, as they
suppose, with their *ipso facto* excommunications; if they
had no stronger weapons for the supporting of their kingdom, it would stand but a short space. If Israel now
were of this world, as it was under the law, then they said
John xvii. something; but if it be not of this world, as it is not, then
14.
the king[6] is not of this world; for when this king came,
the worldly Israel knew him not.

I. I see evidently, that all are but cavils, and that no
mortal man can make any man offer sacrifices under the
new testament, until he be a believer and converted; for
he must be in Christ before he may offer sacrifices; for in
Christ only the Father accepteth us. But what say you?
Have they not power to compel men to come to the place
where the word is publicly taught, that they may be converted?

C. Well then, you see that the example of the kings of
Israel, who had power to compel them to sacrifice, or to
cut them off, applied to earthly princes, is gone, as a mere
doctrine of man, and not of God. And for compelling
men to hear, that they [may] be converted; we can learn
of no better than of him whom if we hear not we shall
have a dreadful recompence. He had all power in heaven
and in earth for converting souls given unto him, and sent
John xx. 21. his disciples, as his Father sent him, charging them that
when they should come into a city, &c., if they would not
receive them nor their word, *to shake off the dust of their*
[Mark vi. *feet for a witness against them,* saying, *it should be easier for*
11.]

uttering nothing but sounds of joy,   earnestness to meet and embrace their
their hands, feet, and all the rest of   new sovereign." (Works, p. 486.)
their members, in their gestures dis-   [5] [though there be; 1662.]
covering a passionate longing, and   [6] [king of Israel; 1662.]

Sodom and Gomorrah in the day of judgment than for that city or house. And so the apostles went from city to city accordingly. Here were no temples made,[7] nor worldly power to compel all to come unto them to hear the word of the Lord, but they [were] commanded to go from city to city, and from house to house.

I. In those days the magistrates were unbelievers, but the question is where magistrates be believers.

C. Christ had all power needful for that work: if magistracy were a power needful for that work, then Christ had not all power. Magistracy is God's blessed ordinance in its right place; but let us not be wiser than God to devise him a means for the publishing of his gospel, which he that had all power had not, nor hath commanded. Magistracy is a power of this world: the kingdom, power, subjects, and means of publishing the gospel, are not of this world.

A A goodly thing, indeed, that men must go about the country to preach.

C. In your estimation it is base and contemptible, your pomp and pride will not bear this; it is more easy for you to hunt after promotion till you come to the highest, in getting to be chief bishop of bishops within these dominions, and then cometh your fall, full low, if you repent not. But the wisdom of God hath appointed the chiefest officers of Christ's kingdom, even the apostles, thus basely to go up and down, to and fro, to preach his gospel; yea, that worthy apostle, Paul, preached this gospel *night and day, with many tears, openly and through-* Acts xx. [20, *out every house.* 31.]

I. But if this be thus, as for my own part I am fully persuaded it is, then I see the high commission

---

[7] [made with hands; 1662.]

cannot stand; for, as I take it, it is only for causes ecclesiastical.[8]

C. So far as it is over church matters it is most unlawful: for the commission for judging and punishing of the transgressors of the laws of Christ's church is given to Christ the monarch thereof, a part whereof he hath left to his disciples, which is no worldly commission or power, but only the power of the Lord Jesus, the uttermost of which commission is excommunication.

1 Cor. v. [5]

A. The high commission is from the king; and dare you once call it into question?

C. If I do take any authority from the king's majesty, let me be judged worthy my desert; but if I defend the authority of Christ Jesus over men's souls, which appertaineth to no mortal man whatsoever, then know you, that whosoever would rob him of that honour which is not of this world, he will tread them under foot. Earthly authority belongeth to earthly kings; but spiritual authority belongeth to that one spiritual King who is KING OF KINGS.

A. Well, all your pleading will not serve your turn, either you must come to church, or else go to prison.

---

[8] [The High Commission Court was established by letters patent, under the powers granted to queen Elizabeth in the "Act restoring to the crown the ancient jurisdiction of the state ecclesiastical and spiritual;" and the first warrant for the same was issued the 19th July, 1559. To the queen, her heirs and successors, was given the power to "visit, reform, repress, order, correct, and amend, all such errors, heresies, schisms, abuses, offences, contempts, and enormities whatsoever, which by any manner of spiritual or ecclesiastical power can ... be reformed ... or amended to the pleasure of Almighty God." In that sacred name she accordingly proceeds to authorize her commissioners to inquire, by all the means they can devise, after heretical opinions, books, seditious books, contempts, conspiracies, false rumours, tales, seditious misbehaviours, slanderous words." All other crimes contrary to law, are included in this sweeping commission, and especially must the commissioners seek for all who "obstinately absent themselves from church." Offenders are to be fined, imprisoned, or other-

C. I have showed you by the law of Christ that your course is most wicked, to compel any by persecution to perform any service to God, as you pretend. Now I desire also to show you, that the statute law of the land requireth only civil obedience, and his majesty's writings, maintaining the oath of allegiance, testifieth the same.

The law of the land requireth, that whosoever cometh not to church, or receiveth not the sacraments, the oath of allegiance is to be tendered to them, which, that it may be manifest to all, that not only I, but all that profess the faith with me, are most willing to subscribe unto it in faithfulness and truth, I have thought good to express it.

The words of the Oath. Anno 3. Jacobi Regis.

" I, *A. B.*, do truly and sincerely acknowledge, profess, and testify, and declare in my conscience before God and the world, that our sovereign lord King James is lawful king of this realm, and of all other his majesty's dominions and countries; and that the pope, neither of himself, nor by any other authority of the church or see of Rome, or by any other means with any other, hath any power or authority to depose the king, or to dispose of any his

---

wise punished at the discretion of their judges. Suspected persons, as well as all others, are to be examined "upon their corporal oath for the better trial and opening of the premises." (Godolphin's Abridg. p. 11. Doc. Annals. i. 223.) Thus " they entangled their prisoners with oaths *ex officio,* and the inextricable mazes of the popish canon law. . . . . These commissioners sported themselves in all the wanton acts of tyranny and oppression, till their very name became odious to the whole nation." (Neal. i. 90.) Even " children were on their oaths interrogated against their own fathers . . . . . and although these accusations were not capital, yet because their parents' credit was so deeply concerned therein, such proceedings had a strong tang of tyranny." (Fuller, iii. 90.) These powers were most oppressively exercised by a succession of commissioners, until their arbitrary and cruel proceedings under Laud, roused the ire of the parliament of 1641, by which this court, with its fellow the Star Chamber, was for ever destroyed.]

majesty's kingdoms or dominions, or to authorize any
foreign prince to invade or annoy him or his countries, or
to discharge any of his subjects of their allegiance and
obedience to his majesty; or to give licence or leave to any
of them to bear arms, raise tumults, or to offer any violence or hurt to his majesty's royal person, state, or
government, or any of his majesty's subjects within his
majesty's dominions. Also I do swear from my heart,
that notwithstanding any declaration or sentence of excommunication, or deprivation made or granted, or to be
made or granted by the pope or his successors, or by any
authority derived, or pretended to be derived from him or
his see, against the said king, his heirs or successors, or
any absolution of the said subjects from their obedience, I
will bear faith and true allegiance to his majesty, his heirs
and successors, and him and them will defend to the uttermost of my power against all conspiracies and attempts
whatsoever which shall be made against his or their persons, their crown and dignity, by reason or colour of any
such sentence or declaration or otherwise, and will do my
best endeavour to disclose and make known unto his
majesty, his heirs and successors, all treasons and traitorous
conspiracies, which I shall know or hear of, to be against
him or any of them. And I do further swear, that I do
from my heart abhor, detest, and abjure, as impious and
heretical, this damnable doctrine and position, that princes
which be excommunicated or deprived by the pope, may
be deposed or murdered by their subjects, or any other
whatsoever. And I do believe, and in conscience am resolved, that neither the pope, nor any person whatsoever,
hath power to absolve me of this oath, or any part thereof,
which I acknowledge by good and full authority to be
lawfully ministered to me, and do renounce all pardons and
dispensations to the contrary. And all these things I do

plainly and sincerely acknowledge and swear, according to
these express words by me spoken, and according to the
plain and common sense and understanding of the same
words, without any equivocation, or mental evasion, or
secret reservation whatsoever. And I do make this recognition and acknowledgment heartily, willingly, and truly,
upon the true faith of a Christian. So help me, God."

A. This oath was intended for the papists, and not
for you.[9]

C. It is not so: for his majesty at the last session of
parliament, anno 1609, saith thus: "Some doubts have
been conceived anent the using of the oath of allegiance;
and that part of the act which ordains the taking thereof is
thought so obscure, that no man can tell who ought to be
pressed therewith.[1] And therefore if there be any scruple

---

[9] [The statute in question is entitled,
"An Act for the better discovering
and repressing of Popish Recusants."
It enacts that every recusant who had
conformed, or should in future conform, should "repair to the church
and continue there during the time of
divine service," under a penalty of
twenty pounds for the first, forty for
the second, and sixty for every subsequent omission ; and "receive the
blessed sacrament of the Lord's supper," at the least once in every year.
It then imposes the oath given above,
and subjects those refusing to take it,
if a female, to imprisonment, and all
other individuals of the age of eighteen
years to the penalties of premunire.
It continues the weekly fine of twelve
pence, imposed by an act of Elizabeth,
for absence from church on Sundays;
and concludes by declaring every
housekeeper, of whatever religion, receiving a visitor or keeping a servant,
who should not repair to some church
or chapel to hear divine service,
should be liable to a penalty of ten
pounds for every month they should
continue to harbour or keep such
stranger or servant. (Tierney's Dodd's
Church History, iv. 67, and App. No.
20.) The king's professions of liberality and horror of persecution, were
strangely in contrast with the oppressive measures which followed in the
train of this intolerant enactment ;
and which in its operation was made
to include all other persons, besides
papists, who hesitated to worship at
the altars of the established church.
Indeed in many cases, "especially of
great men's wives, and their kin and
followers," the catholics were connived
at, while the whole weight of royal
and episcopal authority fell without
mercy upon the puritans. (King
James's Works, pp. 144, 252, 545.)]

[1] ["For I myself, when upon a

touching the ministering thereof, I would wish it now to
be cleared." [2]   And thereupon this statute was made, anno
7, regni regis Jacobi, &c. chap. 6, towards the latter end.

" And if any person or persons whatsoever, of and above
the age of eighteen years, do now stand, or at any time
hereafter shall stand, and be presented, indicted, and convicted, for not coming to church, or receiving the Lord's
supper, according to the laws and statutes of this realm,
before the ordinary, or any other having power to take
such presentments or indictments; or if the minister, petty
constable, or churchwardens, or any two of them, shall at
any time hereafter complain to any justice of peace near
adjoining to the place where any person complained of
shall dwell, and the said justice shall find cause of suspicion; that then any one justice of peace, within whose
commission or power any such person or persons shall at
any time hereafter be, or to whom complaint shall be
made, shall upon notice thereof require such person or
persons to take the said oath.   And that if any person or
persons being of the age of eighteen years or above, shall
refuse to take the said oath, duly tendered unto him or
her, according to the true intent and meaning of this
statute, that then the persons authorized by this law to
give the said oath, shall and may commit the said offender
to the common gaol, &c." [3]

time I called the judges before me at
their going to their circuits, I moved
this question unto them; wherein, as
I thought, they could not resolutely
answer me."]

[2] [Works. Speech at Whitehall,
p. 544.]

[3] [The assassination of Henry IV. of
France, by Ravilliac, at the instigation of the Jesuits, was the occasion
of enacting this statute. It was preceded by a proclamation "strictly
commanding all Jesuits and Roman
catholic priests to depart this kingdom." And all recusants were forbidden to come within ten miles of
the court. Collier, vii. 356, ed. 1840.
Browning's Hist. of the Huguenots,
p. 206.]

Where we see, that if any take the said oath at their first apprehension, they are not to be committed, or if they, being committed, take the said oath at the next open court, they are to be set at liberty; if they will not take the said oath, to be in *premunire,* as is at large in the statute declared, and as is daily practised with papists and others.

A. The king's majesty requireth your allegiance to be testified by your coming to church.

C. I pray let me demand this question: Doth the king require my coming to church to worship and serve God, or to worship and serve the king? If to worship and serve the king, I am ready to obey: if to worship and serve God, which none can do but of conscience, the king himself saith he never intended to lay any thing to the charge of any for the cause of conscience; and this coming to church being a cause of conscience, if not he, why do you lay any thing to my charge for the same? And therefore you wrong his majesty in thus affirming; for his highness requireth only my faithful allegiance to be testified by the aforesaid oath, and therefore hath ordained it, as I shall show by his highness's own testimony.

If I should come to church, and not of conscience, but for other respects, as many papists and other hypocrites do, to God it were most abominable; and what faithfulness can be hoped for in such towards his majesty's person and state? Can any godly, wise man think that he that playeth the dissembling hypocrite with God, that he will do less with men, and will not work any villany, if it were in his power? And therefore herein you compelling me by tyranny, to bring my body whereunto my spirit cannot be brought, you compel me to hypocrisy with God and man: for if my heart were not faithful in sincerity to his majesty's crown and dignity, as I take God to witness

K 2

(before whom I must be condemned or justified) it is, these courses would rather harden my heart to work villany than otherwise.

Now for his majesty's many testimonies in his writings, they are worthy to be recorded with thankfulness to the Highest for guiding his heart and pen to write such things.

In his Apology for the Oath of Allegiance,[4] he saith, speaking of such papists as took the oath of allegiance, " And I gave a good proof that I intended no persecution against them for conscience' cause, but only desired to be secured of them for civil obedience, which for conscience' cause they were bound to perform." And, speaking of Blackwell, the archpriest, he saith,[5] " It was never my intention to lay any thing to the said archpriest's charge, as I have never done to any, for cause of conscience." And, page 336, he saith, " First, [as] for the cause of their punishment, I do constantly maintain that which I [have] said in my Apology, that no man, either in my time, or in the late queen's, ever died here for his conscience : for, let him be never so devout a papist, nay, though he profess the same never so constantly, his life is in no danger by the law, if he break not out into some outward act expressly against the words of the law ; or plot not some unlawful or dangerous practice or attempt," &c. Where we may see in short what is the whole sum that he requireth.

And in his majesty's speech at the last session of parliament, anno Domini, 1609, where he saith he showeth his subjects his heart,[6] he saith thus : " I never found, that

---

[4] [Works, p. 248.]

[5] [Works, p. 268.]

[6] [" As ye made me a fair present indeed in presenting your thanks and loving duties unto me : so have I now called you here, to recompense you again with a great and rare present, which is a fair and crystal mirror. Not such a mirror wherein you may see your own faces, or shadows;

blood and too much severity did good in matters of religion: for, besides [that] it is a sure rule in divinity, that God never loves to plant his church by violence and bloodshed, natural reason may even persuade us, and daily experience proves it true, that when men are severely persecuted for religion, the gallantness of many men's spirits, and the wilfulness of their humours, rather than the justness of their cause, make them to take a pride boldly to endure any torments, or death itself, to gain thereby the reputation of martyrdom, though but in a false shadow."[7]

A most undoubted truth; which if it be (as most manifest it is by the testimony of the Holy Ghost throughout Christ's testament, as before is proved), then how cursed are all the rank of you that continually break this sure rule of God, thus confidently acknowledged by his majesty, planting your church by violence and bloodshed, forcing many thousands against their consciences to be of your church, and to receive your sacraments, by all the persecutions that would follow if they did not yield; and those that fear God more than men, and dare not yield, casting them into noisome prisons, amongst most wicked blasphemers of God, to the wounding of their souls, dividing them from their wives, children, and families, and' from their callings, some a hundred miles and more, utterly consuming that substance they have, which sustaineth the blood of them, their wives and children; seldom or never affording them release, but either by yielding to you against their consciences, or else by consuming their bodies to death in prison, banishment, or the like, leaving them and their wives to horrible temptations of adultery, in

but such a mirror or crystal, as through the transparencies thereof, you may see the heart of your king. . . . . As it is a true axiom in divinity, that *cor*

regis is *in manu Domini,* so will I now set *cor regis in oculis populi.*" Works, pp. 527, 528.]

[7] [Ibid. p. 544.]

parting them and their wives, and to all manner of evil, in taking them from their callings, and so leaving them in continual idleness. Is God's church thus planted? or, do Christ's disciples thus plant?

I. Oh, I see this spiritual power is little inferior in cruelty to the Romish spiritual power: I pray how, or when was this set up?

C. Henry the eighth casting off pope Clement the seventh, and so the pope's power, anno 1534, set up this spiritual power under him.[8]

I. I pray you show the likeness between these two spiritual powers.

C. I will do my best endeavour, which is but small. First, the Romish spiritual power doth make laws to the conscience, and compel all thereunto by excommunication, imprisonment, banishment, death, and the like.   This

---

[8] See Acts and Monuments. [In the parliament assembled in the month of March, it was "most graciously, and by the blessed will of God, enacted, that the pope, and all his college of cardinals, with his pardons and indulgencies, which so long had clogged this realm of England, to the miserable slaughter of so many good men, and which never could be removed away before, was now abolished, eradicate, and exploded out of this land, and sent home again to their own country of Rome, from whence they came. God be everlastingly praised therefore. Amen." The separation from Rome was completed, and the new order of things definitively settled in the following session, by "An act concerning the king's highness to be the supreme head of the church of England." It says, "Albeit the king's majesty justly and rightfully is and ought to be the supreme head of the church of England, and so is recognized by the clergy of this realm in their convocation;" and then proceeds to enact, "that the king our sovereign lord, his heirs and successors, kings of this realm, shall be taken, accepted, and reputed the only supreme head in earth of the church of England, called *Anglicana Ecclesia.* And shall have full power to visit, repress, redress, order, correct, restrain, and amend all such errors, abuses, offences, whatsoever they be, which, by any manner of spiritual authority, ought, or may lawfully be reformed or amended, most to the pleasure of Almighty God, the increase of virtue in Christ's religion, and for the conservation of the peace, unity, and tranquillity of this realm."—Fox, ii. 963, ed. 1610.]

spiritual power doth the like, upon the like penalties, as all know.

The Romish power doth give titles to his ministers, which are the titles of God and Christ, as spiritual lords, great bishop, and many more. This spiritual power doth the like, as all know.

The Romish power doth set up lords over their brethren in spiritual things, unto whom they command honour, and great livings to be given, great pomp and pride. This power doth the like, as all know.[9]

I shall not need to speak of this, in that all books are full, and all consciences (except those that are seared with hot irons) convinced hereof. Let but Master Fox, or any others, who have described the spiritual power of Rome, let but their description thereof be compared with this spiritual power, in all their laws, courts, titles, pomp, pride, and cruelty, and you shall see them very little differ,

[9] [" The pope of Rome writeth himself Father of Fathers, and the head of the church.

The pope of Lambeth writeth Reverend Father Matthew of Canterbury, by the sufferance of God, metropolitan and primate of all England ; as much as to say, as chief head of the church of England.

The pope of Rome doth command superstitious holy days to be kept, contrary to the commandment of God.

The pope of Lambeth doth the same, and compelleth men to break the commandment of God, to observe popish traditions.

The pope of Rome doth rule his church by the cursed canon law, with popish excommunication, the scalding house of conscience.

The pope of Lambeth with his cardinals, the other bishops, doth the same.

The pope of Rome doth make his ministers or priests by his own power, and not by consent of the congregation.

The pope of Lambeth, with his bishops or cardinals, doth the same.

The pope of Rome doth persecute all godly preachers and people that would bring the congregation to the purity and truth of the apostolic church.

The pope of Lambeth, with his clergy, do the same, and that can the Gatehouse, the Fleet, Bridewell, the Marshalsea, the White Lion, and both the Counters testify."—A Viewe of Antichrist, his Lawes and Ceremonies, in A Parte of a Register, pp. 57, 58.]

except in their cruelties, which (glory be to God) the king's majesty, who thirsteth not after blood, hath something restrained, although it is most grievous cruelty to lie divers years in most noisome and filthy prisons, and continual temptations of want, their estates overthrown, and never coming out (many of them) till death; let it be well weighed, and it is little inferior to the cruel sudden death in times of Romish power in this nation.

I. It is very apparent it is that image or similitude of that beast spoken of, Rev. xiii. [15.]

C. Oh yes, for there is no such image of the popish power under the heavens as this. Well, our comfort is, the strong Lord hath said, the kings of the earth, by whose power both the beast and his image is supported, shall take their power from her,[1] then shall she stand naked and desolate. And to this purpose his majesty hath a worthy exhortation to all princes, &c., in his Apology.[2] The words are these: "For as she did fly but with your feathers, borrowing as well her titles of greatness, and forms of honouring her from you, as also enjoying all her temporal living by your liberalities, so if every man do but take his own again, she will stand up naked," &c. Oh that the words of God, might be accepted of his majesty, set down by the Holy Ghost, *Thou that teachest another,* Rom.ii.[21.] *teachest thou not thyself?* For, if he would take but his own, their titles of greatness, and forms of honouring them, and their temporal livings, this spiritual power would stand very naked and desolate.

I. Well, *the hearts of kings are in the hands of the Lord,* [Prov. xxi. 1.] *and he can turn them as the rivers of waters,* but I desire your advice for my own estate. I know every one must

---

[1] [Rev. xvii. 16.]   [2] [Works. Premonition, &c. p. 327.]

bear their own burden: I have a long time remained subject to this spiritual power, partly through ignorance, and partly through fear.

C. I will first declare unto you the judgments of God against such as submit thereunto, that so from an utter abhorring thereof you may come out, never to return thither again. Secondly, I will do the best I can to show you the way the Lord requireth you to walk in, and that only out of his word.

The judgments are so fearful that I tremble to think of them, greater than which is not manifested in the whole book of God. *And the third angel followed them, saying* Rev. xiv. 9, *with a loud voice, If any man worship the beast and his image,* 10, 11 *and receive his mark in his forehead, or on his hand, the same shall drink of the wine of the wrath of God, yea, of the pure wine that is poured into the cup of his wrath, he shall be tormented in fire and brimstone before the holy angels, and before the Lamb. And the smoke of their torments shall ascend evermore, and they shall have no rest day nor night, which worship the beast and his image, and whosoever receiveth the print of his name.*

I. I confess these judgments are to be trembled at; but how do you apply them properly to such as worship in these assemblies?

C. For the satisfaction of all consciences herein, that it may appear plainly, not to be gainsaid, let us consider the words of wisdom, set down in order as they lie. And first, what is meant by worship. Secondly, what by the beast. Thirdly, what his image is. Fourthly, what his mark is. And lastly, what is meant by forehead or hand.

And first, for worship. It is plentifully manifested in the scriptures, that it is service, subjection, or obedience to Matt. iv. 10; such things as are commanded by God or others, and there- Deut. xiii. 4.
Ex. xx. 5 ;

Rom. vi. 16. fore, *his servants we are whom we obey.*   And as the Lord

Mal. i. 6. saith, *If I be your master, where is my fear? if a father, where is mine honour* or worship?

Secondly, by beast, the scripture speaketh sometimes of Dan. vii. 17; cruel men in power and authority.   Sometimes of a blas- Luke xiii. 31, 32 ; 2 phemous spiritual power exercised by men, received of the Tim. iv. 17. dragon exalting itself above God, making war with the saints, and overcoming them, and that hath power over every kindred, and tongue, and nation, so that all that dwell upon the earth worship him, &c.   And this is the beast here spoken of, even that spiritual power or jurisdiction of Rome, which first wrought in a mystery, and by degrees was exalted, till at the last it was exalted to this cruel beast, described Rev. xiii. 1, &c., which beast openeth his mouth in blasphemy against God; saying and practising, that the commandments that God hath given for his service are not to be regarded; but instead thereof, setting up commands of his own, unto which whosoever will not be subject, excommunication and all cruelty, even to death, will ensue, yea, even with gunpowder ere it fail: and for this his cruelty he is called a beast.

Thirdly, by image, is meant any form, shape, similitude, As Deut. iv. or resemblance of the thing spoken of, so that wheresoever 15, 16, &c.; Exod. xx. 4. such a spiritual power is, as this above described, there is the beast's image, as in England; the like power or beast to the first, is not to be found under the heavens in exalta- tion and cruelty.

Fourthly, by mark, is meant profession or practice, As Matt. vii. whereby we are known from others.   As badges or marks 20; 1 John ii. 3; John do put difference between this man's and that man's, in xiii. 35. cattle or servants: as by such a man's mark we know these are · his sheep: and by such a man's badge we know this man belongeth to such a great man: so they Gal. iii. 27. are said to have put on Christ, that have received his baptism, even as a servant is known by putting on his livery.

Lastly, forehead or hand, the Holy Ghost useth that phrase from the old testament, where God's people were commanded, not only to lay up his commands in their hearts and in their souls, but to *bind them for a sign upon* Deut. xi. 18; *their hands, that they might be as frontlets between their eyes.* vi. 6, 8. The wisdom of God therein teaching, that [as] the forehead and hand are the apparentest parts of the body to the view of all men, so that to receive the mark in the forehead or hand, is to make manifest profession of him we obey. The sum of all which is, that whosoever openly professeth obedience and subjection to that spiritual cruel power of Rome, the beast, or to that spiritual cruel power of England, his image, (wheresoever they or either of them are exalted,) such a one, and such persons, shall drink of the wine of God's wrath, and be tormented in fire and brimstone, and shall have no rest day nor night for evermore.

I. Your description of the beast the papists will deny, so will the English lord bishops and their followers deny your description of his image; but thousands will grant both, and some will deny both, as the familists, who say that religion standeth not in outward things, and therefore they would submit to any outward service: and they that do not so, but suffer persecution, say they, are justly persecuted.[3]

C. Those enemies to the cross of Christ are most of them not worth information, because for the most part they are such as do with a high hand sin after enlightening, having forsaken the way wherein they walked, because they would not bear Christ's cross; but in that some simple souls may be seduced by them, let us a little in general compare their opinion with the scriptures.

[3] [See Addenda, A.]

True it is, that religion standeth not in outward things only, for God requireth the heart, and truth in the inward parts; but that God requireth not our subjection, upon fearful punishments, to those outward ordinances which he requireth, is a doctrine of devils, as I shall prove.

And first, for the outward ordinances of the old testament, which were merely shadows, and now are *beggarly rudiments*, what indignation the Lord had towards them that transgressed. Nadab and Abihu offering strange fire, which the Lord hath not commanded, *a fire went out from the Lord and devoured.*[4] The men of Bethshemesh looking into the outward ark, which God had forbidden, the Lord *slew fifty thousand and threescore and ten* of them. Uzza, of a good intent, leaning his shoulder to the same outward ark, which God forbad, the Lord slew him. Uzziah the king offering up outward incense, which God commanded to be done only by the priests, the Lord smote him with leprosy until his death. Korah and his company, what fearful judgments came upon them, though he [was] a Levite, for presuming to meddle with the priest's office, the earth opening and swallowing them up. King Saul likewise offering up incense, in time of need as he thought, the Lord rent his kingdom from him, as also for his disobedience afterwards, touching the fat of Amalek's cattle.

How often was the wrath of the Lord poured down upon the Israelites because of their transgression of his outward ordinances, in place, person, and things? for it was a law, that whoso brought not his sacrifice to the place, viz., *to the door of the tabernacle of the congregation*, but offered it up other where, *blood should be imputed to that man, and he should be cut off from among his people;* yea, such sacrifices

Marginal notes:
Gal. iv. 9.
Lev. x. 1, 2.
Num. iv. 20.
1 Sam.vi. 19.
1 Chron.xiii. 7—10.
Num. xviii. 3, 7.
2 Chron. xxvi. [19.]
Num. xvi. [31—35.]
1 Sam. xiii. [9—14.]
1 Sam. xv. [20—23.]
Lev. xvii. 3, 4.

[4] [destroyed them ; 1662.]

were esteemed of God as offered to devils. And the Lord Verse 7.
caused them to pronounce, *Cursed be he that confirmeth not* Deut. xxvii. 26.
all the words of this law, to do them; and all the people
must say, So be it. Was God thus jealous of Moses's ordinances, and is he less jealous of Christ's? Must he die
that despiseth Moses's law, and shall he escape that despiseth Christ's, upon what pretence soever? And Christ
saith, *it becometh* him, and all his, *to fulfil all righteousness* Matt. iii. 15.
in outward ordinances, as washing with water. And
whosoever saith, he knoweth God, and keepeth not his com- 1 John ii. 4.
mandments, which are outward as well as inward, he *is a*
liar. And *whosoever breaks the least commandment, and* Matt. v. 19.
teacheth men so, he shall be called the least in the kingdom
of heaven. And whosoever *will not hear that prophet,* Christ Acts iii. 22, 23.
Jesus, *in all things that he shall say unto them, shall be*
destroyed out of his people.

The affections of the soul are to be manifested by the
actions of the body, according to God's word, and all other
good intents or affections are abominable. We may not,
neither can we, worship God with our spirits, and the devil
with our bodies; for, *we are bought with a price, and therefore* 1 Cor. vi. 20 vii. 23.
must not be the servants of men, but must glorify God with
our bodies and with our spirits, for they are his. And this
may suffice to satisfy any concerning the overthrow of this
cursed conceit, knowing also that Christ and his apostles,
and all his disciples to the end of the world, might and
may live peaceably enough from persecution, if this
doctrine might be observed, viz., submission with our
bodies to any outward service. The Lord discover such
hypocrites.

I. I bless God I have learned of the apostle, *to say*
nothing against the truth, but for the truth, and therefore 2 Cor. xiii. 8.
when I see things are evidently manifested by the scrip-
tures, am desirous to submit, and not to cavil. But you

know it is pleaded, they have the word and sacraments in the English assemblies.[5]

C. I confess they have the scriptures, in the which God's mysteries are contained, which are locked up from them, and revealed to his saints, which they wofully pervert to their own destruction.   They have also imitations of God's ordinances, as water, bread, and wine, and other things, which they use after their own inventions; which things make them boast so much of their Christianity and of their church, and which maketh them reason thus:

Col. i. 26.

" We are God's people, for we have the word and sacraments."   The Philistines might better have reasoned, who had the true ark of God amongst them, (these have but a show,) " We are God's people, for we have God's ark and holy oracles amongst us." [6]   But I think they had no great cause to rejoice thereof in the end; no more shall

1 Sam. v.

---

[5] [" We have, by God's mercy, the true and right use of the word and sacraments, and all other essential gifts and graces of God ; if there might be some further helps in execution, to make these more effectual, we resist not.—If there be Christ with us, if the Spirit of God in us, if assemblies, if calling by the word ; whatsoever is, or is not else in the constitution, there is whatsoever is required to the essence of a church.—We are true Christians, for we were baptized into the name of Christ ; we truly confess our continuance in the same faith in which we were baptized ; we join together in the public services of God ; we maintain every point of the most ancient creeds ; we overthrow not the foundation by any consequence.   Therefore whatever is wanting to us, whatever is superfluous, in spite of all the gates of hell, we are the true church

of God." An Apologie against Brownists.   Bp. Hall's Works, ed. 1620, pp. 536, 486, 527.]

[6] [" Their having the word and sacraments proves no more their churches to be true, than doth a true man's purse in the hand of a thief prove him to be an honest man.   As the Lord's vessels were of old in the temporal Babylon, so are there sundry of his ordinances now in spiritual Babylon, and therefore the papists can say the like, and all other heretics.   If any should reply, but these have the word preached in an unlawful ministry, and the sacraments unrightly administered, I answer, the same may be said of the English assemblies, as the nonconformists have soundly proved."—A Necessitie of Separation from the Church of England, &c., by John Canne, p. 204, 4to. 1634.]

these have in the end, when God recompenseth all that withhold the truth in unrighteousness. God's dealing is now as it was of old, he now reserveth punishment to the last day, he is patient, and would have men repent; but they despise his bountifulness and long-suffering, preaching peace when there is no peace.

I. It cannot be denied, but that the ministers preach many excellent truths, and do bring people to much reformation in many things.

C. True, it cannot be denied; for, if the devil should come in his own likeness, men would resist him; but because he transformeth himself into an angel of light, therefore he deceiveth. So his ministers, if they should teach all lies, men would not be deceived by them, nor plead for them, but because they teach many truths, people receive them.

But first, for whatsoever they teach, they neither could nor should teach publicly, their mouths should be stopped, if they received not that, their power to teach such truths, from those the dragon sends; and therefore none can receive those truths from them, but they receive the devil by whose power they teach; for, as our Saviour saith, *he that receiveth you, receiveth me, and he that receiveth me,* Matt. x. 40. *receiveth him that sent me.* So, he that receiveth those the beast sends, receiveth the beast; and he that receiveth the beast, receiveth him that sent him, that is the devil. Further, did not that soothsayer Balaam teach excellent Num. xxiii. truths? Yea, the soothsayers of the Philistines the like— xxiv. 1 Sam. vi. [2—9.] yea, those in the gospel preach in Christ's name. As many Matt. vii. 22 more testimonies might be manifested.

And secondly, for their bringing of people to reformation, and therein doing great works. Did not the soothsayers, before recited, show the princes their sin in 1 Sam. vi detaining God's ark, and the judgments against them for [2.] the same, exhorting them to send it away, and not to harden their hearts, as Pharaoh and the Egyptians hardened their hearts? And was not reformation wrought thereby? And did not they that preached in Christ's name cast out devils, and do many and great works, of whom our Saviour testifieth, he never acknowledged them?

But let us a little consider wherein the reformation consisteth, procured by their preaching. In drunkenness, whoredom, swearing, &c., moral duties, which things whosoever is not reformed in, shall never see God's kingdom; yet which things many of the philosophers (that knew not God) abounded in, as they that know the stories cannot deny. But do they teach their hearers to hate vain inventions, and love God's law? In a general manner of teaching they may, but if it come to particular practice, you shall see what they will do. Do they teach any to submit to that one law-giver, Christ Jesus, for the guidance of his church, and not to antichrist's abominations? No, they will tell you, you must sigh and groan till the magistrate will reform; for you are a private person, and must be subject.[7]

And if the powerful working of God's word and Spirit prevail in you, to let you see that the magistrates not reforming will not excuse you at the day of account, but that *that soul that committeth abomination shall die:* and that rather than you will worship the beast or his image, you will suffer with Christ peaceably, separating yourself from such open profanation as neither can nor will be reformed, endeavouring to square yourself both in your entrance and walking in Christ's way, unto that golden rule that he hath left for direction. Then the best of all these preachers and reformers will be hot and bitter, labouring with all the

---

[7] [" A PRIVATE MAN, say they, HATH not to meddle with the public actions and affairs of the church, which, (if they be amiss,) he is patiently to bear, and to mourn and groan with love, until God either amend or correct them, whose office it is to root out the tares."—A Brief Discourse of the False Church, by H. Barrow, p. 32, 1590.]

turning of devices to turn you, and withhold you from reformation;[8] and if they cannot prevail hereby, then publish you in their privileged pulpits, where none may answer them: you are a schismatic, Brownist, anabaptist, and what not, to make the multitude abhor your doings, and not to follow you therein; and some of them, if not all, under a colour, procure your imprisonment and trouble by their canonized lords, or some of their hellish pursuivants. And such preachers of reformation are the best of them all.[9]

I. Oh! how have we been besotted in these things for want of true knowledge and understanding from the scriptures; how have I and others satisfied ourselves with these things, in that our estate was happy, persuading ourselves thereof, when, alas! our fear towards God was taught by the inventions of men; but the reason thereof was, we judged ourselves by our own persuasions, and not by God's word.

C. I pray you let not that seem strange unto you, that people should persuade themselves of their good estate with God, when it is not so. The Israelites, God's people, thought their estate good many times, when, alas! it was otherwise, as the prophets declared unto them; yea, our Saviour testifieth that they boasted of God being their Father, when they not so much as knew him; yea, when <small>John viii. 19.</small>

[8] [" Whom do they take for greater enemies, than the separatists? And why? Because these boldly put in practice, what they do teach, but dare not perform. And for this very thing many of us have received most grievous injuries, both from their tongues and hands, but the Lord forgive them for it."—A Necessitie of Separation, &c., by John Canne, p. 206. Printed 1634.]

[9] [" They pray, *let thy kingdom come*, but how do they think that ever they shall behold the beauty and glory thereof, seeing they resolve not to set their hands unto the raising of it up, but do leave the work wholly to the magistrate? So that if the arm of flesh will not build a spiritual temple for the Lord, he is likely, for their part, to have none at all."—Canne's Necessitie, &c., p. 168.]

PERSECUTION, &c.]   L

Verse 44. they were of their father the devil. The five foolish virgins thought their condition good enough, and that Matt. xxv. 11. they should have been let in, but it was otherwise. The John xvi. 2. wicked thought they did God service that killed Christ's Jer. xvii. 9. disciples. Man's heart is deceitful. Who are more confident of their good estate with God than the papists, notwithstanding all their gross abominations? Even so have you and I (God pardon us) thought beyond all, that we were in a good estate, having such zealous teachers, that teach so many excellent truths under the title of Christ's ministers, till we came to examine them, as the church of Rev. ii. [2.] Ephesus did, then we found them to have no other ministry than that they received from the beast and his image, which Rev. xiii. [4, 15.] the dragon gave.

I. Are all, without exception, in this fearful estate to be cast into the lake that burneth with fire and brimstone?

C. All that submit, obey, or worship the beast without exception, for there is no respect of persons with God. So [Rev.xiv. 9.] saith the Lord, *If any man worship, &c.* These worshippers under the beast's image may be divided into two sorts: first, those that ignorantly persuade themselves that all that is practised is good and acceptable to God; secondly, those that see and acknowledge many things to be evil, which they would gladly have removed, but because they cannot without the cross of Christ, partly for that, and partly by the persuasion of their prophets (that the things are not fundamental, and the like pretences), all submit, and teach men so.

I. Some affirm, there be thousands in England that never worshipped the beast, &c., but be careful to keep the commandment of God, and faith of Jesus.

C. Such are not under these judgments. But if their meaning be of any that submit to these ordinances appointed for these assemblies, such teachers preach peace when there is none, strengthen the wicked that they cannot return from their wicked way, by promising them life, whose reward shall be according to the reward of such false prophets; because they follow their own spirit, and have _{Ezek. xiii. 2;} not received it from the Lord; for thus saith the Lord, ^{xiv. 10.} such *shall drink of the wine of the wrath of God.*   Rev. xiv. 10.

1. It is also affirmed by some, that in respect of personal graces, some of the professors (as they are called) are the children of God, and may be communicated with privately, though in respect of their church-actions they are members of antichrist's body, to whom the judgments of God appertaineth.

C. This opinion proceedeth not from God's word, but from man's vain heart, by the suggestion of the devil: which, that it may evidently appear, let us a little consider of it. In truth, it is to say, that in one respect they have God's promises appertaining to them: in another respect they have God's most fearful torments, pronounced against that beast, and that false prophet, appertaining to them. Rev. xix. 20. In one respect they are God's people, serving him their master: in another respect the devil's people, serving him their master. In one respect they shall be saved; in another respect they shall be damned. But what false doctrine this is God's holy word doth discover. Our Saviour saith, *No man can serve two masters ; ye cannot serve* Matt. vi. 24. *God and riches.* And can any serve Christ and the beast, God and the dragon? When Christ shall come at the last day to give to every man according to his works, will he say to any one, " In respect of thy personal graces, I will save thee; come, thou blessed," as he will say to all his children : " but in respect of thy being a member of antichrist's body, I will damn thee; go, thou cursed," as he will to all that worship or obey the beast? Will not Christ Jesus pronounce absolutely either salvation or con-

L 2

demnation to every one? and that according to this word,
John xii. 48; so as God in his righteousness will either
justify or condemn every man.   So hath he taught us to
know, that no fountain can make salt water and sweet.
And therefore, that by men's fruits we should know and
judge them to be not both good and evil trees at one time,
as this opinion teacheth, but either good or evil: always
taking heed, we justify not the wicked, nor condemn the
innocent, both which are abominable to the Lord.   And
for any communion whatsoever with them, What fellowship hath Christ with antichrist, the righteous with the
wicked, the servants of the Lamb with the servants of the
beast?   But I leave this for further answer to those, who,
although they are nearer to this man that hath published
this opinion than I am, yet hath (according to truth) confessed in writing, "that there is nothing to be expected
from Christ by any member of the church of England, but
a pouring out of his eternal wrath upon them."[10]

I. Well, I praise God, I am much informed in these

[10] Mr. De Cluse, Advertis. page 9.
[This gentleman is called by Paget
the "ancientest and busiest elder" of
Mr. Henry Ainsworth's church at
Amsterdam.   He had been a member of the French reformed church,
and desired the office of the ministry
in that community.   The reasons for
his separation are said to have been,
"their sins in their public worship of
God, and administration of the church,
as praying out of human prescribed
liturgies, preaching from human apo-
cryphal catechisms, baptizing such as
are not in the covenant of Christ, and
the like."   He frequently exercised
his gifts in the church of which he
became an elder, and after the death of
Mr. Ainsworth, appears for a time to
have conducted its affairs, until it
chose for its pastor the celebrated Mr.
John Canne.   Paget's Arrow against
the Separation of the Brownists, pp.
126,46,56.ed.1618. He also translated
into the French language Ainsworth's
treatise on the "Communion of
Saints." Hanbury's Hist. Memorials,
i. 273, 516.   The book referred to
above, was probably written in opposition to the sentiments of Mr. Bright-
man, of which, Paget says, he made
"manifold erroneous collections . . . .
whereof he is also convinced in that
book which was shortly after written
for the refutation and reproof of him."
An Arrow, &c., pp. 88, 89.   See
also Addenda B.]

things; yet one thing more I will desire your answer unto. The case standeth thus with me: in these things I am betwixt faith and doubting; though the rather I believe these things you say are true, and that I may never go to these assemblies again without sin; but I am not so persuaded thereof that I dare suffer for it. What if I should, not having faith to suffer, for fear of persecution, go to their worship again?

C. It were your most fearful sin, which I prove thus; and I pray you observe it well: you must do it, either as being verily persuaded you do well, and then all this beginning of light in you should be extinguished, and so your estate is with the worst, if not worse: or else you must do it, doubting whether you do well or no; for I hope you will not say, you do it knowing you do evil. If you do it doubting, the Lord saith, *it is sin;* which I hope Rom.xiv.23. you will acknowledge, and not approve yourself to do well in sinning, and then God *is merciful to forgive your sin,* 1 John i. 9. either this or any other. But if you say, you sin not therein, doing it doubtingly, you make God a liar, who saith, *it is sin, and your sin remaineth.*

I. What if I should many times go through weakness?

C. If you unfeignedly repent, being through weakness, there is mercy with God, though it should be *seventy times* Matt. xviii. *seven times* in a day. But we had need to take heed of our 21, 22. repentance. The apostle saith, where there is godly sorrow for sin, *what care it worketh in you, yea, what indigna-* 2 Cor. vii. *tion,* &c.; and custom in sin is dangerous, we had need to [11.] take heed we be not *hardened, through the deceitfulness of* Heb. iii. 13. *sin.*

I. Then you hold, that if any man approve himself in sinning, his sin remaineth.

C. If any man sin, and say he hath not sinned, there is 1 John i. 8. no truth in him; and God will enter into judgment with him. Jer. ii. 35.

I. Then absolutely I see, that if any man worship the beast, or his image, &c., as before you have showed, he neither hath faith nor fear of God in him, what show of godliness soever he maketh. But what say you, may not a man that separateth from all uncleanness, though he yet see not the way of Christ in his ordinances, may not such a man be saved?

C. Yes, upon this condition, that he believe in Jesus Christ for his only righteousness, and be willing and ready to hear and obey his ordinances. An example hereof we have in Cornelius. But if any *will not hear that prophet,* Christ Jesus, *in all things whatsoever he shall say unto them,* [*he*] *shall be destroyed out of his people.*

Acts x.
Acts iii. 22, 23.

I. What do you mean by " will not hear?"

C. That when any part of the ways of God is manifest to them, they despise and contemn it, or carelessly neglect it; otherwise men may not receive some of Christ's truth, and yet not be said that they will not receive it.

I. Next after forsaking the ways of wickedness, and embracing Christ for our righteousness, what must we do?

C. Christ's whole testament teacheth this, and no other way; after repentance from dead works, and faith towards God, to be baptized with water; and a cloud of witnesses; calling these the *beginnings of* Christ, and *foundation.*

Mark xvi. 16; Acts ii. 41; viii. 16, 38; ix. 18. Heb. vi. 1, &c.

I. May none be admitted to the church to partake in the ordinances, except they be baptized?

C. If any teach otherwise, he presumeth *above that which is written,* and therefore ought to be held *accursed.* For there was never true church, since Christ's manifesting[1] in the flesh, joined together of unbaptized persons, though some have vainly published the contrary.[2]

1 Cor. iv. 6.
Gal. i. 8, 9.

---

[1] [Christ was manifested; 1662.]

[2] [" Is this so strange to John Robinson? Do we not know the beginnings of his church? That there was first one stood up and made a covenant, and then another, and these

I. True, I think that cannot be denied, where the persons were never baptized; but now the members of the church of Rome, from whence the baptism of the church of England cometh, are baptized, therefore why need they again be baptized?

C. If they be baptized with Christ's baptism, I will acknowledge they need not again be baptized: but that the baptism of the church of Rome is Christ's baptism, that can never be proved; for Christ requireth that only his disciple should baptize his disciple, and into his body: none of which is in Rome's baptism.³ For Christ's adversaries wash with water those that are not Christ's disciples, into the body, not of Christ, but of antichrist.

I. I confess that the church of Rome, and members thereof, are the church and members of antichrist, but they use the water and words in their baptism that Christ appointed.

C. What then? Is it therefore Christ's baptism? The conjurors used the same words that the apostles did, *We* Acts xix. 13, *adjure you by the name of Jesus,* &c.; yet abominable was &c. their action. Also, *Unto the wicked said God, What hast* Ps. l. [16.] *thou to do with my ordinances, or to take my word in thy mouth?* &c. Also the papists use the same words of their church, that Christ hath appointed to be used of his, as also of their ministry; is it therefore Christ's church and

---

two joined together, and so a third, and these became a church, say they; which we deny, except a synagogue of Satan. For was ever church of the new testament made by a covenant without baptism? There is not the least show for it. In this they run to Israel's renewed covenant, wherein again they acknowledge Rome and England true churches in their foundation."—A Description of what

God hath Predestinated Concerning Man. Printed 1620, pp. 169, 170.]

³ [" The church of Rome at this day, and for divers hundred years, not being made by baptizing believers, but by washing fleshly infants upon confession of sureties for them, therefore they have not Christ, but are in God's account as the worst pagans, Egyptians, &c."—A Description, &c. p. 156.]

ministry? They use also the same washing water and words,[4] in baptizing their bells,[5] that they use in their baptizing their infants; is it therefore Christ's baptism? If answer be made, Bells are not to be baptized; I answer, No more are the seed of wicked persecutors, by our opposite's own confession. If this were any thing, you should see what will follow: the baptism of Rome is Christ's baptism, because they use water and these words; so if any use water and these words, as the Jews, or any other of Christ's adversaries (as the papists are), *there* is Christ's baptism. Consider this, and see what truth there is in it.

I. Though the baptism of the church of Rome should be nought, yet the baptism of the church of England may be good, in that there be many thousands that were never baptized in the church of Rome.

C. I answer, that the first beginning of the church of England was made of the members of the church of Rome, as is apparent in the days of king Henry the eighth, and afterwards in the beginning of queen Elizabeth's reign, after queen Mary's death, and so continueth unto this day; and the long continuance of it, maketh it not

---

[4] [words, and washing with water; 1662.]

[5] ["In the blessing and exorcising of a bell, they give him godfathers and godmothers, which hold the rope in their hands; the suffragan asketh certain questions of the bell; they clothe him in white, sprinkle him with holy water and salt; the bishop or his suffragan anoints him with oil, with many signs of the cross, praying God that he will grant power unto the bell against the secret assaults of the devil, against thunder and tempest, and for the comfort of souls departed; then after the singing of certain psalms, he is newly marked again with seven crosses without, and four crosses within, which are made with the chrism with the bishop's or his suffragan's thumb, who at every cross repeats these words: ' Consecretur et sanctificetur Domine signum istud in nomine Patris et Filii, et Spiritus Sancti.' In all this ceremony there is nothing wanting but the word baptism, save that it is done somewhat more diversely."—Du Moulin, Defence of the Catholic Faith, p. 309, ed. 1610. Sleidan, Comment. lib. xxi. fol. 350, ed. 1559.]

approvable.[6]   And the papists themselves bid the protestants prove if they have or hold any other baptism, church,
or ministry, than that they have from them, and show it,
and they will recant.   Besides, the baptism now practised
in the church of England is no better, no otherwise than
that of Rome: for the church of Rome baptizeth all the
infants of the most wicked that are in her dominions; and
so the church of England baptizeth all the infants of the
most wicked that are in the king's majesty's dominions:
and of this timber are both these churches built; and
therefore we may truly say, "As is the mother, so is the
daughter."[7]   And as they are in their first building, so are
they in most of their laws, lords, lawmakers, courts, and
thousands of their abominations, insomuch that it is plain
enough, the latter is the very image of the first; unto
which, whosoever submitteth, or obeyeth, or maintaineth
their baptism, or any other of their human trash, he shall
be tormented in fire and brimstone for evermore, and shall
never have rest day nor night.   And therefore in God's Rev. xiv.
[11.]

[6] [" Their parishes were at first
constituted, as now they stand, of the
members of antichrist, to wit, the
idolatrous papists, and of all other
kind of most notorious sinners, scoff-
ers at religion, &c. This profane
multitude, without any profession of
faith and repentance, were forced and
compelled by human authority in the
beginning of queen Elizabeth's reign,
to be members of their church, and
so have continued, they and their
seed ever since, contrary to the express word of God."—Canne's Necessitie of Separation, p. 196.]

[7] [" That such is and was the estate
of Rome and England when John
Robinson and his company left it, old
Brownism freely confesseth; yea, he

himself acknowledgeth, that the Lord
never made covenant with Rome nor
England; and not only Brownists,
but Calvinists, church of England,
and others, apply all these things—
against Rome; yet being loth to cast
her down to the ground, even all of
them retain and maintain the Baby-
lonish, Egyptian, and Sodomitish
washing of the habitation of devils,
for the outward badge of their Christianity, wherein they take the chief
corner-stone of Babylon for foundation, contrary to the express command
of the Lord......therefore shall they
be destroyed, and are in God's account
so far from being true churches, that
they are synagogues of Satan."—A
Description, &c. pp. 157, 158.]

fear cast away that cursed action of washing, where was neither Christ's disciple administering, nor his disciple upon whom it was administered, nor Christ's body or church baptized into : and obey Christ's voice in becoming his disciple, and [in coming] to his church, that you may be baptized by his disciple, and be made a member of his body or church. This only is Christ's baptism, and of him acknowledged, and ought to be of all his disciples; and the contrary to be held accursed, and in no sort maintained or kept.

I. It is objected, that we must cast away that which is man's ordinance, and retain that which is God's ordinance, namely, washing, and water, and words.

C. I deny that any thing in that action was God's ordinance or appointment. What truth is there in this, to say, that because God appointeth water, and washing, and words in his baptism, therefore, howsoever water, and washing, and these words are used, that is Christ's ordinance ? I confess, water, and washing, and words are God's ordinance, being used as he hath commanded, the which I acknowledge must be held; but this use of them, or action forespoken of, being not the use of them, or action appointed of God (as the adversaries confess) is to be cast away as execrable.

I. Further, it is objected, they repent of that which is evil, and retain that which is good.

C. For the better discovering of this deceit, let us consider what is the evil, they confess and that they repent of. Say they, an unlawful person performed an unlawful action upon an unlawful person; this is the evil. Now this is the question, whether this action thus unlawfully performed may be kept, and yet repented of ? The scrip- Prov. xxviii. 13. ture teacheth, that not only confessing, but forsaking sin, is repentance. Can a thief that hath stolen goods, repent thereof to acceptance with God, and not make restitution to the party wronged, being in his power, or having ability to restore? I would know how this will be maintained; for the one is a greater theft than the other.

I. It is further objected, that Jeroboam's followers had no right to circumcision in their idolatrous estate, yet such as were circumcised in that estate, were not afterwards circumcised when they came to repentance.

C. It is their forgery so to object; for, either they had right to circumcision, being true Israelites, although in transgression, or else none had right to circumcision in the world; no, not Judah. For, what can be said, but that because the ten tribes were in rebellion against God, therefore they had no right to circumcision? May not the same be said in as high a measure of Judah? Was Israel's sin half so great as Judah's? If it be said, that Israel forsook the place of God's worship, the temple; so did Judah too, worshipping under every green tree, and grove, and high place: whatsoever can be said of the one, as much may be said of the other. This is a mere deceitful forgery, raised up by Satan in the hearts of his false prophets, to deceive themselves, and them that shall perish, if they repent not; in that they receive not the love of the truth, but believe these lies, and have pleasure therein; concluding from this false ground, that because the Israelites in transgression were circumcised, and after coming to repentance were not circumcised again: so Egyptians, Sodomites, and Babylonians, never having been Israelites, baptized in the synagogues of Satan, are not to be re-baptized (as they call it), there being no comparison betwixt the persons; the one being true Israelites according to the flesh, God's people, to whom by God's appointment circumcision appertained, and who should have increased their transgressions if they had not performed

it ; and the other true Babylonians, God's adversaries,
unto whom God threateneth his judgments, for taking his
ordinances in their mouths or hands.

I. I see indeed there is no true proportion betwixt the
persons in circumcision and baptism ; for the one were the
persons appointed of God to be circumcised, which circumcision taught them the forsaking of their wicked ways, and

Gal. v. 3. bound them to the observation of the law, and they had
no cause to repent of that their action : the other are not
the persons appointed of God to be baptized, but sinned in
that their action, and must repent thereof, by your opposite's own confession. But if this be granted, this question ariseth, Who shall then baptize after antichrist's
exaltation ?

C. For answer to this, there are three ways professed
in the world ; one by the papists, and their several successors, professing succession from the pope and his ministers ; another by the familists [8] and scattered flock, that
none may intermeddle therewith lawfully, till their extraordinary men come; another, we and others affirm, that
any disciple of Christ, in what part of the world soever,
coming to the Lord's way, he by the word and spirit of
God preaching that way unto others and converting; he
may and ought also to baptize them. The two former I
shall through the help of God confute, and confirm the
latter by the scriptures.

First, to the papists and all their several successors,
some standing for all, by succession from Rome, some for
more, some for less, some for nothing but baptism, being
of our judgment for the appointing of their ministry. To

Ps. l. 16. them all I answer with the words of the Lord, *What have
antichrist's ministers to do to take God's word in their*

<hr>

[8] [See Addenda, note A.]

mouths, or to declare his ordinances, seeing they hate to be reformed, and *have cast God's word behind their backs?*   If they have nothing to do with his word and ordinances, then not with ministry and baptism.   Besides, God hath forbidden that the adversaries of him, his temple, and them that dwell in heaven, should build, according to that of Neh. ii. 20, *The God of heaven, he will prosper us, and we his servants will rise up and build; but as for you, you have no portion, nor right, nor memorial in Jerusalem.*

Secondly, to that fantastical sect I answer; it is their dream and false vision to look for extraordinary men, for God hath not spoken it.   *For if an angel from heaven* Gal. i. 8, 9. *should come and preach otherwise* than those extraordinary men the apostles have preached, which none else could preach, and which is written in Christ's testament, *we are to hold them accursed.*   Which truth none need go into heaven to seek, but every one that searcheth the scriptures may find by the direction of the Holy Ghost, which God Acts v. [32.] hath promised to all that obey him and ask it.   Luke xi. 13.

I. Now I pray you let me hear your confirmation of your practice.

C. As it was in the second building of the material temple, after the captivity of Babylon in Chaldea; so, according to the true proportion, it is to be in the second building of the spiritual temple, after the captivity of spiritual Babylon.   Now this is [to be] observed in the former, that every Israelite with whom the Lord was, and whose spirit the Lord stirred up, was commanded to go and build, Ezra i 3, 5. though some were more excellent in the business than others   So now, every spiritual Israelite with whom the Lord is, and whose spirit the Lord stirreth up, are commanded to go and build, and the Lord will prosper them in rising up and building, though some be more excellent in the business than others; the beginning of which spiri-

tual building is, first, to beget men anew by the immortal
seed of God's word, so making them living stones, and
thereupon to couple them together a spiritual house unto
God, upon the confession of their faith by baptism, as the
scriptures of the new testament every where teach, as
before is showed.

I. It is confessed of many, that any that hath gifts may
preach, and convert, but not baptize.[9]

C. Such our Saviour accounteth hypocrites, and re-
proveth, that held it was lawful to swear by the temple,
but not by the gold of the temple; by the altar, but not
by the offering on the altar: to whom he saith, *Whether is
greater, the gold, or the temple that sanctifies the gold? the
offering, or the altar that sanctifies the offering?* So may I
say, Whether is greater, the water and washing, or the
word that sanctifies the water?

I. What other example have you in the scriptures, that
an unbaptized person may baptize?

C. If there were no other than that aforementioned, it
were sufficient. An Israelite circumcised in flesh, God
stirring up his heart, was to build the temple made with
hands, from the first stone to the last; so an Israelite circumcised in heart, God stirring him up, is to build the
temple made without hands, from the first stone to the

1 Pet. ii. [5.]

Matt. xxiii. [16, 17.]

[9] [" Though a private man might dispense the word alone; yet doth it not follow that he may administer both the word and the seal thereof: both which are joined in baptism, and jointly administered."—Perkins on Galatians, p. 258, ed. 1604.

" John Robinson, preacher to the English at Leyden, hath printed half a sheet of paper, who laboureth to prove, that none may baptize but pastors or elders of a church, and conse-quently, that you and all your com-panies in England, wanting pastors, are unbaptized. . . . . Some of the Brownists acknowledging it lawful for any disciple to preach and convert, but not baptize: though others of them hold, that disciples of Christ, though not in office of pastor or elder, may convert and baptize also, upon which they have been at deadly jars these many years." A Description, &c. pp. 154, 162.]

last, beginning with, *Go, preach and baptize, teaching to* [Matthew xxviii. 19.]
observe all that God commands, as Christ teacheth his disciples to the end of the world. But further, we have the particular example of John Baptist, who being unbaptized, preached, converted, and baptized.

I. But John Baptist was an extraordinary man, it will be objected, for God spake to him extraordinarily.

C. What then, is not his practice written for our instruction? *God hath spoken at several times after sundry* Heb. i. 1, &c. *manners, yet all to one end.* As for this of John Baptist, the same God that spake to John Baptist in the wilderness his word, the same God speaketh to us in his scriptures the same word he spake to John; and therefore seeing the Lord hath spoken, who shall not preach and practise according to his word? seeing now God speaketh to no particular persons; *for whatsoever is written aforetime is written* Rom. xv. 4. *for every man's instruction.*[1]

I. Many famous men, as Mr. Perkins and others, confess that if a Turk should come to the knowledge of the truth in Turkey, he might preach the same to others, and converting them, baptize them, though unbaptized.[2]

[1] ["Every believer hath Christ and his apostles, commanding him to covet to preach, 1 Cor. xiv. 1; and to call all to come, Rev. xxii. 17; and when they come, to baptize them. Here is the King and Lawgiver, the city Jerusalem, the new testament, with her gates open; and the Spirit of God bidding all come freely; and all the faithful made kings and priests unto God, 1 Pet. ii. 5; Rev. i. 6. What should let that they may not baptize till they have officers, or when the officers are sick, die, are in prison, or the like? Doth their power then cease to baptize any? and so to receive them into the church? The primitive churches never knew this, who all were gathered by faith and baptism, and who were without pastors a good while, Acts xiv. 21, 23, for a young disciple may not be a pastor, 1 Tim. iii. 6; and they increased and grew, being left of the apostles for a season, who after their long journeys to other places, came to them again, and taught them 'the order of having pastors in every church."—A Description, &c. p. 164.]

[2] ["If in Turkey or America, or elsewhere, the gospel should be received of men, by the counsel and

C. True, but this mystery of iniquity so prevaileth, persuading many that they are Christians, because they had baptism in their infancy, when it appertained not to them, that they think their case is better than the Turks, though, alas! it is much worse: for it shall be easier for the Turks than for them, if God's word be true. Are not all Jews and Gentiles in one estate by nature? and is there more than one way of coming to Christ for them Gal. iii. 26, 27. both, namely, to be the *sons of God by faith,* and to put on Christ by baptism? Who hath set up his new way? Christ or antichrist?

I. Many of those called Brownists, do confess that they are reasonably persuaded that antichristians coming to the truth may be baptized;[3] and they would not differ with you concerning that, but that you deny infants' baptism.

---

persuasion of private persons, they shall not need to send into Europe for consecrated ministers, but they have power to choose their own ministers from within themselves; because where God gives the word, he gives the power also." Perkins on Galatians, p. 35, ed. 1604. " All which I have showed to this end, to make plain, that if John Rob[inson] and others did walk in the path of the Lord, as they follow the vision of their own hearts, they should be constrained to practise that in the building of the church of Christ, which they disapprove in us ; that is, that when they separated from that habitation of devils, Rome, and were to combine themselves together to be a church, some one must baptize, not being yet pastor or elder. For there must be a flock before a shepherd, as were all the churches of the primitive time, and as was Jo. Rob[inson's] flock before they made him their shepherd." A Description, &c. p. 158.]

[3] [Whether a " Turk coming to the knowledge of Christ, and to faith by reading the new testament, and withal teaching his family, and converting it, and others to Christ, and being in a country whence he cannot easily come to Christian churches, whether he may baptize them whom he hath converted to Christ, he himself being unbaptized ? Zanchius answers, ' I doubt not of it, but that he may, and withal provide, that he himself be baptized of one of the three converted by him.' The reason (he gives) is, because he is a minister of the word stirred up extraordinarily of Christ ; and so, as such a minister may, with the consent of that small church, appoint one of the communicants, and provide that he be baptized by him." Robinson's Justification of Separation, pp. 339, 349, ed. 1639.]

What say you, may not the infants of the faithful be baptized?

C. No, except God have appointed it.

I. You know it is granted that there is neither plain command nor example for it in Christ's testament, but from the consequence of circumcision in that covenant that God made with Abraham and his seed, Gen. xvii. [2,] and other places agreeing therewith.

C. Let us endeavour to put an end to this, if it may be, in short. I demand of you, what covenant the Lord meaneth here? It must be granted, he meaneth either the covenant of the land of Canaan, with all the promises thereof, or the covenant of Christ's coming of his loins concerning the flesh, or else the covenant of life and salvation by Christ; one of these three it must needs be. Let me have your answer, or any man's hereto.

I. The first and second cannot be pleaded, therefore it must be the third, namely, life and salvation by Christ.

C. Well then, I demand, hath the fleshly children of the faithful more privilege to life and salvation than the faithful themselves?

I. No, I think it cannot be said.

C. Well then, I affirm that the faithful have right to this covenant of life and salvation only upon their repentance and faith, and not otherwise: and so have their children, and not otherwise, except you will say they have greater privilege than the faithful, or else that they shall have life and salvation by their parents' faith, or else that they have right and title to it, whether they repent and believe or no. If any say they have right and title to it by God's promise, I answer, God hath promised life and salvation by Christ to none that are under condemnation, but only by repentance and faith; let any show the contrary if they be able. If any say, as some foolishly have

PERSECUTION, &c.]   M

done, being urged, that it is the covenant of the visible church; what covenant is that but the covenant of life and salvation made to the faithful, Christ's body and church? And therefore, seeing they are so confounded herein, some teaching one thing and some another, some that infants have neither faith nor repentance, but by virtue of the covenant made to their parents; others teach that repentance and faith is to be performed of every one that is to be baptized, and that infants may repent and believe by their sureties, till they come to age themselves : seeing, I say, they are thus confounded herein, having nothing in Christ's perfect testament, only some show of a forged consequence, and also that they agree not amongst themselves; let us take heed of profaning the Lord's holy ordinance, administering it where he hath not commanded. Many other things might be said, but this may suffice, seeing much is already written, and more may be ere long, knowing they have nothing to say but their several conceits.

I. But what do you then hold of infants?

C. That they are innocents, as Christ teacheth, that they have no knowledge, that God speaketh not to them, requiring any thing at their hands, and therefore they have not sinned, seeing sin is the breach of God's law.

I. Then you hold they shall be saved?

C. Wherefore should they be condemned?

I. For that original sin, they have received from Adam.

C. Well, it is not my purpose now, time will not serve, to answer all the objections that are made in this matter. In short, I trust to cut down that conceit, that any infant should be condemned, as thus. I demand of you, did any of Adam's posterity fall deeper in that transgression than he himself?

I. No, I never heard it affirmed; but as deep as he.

Matt. xviii. 3, &c.; xix. 14, &c.; 1 Cor. xiv. 20. Deut. i. 39; Jonah iv. 11. Deut. xi. 2; Matt. xiii. 9; Rom vii. 9; 1 Cor. x. 15. 1 John iii. 4; Rom. iv. 15.

C. Well, out of your own ground you shall be convinced: Did God ever purpose or declare that Adam for that transgression should go to hell? Consider it well before you answer.

I. No; for from eternity he purposed that Christ should be betwixt that sin and condemnation.

C. You say true. Then for that sin God never purposed to condemn Adam to hell. If not him for that, why any of his posterity for that? Let this be considered, it is your own ground. Further, I say, and that without contradiction, it was never God's purpose that any should go to hell, but for refusing Christ. *This is condemnation,* John iii. 19. *that light,* or Christ, *is come into the world, and men love darkness* better. And Christ will condemn the world *of* John xvi. 9. *sin, because they believe not* in him.[4]

I. I cannot contradict you in this, I will better consider of it. But, I pray you, what hold you then of predestination?

C. If you conceive the former, you may see what I hold; namely, that, before all beginnings, it was God's purpose, or predestination, that salvation should consist in the receiving, or believing in Christ, and condemnation in refusing of Christ. *He that will not believe shall be* Mark xvi. 16. *damned,* and not otherwise.

---

[4] ["Further, I say, it was never God's purpose to execute upon Adam for that transgression, condemnation to hell; in that, he purposed to send Christ betwixt, in whom, Adam believing, he should be saved. If Adam himself, for his own sin was not condemned to hell without remedy, shall any of his posterity be sent to hell, without remedy, and that for his sin? Seeing they fell no deeper in the transgression than he, if so deep. Is this equal and right for the Judge of all the earth to do? The scripture saith, THIS *is condemnation, that light,* or Christ that true light, *is come into the world, and men love darkness* better. And Christ will condemn the world *of sin, because they believe not* in him. Condemnation consisteth in refusing Christ, *he that will not believe shall be damned,* and not else. For God hath shut up all in unbelief." A Description, &c. p. 115.]

M 2

I. Then you hold that God hath predestinated some to be saved, and some to be damned?

C. Yes, as I told you, namely, the receivers of Christ to be saved, and the refusers of Christ to be damned. But that God hath predestinated or appointed some to the means and end, namely, to be wicked and to be damned, is the most blasphemous conceit that ever Satan foisted into man's heart or brain.

I. But are men left then to their own free-will?

C. What do you mean by free-will?

I. Ability of ourselves to do good or evil.

C. You say well, that truly is free-will. To do evil, and to resist God's word and Spirit, we have free-will or power of ourselves. But to do good, or to receive God's word or Spirit, we have no power of ourselves. God worketh the will and the deed hereunto. We are both begotten again of God, by his abundant mercy in Christ, to that heavenly inheritance, and kept *by his power, through faith, unto salvation.* So that nothing appertaineth to us but shame; to him only appertaineth the glory for our life from death, and for our preservation therein.

Acts xiii. 46; vii. 51.

Phil. ii. 13.

1 Peter i. 3, 4, 5.

I. How comes it then that some do believe, and some do not?

C. That any do believe, I have showed you the cause, without the which none could believe; namely, God's mercy in Christ, in quickening us that were dead, by his powerful and lively word [and] Spirit. That some do not believe, the cause is, they having free-will to do evil, and to resist God's word and Spirit, use the same, and so do not believe. That any believe, it is thus God's mercy; that most believe not, the cause is not God's, but their own wicked, resisting will.

I. It is said that the reason why some believe not, is, because God doth not effectually call them, as he doth the other; for if he did, they should come.

C. This saying is partly blasphemous, partly ignorant. Blasphemous, in that it layeth the cause of their not believing on God, in that he effectually calleth them not, and maketh God a dissembler in his word, who saith, As he liveth, he would have it otherwise. Ignorant it is, in [Ez. xxxiii. 11.] that such persons, as so say, know not God's work in creating man. For if God had made Adam otherwise than he made him, either unchangeably good or evil, he must have made him either a god or a devil. For if he could not have resisted God, by his creation, then what was he but as God, unchangeable? And if he could not have resisted the devil, by his creation, what was he but a devil, unchangeable? Or if he could not have resisted God in eating the forbidden fruit, how could God have manifested his mercy to him in Christ? Or if he could not have resisted the devil therein, how could God justly pour out his judgments upon him for his obedience to Satan, God creating him thereunto.[5]

Now for us, Adam's posterity, it is granted of all, that we have the same will or power to evil that Adam had, or rather worse, though not the will to good he had, and therefore men may, and do resist God in his effectual

[5] [" If God had made Adam that he could not but continue righteous, he must have made him God, like himself, unchangeable; or, if God had made him that he could not but sin, what was he then but as the devils now are, unchangeable? But God, in making man, made a very good creature, yet subject to change, by having his will brought to submit unto evil through the devil's temptations. So that I may conclude, that God could not make man otherwise than he made him, a reasonable creature, yet mutable, able to obey his righteous precepts, which, if he did, he would continue him in that blessed estate he created him in; if not, he would bring upon him his judgments —God not forcing him either way. Further, if God had made Adam unchangeably good, that he could not break his righteous law, then it had been to no purpose to set a penalty to that law, which could not be transgressed. And then had those most holy attributes of God, his justice to punish sin, and his mercy to pardon upon repentance, been utterly without use towards man." A Description, &c. pp. 10, 11.]

calling of them, as Adam did in God's effectual forbidding him that tree. God is no respecter of persons, he calleth all effectually, and in good earnest, and whosoever holdeth otherwise, he hath an evil conceit of God.[6]

I. I praise God you have given me great satisfaction in these things. What must we do after our baptism?

C. As the saints, our predecessors, did; *they that gladly* Acts ii. [41, *received the word, were baptized, and they continued in the* 42.] *apostles' doctrine, fellowship, breaking of bread, and prayers,* walking in fear towards God, and in love, in word and deed, one towards another, according to the blessed rules in Christ's testament; and also justly and unblameably towards all men, that they may cause their conversation, [Matt.v.16.] as well as their doctrine, to shine before men, *that men may see their good works, and glorify their Father which is in heaven,* without the which conversation, all profession is nothing.

I. It is a great stumbling-block to many, that divers who profess religion walk corruptly in their conversation; it is a great cause that the wicked open their mouths against God's truth.

C. Alas, it is most lamentable! But God's people must know, it hath been, and will be so, unto the end of Matt. xviii. the world; and therefore hath Christ Jesus appointed [17]; 1Cor.v. [5,] &c. means for the redressing thereof in his church. And we may not justify nor condemn any religion whatsoever by men's personal walkings. May we say the religion of the

[6] [The whole of the above passages, commencing on page 170 up to this point, on original sin in infants, free-will, and predestination, are to be found in the first edition only, being omitted in all the subsequent reprints. They are important, as placing beyond question the accordance in sentiment of the baptists of the time of James with those of Henry VIII. and Edward VI. As they thought alike on these subjects, so also did their opinions coincide on the main topic of the tract—liberty of conscience. See the Historical Introduction, for the evidence on this subject.]

philosophers was good, because of their moral virtues? or, that the religion that Judah and David professed was evil, because of Judah's incest, and David's adultery and murder? or the religion of Christ evil, because that one that professed it fell into incest? God's people had need Ge. xxxviii. [24]; 2 Sam. xi. [2, 17.] 1 Cor. v. [1.] to take heed of sinning, whereby to cause the adversaries to blaspheme, for the which God may make them examples to all succeeding ages.

I. I give you hearty thanks for your pains with me in these things, and I trust I shall not let them slip, but remember them all my life, and put them in practice.

C. The glory and thanks thereof only belongeth to God, for to him it is due; but this I desire you to consider, that the knowing of the will of God, without practising it, doth us rather hurt than good; the scripture saith, *Not the* Rom. ii. 13; James i. 22. *knowers, but the doers are justified.* And *he that knows his* [Luke xii. 47.] *master's will, and doth it not, shall be beaten with many stripes.* Many there be in this nation, with grief of soul I speak it, that acknowledge and confess the truth, but practise it not, for some respects or other; the Lord persuade all your hearts to the speedy practice thereof, and that by many examples that are left unto you. David, that man of God, saith, *I made haste, and delayed not to* Ps. cxix. 60. *keep thy commandments.* The disciples, immediately, with- Matt iv.[20.] out tarrying, followed Christ. The three thousand, the same day they were informed, obeyed the Lord, and were Acts ii. [41.] baptized. The Samaritans, as soon as they believed, *were* Acts viii. 12. *baptized, both men and women.* The eunuch likewise. The Verse 38. gaoler, Lydia, Paul, and a cloud of witnesses, communing not with flesh and blood, but obeyed the Lord as soon as they believed. Here was no staying to hear what this and that learned man could say against it, as now a days, but as they were confidently persuaded thereof, they obeyed.

And so I am assured it shall be, by little and little, as the kingdom of the beast diminisheth.

I. I hope I shall testify to all, my speedy walking in the steps of these holy men; but one thing there is yet which hath much troubled me and others, and in my judgment hath much hindered the growth of godliness in this kingdom, and that is, that many so soon as they see or fear trouble will ensue, they fly into another nation, who cannot see their conversation, and thereby deprive many poor ignorant souls in their own nation of their information, and of their conversation amongst them.

C. Oh ! that hath been the overthrow of religion in this land, the best able and greater part being gone, and leaving behind them some few, who, by the others' departure, have had their afflictions and contempt increased, which hath been the cause of many falling back, and of the adversaries' exulting.   But they will tell us, we are not to judge things by the effects, therefore we must prove that their flight be unlawful, or we say nothing.

And first, Whereas it is said by some of the fliers, that many of the people of God fled into foreign countries, and that God gave approbation thereof, as Moses, David, our Saviour Christ in his infancy, and others, thinking hereby to justify this their flight: I answer, God preserved Moses and the rest in their flight till the time was come that he employed them in his service, then in no case would he suffer them to fly: as when Moses manifested his exceeding backwardness to the Lord's work, in helping his people out of bondage, using many excuses, Ex. iv. 10— the Lord was very angry with him.   And whither did our Luke i. 80. Saviour fly, when the time came that he was to *show himself to Israel?* If any of these men can prove the Lord requireth no work at their hands to be done for his glory, and the salvation of thousands of ignorant souls in their own nation, let them stay in foreign countries.

But I trust God's people have learned not to say, the time is not yet come that Babel should be destroyed, and the Lord's house builded; but that the time is come to build the Lord's house, and not to dwell in ceiled houses, Hag. i. [2, 4.] nor any way to seek our outward promotion; which, if it be granted, that the time is come, not only to come out of Babel, but to destroy her, all these objections are nothing, except they prove, that when God called any of his people to his work, they left it for fear of trouble. This doctrine was not approved of God, when the time came that his adversaries were to be rooted out, and that his people had gotten some victory. The Reubenites and the Gadites could have been content to have remained to their most peace and commodity, but Moses said unto them, *Shall* Num. xxxii. [6, 7, 14.] *your brethren go to war, and ye tarry here? Wherefore now discourage ye the hearts of the children of Israel?* &c.; sharply reproving them, *as an increase of sinful men, risen up in their fathers' steads, still to augment the fierce wrath of the Lord.* And Moses would not be satisfied, until they had promised that they would go with their brethren to the Lord's work, and would not return to their houses till they had accomplished the same. And the angel of the Lord doth say, *Curse ye Meroz, curse the inhabitants thereof,* Jud. v. 23. *because they came not to help the Lord, to help the Lord against the mighty.* Also, because the men of Jabesh-gilead came not up to the Lord to help their brethren, against the wicked men of Gibeah, all the men were Jud. xxi. 11. destroyed, and all the women that had lain by men, no excuse whatsoever could serve.

Did God thus respect his work and people then, that all must put to their helping hand, and none must withdraw their shoulder lest others were discouraged; and is there no regard to be had thereof now, but any occasion, as fear of a little imprisonment, or the like, may excuse any, both from the Lord's work and the help of their brethren, that for want of their society and comfort are exceedingly weakened, if not overcome? If answer be made, they perform their duty in both, that they do the Lord's work, the pastor feeding his flock, and the people walking [in fellowship] one towards another; I demand, Doth the Lord require no more work of them? doth he not require that they should help to cast down Babel? If reply be made, they do it by their books; I answer, that may be done, and their lights shine by their mouths and conversations also among the wicked, which is the greatest means of converting them, and destroying antichrist's kingdom:

Rev. xii. 11. *They overcame,* not by flying away, [but] *by the blood of the Lamb, and by the word of their testimony; and they loved not their lives unto the death.*

Matt. v. [14, 15.] God's people are the lights of the world, a city set on a hill, a candle set on the candlestick, giving light to all that come in, and therefore must shine by their persons, more than by their books. And great help and encouragement would it be to God's people in affliction of imprisonment and the like, to have their brethren's presence, to administer to their souls or bodies, and for which cause Matt. xxv. 36, 41. Christ will say, *I was in prison, and ye visited me; in distress, and ye comforted me*; and unto those that do not so, according to their ability, *Go, ye cursed.* If men had greater love to God's commands, or the salvation of thousands of ignorant souls in our nation, that for want of instruction perish, than to a little temporal affliction, they would neither publish nor practise as they do in this thing.

Thus have I, in short, showed you my poor ability in these things. And for all other things we hold; as the lawfulness of magistracy, God's blessed ordinance : of Christ our Saviour, taking his flesh of the virgin Mary, by the wonderful work of the Holy Ghost, &c.: you may see them in our Confession in print, published four years ago.[7]

I. Many that be called anabaptists hold the contrary, and many other strange things.

C. We cannot but lament for it; so did many in Christ's churches in the primitive times hold strange opinions; as some of the Corinths denied the resurrection; and in many of the seven churches were grievous things, which the Lord by his servants warned them of, upon pain of his displeasure and removing of his presence from them; nevertheless, others professing the same general cause of Christ, were commended.

I. Well, you will yet be called anabaptists, because you deny baptism to infants.

C. So were Christians before us called sects: and so they may [call] John Baptist, Jesus Christ himself, and his apostles anabaptists; for we profess and practise no otherwise herein than they, namely, the baptizing of such as confess with the mouth the belief of the heart. And if they be anabaptists that deny baptism where God hath appointed it, they, and not we, are anabaptists. But the Lord give them repentance, that their sins may be put

---

[7] [" A little after Mr. Smith's death, Mr. Helwisse and his people published a confession of their faith.......It was supposed to have been chiefly drawn up by Mr. Smith himself, before his decease; but it was called, *The Confession of Faith, published in certain conclusions, by the remainder of Mr. Smith's company,* and came out in the year 1611. At the end of it there was an appendix, giving some account of Mr. Smith's last sickness and death." Crosby, Hist. of Eng. Baptists, i. 271. At the end of his first volume, Crosby gives some particulars of this Confession, collected from a work of Mr. John Robinson, written in reply : and in the appendix of the second volume, the Confession itself entire, which he obtained subsequent to the publication of his first volume. See Addenda, C.]

away, and never laid to their charge, even for his Christ's
sake.   Amen.

Thus have we in this dialogue, according to our poor
ability, answered such objections, as, hitherto in our poor
and unworthy testimony, have been objected against any
of us concerning persecution for religion: as also with
good consciences pointed at the principal things of Mr.
Robinson's late book till further time.[8]

[8] [This paragraph was omitted in all subsequent editions.]

FINIS.

AN HUMBLE

SUPPLICATION

TO THE

KING'S MAJESTY.

1620.

A MOST

HUMBLE SUPPLICATION

OF MANY OF THE

KING'S MAJESTY'S LOYAL SUBJECTS,

READY TO TESTIFY ALL

CIVIL OBEDIENCE,.

BY THE

OATH OF ALLEGIANCE,

OR OTHERWISE,

AND THAT OF CONSCIENCE;

WHO ARE

PERSECUTED (ONLY FOR DIFFERING IN RELIGION),

CONTRARY TO DIVINE AND HUMAN TESTIMONIES.

As followeth.

PRINTED 1620.

[This is the title-page of the original edition, according to Crosby.]

INTRODUCTORY NOTICE.

SINCE the year 1614, when Leonard Busher presented his petition for liberty of conscience to king James, and to the parliament then assembled, there had been no session of the great council of the nation. In the mean time, the baptists had been called to endure, in many parts of the country, severe persecutions, imprisonments, loss of goods and life; "not for any disloyalty, nor hurt to mortal man," but because they dared not assent to, nor practice in the worship of God, such things as they deemed contrary to, or unsanctioned by, his word.

Constrained by his urgent necessities, James in 1620 summoned the houses of Lords and Commons; but was most unwilling that they should enter upon a consideration of the domestic wants and grievances of his people. His inaugural speech promised no relief to tender consciences; his former professions of liberality were unheeded or forgotten. "For religion," says he, "there are laws enough, so as the true intent and execution follow. The maintenance of religion stands in two points: 1. Persuasion, which must precede. 2. Compulsion, which must follow; for as all the world cannot create a new creature, be it never so little, so no law of man can make a good Christian in heart, without inward grace. Yet it is not enough to trust to a good cause, and let it go alone. Likewise the busypuritans; do but see how busy they are in persuading the people. But God forbid that I should compel men's consciences, but leave them to the laws of the kingdom; for the rumour that is spread, that I should tolerate religion in respect of this match which hath been long intreated with Spain for my son, I profess I will do nothing therein which shall not be honourable, and for the good of religion."[1]

The wavering of the king between his hopes and fears, and his feigned unwillingness to tolerate popery, did not deceive the Commons, nor prevent them from exhibiting a determined resolution to put down recusancy by yet stronger measures. Moreover, they boldly expressed their sympathy with the misfortunes of the Elector Palatine, whose cause was regarded as that of all true protestants. They determined to assist him, however distasteful it might be to James, his father-in-law, or adverse to the secret intrigues of their sovereign with France and Spain. There were besides, grievances to be redressed, attacks on the liberty of speech to be resented, and peculators to be brought to justice. They rendered their sessions ever memorable, by the impeachment and humiliation of the renowned lord chancellor Bacon.[2]

[1] Parliamentary History, vol. v. p. 315.

[2] Parl. Hist. vol. v. pp. 309, 322, 331, 334, 350.

Amid these exciting events the cry of the oppressed could not be heard, and the earnest and loyal " Supplication" of the baptists passed unheeded. But if they suffered much, they were *in labours more abundant;* they kept up their separate meetings, and many persons embraced their sentiments. An opponent says of them, that at this time they had multitudes of disciples; that it was their custom to produce a great number of scriptures to prove their doctrines; and that they were in appearance more holy than those of the established church.[3] Of their attachment to a scriptural faith the following pages testify. Their temperate, yet noble assertion of the rights of conscience, deserves our admiration and esteem. In this they stood alone among all their contemporaries.

A comparison of some passages with others occurring in " A Description of what God hath predestinated concerning Man,"[4] which book is understood to be the production of Mr. John Murton and his friends, would indicate the same authorship for the ensuing " Humble Supplication." No copy of the original publication is known to exist. The present edition is reprinted from that of 1662, collated and corrected by the reprint of Crosby, who has inserted it in the appendix of the second volume of his History of the English Baptists, and apparently from the first edition of 1620.

It was also reprinted by the late Rev. Joseph Ivimey, in 1827, with " Persecution for Religion judged and condemned."

---

[3] Crosby, Hist. of Eng. Baptists, i. 139.   [4] See before p. 89.

N 2

Some difficulty has been experienced in verifying the references, from the indefinite manner of quotation adopted, as also from the quotations being taken in some instances from secondary sources. In two or three cases the search has altogether failed.

AN

HUMBLE SUPPLICATION

TO

THE KING'S MAJESTY;

AS IT WAS PRESENTED 1620.

To the high and mighty King, JAMES, *by the grace of God,
King of Great Britain, France, and Ireland,* [*our sovereign lord on earth ;*] [1]

To the right excellent and noble Prince, CHARLES, *Prince of
Wales, &c. ;*

To all the right honourable NOBILITY, *grave and honourable*
JUDGES, *and to all other the right worshipful* GENTRY, *of
all estates and degrees, assembled in this present Parliament.*

Right high and mighty, right excellent and noble, right
honourable, and right worshipful ;

AS the consideration of that divine commandment of
the King of kings, *Let supplications, prayers, inter-* [1 Tim. ii.
cessions, and giving of thanks, be made for kings, and for all 1, 2.] ;
*that are in authority ; that we may lead a quiet and a peace-
able life, in all godliness and honesty,* doth cause in us a
daily practice thereof in our secret chambers for you all, as
in duty we are bound, of which the Searcher of all hearts

[1] [Crosby.]

beareth us witness; so let it be pleasing unto your majesty, and the rest in authority, that we make humble supplications and prayers to you, for such our bodily miseries and wants as are upon us, in that it is in your power to redress them; and especially at this present, in this high meeting, assembled for the public weal of all your loyal subjects. Our miseries are long and linger-ing imprisonments for many years in divers counties of England,[2] in which many have died and left behind them widows, and many small children: taking away our goods, and others the like, of which we can make good probation; not for any disloyalty to your majesty, nor hurt to any mortal man, our adversaries themselves being judges; but only because we dare not assent unto, and practise in the worship of God, such things as we have not faith in, Heb. xi. 6; because it is sin against the Most High. As your majesty Rom. xiv.23. well observeth in these words: " It is a good and safe rule in theology, that in matters of the worship of God, Rom. xiv. 5. *quod dubitas, ne feceris,* according to Paul's rule, *Let every man be fully persuaded in his own mind.*" [3]

If we were in error herein, these courses of afflicting our bodies for conscience' cause, are not of Christ, but of anti-christ, as hereafter is most plainly showed. And if no

---

[2] [" They were not only railed against in the pulpits under the names of heretics, schismatics, and anabap-tists, and harassed in the spiritual courts ; but the temporal sword was used against them; their goods seized, their persons confined for many years in stinking gaols, where they were deprived of their wives, children, and friends, till the Divine Majesty was pleased to release several of them by death." Crosby, i. p. 128.]

[3] Medit. on Lord's Prayer. [Works, p. 581, " Surely we that are upon this earth are commanded to pray one for another; but no mention is made of saints nor angels in that precept, nor any where else in the word of God : and it is a good sure rule in theology, in matter of worship of God, quod dubitas, ne feceris (that which is doubtful, ought not to be done) ; ac-cording to that of Saint Paul, Rom. xiv. 5, Let every man be fully per-suaded in his own mind."]

church be the rule of faith, but only the holy scriptures, as the learned protestants do truly confess; and that therefore the doctrine of the church of Rome, that all must believe as the church believes, and so practise, or else be cruelly persecuted, be most ungodly, as it is; then how can they avoid the like censure that practise the same thing, contrary to their own judgment? For the learned protestants do say, it is high cruelty for the papists to constrain them to practise those things in God's worship which they have not faith in, nay, which they know to be evil, with imprisonment, fire, and faggot. And therefore why may not *we* say, it is great cruelty for the learned protestants to constrain us to practise those things in God's worship which *we* have not faith in? nay, which we certainly know to be evil, with lingering imprisonment, loss of goods, and what other cruelties they can procure against us of your majesty and the civil state. If your learned say, they have the truth, and we are in error, that resteth to be tried by the true touchstone, the holy scriptures. If they be our judges, the verdict must needs go against us. If their sayings be a safe rule for us to be saved by, we will rest upon them. And then why may not the sayings of the papists be sure also, and they be the protestants' judges, and so bring us all to believe as the church believes? The iniquity of which we have discovered as briefly as we could; beseeching your majesty and all that are in authority, to hear us. IT CONCERNETH OUR ETERNAL SALVATION, OR CONDEMNATION, AND IS THEREFORE OF GREAT IMPORTANCE; FOR WHAT CAN A MAN GIVE FOR THE RANSOM OF HIS SOUL?

Oh! be pleased to remember the saying of that great and good man, Job; *I delivered the poor that cried, and the* ^{Chap. xxix.} *fatherless, and him that had none to help him: the blessing of* [12—17.]

him that was ready to perish came upon me, and I caused
the widow's heart to rejoice. I was a father to the poor;
and when I knew not the cause, I sought it out diligently. I
brake also the jaws of the unrighteous man, and plucked the
prey out of his teeth.

Our prayers are and shall be for you day and night, to
that God of glory by whom you reign and are advanced,
that he will put it into your hearts to let these things
enter into your thoughts; and then we doubt not, the
evidence of them being such, that you will be moved to
repeal and make void all those cruel laws, which we most
humbly beseech, that persecute poor men, only for matters
of conscience. Not that we any way desire for ourselves
or others, any the least liberty from the strict observation
of any civil, temporal, or human law, made or to be made,
for the preservation of your majesty's person, crown, state,
or dignity; for all that give not to Cæsar that which is
his, let them bear their burden. But we only desire, that
God might have that which is his, which is the heart and
soul in that worship that he requireth, over which *there is*
but one Lord, and *one Lawgiver, who is able to save it, or*
to destroy it, which no mortal can do. It is not in your
power to compel the heart; you may compel men to be
hypocrites, as a great many are, who are falsehearted both
towards God and the state; which is sin both in you and
them.

The vileness of persecuting the body of any man, only
for cause of conscience, is against the word of God and
law of Christ. It is against the profession of your
majesty; against the profession and practice of famous
princes; the ancient and later approved writers witness
against it; so do the puritans; yea, the establishers of it,
the papists themselves, inveigh against it: so that God
and all men do detest it, as is herein showed. And there-

Eph. iv. 5.
Jas. iv. 12.

fore, in most humble manner, we do beseech your majesty, your highness, your honours, your worships, to consider of it, and do as God directeth you in his word, that cannot lie. *Let the wheat and tares grow together in the world,* Matt. xiii. [30.] *until the harvest.*

And so in humble manner we proceed.

CHAPTER I.

The rule of faith is the doctrine of the Holy Ghost contained in the sacred scriptures, and not any church, council, prince, or potentate, nor any mortal man whatsoever.

PROVED, by the scriptures themselves, which are the writings of Moses and the prophets, the evangelists and apostles; these are a sufficient rule alone, to try all faith and religion by. Our reasons are, 1. They are inspired of God, and *are able to make us wise unto salvation, and perfect* 2 Tim. iii. 15, &c. *to every good work.* 2. Because these writings are written, that we might have *certainty of the things whereof we are* Luke i. 4. *instructed, that our joy might be full;* and *that we might* 1 John i. 4. *believe, and in believing might have life.* 3. We are com- John xx. 31. manded not to presume, *or be wise above what is written.* 1 Cor. iv. 6. For, with this weapon Christ put to flight the devil; and Matt. iv. 4. taught his disciples; and Paul, taught Christ Jesus. The Luke xxiv. 27. godly are commended for searching the scriptures. All Acts xvii. 2. Verse 11. are commanded to search them; and they that will not John v. 39. Verse 47. believe these writings, will not believe Christ's words, nor Luke xvi. 31. one that should come from the dead. If any ask, how we know all, or any of these scriptures to be inspired of God? We answer, *The ear discerneth words, and the mouth tasteth* Job xii. 11. *meat for itself;* and as the eye discerneth the light of the sun, so doth our spirit discern these scriptures to be inspired of God.

And that for these reasons : 1. In regard of the majesty, wisdom, and grace of them above all other writings; for there is as great glory in these scriptures as in the making of this wonderful world, which is most evidently discerned. 2. By their teachings, which excelleth all human teachings, leading us from Satan, from this world and ourselves, to God, in holiness, faith, love, fear, obedience, humility. 3. The true events of them, or fulfilling of the prophecies contained in them.   4. The consent and agreement of all the parts of them, the like whereof cannot be shown of so many several writers since the world began. 5. The admirable preservation thereof against time and tyrants; all which could not extinguish them.   6. The devil and his instruments rage against those that practise the doctrines contained in them.   7. The conversion of thousands to God, by the power of their doctrine. 8. The vengeance that hath come upon such as have not obeyed them.   9. The acknowledgment of them by the very professed adversaries thereof.   10. The miracles confirming them from heaven.   11. The sight of a Saviour to man is only by and from them.   And lastly, the simplicity of the writers and plainness of the writings; for God hath chosen the mean, contemptible, and despised, to manifest unto the world his mysteries.

Heb. xi. 3.

1 Cor. i. [26, 27.]

These are sufficient to persuade, that these holy writings are inspired of God, and so able to make wise unto salvation, and perfect to every good work.   These scriptures contain the law and testimony ; and if any church, council, prince, or potentate, *speak not according to this word, it is because there is no light in them.*   And we are commanded to hold them accursed.   For, *whosoever shall add unto these things, God shall add the plagues written herein;* and *who-*

Isa. viii. 20.

Gal. i. 8, 9.
Rev. xxii.
[18, 19.]

soever shall take away from these things, God shall take his name out of the book of life, and out of the holy city, and from those things that are written.

Much by us shall not need to be written on this subject, the thing is so evident, and so generally acknowledged, at least in words, excepting the papists, with whom we have not here to do; only we will add some human testimonies.

The learned protestants affirm and prove, that it is the doctrine of the church of England,[4] Art. vi. [The doctrine of holy scripture] "That the scripture comprehended in the [canonical books of the] old and new testament, is the rule of faith so far, that whatsoever is not read therein, or cannot be proved thereby, is not to be accepted as any point of faith, nor needful to be followed; but by it all doctrines taught, and the church's practice must be examined, and that rejected which is contrary to it, under what title or pretence soever it come unto us." And further they say,[5] that the pope, or any mortal man, should be the rule that must resolve in questions and controversies of faith, is " an unreasonable position, void of all indifferency ; when common sense teacheth, that he which is a party, cannot be judge." And again,[6] " Which is the church is controversal, which is the scriptures is not; therefore, let that be the rule which is out of doubt." And again, " The scriptures contain the principles of our faith, and shall we not believe them? Or, cannot we

---

[4] White's Way to the Church, dedicated to two bishops, page 12. [The Way to the True Church; wherein the principall motives perswading to Romanisme, and Questions touching the nature and authoritie of the Church and Scriptures, are familiarly disputed, and driven to their issues, where this day they sticke betweene the papists and us : &c., &c., by John White, minister of God's word at Eccles. London : 1610, 4to. Dedicated to Tobie, the Lord Archbishop of Yorke, and to George, Lord Bishop of Chester.]

[5] Page 1.   [6] Page 17.

know them infallibly of themselves, without we let in the authority of the church?" This, and much more, the learned protestants have written, and sufficiently confirmeth, that no church nor man whatsoever may be the judge, rule, or umpire, in matters of faith, but only the holy scriptures; and whosoever teacheth and practiseth otherwise, they must hold and maintain the papists' creed, or collier's faith, which the protestants so much in words detest, and mention out of Staphilus his Apology,[7] thus: " The collier being at the point of death, and tempted of the devil, what his faith was; answered, 'I believe, and die in the faith of Christ's church.' Being again demanded, what the faith of Christ's church was: 'That faith,' said he, 'that I believe in.' Thus the devil, getting no other answer, was overcome and put to flight. By this faith of the collier, every unlearned man may try the spirits of men, whether they be of God or no; by this faith he may resist the devil, and judge the true interpretation from the false, and discern the catholic from the heretical minister, the true doctrine from the forged."

If the answer of the collier, and the papist's conclusion upon it be not sound, but detestable, as the protestants confess, and cry woe unto the papists for the same, and

---

[7] White's Way to the True Church, p. 6. [Apologia D. Frederici Staphyli, Coloniæ, 1562, fol. 82, 83. " Carbonarii fides optima. Et hæc est carbonarii illius fides, quem ferunt in supremo spiritu constitutum, cùm à malo spiritu de fide tentaretur, hoc pacto respondisse : Ego credo, et jam animam reddo in ea fide, quam habet Christi ecclesia. Porro percontanti dæmoni quod Christi ecclesia crederet, iterum dixisse, Id quod ego credo.

Atque hac simplici ejus carbonarii fide victus et profligatus est teter spiritus. Eadem carbonarii fide potest quilibet è vulgo idiota probare spiritus utrùm ex Deo sint: potest resistere et contradicere diabolo, potest dijudicare veram et catholicam, a falsa et hæretica interpretatione, potest ferre sententiam, quis catholicus, quis hæreticus sit concionator, quis seductor, factiosus et hæresiarcha."]

that justly; then is it no less detestable in the protestants or any other to require, or any to yield so far in religion and faith, that upon such a temptation he hath no better answer to make than as the collier, to say, " I believe and die in the faith of the church, or of the prince, or of the learned." For, being demanded, what that faith is? if he be not able to prove it by God's word, contained in the scriptures, it is no better, nor other, than the answer of the collier, " The faith that I believe in." Oh! how many millions of souls in this nation, not papists but protestants, live and die, and have never other faith than this, where-unto they are constrained and compelled by persecution, without either faith or knowledge.

CHAPTER II.

The interpreter of this rule is the scriptures, and Spirit of God in whomsoever.

THE next thing, as the immediate question from this former, is, Who must interpret this rule? Because, as is objected, there are many dark places in it, *hard to be* 2 Pet. iii. *understood.* Unto which we answer: the two witnesses of [16.] God shall be the only interpreters thereof; which are, the word of God contained in the same scriptures, and the John xv. 26, Spirit of God; so are they called. 27; Acts v. 32.

First, for the scriptures themselves; though some doc-trines in some places be dark and obscure, as Peter speaketh, yet the self-same doctrines in other places are plain and manifest: for, all the words of the Lord *are* Prov. viii. 9. *plain to him that will understand, and straight to them that*

Prov. xiv. 6. *would find knowledge ;* and *knowledge is easy to him that will understand.*

1 John v. 6. Secondly, The Spirit of God; so saith the apostle : *It is the Spirit that beareth witness : for the Spirit is truth.*

John xiv. 26. *But the Comforter, which is the Holy Ghost, whom the Father will send in my name, he shall teach you all things, and bring all things to your remembrance, which I have told you.*

John xvi. 13. *Howbeit when he is come, which is the Spirit of truth, he will lead you into all truth; for he shall not speak of himself; but whatsoever he shall hear, shall he speak, and he*

1 Cor. ii. 10, 11. *will show you of the things to come. For the Spirit searcheth all things, even the deep things of God. For the things of*

1 John ii. 27. *God knoweth no man, but the Spirit of God. But the anointing that ye have received of him dwelleth in you, and ye need not that any man teach you ; but as the same anointing teacheth you of all things, and it is true, and is not lying ; and as it hath taught you, you shall abide in him.*

1 John iii. 24. *Hereby we know that he abideth in us, even by the Spirit*

1 Cor. xii. 8. *that he hath given us. For to one is given by the Spirit, the word of wisdom ; and to another the word of knowledge, by the same Spirit.*

The scriptures be so plain in this, that the greatest adversaries thereof do acknowledge the truth of it : only herein lieth the difficulty, who it is that hath this Spirit of God to interpret the scriptures, which is this sure rule ? Which in the next place is to be handled.

CHAPTER III.

That the Spirit of God, to understand and interpret the scriptures, is given to all and every particular person that fear and obey God, of what degree soever they be; and not to the wicked.

PROVED. *What man is he that feareth the Lord? him* Ps. xxv. 12, 14. *will he teach the way that he shall choose. The secret of the Lord is revealed to them that fear him, and his covenant to give them understanding. Who is wise that he may ob-* Ps. cvii. 43. *serve these things? he shall understand the lovingkindness of the Lord. None of the wicked shall have understanding; but* Dan xii. 10. *the wise shall understand. For God will do nothing, but* Amos iii. 7. *he revealeth his secrets to his servants. I have had more* Ps. cxix. 99, 100. *understanding than all my teachers, and than all the ancients; because I kept thy precepts. For he that keepeth the law is* Prov. xxviii 7. *a child of understanding. If ye love me, keep my command-* John xiv. 15 16, 23. *ments, and I will pray the Father, and he shall give you the Spirit of truth. If any man love me, he will keep my word, and my Father and I will come unto him and will dwell with him. If any man will do his will, he shall* John vii. 17. *know of the doctrine, whether it be of God or no. Yea, and* Acts v. 32. *the Holy Ghost, whom God hath given to all that obey him. I will give you,* my disciples that obey me, and suffer for Luke xxi.15 my sake, *a mouth, and wisdom, &c. The Holy Ghost shall* Luke xii. 12. *teach you what ye shall say. For, it is not you that speak,* Matt. x. 20. *but the Spirit of my Father that speaketh in you. And, to* Mark iv. 11. *you,* my followers, *is given to know the mysteries of the kingdom of God; but not to them that are without:* for the Col. i. 26. mystery of the gospel is made manifest to the saints.

The church and saints of God have revealed unto them *by the Spirit,* the things *that eye hath not seen, &c.* And 1 Cor. ii. 9, 10, [12,] 14, *they have received the Spirit of God, that they might know* [15.]

the things that are given them of God.   But *the natural man perceiveth not the things of the Spirit of God, for they are foolishness to him; neither can he know them, because they are spiritually discerned: but he that is spiritual, discerneth all things,* &c.

Hence it is most plain to whom the Spirit of God is given, even to every particular saint of God. And it is 2 Pet. i. 20. no private spirit, but even the public Spirit of God which is in him, which enableth him to understand, and so to declare the things given him of God. That is a private spirit that is not of God, though it be in multitudes; but the Spirit of God, though but in one saint, is not private. God's Spirit is not private, for it is not comprehended only within one place, person, or time, as man's is, but it is universal and eternal; so is not man's: therefore man's is private, though they be many; God's is public, though but in one person.

CHAPTER IV.

Those that fear and obey God, and so have the Spirit of God to search out and know the mind of God in the scriptures, are commonly, and for the most part, the simple, poor, despised, &c.

Matt. xi. 5, 25, [26.]   PROVED, our Saviour saith, *The poor receive the gospel; and, I thank thee, Father, because thou hast opened these things unto babes; it is so, O Father, because thy good plea-* James ii. 5. *sure was such. Hearken, my beloved brethren, hath not God chosen the poor of this world, that they should be rich in faith, and heirs of the kingdom which he hath promised ? &c. Bre-* 1 Cor. i. 26, *thren, you see your calling, that God hath chosen the foolish* &c.

of this world, the weak of this world, the vile of this world and despised, and which are not. God's dealing is, to give unto the *simple sharpness of wit, and to the child knowledge and* Prov. i. 4. *discretion. The Spirit bloweth where it listeth,* and is not John iii. 8. tied to the learned. Poor persecuted Micaiah had the truth against four hundred of king Ahab's prophets; so 1Kings xxii. [8.] had Jeremiah against all the priests and prophets of Israel.

The Lord of life himself, in his fleshly being, what was he but a man full of sorrows? in his birth laid in a cratch, because *there was no room for him in the inn ; a carpenter* Luke ii. 7. by trade, *having not a hole to rest his head in ; and in his* Mark vi. 3. Matt.viii 20. death, contemned and despised. His apostles, in like manner, what were they but mean men, fishermen, tent-makers, and such like, *having no certain dwelling-place?* 1 Cor. iv. 11. Which the worldly-wise scribes and pharisees took notice of, and reproachfully said, *Do any of the rulers, or of the* John vii, 48, 49. *pharisees, believe in him ?* but *this people that know not the law are accursed.*

The truth of this is as plain as may be, that the scriptures being the rule of faith, perfect and absolute, and that the plainness of them is such, as by the Spirit of God they may be easily understood of those that fear and obey God, but of none else, and that such are most commonly the poor and despised; for, *if any man want wisdom,* be he James i. 5. never so simple, *let him ask of God,* and he will give him. Which is also confirmed by human testimonies.

The protestants confess,[8] that "in the primitive church, the doctrines and several points of religion, were known and discoursed by the meanest of the people, and the bishops exhorted them thereunto," &c. Also, [9] "that this rule is of that nature, that it is ABLE to direct any man, be he never so simple; *yea,* the most unlearned alive

---

[8] White's Way to the True Church,   [9] White's Way, p. 9.
p. 7.

HUMBLE SUPPLICATION.]   O

may conceive and understand it sufficiently for his salvation."

And they relate the sayings of the ancients in this thing; first, Clemens Alexandrinus : " The word is not hid from any, it is a common light that shineth unto all men, there is no obscurity in it; hear it you that be far off, and hear it you that be nigh." [1]

Next him, Austin : " God hath bowed down the scriptures, [even] to the capacity of babes and sucklings, that when proud men will not speak to their capacity, yet himself might." [2]

After him, Chrysostom : " The scriptures are easy to understand, and exposed to the capacity of every servant, and ploughman, and widow, and boy, and him that is most unwise." [3] " Therefore God penned the scriptures by the hands of publicans, fishermen, tentmakers, shepherds, neatherds, and unlearned men, that none of the simple people might have any excuse to keep them from reading, and that so they might be easy to be understood of all men, the artificer, the householder and widow woman, and him that is most unlearned. Yea, the apostles and prophets, as schoolmasters to all the world, made their writings plain and evident to all men, so that every man of himself, only by reading them, might learn the things spoken therein." [4]

[1] White's Way, &c. p. 32. [" Ἀκού-σατε οὖν οἱ μακρὰν, ἀκούσατε οἱ ἐγγύς. Οὐκ ἀπεκρύβη τινὰς ὁ λόγος· φῶς ἐστι κοινὸν, ἐπιλαμβάνει πᾶσιν ἀνθρώποις· οὐδεὶς κιμμέριος ἐν λόγῳ." Clem. Alex. Opera, Protrept. p. 42. Lugduni, 1616.]

[2] [" Inclinavit ergo scripturas Deus usque ad infantium et lactentium capacitatem, sicut in alio Psalmo canitur, et inclinavit cœlos et descendit, et hoc fecit propter inimicos, qui superba loquacitate inimici crucis Christi, etiam cum aliqua vera dicunt, parvulis tamen et lactentibus prodesse non possunt." Enarrat. in Psal. viii. Opera, tom. 8. fol. 12. Venetiis, 1551.]

[3] [" Ὅπου καὶ γηπόνῳ, καὶ οἰκέτῃ, καὶ γυναικὶ χήρᾳ, καὶ παιδὶ αὐτῷ, καὶ τῷ σφόδρα ἀνοήτῳ δοκοῦνται εἶναι, πάντα εὐσύνοπτα καὶ ῥᾴδια καταμαθεῖν." Homil. I. in Matt. Commentaria. Tom. i. p. 9. Parisiis, 1636.]

[4] [" Διὰ γὰρ τοῦτο ἡ τοῦ πνεύματος ᾠκονόμησε χάρις τελώνας

Next, Justin Martyr saith: "Hear the words of the scripture, which be so easy that it needs no exposition, but only to be rehearsed." [5]

And this, the protestants say, "was the perpetual and constant judgment of the ancient church," &c.

And further, he allegeth Theodoret, who wrote of his times, "You shall everywhere see these points of our faith to be known and understood, not only by such as are teachers in the church, but even of cobblers, and smiths, and websters, and all kinds of artificers; yea, all our women, not they only which are book-learned, but they also that get their living by their needle; yea, maid-servants and waiting-women; and not citizens only, but husbandmen of the country are very skilful in these things; yea, you may hear among us ditchers, and neat-herds, and woodsetters, discoursing of the Trinity and the creation," &c.[6] "The like is reported by others."

καὶ σκηνοποιοὺς, καὶ ποιμένας, καὶ αἰπόλους, καὶ ἰδιώτας, καὶ ἀγραμμάτους ταῦτα συνθεῖναι τὰ βιβλία, ἵνα μηδεὶς τῶν ἰδιωτῶν εἰς ταύτην ἔχῃ καταφεύγειν τὴν πρόφασιν ἵνα πᾶσιν εὐσύνοπτα ᾖ τὰ λεγόμενα. ἵνα καὶ ὁ χειροτέχνης, καὶ οἰκέτης, καὶ ἡ χήρα γυνὴ, καὶ ὁ πάντων ἀνθρώπων ἀμαθέστατος, κερδάνῃ τε καὶ ὠφεληθῇ παρὰ τῆς ἀκροάσεως.

"Οἱ δὲ ἀπόστολοι καὶ οἱ προφῆται τοὐναντίον ἅπαν ἐποίησαν. Σαφῆ γὰρ καὶ δῆλά τὰ παρὰ ἑαυτῶν κατέστησαν ἅπασιν, ἅ τε κοινοὶ τῆς οἰκουμένης ὄντες διδάσκαλοι, ἵνα ἕκαστος καὶ δι' ἑαυτοῦ μανθάνειν δύνηται ἐκ τῆς ἀναγνώσεως μόνης τὰ λεγόμενα." Concio III. de Laz. Opera, tom. 5. p. 58. Parisiis, 1636.]

[5] White's Way, p. 33. ["Προσ-

ἔχετε τοιγαροῦν, ὥσπερ μέλλω ἀναμιμνήσκειν ἀπὸ τῶν ἁγίων γραφῶν, οὐδὲ ἐξηγηθῆναι δεομένων, ἀλλὰ μόνον ἀκουσθῆναι." Dialog. cum Tryphon. Opera, p. 150. Parisiis, 1742.]

[6] White's Way, p. 21. ["Καὶ ἔστιν ἰδεῖν ταῦτα εἰδότας τὰ δόγματα οὐ μόνοις γε τῆς ἐκκλησίας τοῖς διδασκάλοις, ἀλλὰ καὶ σκυτοτόμοις καὶ χαλκοτύποις καὶ ταλασιουργοῖς καὶ τοῖς ἄλλοις ἀποχειροβιώτοις· καὶ γυναῖκας ὡσαύτως, οὐ μόνον τὰς λόγων μετεσχηκυίας· ἀλλὰ δὲ χερνητίδας καὶ ἀκεστρίδας καὶ μέντοι θεραπαίνας. Καὶ οὐ μόνον ἀστοὶ, ἀλλὰ δὲ χωρητικοὶ τήνδε γνῶσιν ἐσχήκασι. Ἔστι δὴ εὑρεῖν καὶ σκαπανέας καὶ βοηλάτας καὶ φυτουργοὺς περὶ τῆς θείας λεγομένους Τριάδος: καὶ περὶ τῆς τῶν

And, say the protestants, " his doctrine that was president in the Trent conspiracy, 'that a distaff was fitter for
women than a bible,' was not yet hatched." [7]

Oh! it were well if the contempt of these pious practices
were paled only within the Romish profession, and were
not practised in and among those that profess themselves
to be separated therefrom. And what is more frequent in
the mouths of many protestants, yea, the bishops themselves, than these and such like words : Must every base
fellow, cobbler, tailor, weaver, &c. meddle with the exposition or discoursing of the scriptures, which appertain to
none but to the learned? Yea, do they not forbid their own
ministers to expound or discourse of the scriptures? Read
their forty-ninth canon : [8] which is, " No person whatsoever,
not examined and approved by the bishop of the diocese,
or not licensed, as is aforesaid, for a sufficient or convenient
preacher, shall take upon him to expound in his own cure,
or elsewhere, any scripture, or matter, or doctrine; but
shall only study to read plainly and aptly, without glossing
or adding, the homilies already set forth, or hereafter to be
published by lawful authority, [for the confirmation of the
true faith, and for the good instruction and edification of
the people.]"

So that not only Jesus Christ and his apostles, who are
alive in their doctrine, though not in their persons, are
forbidden all exposition of the holy scriptures, or matter,
or doctrine, not being licensed by the bishops, but also
their own ministers, who have sworn canonical obedience
to them. Yet, when they are put to answer the papists
who practise the same thing, they take up both scriptures
and ancient writers to confute it.

ὅλων δημιουργίας." Theodoret.   [7] [White's Way, &c. p. 21.]
Græcarum Affect. Curatio. Serm. V.   [8] [Constitutions and Canons Ec-
Opera, tom. iv. p. 556. Paris. 1642.]   clesiastical, &c. canon xlix.]

CHAPTER V.

The learned in human learning, do commonly and for the most part err, and know not the truth, but persecute it, and the professors of it: and therefore are no further to be followed than we see them agree with truth.

THE next thing in order is, seeing the Lord revealeth his secrets to the humble, though wanting human learning, that we now prove on the contrary; that God usually, and for the most part, hideth his secrets from the learned, and suffereth them to err and resist the truth, yea, so far as to persecute it, and the professors of it.

And first, let us begin with the learned heathen, who were behind none in human learning; the wise men of Egypt, how did they resist the glorious and powerful truth of God delivered by Moses! Yea, they resisted it Exod.vii.11, with such signs and lying wonders, that the heart of 12, 13; viii. 7. Pharaoh and all his people were hardened against it. And what was the cause of Babel's destruction, but their trusting in the learned? *Thou art wearied in the multitude* Isaiah xlvii. *of thy counsels,* &c. *I destroy the tokens of the soothsayers,* Isaiah xliv. *and make them that conjecture fools, and turn the wise men* 25. *backward, and make their knowledge foolishness.* The things of God's dealing none of the learned of Egypt or Babel could interpret, but Joseph and Daniel.

Next come to the learned priests and prophets of the Jews, whose lips should have preserved knowledge, and at whose mouth the people should have sought the law; *but,* Mal. ii. 7, 8 saith the Lord, *they are gone out of the way, they have caused many to fall by the law,* &c. Also, *Stay yourselves* Isaiah xxix. *and wonder: they are blind, and make you blind; they are* [9, 10,13, 14.] *drunken, but not with wine; they stagger, but not with strong*

*drink ; for the Lord hath covered you with a spirit of slumber,
and hath shut up your eyes, the prophets, and your chief
seers,* &c.   *Therefore the Lord said, Because this people come
near to me with their mouth, and honour me with their lips,
but have removed their heart far from me, and their fear
towards me was taught by the precepts of men ; therefore,
behold, I will again do a marvellous work in this people, a
marvellous work and a wonder, for the wisdom of their wise
men shall perish, and the understanding of the prudent shall*
be hid, &c.   *Their watchmen are all blind, they have no
knowledge,* &c.   And these *shepherds cannot understand, for
they all look to their own way, every one for his own advantage,
and for his own purpose.   The wise men are ashamed, they
are afraid and taken ; lo, they have rejected the word of the
Lord, and what wisdom is in them,* &c. ?   *My people have
been as lost sheep, their shepherds have caused them to go
astray, and have turned them away to the mountains,* &c.
*Night shall be unto them for a vision, and darkness for a divi-
nation ; the sun shall go down over the prophets, and the day
shall be dark over them,* &c. *for they have no answer of God.
They build up Zion with blood, and Jerusalem with iniquity,*
&c.   *Her prophets are light and wicked persons, her priests
have polluted the sanctuary, they have wrested the law.*

And in the time of our Saviour, how had they *made the
commandments of God of no authority by their traditions.*
The rulers of Jerusalem, the high priests, scribes, and
pharisees, knew not Christ, *nor yet the words of the prophets,
which they heard read every sabbath, but fulfilled them in
condemning him.*   And our Saviour saith, *I thank thee,
Father, Lord of heaven and earth, because thou hast hid
these things from the wise, and men of understanding.*   And
none of the pharisees nor rulers believed on him.   *Where
is the wise ?   Where is the scribe ?   Where is the disputer of
this world ?   Hath not God made the wisdom of this world*

Isaiah lvi.10, &c.

Jer. viii. 9, &c.

Jer. xiv. 14, &c. ; l. 6.

Micah iii. [6, 7, 10.]

Zeph. iii. 4.

Matt. xv. 6; Acts xiii. 27.

Matthew xi. [25.]

John vii. 48; 1 Cor. i. 20, 26.

foolishness ? Not many wise men after the flesh, not many mighty, not many noble, are called, &c.

And for the learned since the time of our Saviour. At the council of Ephesus, where were one hundred and thirty-two bishops ; of Seleucia, where were one hundred and sixty bishops, related by the protestants. How grievously did they err in decreeing the detestable error of Arianism ?[9] Who is ignorant, knowing the histories, that from time to time, both particular popes and general councils have grossly erred in many things? Only one we will mention, passing by Trent and others. The council Lateran we mean,—Pope Innocent, 1215,—which, for universality, was behind none, " where were present two patriarchs, seventy archbishops metropolitans, four hundred bishops, twelve abbots, eight hundred conventual priors, the legates of the Greek and Roman empire, besides the ambassadors and orators of the kings of Jerusalem, of France, of Spain, of England, and of Cyprus. In this council it was decreed, that all heretics, and so many as did in any point resist the catholic faith, should be condemned [as schismatics, and delivered to the secular power, to be punished accordingly]."[1] And also, " that

---

[9] [" For what bishops, what pastors, what councils, what men, what churches, have not erred ; though God have bidden us inquire their judgment, and seek unto them ? (Mal. ii. 7 ; Eph. iv. 11 ; Heb. xiii. 17.) The papists will say particular churches may err, but how did the councils of Ephesus, Seleucia, and Remino, (Ariminum,) miss it, where the flower of all the Christian pastors of the world were assembled ? whereof Jerome complained, *The whole world groaned and wondered to see itself Arian.*" White's Way, p. 82, 83.]

[1] [" The famous general council of Lateran [was] celebrated above three hundred years since, wherein there were patriarchs and archbishops, seventy ; bishops, four hundred and twelve ; and other prelates, eight hundred. In all, of the most chosen men of all nations, twelve hundred and eighty-two, with the ambassadors of the Roman emperor, of the king of Jerusalem, of England, of France, of Spain, and of Cyprus, as also of other Christian states. Than which there can be no surer judgment upon earth, which assembly representing the whole

the secular powers, of whatsoever office or degree they be,
should be compelled openly to swear for the defence of the
faith, that they shall to the uttermost of their power root
out and destroy in all their kingdoms, all such persons as
the catholic church hath condemned for heretics ;" and if
they do not, they shall be excommunicated; and if they
do not reform within one whole year, then the pope
may denounce all their "subjects absolved, and utterly
delivered from showing, or owing, any fidelity or obedience towards them. Again, that the pope may give that
land, to be occupied and enjoyed of the catholics, to possess
it, all heretics being rooted out, quietly and without any
contradiction." [2]   And the protestants confess, that this
"imperfection hath hung so fast upon all councils and
churches, that Nazianzen saith, 'He never saw any
council have a good end.'" [3]

    Thus are here sufficient testimonies proved from scrip-
tures and experience, that the learned may, and have
usually erred ; and therefore the holy scriptures often
warn us, to *beware of false prophets, for many are gone out
into the world.*

Matt. xxiv.
[11]; 1 John
iv. [1.]

    And will not your majesty, your highness, your honours,

Christian world, would never agree
upon any assertion traitorous. These
then are the words of their most renowned decree, 'If any lord temporal, required and admonished by
the church, neglect to purge his state
from heretical filth, let him he excommunicated by the metropolitan
and conprovincial bishops. But if he
contemn to come to order within one
year's space, let relation be made to
the supreme bishop, that from thence-
forth he may declare all his subjects
to be discharged of their fealty
towards him, and give up his land
to be possessed by catholics ; which

catholics, without all contradiction,
when they have driven out the heretics, shall have and hold the same,
and so preserve it in purity of faith."
Cardinal Allen's Defence of English
Catholics, quoted by Dr. Bilson in
his True Difference, &c. p. 316, 4to
ed. 1585.]
    [2] Tho. Becon, in his Reliques of
Rome, printed 1563, [fol. 216, 217.]
    [3] [White's Way, &c. p. 83. " "Ὅτι
μηδεμιᾶς συνόδου τέλος εἶδον
χρηστὸν μηδὲ λύσιν κακῶν μᾶλλον
ἐχηκυίας, ἢ προσθήκην." Greg.
Nazianzen. Op. Parisiis. 1630, Ep.
ad Procop. p. 814.]

your worships, be pleased to consider of these things?
But will yourselves submit the guidance of your souls to
the learned spirituality, as they are called, without due
examination by the scriptures? Which, if you will still
do, we can but bewail with the sorrows of our hearts.
And not so only, but will you with your power which
God hath given you to use well, compel and constrain
your subjects and underlings to believe as the learned
believe, not suffering us to read or search the scriptures?
Which, if you abhor, as being the Romish practice, will
you do that which is worse, letting us read the scriptures,
whereby we may know the will of our heavenly Master,
and have our consciences enlightened and convinced, but
not suffer us to practise that we learn and know? whereby
our sin and condemnation is made greater than the blind
papists', as is proved. And not only so, but will you Luke xii. 47
constrain us to captivate our consciences, and practise in
that, which in our souls we know to be evil, and contrary
to the manifest law of the Lord, and that only because the
learned have so decreed—whom you acknowledge are
subject to err as well as others—or else lie in perpetual
imprisonment, and be otherwise grievously persecuted?

May it please you to observe that the church of Rome
seeth and acknowledgeth in words, that *Jesus Christ is
come in the flesh,* and hath abolished the priesthood of
Aaron, and the legal sacrifices. But the Jews see it not
to this day; nay, the high priest, scribes, and pharisees,
saw it not; but, for the publishing thereof, persecuted
Christ the Lord, and his apostles, unto the death, calling
their doctrine heresy, and them seditious enemies to Cæsar,
&c. For the which we all justly condemn them for their
wickedness, so often as we read the holy history.

And the church of England seeth and acknowledgeth
divers damnable doctrines of the church of Rome. This,

among many, That the scriptures are not the only rule of faith; but that men ought to be constrained to believe as the church believes.[4] The protestants see the iniquity of this, because they see and acknowledge all churches are subject to err.[5] But the learned papists see it not, but have decreed, that whosoever resisteth in any point shall be judged as an heretic, and suffer fire and faggot; and every temporal magistrate that doth not root such heretics out of their dominions, shall be excommunicated, and if he do not reform, he shall be expelled his earthly possessions, and his subjects freed from owing any fidelity or obedience towards him, &c.[6] For the which height of iniquity, the protestants and we justly cry out against them, for all the innocent blood that they have shed.

Rom. xiv. 23.
Heb. xi. 6.

And we see most manifestly, that *whatsoever is not of faith is sin,* and *without faith it is impossible to please God.* And therefore, that no mortal man may make a law to the conscience, and force unto it by persecutions, and consequently may not compel unto any religion where faith is wanting, as hereafter more largely we prove. But the learned of this land see it not, or rather will not practise it; but, for our not submitting herein, procure your temporal sword to persecute us, by casting us in prisons,

[4] ["No man ought to be so arrogant and presumptuous to affirm for a certain truth in religion, any thing which is not spoken of in holy scripture. And this is spoken to the great and utter condemnation of the papists, which make and unmake new articles of our faith from time to time at their pleasure, without any scripture at all, yea quite and clean contrary to scripture. And yet will they have all men bound to believe whatsoever they invent, upon peril of damnation and everlasting fire. And they would constrain with fire and faggot all men to consent, contrary to the manifest words of God, to these their errors in this matter of the holy sacrament of Christ's body and blood." Cranmer's Works, by Jenkyns, ii. 395.]

[5] [Article xix.—"As the church of Jerusalem, Alexandria, and Antioch, have erred, so also the church of Rome hath erred, not only in their living, and manner of ceremonies, but also in matters of faith."]

[6] [See before, p. 208.]

where many of us have remained divers years in lingering imprisonment, deprived of all earthly comforts, as wives, children, callings, &c. without hope of release, till our God, for the practice of whose commandments we are thus persecuted, persuade the hearts of your majesty, your highness, your honours, your worships, to take pity upon us, our poor wives and children, or his heavenly Majesty release us by death. Will not succeeding ages cry out against the cruelty of the learned protestants herein, as well as they cry out against the cruelty of the learned Jews and papists? Yes, we are assured they will, as many millions do in other nations at this day.

The scriptures declare the cause of the Jews' blindness, John xi. 48. was not the obscurity of the scriptures, but that they winked with their eyes, lest they should see that which would deprive them of their honours and profits : and because their fear towards God was taught by men's precepts, and because they looked to their own way, and to their own advantage, and had rejected the word of the Lord, and because they builded their Zion with blood, and Jerusalem with iniquity, and sought their own honour, and not God's, as before is proved. So the cause of the blindness of the learned papists in denying the scriptures, the only rule of faith, is not the obscurity of the scriptures, but their winking with their eyes, lest they should see that, that would bring them from their honours and profits, and all the forenamed in the Jews. And also as the protestants well observe, "First, that they might make themselves judges in their own cause, for who seeth not, that if the church be the rule of faith, and theirs be the church, which way the verdict will go?" "Next, for that [they know and confess] the [most and] greatest points of their religion, [even well nigh all wherein they dissent from us] have no foundation on the scriptures;"[7] so that take away the scriptures and establish their religion; but establish the scriptures, and their religion vanisheth; and that mother

Rev. xviii.
[7.]

of whoredoms, that glorified herself as a queen, shall be consumed, and her merchants that were waxed rich through her pleasures and profits, shall wail and weep, the which they now seeing, shut their eyes, lest they should see that which would bring them from these honours, profits and pleasures.

In like manner, it may easily be judged by every indifferent man, that the cause why the learned of this land will not see, or at least practise,—that seeing there is but

Eph. iv. 5.
James iv. 12.

one *Lord,* and one *Lawgiver* over the conscience, therefore no man ought to be compelled to a worship, wherein he hath not faith, by persecution—is not the obscurity of the scriptures, but their winking with their eyes, lest they should see that, that would take away their honours and

Deut.xvi 19.

profits? for, if *bribes blind the eyes of the wise,* then honours and profits much more. For, who seeth not, if none should be compelled by persecution to worship, till the power of God's word had begotten faith in them, to wor-

John iv. 23.

ship God in spirit and in truth—*such only worship him,* and none but such are required *to worship him*—that these learned would lose their honours and profits, in being lords and law-makers over the conscience and souls of men: although your majesty might lawfully give them what temporal honours and profit your highness liked of. These are the true causes of the blindness of the learned;

John v. 44.

for so Christ saith, *How can ye believe when ye seek honour one of another, and seek not the honour that cometh from God alone?* And how can men but be blind in God's mysteries, when they look to their own way, for their own

---

[7] White's Way, &c. p. 18.

advantage, and for their own purpose; for, having rejected the word of the Lord, what wisdom is in them? they have no answer of God, that build up their Zion,—for so they account their churches and professions,—with blood, and Jerusalem with iniquity, as before is proved.

If these learned could free us from the Lord's wrath, or if they might answer for us, and we be free, it were safe for us to submit ourselves, and captivate our judgments and practice to them. But seeing they cannot so much as deliver their own souls, and that *if the blind lead the blind,* Matt. xv. 14. *both must fall into the ditch,* and *every one must give account of himself to God,* and *be judged by his own works done in the* [2 Cor. v. 10.] *flesh,* and that *the soul that sinneth shall die;* we dare not [Ezek. xviii. 20] follow any mortal man in matters of salvation further than we know him to agree with the meaning of God in the scriptures.

Paul, the holy apostle of Jesus Christ, taught, that we should follow him no otherwise than he followed Christ. 1 Cor. xi. 1. Yea, Christ himself sent men to the scriptures to try his doctrine. The apostles suffered their doctrine to be tried, and commend them that try it. And the protestants confess, this doctrine " was never misliked, till a church arose, whose silver being dross, and whose milk poison, might not endure the trial."[s] Which being true, that we may try, why may we not also judge and practise according as God's Spirit shall direct us in our trial? If a man should drink poison, and know it to be poison, were he not in a worse estate than he that should drink it ignonorantly, not knowing thereof; even a murderer of himself in the highest degree? So he that drinketh spiritual poison, knowing it,—for according unto men's faith it is unto them—he is in a worse estate, and a murderer of his own soul in the highest degree. And therefore that

[s] White's Way, &c. p. 127

church, or those learned, that will suffer their doctrine to be tried, and yet constrain men to receive and practise it, when upon examination their consciences are convinced of the falsehood thereof, are worse, and do more highly sin, than they that constrain a blind conscience, though both be evil.

We despise not learning, nor learned men, but do reverence it and them, according to their worthiness; only when it is advanced into the seat of God, and that given to it which appertaineth unto the Holy Ghost, which is to lead into all truth, then ought all, as Hezekiah did unto the brazen serpent, detest it, and contemn it.

CHAPTER VI.

Persecution for cause of conscience, is against the doctrine of Jesus Christ, King of kings.

Matt. xiii. 30, 38, &c.   1. CHRIST commandeth, that the tares and wheat, which are those that walk in the truth, and those that walk in falsehood, should be let alone in the world, and not plucked up until the harvest, which is the end of the world.

Matt. xv. 14.   2. The same commandeth, that they that are blindly led on in false religion, and are offended with him for teaching true religion, should be let alone, referring their punishment unto their falling into the ditch.

Luke ix 54, 55.   3. Again, he reproved his disciples, who would have had fire come down from heaven, and devoured those Samaritans that would not receive him, in these words, *Ye know not of what spirit ye are: the Son of man is not come to destroy men's lives, but to save them.*

4. Paul, the apostle of our Lord, teacheth, *that the servant* 2 Tim. ii. 24, [25, 26.] *of the Lord must not strive, but must be gentle towards all men, suffering the evil men, instructing them with meekness that are contrary-minded; proving if God at any time will give them repentance, that they may acknowledge the truth, and come to amendment out of that snare of the devil,* &c.

5. According to these aforesaid commandments, the holy prophets foretold, that when the law of Moses concerning worship should cease, and Christ's kingdom be established, then all carnal weapons should cease. *They* Isaiah ii. 4; Mic. iv. 3, 4. *shall break their swords into mattocks, and their spears into scythes,* &c. *Then shall none hurt nor destroy in all the* Is. xi. 9 *mountain of my holiness,* &c. And when he came, the same he taught and practised, as before. So did his apostles after him; for *the weapons of his warfare are not* 2 Cor. x. 4. *carnal,* &c. But he charged straitly, that his disciples should be so far from persecuting those that would not be of their religion, that when they were persecuted they Matt. v. [44.] should pray; when they were cursed, they should bless. The reason is, because they that are now tares may hereafter become wheat; they who are now blind, may hereafter see; they that now resist him, may hereafter receive him; they that are now in the devil's snare, in adverseness to the truth, may hereafter come to repentance; they that are now blasphemers, persecutors, and oppressors, as Paul was, may in time become faithful as he; they that are now idolaters, as the Corinthians once were, may hereafter 1 Cor. vi. 9. become true worshippers as they; they that are now no people of God, nor under mercy, as the saints sometimes 1 Pet. ii. 10 were, may hereafter become the people of God, and obtain mercy, as they. Some come not till the eleventh hour: Matt. xx. 6. if those that come not till the last hour should be destroyed because they came not at the first, then should they never come, but be prevented. And why do men call themselves Christians, and do not the things Christ would?

CHAPTER VII.

Persecution for cause of conscience is against the profession and practice of famous princes.

FIRST, we beseech your majesty, we may relate your own worthy sayings, in your majesty's speech at parliament, 1609.[1] Your highness saith, " It is a sure rule in divinity, that God never loves to plant his church by violence and bloodshed," &c. And in your highness's Apology,[2] speaking of such papists as took the oath, thus : " I gave a good proof that I intended no persecution against them for conscience' cause, but only desired to be secured [of them] for civil obedience, which for conscience' cause they were bound to perform." And, speaking of Blackwell, the archpriest,[3] your majesty saith, " It was never my intention to lay any thing to the said archpriest's charge, as I have never done to any, for cause of conscience," &c. And in your highness's Exposition on Rev. xx. printed 1588, and after, in 1603,[4] your majesty truly writeth thus : " Sixthly, the compassing of the saints, and besieging of the beloved city, declareth unto us a certain note of a false church to be persecution ; for they come to seek the faithful, the faithful are those that are sought : the wicked are the besiegers, the faithful the besieged."

Secondly, the saying of Stephen, king of Poland : " I am king of men, not of consciences ; a commander of bodies, not of souls," &c.[5]

[1 See before, p. 100.]
[2 See before, p. 140.]
[3 See before, p. 140.]
[4 Works, Meditation, &c. p. 79.]
[5 Stephen Bathori was one of the most distinguished of the sovereigns of Poland. He died on the 12th December, 1586, after a vigorous and successful reign of ten years. Himself a convert to Romanism, he was

Thirdly, the king of Bohemia hath thus written : "And, notwithstanding, the success of the latter time, wherein sundry opinions have been hatched about the subject of religion, may make one clearly discern with his eye, and (as it were) touch with his finger, that according to the verity of holy scripture, and a maxim heretofore held and maintained by the ancient doctors of the church, that men's consciences ought in no sort to be violated, urged, or constrained ; and whensoever men have attempted any thing by this violent course, whether openly or by secret means, the issue hath been pernicious, and the cause of great and wonderful innovations in the principallest and mightiest kingdoms and countries of all Christendom," &c. And further, his majesty saith: "So that once more we do protest, before God and the whole world, that from this time forward we are firmly resolved, not to persecute nor molest, nor suffer to be persecuted or molested, any person whosoever, for matter of religion, no, not they that profess themselves to be of the Roman church, neither to trouble nor disturb them in the exercise of their religion, so they live conformably to the laws of the states," &c.[6]

especially tolerant towards his protestant subjects, and though strongly urged to the contrary course by the Jesuits, all persecution was withheld. It was his favourite saying, " There are three things which God has reserved to himself: creative power, the knowledge of future events, and dominion over conscience."—Robinson's Eccles. Researches, p. 613. Pop. Cyclop. Art. Stephen.]

[6] [The elector palatine, count Frederic the fifth, was chosen king of Bohemia by the States of that country, instead of Ferdinand, archduke of Austria and emperor of Ger-

many, who would have deprived the protestants of their liberty in matters of religion. His father-in-law, king James the first, was much displeased with his acceptance of the crown. " It was a rash and too hasty resolution." The sovereignty being conferred by election, was opposed to the views of James on the hereditary rights and *jus divinum* of kings. He ordered that his son should not be styled king in the public prayers, but only elector palatine. After his coronation, the newly elected sovereign issued, in a public manifesto, the above-cited sentiments touching coercion of

HUMBLE SUPPLICATION.] P

And for the practice of this, where is persecution for the cause of conscience, except in England, and where popery reigns? and not there neither in all places, as appeareth by France, Poland, and other places. Nay, it is not practised among the heathen, that acknowledge not the true God, as the Turk, Persian, and others.[7]

CHAPTER VIII.

Persecution for cause of conscience is condemned by the ancient and later writers, yea, by puritans and papists.

HILARY against Auxentius, saith thus: "The Christian church doth not persecute, but is persecuted; and lamentable it is to see the great folly of these times, and to sigh at the foolish opinion of this world, in that men think by human aid to help God, and with worldly pomp and power to undertake to defend the Christian church. I ask of you bishops, what help used the apostles in the publishing of the gospel? With the aid of what power did they preach Christ, and convert the heathen from their idolatry to God? When they were imprisoned and lay in chains,

conscience, in which he shows himself superior to his father-in-law in moderation and comprehensiveness of views. Brandt, Hist. of Reformation in Low Countries, iii. 200.]

[7] [" This course of toleration is held by Henry the fourth now reigning in France, by the present emperor in divers parts of his territories, by the king of Poland, and allowed of by the Spaniard in his late treaty with the states of Holland, and other

the united provinces. The liberty of the gospel and the free exercise of every part thereof, both for doctrine and government, is observed to be of so harmless and peaceable a nature and carriage, and so far from wronging any monarch in his sovereignty and public interest, that the very heathen, the Persian namely, and the Turk, give passage and entertainment thereunto."—An Humble Supplication to his Majesty, 1609, p. 23.]

did they praise and give thanks to God for any dignities, graces, and favours received from the court? Or, do you think that Paul went about with regal mandates, or kingly authority, to gather and establish the church of Christ? Sought he protection from Nero Vespasian?" &c.

" The apostles wrought with their hands for their own maintenance, travelling by land and water, from town to city, to preach Christ; yea, the more they were forbidden, the more they taught and preached Christ. But now, alas! human help must assist and protect the faith, and give the same countenance. To and by vain and worldly honours do men seek to defend the church of Christ, as if he by his power were unable to perform it."[8]

The same, against the Arians: " The church now, which formerly by enduring misery and imprisonment, was known to be a true church, doth now terrify others, by imprisonment, banishment, and misery, and boasteth that she is

[8] [" Ac primùm miserari licet nostræ ætatis laborem et præsentium temporum stultas opiniones congemiscere quibus patrocinari Deo humano creduntur, et ad tuendam Christi ecclesiam ambitione seculari laboratur. Oro vos episcopi qui hoc esse vos creditis quibusnam suffragiis ad prædicandum evangelium apostoli usi sunt? Quibus adjuti potestatibus Christum prædicaverunt gentesque fere omnes ex idolis ad Deum transtulerunt? Anne aliquam sibi assumebant è palatio dignitatem, hymnum Deo in carcere inter catenas et post flagella cantantes? Edictisque regis Paulus cum in theatro spectaculum ipse esset Christo ecclesiam congregabat? Nerone se, credo, aut Vespasiano, aut Decio patrocinantibus tuebatur? Quorum in nos odiis confessio divinæ prædicationis effloruit.—Illi manû atque opere se alentes, intra cœnacula secretaque coëuntes, vicos et castella, gentesque fere omnes terrâ ac mari contra senatus-consulta et regum edicta peragrantes, claves credo regni cœlorum non habebant? Aut non manifesta se tum Dei virtus contra odia humana porrexit, cùm tanto magis Christus prædicaretur quanto magis prædicari inhiberetur? At nunc, proh dolor! divinam fidem suffragia terrena commendant, inopsque virtutis suæ Christus dum ambitio nomini suo conciliatur, arguitur." S. Hilarii Opera, cap. 3, 4, edit. Paris. 1693.]

highly esteemed of the world; whereas the true church cannot but be hated of the same."[9]

Tertullian ad Scapulam. "It agreeth both with human equity and natural reason, that every man worship God uncompelled, and believe what he will; for, another man's religion or belief neither hurteth nor profiteth any man: neither beseemeth it any religion to compel another to be of their religion, which willingly and freely should be embraced, and not by constraint: forasmuch as the offerings were required of those that freely, and with a good will offered, and not from the contrary."[1]

Jerome in Proem. lib. 4. in Jeremiam.[2] "Heresy must be cut off with the sword of the Spirit; let us strike through with the arrows of the Spirit all sons and disciples of misled heretics, that is, with testimonies of holy scriptures: the slaughter of heretics is by the word of God."

Brentius on 1 Cor. iii. "No man hath power to make or give laws to Christians, whereby to bind their consciences; for willingly, freely, and uncompelled, with a ready desire and cheerful mind, must those that come, run unto Christ."

Luther, in his book of the civil magistrate. "The laws of the civil government extend no further than over the body or goods, and to that which is external: for, over

---

[9] ["Terret exiliis et carceribus ecclesia, credique sibi cogit, quæ exiliis et carceribus est credita. Pendet ad dignationem communicantium quæ persequentium est consecrata terrore. .... Diligi se gloriatur à mundo quæ Christi esse non potuit nisi eam mundus odisset."—Ibid. cap. 4.]

[1] ["Tamen humani juris et naturalis potestatis est unicuique quod putaverit colere: nec alii obest aut prodest alterius religio. Sed nec religionis est cogere religionem, quæ sponte suscipi debeat, non vi: cum et hostiæ ab animo libenti expostulentur."—Tertullian. ad Scap. tom. i. 152. Opera. Paris. 1829.]

[2] ["Superbissimam hæresim spirituali mucrone truncemus." S. Hieron. Opera, tom. ii. p. 584. Parisiis, 1609. The remainder of the quotation does not occur in the place cited, nor in any other of the proems to Jeremiah.]

the soul God will not suffer any man to rule, only he himself will rule there: therefore, wheresoever the civil magistrate doth undertake to give laws unto the soul and consciences of men, he usurpeth that government to himself, which appertaineth to God," &c. The same upon 1 Kings vi. "In the building of the temple there was no sound of iron heard, to signify that Christ will have in his church a free and willing people, not compelled and constrained by laws and statutes." [3]

Again, he saith upon Luke xxii. "It is not the true catholic church which is defended by the secular arm or human power, but the false and feigned church; which although it carries the name of a church, yet it denieth the power thereof."[4] And upon Psalm xvii. he saith, "For the true church of Christ knoweth not *brachium seculare*, which the bishops now-a-days chiefly use."[5] Again, in Postil. Dom. i. post. Epiph. he saith, "Let not Christians be commanded, but exhorted; for he that will not wil-

---

[3] ["Das weltliche Regiment hat Gesetze, die sich nicht weiter erstrecken, denn über Leib und Gut, und was äusserlich ist auf Erden. Denn über die Seele kann und will Gott niemand lassen regieren, denn sich selbst alleine. Darum wo weltliche Gewalt sich vermisset, der Seelen Gesetz zu geben, da greift sie Gott in sein Regiment, und verführet und verderbet nur die Seelen."

"Am ganzen Bau des Temples hörete man nie kein Eisen, spricht der Text 1 Kön. vi. 7. alles darum, dass Christus ohne Zwang und Drang, ohne Gesetze und Schwerdt ein freiwillig Volk haben sollte." Luther's Sämmtliche Schriften 10ʳ. Th. ss. 438, 452. herausgegeben Walch, Halle, 1742, &c.]

[4] [The following is the passage nearest in sense that we have been able to find. "Gott seine Kirche will erhalten und regieren allein durch sein Wort und nicht durch menschliche Macht. Die nun in Kirchenämtern sind und das Predigamt haben, die haben das Wort allein dazu, dass sie andern damit dienen; und nicht dazu, dass sie dadurch sich zu Herren machen sollen." Evangelium Luc. am xxii. v. 24—30, s. 2818. Schriften 13ʳ. Th.]

[5] ["Ecce vera Christi ecclesia nescit brachium seculare, quod hodie impii pontifices unicè amplectuntur, invocant et metuunt. Quàm pulchrè concordat eorum vita et sensus cum divinis scripturis?"—Lutheri Opera Omnia, tom. iii. fol. 302, Witeb: 1552, &c.]

lingly do that whereunto he is friendly exhorted, he is no
Christian : therefore those that do compel them that are
not willing, show thereby that they are not Christian
preachers, but worldly beadles."[6]

Again, upon 1 Peter iii. he saith, " If the civil magistrate would command me to believe thus or thus, I should
answer him after this manner; Lord, or Sir, look you to your
civil or worldly government, your power extends not so
far, to command any thing in God's kingdom, therefore
herein I may not hear you: for if you cannot suffer that
any man should usurp authority where you have to command, how do you think that God should suffer you to
thrust him from his seat, and to seat yourself therein ?"[7]

The puritans, as appeareth in the Answer to Admonition
to Parliament,[8] "That papists nor others, neither con-

[6] [" Ich ermahne euch, lieben
Brüder.—Er spricht nicht: Ich ge-
biete euch; denn er prediget denen,
die schon Christen und fromm sind
durch den Glauben im neuen Mensch-
en, die nicht mit Geboten zu zwingen,
sondern zu ermahnen sind, dass sie
williglich thun, was mit dem sünd-
lichen alten Menschen zu thun ist.
Denn wer es nicht williglich thut, allein aus freundlichem Ermahnen, der
ist kein Christ: und wers mit Gesetz-
en erzwinget von den Unwilligen, der
ist schon kein christlicher Prediger
noch Regierer, sondern ein weltlicher
Stockmeister."—Die Epist. am ersten
Sonntage nach Epiph. Schrift. s. 429.
12r. Th.]

[7] [" Idcirco, siquis jam me Cæsar
vel princeps rogaret, quæ mea fides
sit, deberem planè id ei fateri . . . .
Si autem vellet pergere, et mihi man-
dare, ut hoc, aut illo pacto crederem,
jam dicendem ei est : Optime Princeps,

cura tu imperium istud externum,
haud tibi licet, ut Dei regnum invadas,
aut quod ipsius solius est, tibi usurpes;
ideo nullus tibi parebo. Ipse tamen
non potes ferre, ut quis in tuam ditio-
nem sibi aliquid vendicet potestatis,
si quis tantum tuas excubias præ-
tereat, nolens eas sibi statuto pretio
adesse custodes, insequeris eum bom-
bardis. Qui igitur potes in animum
inducere, laturum Deum, quòd tu
dejicere eum solio conaris, et te in
ejus locum sustollere ?"— Enarrat.
M. Lutheri in Epist. Petri, fol. 62.
Argent. anno 1525.]

[8] Page 109. [This is quoted from
the Admonition to Parliament, the
whole of which is inserted in Whitgift's " Answer to the Admonition,
&c." ed. Lond. 1572. " Surely,"
says Whitgift in reply, " the papists
have to thank you, that you would
not have them constrained to come
to the communion. This one lesson

strainedly nor customably communicate in the mysteries of salvation." Also in their supplication, printed 1609, much they write for toleration.[9]

Lastly, the papists, the inventors of persecution; in a wicked book lately set forth, thus they write: "Moreover, the means which almighty God appointed his officers to use in the conversion of kingdoms and people, were, humility, patience, charity, &c., saying, *Behold, I send you as* Matt. x. 16. *sheep in the midst of wolves.* He did not say, 'I send you as wolves among sheep, to kill, imprison, spoil, and devour those unto whom they were sent.' Again, he saith, *They* Verse 17. to whom I send you *will deliver you up in councils, and in their synagogues they will scourge you; and to presidents and to kings shall you be led for my sake.* He doth not say, 'You whom I send shall deliver the people, whom you ought to convert, into councils, and put them in prisons, and lead them to presidents and tribunal seats, and make their religion felony and treason.' Again, he saith, *When* Verse 12. *ye enter into the house, salute it, saying, Peace be to this house.* He doth not say, 'You shall send pursuivants to ransack and spoil the house.' Again, he saith, *The good* John x. [11, *pastor giveth his life for his sheep; the thief cometh not but to steal, kill, and destroy.* He doth not say, 'The thief giveth

---

of liberty hath made all the stubborn and stiffnecked papists in England, great patrons and fautors of your book: you might as well have said that you would have every man freely profess what religion he list, without controlment, and so let all at liberty, which is your seeking," p. 110. In this, however, Whitgift mistook the desire of the puritans. They were altogether unwilling to grant that liberty they themselves sought.]

[9] Page 21, &c. ["That the said toleration is for pacifying contentions, in the matter of religion professed by us, a ready mean, may appear hereby, in that it removeth both the original cause and nourishment thereof: and in that it hath been for this excellent service entertained by great monarchs and potentates both in ancient times and of late years."—An Humble Supplication for Toleration, &c.]

his life for his sheep, and the good pastor cometh not but to steal, kill, and destroy,' " &c.[1]

So that we holding our peace, our adversaries themselves speak for us, or rather for the truth.

CHAPTER IX.

It is no prejudice to the commonwealth if freedom of religion were suffered, but would make it flourish.

BE pleased not to hearken to men's leasings, but to what God and experience teacheth in this thing. Abra-
Gen. xiii. 7; ham abode among the Canaanites a long time, yet contrary
xvi. 3.
Gen. xx. [1, to them in religion. Again, *he sojourned in Gerar*, and
15]; xxi. 33,
34. king Abimelech gave him leave to abide in his land.
Gen. xxvi. Isaac also dwelt in the same land, yet contrary in religion.
[6.]
Gen. xxxi. Jacob lived twenty years in one house with his uncle
[19.]
Ex. xii. [41] Laban, yet differed in religion. The people of Israel were four hundred and thirty years in that famous land of
2 Chron. Egypt, and afterwards seventy years in Babylon, all which
xxxvi. [6.] time they differed in religion from the states.

Come to the time of Christ, where Israel was under the Romans, where lived divers sects of religions, as Herodians, scribes and pharisees, sadducees, libertines, Theudæans, Samaritans, besides the common religion of the Jews, Christ and his apostles; all which differed from the common religion of the state, which, is like, was the
Acts xix. 27. worship of Diana, which almost the whole world then worshipped. All these lived under the government of Cæsar, being nothing hurtful to the state and common-

---

[1] [These passages of scripture are quoted from the Douay version.]

wealth; for they gave unto Cæsar that which was his; and for religion to God, he left them to themselves, as having no domination therein. And when the enemies of the truth raised up any tumults, the wisdom of the magis- ^Acts xviii, 14; xix. 35, &c.^ trates most wisely appeased them.

Again, be pleased to look into the neighbour nations who tolerate religion, how their wealths and states are governed. Many sorts of religions are in their dominions; yet no trouble of state, no treason, no hinderance at all of any good; but much prosperity brought unto their countries, they having all one harmony in matters of state, giving unto Cæsar his due, and for religion they suffer one another.

If any object, the troubles of France, Germany, &c., we answer: they are such as have been procured by the learned, but most bloody Jesuits, who seek to establish their religion by blood, for the subversion of whom your wisdoms are wise to deal in. Yet be pleased not to let faithful subjects be punished for their wickedness: but let most severe laws be made for the maintenance of civil and human peace and welfare, as to your majesty and others shall seem expedient. And if it be well observed, it is the learned that raise up all the bloody wars among the princes of the earth.

CHAPTER X.

Kings are not deprived of any power given them of God, when they maintain freedom for cause of conscience.

WE know the learned do persuade, that kings have power from God to maintain the worship and service of

God, as they have power to maintain right and justice between man and man; for Christian kings, say they, have the same power, that the kings of Israel had under the law.[2]

For answer to which, first, let it be observed, the kings of Israel had never power from God to make new laws, or set up new worships, which God's word required not; nor to set high priests, or spiritual lords, for the performance of the services, other than such as God by Moses had expressly commanded; and therefore the power of the kings of Israel will warrant no kings to make or confirm canons, set up new worships, and appoint spiritual lords and lawgivers to the conscience, and persecute all that submit not unto them.

Secondly, let it be well observed, only the kings of Israel had this power, but no other kings, whose commonwealths did flourish to them and their seeds after them to many generations. And it must be granted, that he that is king of Israel now, which is Jesus Christ, the truth of those typical kings of Israel, he hath the power according to the proportion. The temporal kings had temporal power to compel all to the observation of those carnal or temporal commandments. So Christ, the spiritual king, hath spiritual power to compel all to the observation of his spiritual commandments. For when he came, himself

Heb. vii. 16; ix. 10.

[2] ["To remove idols, and all abominations out of the land; to enter [into] a covenant with God, and to walk in his ways; to proclaim fasts, and make public prayers; to sanctify the temple and celebrate the passover; to seek and serve God according to his law; be matters ecclesiastical and not temporal. And yet in the same cases the godly kings of Judah commanded and compelled all that were found in Judah, priest and prophet, man and woman, to stand to that order, which they took for the better accomplishing of those their enterprises. Acknowledge that right and power in Christian princes at this day, to meddle with matters of religion, which the scriptures report and commend in kings of religious and famous memory, we press you no farther."—Bilson's True Difference, &c. p. 198, ed. 1585.]

said, *The hour cometh, and now is, when the true worship-* John iv. 23.
pers shall worship the Father in spirit and in truth; for the
Father requireth even such to worship him. If Christ be
[the] only king of Israel, that sits upon David's throne for Acts ii. 30.
ever, as he is, far be it from any king to take Christ's seat
from him.

The wisdom of God foresaw, that seeing the mysteries
of the gospel are such spiritual things, as no natural men,
though they be princes of this world, can know them; he
left not kings and princes to be lords and judges thereof,
seeing they are subject to err. But he left that power to
his beloved Son, who could not err; and the Son left his
only deputy, the Holy Ghost, and no mortal man whatsoever; as your highness worthily acknowledgeth, in [your]
Apology,[3] "I utterly deny that there is any earthly monarch over the church, whose word must be a law, and
who cannot err by an infallibility of spirit. Because
earthly kingdoms must have earthly monarchs, it doth not
follow the church must have a visible monarch too. Christ
is the church's monarch, and the Holy Ghost his deputy.
The kings of the nations reign over them, but you shall not be Luke xxii.
[25, 26.]
so, &c. Christ, when he ascended, left not Peter with
them to direct them into all truth, but promised to send
the Holy Ghost unto them for that end," &c.

Further, these learned allege the commandments, where Ex. xxiii.
Israel are commanded to destroy all the inhabitants of the 33; Deut. vii.
[2]; xiii. [6,
land, lest they entice them to serve their gods; and to 7.]
slay all false prophets, &c. These they collect from the
time of the law, for in the time of the gospel they have
nothing to allege: for Rom. xiii. [1—7], maketh nothing
for their purpose, Cæsar being a heathen king.

For answer unto the places of Moses: first, the sins of

---

[3] [See before, p. 109.]

this people, the Canaanites, were full, and the Lord would destroy them, and give their possessions unto the Israelites; but the sins of the refusers of Christ are not full until the end, or last hour; as before is proved.

Secondly. The children of Israel had a special commandment from the Lord to destroy them : but the kings of the nations have no command at all to destroy the bodies of the contrary-minded; nay, they are expressly forbidden it.

Matt. xiii. 29.

Thirdly. The Canaanites would have rebelled against Israel, and have destroyed them ; but the contrary-minded will not rebel against their kings, but give unto them the things that belong unto them ; not so much for fear, as of conscience : and of this the God of gods is witness.   If any do or teach otherwise, let them be destroyed.

Fourthly. The heads and rulers of Israel could command and compel the people to observe those carnal rites and ordinances of the law, even as Christ, the head and ruler of Israel, can compel to the observation of his spiritual ordinances of the gospel; but the heads of the nations cannot compel their subjects to believe the gospel ; for *faith is the gift of God :* which faith, if they want, all they do in God's worship is sin.   Therefore they cannot compel any to worship, because they cannot give them faith ; for which cause the Lord in wisdom saw it not meet to charge kings with a duty which they cannot perform.   God will never require it at their hands; the blood of the faithless and unbelieving shall be on their own heads ; *he that will not believe, shall be damned.*

Rom.   xiv. 23 ; Heb. xi. 6.

Mark xvi. 16.

Again. Seeing it is true, as your majesty well observeth in your highness's speech at parliament, 1609,[4] " That the

---

[4] [Works, p. 533. " For God governed his selected people by these   three laws, ceremonial, moral, and judicial. The judicial, being only fit

judicials of Moses were only fit for that time, and those persons." And also it is confessed, the law for adultery, theft, and the like, is not now to be executed according to the judicials of Moses, nor directions for the magistrates of the earth to walk by. Why should these be any directions for them, seeing also our Saviour and his apostles have taught the contrary, as before hath been proved? If all false prophets should be now executed, according to Deut. xiii. [15, 16,] the kings of the earth would not only be deprived of many of their subjects; but the cities of their habitation, with all the inhabitants of the cities, must be destroyed with the edge of the sword; the cattle thereof, and all the spoil thereof, must be brought into the midst of the city, and the city and all therein be burnt with fire, be made a heap of stones for ever, and never be built again: which God forbid such execration should ever be seen. And if these judicials of Moses be not now directions for the kings of nations, we read not in all the book of God, any directions given to kings to rule in matters of conscience and spiritual worship to God. But often we read that the kings of the nations shall give their power to the beast, and fight against the Lamb, as lamentable experience hath plainly taught it. ^{Rev. xvi. 14; xvii. 2, 12, 13, 14, 18; xviii. 3, 9; xix. 19.}

Thus all men, may see there is only deceit in these learned men's comparisons of the kings of Israel in the law, with the kings of nations in time of the gospel, in matters of religion. Much might be written to prove, that kings are not deprived of their power by permitting of freedom of religion; but are rather deprived thereof by

for a certain people, and a certain time, which could not serve for the general of all other people and times. As for example, if the law of hanging for theft, were turned here to restitution of treble, or quadruple, as it was in the law of Moses, what would become of all the middle shires, and all the Irishry and Highlanders?"]

using compulsion to the contrary-minded, and do sin grievously, in causing them to sin for want of faith. But this may suffice, the Almighty blessing it with his blessing, which we humbly beseech him for his Christ's sake, for his own glory's sake, for the prosperity and welfare of these kingdoms, and for the comfort of your faithful and true-hearted subjects, that are now distressed by long and lingering imprisonments, and otherwise; who of conscience give unto Cæsar the things which are his: which is, to be lord and lawgiver to the bodies of his subjects, and all belonging to their outward man, for the preservation of himself, and his good subjects, and for the punishment of the evil. In which preservation, the church of Christ hath a special part, when their outward peace is thereby preserved from the fury of all adversaries; in which respect princes are called nursing fathers, as many are at this day; blessed be the Lord.

Oh! be pleased to consider, why you should persecute us for humbly beseeching you, in the words of the King of kings, *to give unto God the things which are God's;* which is, to be Lord and Lawgiver to the soul in that spiritual worship and service which he requireth. If you will take away this from God, what is it that is God's? Far be it from you to desire to sit in the consciences of men, to be lawgiver and judge therein. This is antichrist's practice, persuading the kings of the earth to give him their power to compel all hereunto: but whosoever submitteth, shall drink of God's fierce wrath. You may make and mend your own laws, and be judge and punisher of the transgressors thereof; but you cannot make or mend God's laws, they are perfect already; you may not add nor diminish; nor be judge nor monarch of his church; that is Christ's right. He left neither you nor any mortal man his deputy, but only the Holy Ghost, as your highness

Matt. xxii.
21.

Rev. xiv. 9,
10.

Ps. xix. 7.
Deut. iv. 2;
Rev.   xxii.
18, 19.

acknowledgeth. And whosoever erreth from the truth, his judgment is set down, and the time thereof.

2 Thess. i. 8,
&c. ; Rom.
ii. 8, &c.
Matt. xiii.
40 ; xxv. 31,
&c. ; Rom.
ii. 16.

This is the sum of our humble petition; that your majesty would be pleased not to persecute your faithful subjects, who are obedient to you in all civil worship and service, for walking in the practice of what God's word requireth of us, for his spiritual worship, as we have faith; knowing, as your majesty truly writeth in your Meditations on Matthew xxvii. in these words, " We can use no spiritual worship nor prayer, that can be available to us without faith."[5]

This is the sum of our most humble petition, thus manifoldly proved to be just.

O LORD God of glory! raise up in this high assembly, the heart of some Nehemiah, of some Ebed-melech, that may open their mouths for the dumb, that cannot speak for themselves, in a truth so apparent as this is; lest it be said, as Isa. lix. 16, *And when he saw that there was no man, he wondered that none would offer himself; therefore his arm did save it, and his righteousness itself did sustain it.*

And now we cease not to pray for the king, and his son, and his seed, and this whole high and honourable assembly, now and always.

Calling the all-seeing God to witness, that we are your majesty's loyal subjects, not for fear only, but for conscience' sake,

Unjustly called,

ANA-BAPTISTS.

---

[5] [Works, p. 615. " But we can use no spiritual worship nor prayer that can be available unto us without faith. Let the school distinctions of δουλεία, ὑποδουλεία, and λατρεία, deceive them that list to be deceived with them ; for all prayer in faith is due to God only.]

THE NECESSITY

OF

TOLERATION

IN

MATTERS OF RELIGION.

1647.

Q

THE

NECESSITY OF TOLERATION

IN

MATTERS OF RELIGION;

OR,

Certain questions propounded to
the Synod, tending to prove that Corporall Punishments
ought not to be inflicted upon such as hold Errors
in Religion, and that in matters of Religion,
men ought not to be compelled, but
have liberty and freedom.

Here is also the copy of the Edict of the Emperours Constantinus and Licinius, and containing the Reasons that
inforced them to grant unto all men liberty to choose,
and follow what Religion they thought best.

Also, here is the faith of the Assembly of Divines, as it was
taken out of the exactest copy of their practice, with
the Nonconformists' Answer why they cannot
receive and submit to the said faith.

*For such are false Apostles, deceitful workers, transforming themselves into the Apostles of
Christ, and no marvell, for Satan himself is transformed into an Angel of Light; therefore
it is no great thing if his ministers also be transformed as the ministers of Righteousnesse,
whose end shal be according to their workes, 2 Cor. xi. 13, 14, 15.*

Ye are bought with a price, be not the servants of men, 1 Cor. vii. 23.

Ye suffer fooles gladly, 2 Cor. xi. 19.　　　　　　First peruse, then refuse.

By SAMUEL RICHARDSON.

Where Romish Tyrannie hath the upper hand,
Darknesse of minde, and superstition stand.

London : Printed in the yeare of Jubilee, 1647.

Q 2

INTRODUCTORY NOTICE.

MR. RICHARDSON is known to us only as an author. No memorials exist of his private life, nor of his religious connexions, and his works afford but scanty materials to supply their place. From one of the earliest of them it may be presumed that he had suffered somewhat for the truth. "Mistress Ann Wilson," he says, "oft refreshed me in the days of my pilgrimage." [1] He must have been a leading person in one of the seven churches in London, which, in 1643, 1644, and 1646, put forth a Confession of Faith, as his name there stands in connexion with that of Mr. Spilsbury. This excellent man was the pastor of a church, formed by a peaceful separation from the community established originally as an independent church by Mr. Henry Jacob, in the year 1616. At the time of the secession, Mr. Lathorp was its pastor, and after his decease, the eminent Mr. Henry Jessey. [2]

As the early baptist churches frequently enjoyed the services of more than one pastor or teacher, Mr. Richardson may probably have been the colleague of Mr. Spilsbury. The church over which they presided is usually regarded

---

[1] The Life of Faith, p. 45.   [2] Crosby, i. 149, 309.

as the first baptist community which held Calvinistic sentiments in this country. Our author was their warm advocate, as appears from a nervous and well-written tract, published in 1647, on "Justification by Christ alone, a fountain of life and comfort." The tract here reprinted issued from the press in the same year.

Early in 1646, he produced a brief but able reply to the scurrilous work of Dr. Featley, "The Dipper Dipt," &c. In this he gives the following interesting account of the mode of administration used at that time in the ordinance of baptism. It had been grossly libelled by his opponent as a "kind of spell." "We confess," says Mr. Richardson, "when any is to be baptized, at the water-side the administrator goeth to prayer suitable to the occasion, and after go both into the water, and useth the words, Matt. chap. xxviii. part of the 19th verse; and coming forth again, they go to prayer, and also return thanks to God. And how this can be a spell we cannot see." [3]

Several of his subsequent publications were devoted to the defence of the army, and of the government of Cromwell. He endeavoured to justify the violent proceeding known as 'Pride's purge,' and dedicated his production to "Honest and faithful Fairfax and Cromwell." He thought that greater evils than this were impending over the nation, from tyranny, bigotry, and oppression—the certain fruits of presbyterian ascendancy. The army had preserved the lives of the people, prevented persecution in matters of religion, broken the fetters of the priest and

---

[3] Some Brief Considerations, &c. p. 4.

despot, and was the only safeguard of the nation's nascent
liberties. Its leaders were justly endeared to the hearts of
hundreds of thousands, and worthy of the highest commendation. "Because, therefore, you have saved our lives,
and more, have not esteemed your lives too much for us,
but often have offered them up for us, we resolve to live
and die with you." [4]

Mr. Richardson regarded the deeds and character of the
Protector with unfeigned and ardent admiration. Then,
as now, the gentle birth of Cromwell was often called in
question, his private character assailed, and the most
calumnious assertions freely uttered, even from the pulpit.
We may be permitted to quote our author's defence of
this remarkable man, to whom he was contemporary. To
this a sense of duty prompted him. " I and others," says
Mr. Richardson, " owe him this service as a neighbour,
as a friend, as a Christian, as he is under God our chief
governor and protector; " and he appeals solemnly to
the divine Being for the truth of that which he had
written :—

" One of the opposers said in a pulpit, speaking of his
Highness, that he was the son of a beggar ; which is neither
true in itself, nor comparatively. For he was the son of a
gentleman, an esquire, and was offered to be knighted, and
refused it. He had a considerable estate of yearly means,
more than enough. His father was a knight, Sir Henry
Cromwell, and had an estate of yearly means of sixteen
thousand pounds a year. Sir Philip and Sir Oliver were

<hr>

[4] Answer to London Ministers, &c. Dedication.

brothers to his Highness's father. The said Sir Oliver Cromwell, his Highness's uncle, had twelve thousand pounds a year in old rents, and his Highness's mother was sister to Sir Thomas Stewart, who was of the kindred and family of the late king. We glory not in the flesh, we glory in God, in being the children of God, heirs of heaven, and of an eternal and unspeakable weight of glory. But this is said to convince them, that what they say is false, and that they and others may see by what spirit they are led in opposing him."

In the following passage we have Mr. Richardson's estimate of the services Cromwell had rendered to his country, and of his personal qualities as a man and governor. "His Highness aimeth at the general good of the nation, and just liberty of every man. He is also a godly man, one that feareth God and escheweth evil; though he is, nor no man else, without human frailty. He is faithful to the saints, and to these nations in whatsoever he hath undertaken from the beginning of the wars. He hath owned the poor despised people of God, and advanced many of them to a better way and means of living. He hath been an advocate for the Christians, and hath done them much good in writing, speaking, pleading for their liberty in the Long Parliament, and fighting for their liberty. He, with others, hath hazarded his life, estate, family; and since he hath refused great offers of wealth, and worldly glory for the sake and welfare of the people of God: God hath given him more than ordinary wisdom, strength, courage, and valour. God hath been always with him, and given him great successes. He is fitted to bear burdens, and to endure all opposition and contradictions that may stand with public safety. He is a terror to his enemies; he hath a large heart, spirit, and principle, that will hold all that fear the Lord, though of different opinions and practices in religion, and seek their welfare. It is the honour of princes to pity the miserable, to relieve the oppressed, and the wrongs of the poor; he is humble, and despiseth not any because poor, and is ready to hear and help them. He is a merciful man, full of pity and bounty to the poor. A liberal heart is more precious than heaven or earth. He gives in money to maimed soldiers, widows and orphans, and poor families, a thousand pound a week to supply their wants; he is not a lover of money, which is a singular and extraordinary thing. He will give, and not hoard up money as some do. I am persuaded there is not a better friend to these nations and people of God among men, and that there is not any man so unjustly censured and abused as he is. And some that now find fault with him may live to see and confess that what I have herein written is truth, and when he is gathered to his fathers, shall weep for want of him." [5]

This, be it remembered, is the language of one personally acquainted with the protector, and an eye-witness of the facts he relates. If it be thought that a too laudatory strain is indulged in, it may be truly said that these were the qualities of Cromwell as a man, his faults were consequent upon his exalted position. If the admirers of the

[5] Plain Dealing, &c. pp. 17, 18, 20, 21.

Stuart demand that the display of many moral and social virtues should veil the obliquities of his regal career, impartiality requires that the protector's defects be also covered with their folds, and that his active godliness receive its fair meed of praise, with the passive piety of Charles.

With such views of the government, and the governor, our author would look with regret upon the wild and visionary attempts of the fifth monarchists to overthrow them. Among these were many who were his brethren in the faith, but who openly and strongly expressed their disapprobation of the protectorate, and sought its dissolution. In an address to Mr. Vavasor Powell and others, he endeavoured to reconcile them to the governing authority. He asserted that there was no just reason for their opposition, and that scripture did not sanction their hostility. On the contrary, the divine record confirmed the authority exercised by the Protector and his council, and required their hearty and conscientious obedience to it. Besides which, there were other and sufficient reasons why the legislative power should be exercised by them, according to the provisions of the ' Instrument of Government.' Two of the most violent, Mr. Rogers and Mr. Feake, both independents, had been selected by Cromwell as worthy of imprisonment; Mr. Richardson assures them that they were not suffering for conscience' sake, as they mistakenly supposed, but for the "safety of the civil peace" of the community. It is worthy of remark, that the principal ground of defence, taken by our author, is, that liberty of conscience and freedom of religion were fully guaranteed under the protectorate, " which," says he, " is so great, it is even unspeakable."

In one part of his writings, Mr. Richardson seems to think that it might possibly be right and beneficial for a government to maintain a body of religious teachers as a moral police, provided that ample provision were made for the full and perfect liberty of all to worship God as conscience in each case should dictate. But the purity and glory of true religion rejects such an alliance in any form, while it would be absolutely useless for the end in view.

All Mr. Richardson's productions are pervaded by an ardent attachment to complete liberty of conscience. He sought for no meagre toleration, which should be confined to his party alone, or even to those only who received, what were called, the fundamentals of the gospel. He desired that all, of any and every sentiment, should be embraced within the compass of the blessing. Other baptists had preceded him in the bold assertion of the truth, and many more came forward at this period to take part in the mighty conflict. Mr. Christopher Blackwood, in 1644, proclaimed that compulsion of conscience and the baptism of babes, were the two great pillars of antichrist. The eloquent exposure of the fallacies of Mr. Cotton, by Mr. Roger Williams, in his " Bloudy Tenent of Persecution, for cause of conscience, discussed," issued from the press in the same year, and rendered signal service to the cause of liberty. Mr. John Goodwin was as yet the only independent who had fully placed himself on the high ground of truth, Dr. Owen not appearing in the field till the year 1649.

The clear, decided, and admirable sermon of Mr. Dell, was preached before the House of Commons in 1646; and the same year, which brought to light the questions of Mr. Richardson, witnessed the publication of Dr. Jeremy Taylor's well known work, " The Liberty of Prophesying." Nor must we omit to mention the Confession of Faith now put forth by the baptists, as containing this noble claim. In this it stands alone among all the confessions and creeds of Christendom, in none of which does a similar article appear.

The friends of religious freedom had every reason to dread the ascendancy of the presbyterian party. The establishment of their church polity was urged with great pertinacity upon the House of Commons, by the assembly of divines, and their adherents in the city of London. Their pulpits echoed with bitter invectives against the toleration of the sectaries. It was evident, from the measures they had succeeded in rendering legal and obligatory on the nation, that a yoke more heavy than that of prelacy, so successfully broken, was prepared for the necks of the people. But immunities so lately purchased, at the cost of England's noblest blood, were not to be tamely surrendered to the grasp of an intolerant priesthood. Men, animated by a noble spirit of Christian patriotism, came forth to dam up the rushing torrent of persecution, which threatened to engulph their religious liberties. The army, with its leaders, to whom the nation had been already indebted for its triumph over civil and prelatic despotism, now again appeared as its shield against the assaults of presbyterian intolerance and assumption, and won the applause of those to whom the cause of liberty was dear.[6]

Some portions of the following work were first issued under the title of " Fifty Questions propounded to the Assembly, &c., by S. R." 1647, 4to. This work was subsequently enlarged and published at a later period of the same year in its present form, but without the name of the printer, or the license of the presbyterian censor. The reprint of this rare tract has been taken from a copy in the British Museum.

The following is a list of Mr. Richardson's works, of which two or three only are noticed by Mr. Ivimey in his History of the Baptists :—

1. Newes from Heaven of a Treaty of Peace. Or, a cordiall for a fainting heart. Wherein is manifested, that Jesus Christ, and all that is his, is freely offered to all who see a need of him, &c. 1643. 16mo. pp. 118.

2. The Life of Faith, in justification, in glorification, in sanctification, in infirmities, in time past, in all ordinances, &c. 1643. 16mo. pp. 70.

3. Some Brief Considerations on Dr. Featley his book, intituled *The Dipper Dipt.* Wherein in some measure is discovered his many great and false accusations of divers persons, commonly called Anabaptists, &c. 1645. 4to. pp. 18.

---

[6] Towards the close of Cromwell's life, and during the short protectorate of his son, the predominance of the army became at last fatal to the true interests of the nation, and prevented that settlement of the civil affairs of the country, earnestly desired and endeavoured by Cromwell. See Rogers's Life of Howe, p. 120, &c.

4. The Saint's Desire; mentioned in the epistle to the reader, prefacing the following work.

5. Justification by Christ alone, a Fountaine of Life and Comfort. Declaring that the whole worke of man's salvation was accomplished by Jesus Christ upon the crosse, &c. 1647. 4to. pp. 73. In this he replies to some objections of Mr. Huet and Dr. Homes, made against his former work.

6. Fifty Questions propounded to the Assembly. 1647. 4to.

7. The Necessity of Toleration in matters of Religion, &c. 1647. 4to. pp. 22. The present reprint.

8. An Answer to the London Ministers' Letter: from them to His Excellency and his Council of War, as also an answer to John Geree's book, entituled *Might overcoming Right*, &c. 1649. 4to. pp. 38.

9. The Cause of the Poor pleaded. 1653. 4to. pp. 15. He gives a painful account of the destitution of the poor, and holds forth Cromwell as an example worthy of imitation, for his abounding liberality.

10. An Apology for the present Government and Governour, with an answer to severall objections against them, and twenty queries propounded, &c. 1654. 4to. pp. 15. Against the fifth monarchy men.

11. Plain Dealing, or the unvailing of the opposers of the present government and governors. In answer of several things affirmed by Mr. Vavasor Powell and others, &c. 1656. 4to. pp. 24.

12. Of the Torments of Hell. The foundation and pillars thereof discovered, searched, shaken, and removed,

&c. 1658 and 1660, 12mo. This is an anonymous publication. We are not aware on what authority it is attributed to our author. It was reprinted in 1708 in the
second volume of the Phenix, p. 427. In their preface,
the editors say, " This discourse is written, or supposed to
be written, by one Mr. Richardson :" we have also seen
his name in old-hand writing attached to a copy of the
first edition.

THE IMPERIAL CONSTITUTION

OF

CONSTANTINUS AND LICINIUS,

Containing the reasons that moved them to grant unto all their subjects free liberty in matters of religion, which is worthy the view, and consideration of all men, especially those in authority.

———

" Not long ago we weighed with ourselves, that the liberty and freedom of religion ought not in any case to be prohibited; but that free leave ought to be given to every man, to do therein according to his will and mind. We have given commandment to all men to qualify matters of religion, as they themselves thought good, and that also the Christians should keep the opinions and faith of their religion. But because that many and sundry opinions by the same our first license, spring, and increase through such liberty granted, we thought good manifestly to add thereunto, and make plain such things, whereby perchance some of them in time to come, may from such their observance be let, or hindered. When, therefore, by prosperous success, I, Constantinus Augustus, and I, Licinius Augustus, came to Mediolanum, and there sat in council upon such things as served for the utility and profit of the common weal; these things amongst others

we thought would be beneficial to all men; yea, and
before all other things we purposed to establish those
things wherein the true reverence and worship of God is
comprehended, that is, to give unto Christians free choice
to follow what religion they think good, and whereby the
same sincerity and celestial grace, which is in every place
received, may also be embraced and accepted of all our
loving subjects. According therefore unto this our pleasure, upon good advisement, and sound judgment, we have
decreed, that no man so hardly[1] be denied to choose, and
follow the Christian [observance or religion; but that this
liberty be given to every man that he may apply his] mind
to what religion he thinketh meet himself, whereby God
may perform upon us, all his accustomed care and goodness. To the intent therefore, you might know that this
is our pleasure, we thought it necessary to write this unto
you, whereby all such errors and opinions being removed,
which in our former letters, being sent unto you in the
behalf of the Christians, are contained, and which seem
very indiscreet, and contrary to our clemency, may be
made frustrate and annihilate. Now therefore, firmly and
freely, we will and command, that every man have a free
liberty to observe the Christian religion, and that without
any grief, or molestation, he may be suffered to do the
same. These things have we thought good to signify
unto you by as plain words as we may, that we have
given to the Christians free and absolute power to keep
and use their religion. And for so much as this liberty is
absolutely given of us unto them, to use and exercise their
former observance, *if any be disposed,* it is manifest that

[1] [*hardie,* i. e. oppressively, Fox; "We have decreed—that license and liberty be henceforth denied unto none at all, of choosing or following the Christian service or religion."—Euseb. Eccles. Hist. translated by Hanmer, p. 202, fol. edit. 1650.].

the same helpeth much to establish the public tranquillity of our lives;[2] every man to have license, and liberty to use, and choose what kind of worshipping he list himself. And this is done of us, only for the intent, that we would have no man to be enforced to one religion more than another. And this thing also, amongst others, we have provided for the Christians, that they may have again the possession of such places, in which heretofore they have been accustomed to make their assemblies. So that if any have bought or purchased the same, either of us or of any other; the same places, without either money, or other recompense, forthwith, and without delay, we will to be restored again to the said Christians. And if any man have obtained the same by gift from us, and shall require any recompense to be made to them in that behalf: then let the Christians repair to the president, being the judge appointed for that place, that consideration may be had of those men by our benignity; all which things we will and command, that you see to be given, and restored freely, and with diligence, unto the society of the Christians, all delay set apart. And because the Christians themselves are understood to have had, not only those places wherein they were accustomed to resort together, but certain other peculiar places also, not being private to any one man, but belonging to the right of their congregation and society; you shall see also all those to be restored to the Christians, that is to say, to every fellowship and company of them, according to the decree, whereof we have made mention, all delay set apart. Provided, that the order we have taken in the mean time be observed, that if any, taking no recompense, shall restore the same lands and possessions, they shall not mistrust, but be sure to be saved harmless by us. In all these things, it shall be your part to employ

2 [time. Fox.]

your diligence in the behalf of the aforesaid company of the Christians, whereby this our commandment may speedily be accomplished, and also in this case by our clemency, the common and public peace may be preserved; for undoubtedly by this means, as before we have said, the goodwill and favour of God towards us, whereof in many cases we have had good experience, shall always continue with us. And to the intent, that this our constitution may be notified to all men; it shall be requisite, that the copy of these our letters be set up in all places, that men may read and know the same, lest any should be ignorant thereof." [3]

So also Maximinus the emperor, after he had persecuted the Christians, sent forth his edict to the contrary; that all men should have liberty to use what religion they like best, seeing that before that time, " upon the occasion, that Dioclesianus, and Maximinianus, our progenitors, commanded the assemblies and meetings of Christians to be cut off, so that there were many of them spoiled and robbed ;" lest our subjects " should be spoiled of their goods and sustenance, which thing chiefly to prevent is our only endeavour," &c. [4] Which thing was very well taken, and highly allowed of the Romans, and wise men.

By reason of these edicts, great tranquillity followed, and long-continued persecution ceased: so, as Fox declares, [5] that the church continued without any open slaughter for a thousand years together, till anno 1300 ; [6]

---

[3] Eusebius Eccles. Hist. lib. x. cap. 5. [Fox, Acts and Monuments, i. 78. edition, 1610.]

[4] Euseb. lib. ix. cap. 10. Fox, Acts and Mon. i. p. 78.

[5] [Acts and Monuments, i. p. 91, 391, 551.]

[6] [The crusades for the extirpation of the Albigenses, which began about A.D. 1209, and the persecutions raised by St. Bernard against the Henricians and Petrobrussians about 1170, alone excepted.]

when the burning of John Huss, and Jeremy of Prague, for heretics, by the council of Constance, caused the Bohemians to raise an army against the authors of their death: and God was so with the Bohemian army under Zisca, that they always conquered.[7] So that God hath caused much evil to come upon them who have compelled men in matters of religion.

THAT RELIGION OUGHT TO BE FREE.

1. Because it is God's way to have religion free, and only to flow from an inward principle of faith and love, neither would God be worshipped of unwilling worshippers. John iv. 24

2. It is God's prerogative only, to force to religion, by working faith in men's hearts; for though religion be natural, yet true religion is supernatural, and proceeds from the Spirit of God.

3. Because the end why God hath a church is, that he might have a people separated from others in the world, to glorify him in a holy conversation, to the convincing of

[7] [The council of Constance was assembled in 1414 to put an end to the schism then reigning in the papacy, from the claims of no less than three rival popes to the supreme government of the church. Notwithstanding the emperor Sigismund's safe-conduct, Huss was arrested by the council, and his doctrines denounced as heretical. Refusing to recant, he was consigned to the secular arm, and burnt by the emperor's order. Jerome of Prague, his disciple, at first retracted his sentiments, but recovering his courage and his faith in the divine promises, after an interval of imprisonment, followed his master to the stake. These cruel and nefarious transactions roused the Bohemians, the countrymen of the martyrs, to arms, and under Ziska, a man of high reputation for wisdom, courage, patriotism, and the fear of God, not only seized the city of Prague, but obtained important successes over the imperial armies. After great losses, the emperor came to terms favourable to the liberties and religious rights of the people. —Robinson's Eccles. Researches, pp. 483, 486.]

those that are out of the church; therefore, there must be a world, before whom the church must walk, to whom such as walk disorderly are to be cast by excommunication, and the church is to wait for their repentance.

4. Because, if there should be an established law for all persons to submit unto, it would tend to the wounding of the souls, and undoing the bodies of very many that could not submit to any one way, because their judgments so much differ. Also, if there should be any defect in the established law, as it is possible to be—as we know by woful experience—the godly shall suffer oppression for conscience of the truth against that defect, by the execution of that law; which, I suppose, would be a grief to honest hearts, seeing, we find, that when laws are made concerning religion, such as make conscience are caught, [Dan. iii. 8; vi. 10.] as Daniel and the three children were.

5. Because, it is the best for the public peace to give every one content, for if there be set up an order in religion for a law, and thereby please one sort of people, another sort will be displeased, who it may be, have as many good reasons for that they would have, as the others; and such as like not a toleration, it is to be feared, they are not rightly principled themselves, and so are not competent judges.

And as for those who think otherwise, I desire they would seriously consider, and answer these questions by the scriptures.

QUESTIONS

Propounded to the Synod, and all honest-hearted and conscientious people, whether corporal punishments ought to be inflicted upon such as hold errors in religion.[8]

QUEST. 1.

Whether corporal punishments can open blind eyes, and give light to dark understandings?

2. Whether carnal punishments can produce any more than a carnal repentance and obedience?

3. Whether the destroying of men's bodies for errors, be not a means to prevent their conversion; seeing some are not called until the eleventh hour, and if they should Matt. xx. 7. be cut off for their errors [at] the seventh, how should they come in?

4. Whether those who would force other men's consciences, be willing to have their own forced?

5. Whether it be wisdom and safe to make such sole judges in matters of religion who are not infallible, but as liable to err as others?[9]

6. If a father or magistrate have not power to force a virgin to marry one she cannot love, whether they have

[8] The celebrated John Goodwin had preceded Mr. Richardson, in presenting to the synod a series of "modest and humble queries" on the same subject, in 1646, equally adapted to expose intolerance and further liberty of conscience. Life of John Goodwin, by Thos. Jackson, p. 123.]

[9] ["Whether twelve simple countrymen, such as our ordinary juries usually consist of at country assizes, be of any competent faculty or interest to pass upon the life or liberty of a studious, learned, and conscientious man, in such cases, which the greatest and ablest professors of divinity in the world are not able clearly, or with any competent satisfaction to the scrupulous, many times to resolve or determine?" Some Modest and Humble Queries, p. 5, qu. 22. London, 1646, 4to.]

power to force one where they cannot believe, against the light and checks of their own consciences?

7. Whether the scripture makes the magistrate judge of our faith?[1]

8. If the magistrates may determine what is truth, whether we must not believe, and live by the magistrates' faith, and change our religion at their pleasures? And if nothing must be preached, nor printed, nor allowed to pass, unless certain men please to approve, and give their allowance thereto, under their hands, whether such do not by this practice tell God that unless he will reveal his truth first to them, they will not suffer it to be published, and so not to be known? And whether the licenser setting his hand to the book to license it, he being a priest by his ordination, and from the pope, be not the mark of the beast, spoken of Rev. xiii. 17? And whether it be not worse than any of our former patents before this parliament?[2] Is not this a spiritual wickedness in high places, which strikes at the truth? Are they fit to be licensers of the truth, who, when the truth hath been tendered to be licensed, have confessed the truth of it, as they have been free to license it, but refused, because they durst not? And whether it can be made to appear that God hath revealed

---

[1] [" Whether did God ever give any power or authority to civil magistrates, or others, either in the old testament or the new, to make any controverted exposition of any clause or clauses in the law—punishable either with imprisonment or death?" Modest and Humble Queries, p. 12, qu. 38.]

[2] [The long parliament. By letters patent, grounded on the royal letters patent, by which the ecclesiastical commission was constituted, the commissioners could fine, imprison, and exercise other authorities not belonging to the ecclesiastical jurisdiction. Monopolies had been also granted to various persons and companies, by letters patent, of almost every article in daily use. These companies were often invested with inquisitorial powers, which were extremely unpopular, and hostile to liberty. The whole of these grievances and oppressions were swept away by this parliament. Neal's History of Puritans, i. 445. Vaughan's Hist. of England, i. 262.]

his truth first to these ministers of England, and so [they are] the first spreaders of it? Instance those who opposed the prelates, the ministers or the people first. And so of the rest.

9. Whether it be not the command of Christ that the tares—those that walk in lies, and the wheat—those that walk in the truth, should be let alone; and the blind [also] —led in a false religion—which are offended at the declaring of the truth, should be let alone? Matt. xiii. 30, 38; xv. 14

10. Whether he was not reproved, that would have fire from heaven to devour those that reject Christ? Luke ix. 54, 55.

11. Whether the servants of the Lord are not forbidden to strive, but to be gentle towards all? 2 Tim. ii. 24.

12. Whether the saints' weapons against errors, be carnal or no?[3] 2 Cor. x. 4.

13. Whether it was not Christ's command that his disciples, when they were persecuted, they should pray, and if cursed, bless?

14. Whether the scriptures declare that the saints should persecute others, and whether the gentle lambs of Christ will or can serve the wolves so, seeing he sent his as sheep among wolves, and not as wolves among sheep, to kill and imprison? Matt. x. 16.

15. Whether Christ hath said, He will have an unwilling people compelled to serve him?[4]

---

[3] [" Whether are errors and heresies any other things than some of those *strongholds and imaginations* in men, *which*, as the apostle saith, *exalt themselves against the knowledge of God*? Or whether can they be better thrown down, than by those weapons, which are *mighty through God* for that very purpose? And whether are these weapons carnal or spiritual?" Modest and Humble Queries, p. 2, qu. 7.]

[4] [" What needs outward power to force a people made willing by the Spirit? *Thy people shall be willing in the day of thy power.* The very day of Christ's power is not to force men against their wills, but to make them willing. They that are not a willing people, belong not to Christ's

16. Whether ever God did plant his church by violence and bloodshed?

17. Whether tares may not become wheat, and the blind see, and those that now oppose and resist Christ afterwards receive him, and he that is now in the devil's snare may get out, and come to repentance, and such as are idolaters, as the Corinthians were, may become true worshippers, as they that are strangers may become God's people?

18. Whether to convert an heretic, and to cast out unclean spirits, be done any other way than by the finger of God, by the mighty power of the Spirit in the word?

19. Whether he that is not conformable to Christ may not at the same time be a good subject to the state, and as profitable to it?

20. Whether men that differ in religion may not be tolerated, seeing "Abraham abode among the Canaanites a long time, yet contrary to them in religion; and *he sojourned in Gerar*, and king Abimelech gave him leave to abide in his land. And Isaac dwelt in the same land, yet contrary in religion." "The people of Israel were about four hundred and thirty years in Egypt, and afterwards in Babylon, all which time they differed in religion from the state." "Christ and his disciples differed from the common religion of the state." "And when the enemies of the truth raised up any tumults, the wisdom of the magistrate most wisely appeased them." [5]

Marginal references: Gen. xiii. 7; xiv. 13. Gen. xx. [1, 15]; xxi. 33, 34. Gen. xxvi. 1. Ex. xii. [41]; 2 Chronicles xxxvi. [20.] Acts xix. 27. Acts xviii. 14; xix. 35.

21. Whether it be not better for us that a patent were granted to monopolize all the corn and cloth, and to have it measured out unto us at their price and pleasure, which yet were intolerable, as for some men to appoint and mea-

kingdom, but to the world." Dell's Right Reformation, &c. p. 22, 4to. ed. 1646.]

[5] [See the Humble Supplication, *ante*, p. 225.]

sure out unto us, what and how much we shall believe and practise in matters of religion?

22. Whether there be not the same reason that they should be appointed by us, what they shall believe and practise in religion, as for them to do so to us; seeing we can give as good grounds for what we believe and practise, as they can do for what they would have, if not better?

23. Whether men heretofore have not in zeal for religion, persecuted the Son of God, instead of the son of perdition?

24. Whether it is not a burden great enough for the magistrate to govern and judge in civil causes, to preserve the subjects' rights, peace, and safety?

25. If the magistrate must judge and punish in matters of religion, the magistrate must ever be troubled with such persons, and such causes. And, if after his conscience be convinced [that] he had no such power, or see that it was truth he punished; what horrors of conscience is he like to possess?

26. Whether he is fit to appoint punishments, that is not fit to judge?

27. If the magistrate must punish errors in religion, whether it doth not impose a necessity, that the magistrate is to have a certainty of knowledge in all intricate cases? And whether God calls such to that place, whom he hath not furnished with abilities for that place? And if a magistrate in darkness, and spiritually blind, and dead, be fit to judge of light, of truth, and error? And whether such be fit for the place of the magistracy? Then, whether it be not a scruple to a tender conscience to submit to such in civil causes, because not appointed to that place by God? Whereas, if the magistrates' power be only civil, the doubt is resolved; because such as may be fit for magistrates, men ought in conscience, in civil

Rom. xiii. 1
—7.]things, to submit unto them, so far as their commands are good.[6]

28. Whether there be any scripture that saith, that any man's conscience is to be constrained; and whether the magistrate can reach men's consciences; and whether he be fit to make a law to conscience, who cannot know when conscience keeps it, and that cannot reward conscience for keeping it, nor punish the conscience for the breaking of it?[7]

29. Whether it be not in vain for us to have bibles in English, if, contrary to our understanding of them, we must believe as the church believes, whether it be right or wrong?[8]

30. Whether the magistrate be not wronged, to give him the title of civil magistrate only, if his power be spiritual?

31. Whether laws made merely concerning spiritual things, be not spiritual also?

32. Whether if no civil law be broken, the civil peace be hurt or no?

33. Whether in compulsion for conscience, not only the guilty, but the innocent suffer also? As if the husband

[6] [" That genuine end of civil society...is no other than SECURITY TO THE TEMPORAL LIBERTY AND PROPERTY OF MAN. For this end civil society was invented; and this, civil society alone is able to procure. The great, but spurious rival of this end, the salvation of souls....belongs to the other division." Warburton's Alliance between Church and State, &c. p. 33. edit. 1748.]

[7] [" In judicially rewarding, therefore, the motives must be known; but human judicatures cannot know them, but by accident. It is only that tribunal, which searches the heart, that can penetrate thus far." Warburton's Alliance between Church and State,

p. 22. The laws of civil society, " can have no further efficacy than to restrain men from open transgression; while what is done amiss in private, though equally tending to the public prejudice, escapes their censure," p. 10.]

[8] [" In vain have English parliaments permitted English bibles in the poorest English houses, and the simplest man or woman to search the scriptures, if yet against their souls' persuasion from the scripture, they should be forced, as if they lived in Spain or Rome itself without the sight of a bible, to believe as the church believes." Preface to Roger Williams' Bloudy Tenent of Persecution discussed, &c. ed. 1644, 4to.]

be an heretic, his sufferings may cause the innocent wife and children to suffer also?

34. Whether such as are spiritually dead, be capable of being spiritually infected?[9]

35. Whether God will accept of a painted sepulchre, a shadow, a mere compliment of obedience, when the heart is dead and rotten, and hates God, and all that is good? God hath no need of hypocrites, much less of forced ones: God John iv.[23.] will have those to worship him that can worship him in spirit and truth.

36. Whether the scriptures appoint any other punishment to be inflicted upon heretics, than rejection and excommu- Tit. iii 10. nication?

37. Whether freedom of conscience would not join all sorts of persons to the magistrate, because each shared in the benefit?

38. Whether those states (as the Low Countries), who grant such liberty, do not live quietly, and flourish in great prosperity?[1]

39. Whether persecution for conscience, do not harden men in their way, and make them cry out of oppression and tyranny?

40. Whether some corporal punishments would not make thousands in England face about to popery, as it did in Queen Mary's time?[2]

---

[9] [affected?]

[1] ["It causes disturbances and tumults in the world, when men are forced by outward power to act against their inward principles in the things of God. What disturbances and tumults this hath bred in state and kingdoms who knows not?" Dell's Right Reformation, &c. p. 24.]

[2] ["Now, after that God had plagued this realm with the most grievous plague that ever came to it, in taking away from it so godly a king as he was, yea, such an one as hath not been read of, of his age, in any realm, both for wit, learning, soberness, and godliness; in his stead he hath set up queen Mary, who in short time hath pulled down that was not builded in many years, and brought in the bishop of Rome, before justly and by law of parliament abolished, *with open per-*

41. Whether laws made concerning religion, have not always caught the most holy men; witness Daniel and the three children? The rest will be of what religion you will.

42. Whether the saints crave the help of the powers of this world to bring Christ to them, or fear their powers to keep him from them?

43. If no religion is to be practised, but that which the commonwealth shall approve on; what if they will approve of no religion? Shall men have no religion at all?

44. Whether the saints ought not to continue their assemblies for the worship of God, without, or against the consent of the magistrates; they being commanded to do so? Matt. xxviii. 18, 19, 20; Heb. x. 25. By an angel from God, Acts v. 20. It was the apostles' practice, who were not rebellious nor seditious.

Acts iv. 18, 19, 20, 23; v. 22. 28.

45. Whether uniformity in religion in the state, do not oppress millions of souls, and impoverish the saints' bodies?

46. Whether God's people have not disputed and taught a new religion and worship, contrary to the state they lived in, and spread it in travelling and [in] open places; as appears, Acts xvii. 2, 17, and xviii. 28; yet [with] no arrogancy and impetuousness? Yea, contrary to public authority in the nation's uniformity in false worship, as the three children; so the apostles, Acts iv. 5, 13. The saints have openly witnessed, that in matters spiritual, Jesus was king. And for this Christ suffered, as appears by his accusation, JESUS OF NAZARETH, THE KING OF THE JEWS. God's people have seemed the disturbers of the civil state. Upon the apostles

Dan. iii. 16 —18.

Acts xvii. 7.

John xix.19; Ps. ii.6; Acts ii. 36.

jury of so many as gave their voices and consent to the same. For they had all made a solemn oath before never to receive his unjust usurped power into the realm again." From Preface of the translator of Archbishop Cranmer's Unwritten Verities, printed in the reign of Queen Mary. Jenkyn's Cranmer's Remains, iv. 164.]

preaching, there followed uproars and tumults, at Iconium, Acts xiv. 4; xix. 29, 40; xxi. 30, 31. at Ephesus, at Jerusalem.

47. Whether Jesus Christ appointed any material prisons for blasphemers of him? Whether, notwithstanding the confidence of the truth they have, to which they would force others: whether the bishops, their fathers, have not been as deeply mistaken; for now they see and say they are anti-christian?

48. Whether it be not a natural law for every man that liveth, to worship that which he thinketh is God, and as he thinketh he ought to worship; and to force otherwise, will be concluded an oppression of those persons so forced?

49. And whether it is best for us to put out our eyes, and see by the eyes of others, who are as dim-sighted?

In my judgment, your judgment is a lie; will ye compel me to believe a lie? Compel ye a man to be present at a worship which he loathes? Or will ye force my tongue to speak that which my ears cannot affect?

50. Whether it be in the power of any man to believe what he will, and as he will? The mind of man being per-suaded with great reasons, is captivated, will he, nill he. I am fully persuaded of the truth of the religion I profess; if I should follow your religion, I should deceive men, and go contrary to my conscience, but I cannot deceive God.

51. Whether the ordinance against preaching[3] is not only

---

[3] [An ordinance of parliament was issued on the 26th April, 1645, for the silencing of all such preachers as were not ordained, nor allowed, " by those who shall be appointed thereunto by both houses of parliament." A still more stringent ordinance was passed to the same effect, on December 26th, 1646. All preaching or expo-sition of scripture was forbidden except by ordained persons; and due punish-ment was to be inflicted on all who spake aught in " derogation of the church government" then established. Many baptists were prosecuted and imprisoned under these intolerant laws, among whom may be mentioned, Mr. Denne, Mr. Coppe, Mr. Lamb, and Mr. Hanserd Knollys. " The presby-terian clergy would authorize none to preach, except such as would take the covenant, and consent to their dis-

the way to ensnare the choicest men; but it cannot catch the worst? Who shall judge what is error, and what is truth? I answer, if our enemies must judge, we must always be persecuted, and abused by the worst of men : for they will judge it fit to persecute us; they will call truth error, and error truth. And sometimes truth shall be esteemed no less than blasphemy ; and that which one man shall do as his duty, in conscience to God's command, may be called obstinacy, though unjustly. So that if any demand who is the most orthodox and sound man, and freest from errors, the answer is now, if you will put it to the vote, it is the major voice, the strongest side, that side that hath the authority to back it ; so that we must follow a multitude. Once a king being sick, it was demanded of him who should succeed him in the crown; he answered, he that had the longest sword. So it is now ; and if truth hath but a few followers, it must be esteemed error and rejected.

52. If the magistrate, as a magistrate, have a power from Christ, to punish such as he is persuaded in his conscience are erroneous and heretical, or because he differs in religion from the magistrate, then queen Mary and her parliament did well, in burning the martyrs for differing from her established religion ; they being as contrary to her religion as any are now in the magistrates' eyes.

53. Either the civil, or the spiritual state must be supreme; which of these must judge the other in spiritual matters? If the magistrate, then he is above the church, and so the head of the church.[4] And [if] he hath his power

cipline." Crosby, Hist. of Eng. Baptists, i. 192, 194, 221, &c. Neal, Hist. of the Puritans, ii. 494. Scobell's Collection of Acts, &c. p. 92.]

[4] ["The state, by this alliance, having undertaken the protection of the church ; and protection not being to be afforded to any community, without power over it, in the community protecting ; it necessarily follows, that the civil magistrate must be supreme." Warburton's Alliance, &c. p. 148.]

from the people to govern the church, whether it will not
follow that the people, as a people, have originally as men
a power to govern the church, to see her do her duty, to
reform and correct her; and so the spouse of Christ, the
wife of Christ, must be corrected according to the pleasure
of the world, which lieth in wickedness? [1Johnv.19.]

54. Whether every man doth not venture his soul upon
the truth of that religion which in his conscience he is persuaded of the truth of?

55. Whether these kingdoms haveany sufficient ground
to believe they shall enjoy their outward rights and liberties,
so long as any one religion is set up, and men forced under
great penalties to be subject to it?

56. Whether it be not a horrible thing that a free division
of England may not have so much liberty as is permitted
to a Turk in this kingdom; who, although he denies Christ,
yet he can live quietly amongst us here? And is it not a
great ingratitude of this kingdom to deny this liberty to
such as are friends, and have been a means in their persons
and estates to save this kingdom from destruction and
desolation? Oh, England, England! Oh that thou wert
wise to know the things that belong to thy prosperity and
peace, before it be too late! The hand of God is against
thee. How have we slain one another; and who knows but
this is come upon us for troubling, undoing, despising, and
banishing the people of God into so many wildernesses?[5]

57. Whether men are bound in conscience to be perse-

---

[5] ["God hath blasted them that
would have kept us from our sweetest
liberty. The king and his bishops
denied it to us, and God hath blasted
them. Those of the parliament promised liberty to us, but did not give it
us; God hath blasted them. The
synod, with the ministry of England,
should have spoken for us, and they
spake against us, and God hath blasted
them—and if the army had neglected
us herein, God would have blasted
them. *Jerusalem is a burdensome stone,*
all that oppose it, dash themselves in
pieces." Richardson's Answer to the
London Ministers, p. 29, ed. 1649.]

TOLERATION.]   S

cuted, when they can help it, for omitting of that they judge sinful? And whether a man may not take that which is his right, or use means to take it by force, in case they who should give it deny it, and he cannot have it otherwise? Thus I would keep my estate, my liberty, my life, by force, if I (can, and) cannot keep it otherwise.[6]

58. Whether there be any man that judgeth his own judgment erroneous?

59. Whether, if any man will take upon him to punish men for errors, it be not fit [that] he show his authority from God, to warrant his practice; and if one man is to be punished for error, must it not of necessity follow, that all men are to be punished; because all men have errors, no man is free from them; and therefore, all men are to be punished with corporal punishments for their errors, either more or less? So that, if Luther and Calvin, and other good men were now amongst us, they should be punished for the errors they held, as well as others are for the truth?

60. Whether the priests of England, in assuming to themselves to be Christ's ministers, and the apostles' successors, and a godly reformed presbytery, be not a cunning trick, and a mere cheat to deceive the simple?[7]

61. Whether the priests' practice be not contrary to the

---

[6] [" A man, when he sins not against the state, may justly stand for his state-freedom ; and to deprive a man of his state-liberty for the kingdom of Christ's sake, as it causeth disturbances in the world, so let any man show me any such thing in the gospel." Dell's Right Reformation, &c. p. 24.]

[7] [In April, 1646, parliament propounded to the assembly of divines, certain questions of a similar tendency, as, " Whether the parochial and congregational elderships appointed by ordinance of parliament, or any other congregational or presbyterial elder-ships, are *jure divino*, and by the will and appointment of Jesus Christ? Whether all the members of the said elderships, as members thereof, or which of them, are *jure divino*, and by the will and appointment of Jesus Christ?" These questions much " retarded" the intolerant courses of the synod. Hanbury's Hist. Memorials, iii. 212.]

apostles' practice? Take one instance: the apostles dipped, viz. baptized, persons, after they believed and confessed their faith; whereas these sprinkle persons before they believe, yea, before they can speak. They baptized persons in a river; these sprinkle water upon their faces. Yet if you will believe them, they are the successors of the apostles, and follow their steps. ^{Acts ii.; viii. [36;] Matt. iii. [6.]}

Acts ii.; viii. [36;] Matt. iii. [6.]

62. Wherefore do the priests of England assume to themselves the title of divines? Is it because they are exercised in divine truths, or because they partake of the divine nature, or both? If so, then many tradesmen may as well have the title of divine given them, as well as they, because they partake of the divine nature, and are as much exercised in matters divine, as the most of them. But it is a question, whether the title divine is to be given to any man, but only to God, whose being only is divine.

63. Whether the name of settling religion be not a fine pretence to establish error and tyranny? We desire not liberty of conscience of any man. Let us enjoy our right, our liberty of persons and estates, and we will give them leave to hang our religion, and consciences too, if they can. They desire not our religion, nor can they see, nor reach our consciences, as Ques. 28. And I am persuaded, that the hand of God and man will be against England and Scotland, till they cease troubling of men for matters of religion.[8]

64. Whether any that are contrary to the synod, did ever

[8] [Baillie, one of the Scots' commissioners to the assembly, in a work printed in 1647, particularly inveighs against the baptists for their opposition to its proceedings. "This immoderate love of licentiousness," he says, "puts them upon a high degree of hatred and indignation against the Solemn League and Covenant, against the Scottish nation whence it came; as two great impediments to their quiet enjoying of that self-destroying and God-provoking liberty, which, so passionately, they lust after." Hanbury's Hist. Memor. iii. 223.]

s 2

sue the parliament to have the presbyters punished for any of their errors, though in them they abound? And whether some of them do not tend to the destruction of the state, if they might have their wills?[9]

65. Whether it be not a great error to slight and disgrace the holy scriptures? And whether the synod are not guilty of this error, in that they do not make the scriptures the ground and rule of what they do? And this appears: 1. In that what they affirm is not in the scriptures. 2. In that they keep not the form of sound words, as the scriptures require. We cannot read it in the scripture what they impose upon others; nor can we find the substance of what they impose upon others in the whole scriptures. 3. Neither do they allege the words nor texts of scripture to prove, what they maintain, as appears by their Directory,[1] what is their authority above the scriptures; if they think so, it is no small error.

66. Whether it doth not appear, that the priesthood, for the most part, do hate and despise the suffering saints of Christ? And this appears: 1. Because they speak not

[9] [" We exalt Jesus Christ alone in the spiritual church; and attribute to the magistrate his full power in the world. But they (the presbyterians) exalt themselves in Christ's stead in the church; and set under their feet the magistrate's power in the world." Dell's Right Reformation, p. 42.]

[1] [On the 3rd January, 1645, the parliament issued an ordinance for the abolition of the Common Prayer Book in the public worship, and for the imposition, in its stead, of the Directory, which had been prepared by the assembly of divines. Therein directions are given for every part of divine service, as the reading of the scriptures, the mode and matter of prayer, the administration of baptism and the Lord's supper, visiting the sick, burials, singing, days and places of public worship, &c.; but liturgical forms were in all cases to be disused. As intimated above, no scripture authority is produced or referred to, either for the sentiments contained in it, or for its use by the clergy. An additional ordinance in the following September rendered the use of it compulsory in all the parishes of the land; persons preaching or writing against it were to be fined, and penalties were attached to the use of the book of Common Prayer, whether used in public or in private. Scobell's Collection of Acts and Ordinances, pp. 75, 97.]

for them. But, 2. Speak against them. 3. They preach against them. 4. They persecute them, and cause others to persecute them. 5. When they are in prison, they do not visit them. 6. Nor allow them any means, when they are in want, to maintain them.

67. Whether it doth appear, that the priests oppose errors and sects out of conscience, or out of bye and self ends? It appears to be the latter: because they write and preach, and bend their strength against those truths that oppose their profit, honour, ease; as tithes, false ministry, and cozening of people. But as for errors, indeed—as to deny the resurrection of the body, the truth of the scriptures, to deny Christ to be God, and the like —which of them hath written one sheet against any of these errors; notwithstanding they have written volumes against good men, for doing that [which] Christ commanded them?

68. Whether those priests are not false priests, in prophesying in their pulpits, that London should be plundered, and their wives, &c., ravished, when Sir Thomas his army came into London?[2] You see apparently they

---

[2] [The war being ended, the presbyterians endeavoured to get rid of the army. But fearing the loss of that liberty for which they had fought, and dreading the intolerant spirit of presbytery, under the direction of the council of agitators, the army resolved not to disband, until the civil and religious liberties of the nation were placed in security. To the dismay of the presbyterians, they seized the person of the king, and advanced towards London; and finally, under the command of Sir Thomas Fairfax and Cromwell, marched through the city, without any disorder, putting an end to presbyterian ascendancy. "The odium of this grand revolution, by which the army became masters of the city of London, and of the parliament itself, fell chiefly on the presbyterians themselves, whose intemperate zeal for covenant-uniformity carried them to very impolitic excesses. The sermons of their ministers were filled with invectives against the army; in their public prayers they entreated the Almighty to incline the hearts of the Scots to return to their relief; and the conversation of their people was riotous and disorderly." Neal, ii. 441, 447.]

prophesy the vision of their own hearts; so they say, "Thus saith the Lord," when he hath not spoken unto them.

[69.] Whether the priests were not the cause of the burning of the book, entitled "The Bloudy Tenent," because it was against persecution? [3] And whether their consciences would not have dispensed with the burning of the author of it? And I wish they would seriously consider Dell's Book of Right Reformation. [4]

70. Whether men's eyes are not so opened, and the priests' deeds so manifest, that it is but in vain for them to think that all men will be led by them evermore?

---

[3] ["The Bloudy Tenent of Persecution for the Cause of Conscience discussed," &c. 4to. 1644, pp. 247, was the work of the noble-minded Roger Williams, published in reply to a letter of Mr. John Cotton, the American congregationalist, advocating persecution. It gave very great offence to the presbyterians, who exclaimed against it as full of heresy and blasphemy. According to Baillie, it did not even meet with the approbation of the English independents. "Liberty of conscience, and toleration of all or any religion, is so prodigious an impiety, that this religious parliament cannot but abhor the very naming of it. *Whatever may be the opinions of John Goodwin, Mr. Williams, and some of that stamp, yet Mr. Burroughes, in his late ' Irenicum,' upon many unanswerable arguments, explodes that abomination.*" Mr. Burroughes was one of the five dissenting brethren.—Brook's Lives, iii. 481. Hanbury's Hist. Memor. iii. 127, 110.]

[4] ["Right Reformation: or, The Reformation of the Church of the New Testament, represented in Gospel-light. In a sermon preached to the Honourable House of Commons, on Wednesday, November 25, 1646, &c." 4to. 1646. pp. 42. He urges on [the parliament, "That as Christ's kingdom and the kingdoms of the world are distinct, so you would be pleased to keep them so; not mingle them together yourselves, nor suffer others to do it, to the great prejudice and disturbance of both." That Christ is the only reformer, his instruments the word and Spirit, and to him all reformation must be left: here no earthly power must interfere.—p. 28. Mr. Dell was one of the ejected ministers, losing a living and the mastership of Caius College, Cambridge. He is usually regarded as a baptist, although his sentiments approximated in some points to those of the quakers. Ivimey, ii. 55.]

IF THE MAGISTRATE BE A MEMBER OF A CHURCH,
YET HE OUGHT TO BE EXCOMMUNICATED, IF HE
DESERVE IT.

REASONS.

1. Because magistrates must be subject to Christ; but 1 Cor. v. 4, 5.
Christ censures all offenders.

2. Every brother must be subject to Christ's censure: Matt. xviii.
but magistrates are brethren.
 15, 16, 17; Deut. xvii. 15.

3. They may censure all within the church. 1 Cor. v. 12.

4. The church hath a charge of all the souls of the Heb. xiii. 17.
church, and must give account of them.

5. Christ's censures are for the good of souls: but ma- 1 Cor. v. 5.
gistrates must not be denied any privilege for their souls,
else they, by being magistrates, should lose a privilege of
Christ's.

6. In which privileges, Christians are all one. Gal. iii. 28; Col. iii. 11.

Sins of magistrates are hateful and condemned. It is a Is. x. 1; Mic. iii. 1.
paradox, that a magistrate may be punished by the church,
and yet that they are judges of the church.

If that religion be true [of which] the magistrate is persuaded: he owes a threefold duty.

First, approbation, with a tender respect to the truth Is. xlix.[23;] Rev. xxi. [24.]
and the professors of it.

Secondly, personal submission of his soul to the power Matt. xviii. [15—20;] 1 Cor. v.
of Jesus his government.

Thirdly, protection of them and their estates from vio- Rom. xiii. [1—7.]
lence and injury.

To a false religion he owes:

1. Permission, — for approbation he owes not to
what is evil, — as Matt. xiii. 30, for public peace and
quietness.

2. Protection of the persons of his subjects, though of a

false worship, that no injury be offered to the persons or goods of any.[5]

OBJECTION I.

The kings of Judah compelled men to serve the Lord: ergo, kings may now compel, &c.

ANSWER I.

They only who lived under the Jewish worship were compelled; strangers were not.

Secondly, they were not compelled to any thing, but what they knew and confessed was their duty.

2 Chron. vi. 12—15.

Thirdly, if they did compel, their actions were not moral, to oblige other kings to do so, see Deut. xiii. 3, 9, 15, 16. Surely they will not do so.

See Lev. xx. 10; Deut. xxii. 22; with 1 Cor. xii.

Fourthly, the kings of Israel did not imprison schismatics, pharisees, Herodians, &c.

Fifthly, the kings of Israel had extraordinary prophets, to direct them what to do infallibly; these kings have none such to direct them.

Sixthly, if the law be moral; where is it set down in Christ's testament, which is to be our rule, that the magistrate shall compel all to *his* religion, for to another he will not?

Obj. 2. It seems you would have no government, no law?

---

[5] [Dr. John Owen answers in the affirmative the following questions :— " Whether the supreme magistrate in a nation, or commonwealth, of men professing the religion of Jesus Christ, may, or ought, to exert his power, legislative and executive, for the supportment, preservation, and furtherance of the profession of the faith and worship of God ; and whether he may and ought to forbid, coerce, or restrain such principles and practices as are contrary to them, and destructive of them ?" He asserts that the law of nature and of nations, God's institutions, the example of godly magistrates, the promises and equity of the gospel, and the confessions of all protestant churches, with that of the independents, prove the duty of secular and magisterial interference in religion to the extent indicated in the question.—Works, edited by Russell, vol. xix. p. 385—390.]

Answ. 2. None but Christ's for his house.[6]

Obj. 3. Then every man may live as he list?

Answ. 3. Had not he as good live as he list, as live as you list?[7]

Obj. 4. But we are bound by oath to a reformation, in suppressing errors, &c.

Answ. 4. But still, according to the word of God, not against it. Show us the pattern of your reformation in Christ's testament, in his gospel, and we will embrace it; for we are not under the law but under grace.

Obj. 5. Then it seems errors may be suffered?

Answ. 5. We must suffer that which we cannot help, necessity hath no law. It is no more in our power to hinder errors, than it was in the power of the prelates, to hinder men's preaching, writing, and speaking against them.

It is not in the power of man to suppress errors. If you can, first, so speak to the blind, and open the eyes of our understandings, as to expel the darkness that is in them; secondly, if you can command the heart, and reform it; thirdly, if you can hinder and destroy the vain imaginations of men's hearts, and hinder Satan's suggestions of errors, and men's speakings each to others; if you can place light in the soul, for there is no light till God give light: till God speak, all is nothing; if you can give the Holy Spirit to men to direct and reform them, for till the

---

[6] [" But would you have no government? Yes; but the government of Christ the head, and the Holy Ghost the Spirit, in and over the church, the body.—But would you have no law? No laws in God's kingdom, but God's laws . . . and they are these three: the law of a new nature; the law of the spirit of life that is in Christ; the law of love."—Dell's Right Reformation, &c., p. 26.]

[7] [" May a Christian then live as he list? No, by no means; for he hath the word and Spirit in him to keep him from living as he list; and he knows that no man in God's kingdom may live as he wills, but as God wills."—Ibid. p. 26.]

Spirit comes there is no reformation to purpose: then are you able to suppress errors. If you cannot do these things, give place to him that can and will do these things in his time; and, in the meantime, will so order all errors to his glory, and the good of his elect.

And for the reformation that some men cry up to suppress errors, what is it but, first, a sinful reformation, in that it forceth men to sin even against their own knowledge and conscience, for many men before they will suffer death, or be undone, will say and do any thing? Secondly, it is a foolish reformation, in going the wrong way to work, in offering to reform the outside first. Whereas God, when he reforms, begins within, at the heart, because if that be not first reformed, it is no spiritual reformation, but a carnal and hypocritical one, as the pharisees made clean the out- side, and [remained] filthy within.[8] Thirdly, it is a carnal reformation, and therefore it is attended with carnal instru- ments, prison and swords, &c. Whereas Christ's kingdom is spiritual, and all that belongs unto it. Fourthly, it is a cruel reformation, that hath more destruction than edifi- cation in it. It is a terrible reformation, there waiteth on it confiscation of goods, fines, imprisonment, banishment, death with fire and sword.[9] Is there no better cure of the pain of the head than beating out one's brains? Lastly, it is a deceitful reformation, in that it makes men to appear to be sheep, when they are wolves; also, in that under the notion of suppressing errors, it suppresseth the

Matt. xxiii. 3.

---

[8] [" So civil-ecclesiastical reformation makes a man clean outwardly, with an outward confession of faith, when inwardly he is all filthy through un- belief: and whites him over with a few handsome forms of worship, when inwardly he is full of ignorance of God and atheism." — Dell's Right Reformation, &c. p. 7.]

[9] [" Civil-ecclesiastical reformation reforms by breathing out threatenings, punishments, prisons, fire, and death; but the gospel by preaching peace."— Ibid. p. 21.]

truth, and stoppeth the passage of the gospel, which, instead of running, cannot go by reason of it.

Obj. 6. Then errors will prevail?

Ans. 6. If truth may be suffered, it will prevail against errors. Corporal punishments cannot suppress errors, neither doth truth need any such help to maintain it. If truth may have liberty, it can maintain itself. Let neither of them have the sword, and let them try it out. I will venture my life truth will prevail. Are there not men as able to write and speak for truth, as any are to write and speak against it?

Lastly, Whether the presbyters to maintain their way do not expound the scriptures as followeth: *peace be to this house*, be presbyters and ye shall be in peace; *if they refuse this doctrine*, if they refuse presbytery; and *shake off the dust of your feet*, speak against them, and bid the magistrate kill, imprison, and undo them; *if they hear not the church*, viz. the assembly of devisers, *let him be to thee as a heathen*, and let him be stripped naked, and be banished among the heathens; *compel them to come in*, let restraint of liberty, with hunger, cold, and nakedness, force them to be presbyters; *avoid a heretic*, one that will not pay tithes, &c. nor comply with the priests; *after once and twice admonition*, after once and twice imprisonment, hang him, or banish him; *he that believeth not*—what we say—*shall be damned*, shall be condemned to death for a heretic?

It is no more in the power of the synod, or the parliament, to hinder errors, than it was in the power of the prelates to hinder men's preaching, writing, and speaking against them. 1. If you can hinder Satan's suggestions. And 2, hinder the vain imaginations of men's hearts. 3. And expel the darkness in men. 4. And place light instead thereof. 5. And hinder men from speaking each to other; then you can suppress errors, else not. The

Lord only can suppress errors by the mighty power of his Spirit, with his word, and we believe he will certainly do it in his time, to his glory, and the comfort of his people. Amen.

I DESIRE TO KNOW WHETHER THE ASSEMBLY OF DIVINES DO NOT BELIEVE, DESIRE, AND PROFESS, AS SOME OF THE ARTICLES OF THEIR FAITH, AS FOLLOWETH ? AND WHETHER THEY HAVE NOT DECLARED THIS TO BE THEIR FAITH BY THEIR WORKS THAT ARE MANIFEST ?

Imprimis. That it be frequently taught, that so it may become natural, that all England, of what age or estate soever they are, [ought] to believe and confess us to be the church, the spouse and wife of Christ, their dear and tender mother, at whose breasts they are to suck all their days. And that such as refuse, ought to be forced, by the authority of our keys, or rod of iron, from their religion, liberties, estates, and lives.

2. That they only have power in all spiritual causes, and are the only law-givers of rules for worship, doctrine, and discipline. This is so clear, that it is confessed of all men, except only a few heretics and infidels, who are so imprudent [as] to affirm that religion and tyranny never grew upon the stock of truth.

3. That all men ought to ascribe to the place where they sit, that which the pope doth to his seat, viz. the infallible chair ; seeing their priesthood and ordination is one and the same with his. So that no man ought to question the truth or goodness of any of their decrees, seeing they are infallible, and so cannot err.

4. That to them only God doth discover his mysteries and secrets, with all the revelations of heaven. So that they know more than all other men, yea, they are not ignorant in any thing, but are able to determine in the deepest and most intricate controversies what is truth, and what is error. Also they are able to cure all sorts of sects and heresies, &c.

5. That notwithstanding this eighty years' preaching in England, the people are so ignorant that they know not in what way they ought to worship God; so that they were constrained to thrust together their late learned, pious, and holy Directory, to enlighten our dark understandings, the scriptures not being able nor fit to do it.[1] And because they see that there is in the people no understanding, out of their care and love to us they have taken upon them, to judge and determine what is right and wrong for us; that so we may see, by their eyes, which is the safest and easiest for the people.

6. That all England, high and low, rich and poor, &c. ought to fall down before them, and make them their gods, and always lie at their feet to receive such directions, instructions, and destructions from them, as they shall think fit, and obey them without any questioning, whether they be right or wrong, good or evil.

7. That the kings and rulers of the earth may have their title, viz. defenders of the faith, that so they may continually incite them to defend *their* faith. It being the faith of Cambridge and Oxford, the most learned and black faith, the only faith; and all else is heresy, schism, if not blasphemy, in comparison with theirs.

8. That as they do so, they will endeavour to reduce all to the unity of the aforesaid faith, under one universal and

---

[1] [See before, p. 268.]

spiritual head.   They do not mean the pope, for that were treason, but themselves ; and this they know is far from treason, for who dare determine contrary to them ?

9. That whatsoever their apprehensions and intentions are, they are all agreed to pretend uniformity in religion, to satisfy the people, and to effect their own ends.   Though they are not so ignorant [as] to think that all men can ever be reconciled in one way, because their ends, principles, opinions, and affections, are so diverse.

10. That seeing they judge it not fit, nor safe, to trust God or man for food and raiment ; they have thought it fit to get an ordinance of parliament, to secure unto them our tithes.   And when they had served themselves, [their] backs and bellies,[2] it was their care that God might be served with their Directory.   And although some are persuaded that tradesmen may make a better ; yet they judge it not fit nor safe, that any be permitted to say so, lest it be made good, inasmuch as it tends to their disgrace.[3]

11. That there is so much light abroad, which is sufficient to overthrow them, (and do judge that too much and

[2] [In 1644, parliament had directed that tithes and other legal payments should be rendered as usual, and by a subsequent act ordered them to be paid to whomsoever might be placed in the living by their authority. Speaking of the assembly of divines, Milton says : " The most part of them were such as had preached and cried down, with great show of zeal, the avarice and pluralities of bishops and prelates; that one cure of souls was a full employment for one spiritual pastor, how able soever, if not a charge rather above human strength. Yet these conscientious men (ere any part of the work was done, for which they came together, and that on the public salary), wanted not boldness, to the ignominy and scandal of their pastor-like {profession, to seize into their hands, or not unwillingly accept, (besides one, sometimes two or more of the best livings) collegiate masterships in the universities, rich lectures in the city, setting sail to all winds that might blow gain into their covetous bosoms."—Scobell's Collection, &c., pp. 74, 131.   Milton's Prose Works, iv. 84.]

[3] [See before, note 1, p. 268.

declare) that it is their wills and pleasures, that nothing
be printed, unless it be licensed by them, lest their profitable traditions, with their plots and devices, be discovered.[4]

12. That as they believe, so they judge it not lawful
for any but themselves to speak or preach from the scriptures, seeing it is their trade, and they have served for it
so many years, that they have reason to monopolize it to
themselves, and to their black coats.

THE NONCONFORMISTS' ANSWER WHY THEY CANNOT RECEIVE AND SUBMIT TO THE AFORESAID FAITH.

I. In respect of the institutors of it. II. The matter of
their faith.

I. We cannot believe what you say : 1. Because you
are the men that have often deluded us, and thrust upon
us errors for truths, and so have deceived us and yourselves.

2. You appear to us to be carnal, in that you are so
full of strife, and envy against others, in seeking their
destruction, who do differ from you. Also, you serve not
the Lord Jesus, but your own bellies. Neither did we
ever hear of any action that you ever did, in which the
least measure or degree of self-denial did appear.

3. We have had very much experience of you to be

---

[4] [By an ordinance of parliament,
dated 14th June, 1643, no books or
pamphlets of any kind were to be
printed without due license. Private
presses were to be strictly inquired
after, and suspected shops and ware-
houses searched for unlicensed books
and pamphlets, and the printers and
authors to be committed to prison.
The censorship was placed in the
hands of staunch presbyterians only.
—Scobell's Collection, p. 44. Neal's
Puritans, ii. 205.]

the greatest timeservers among men, and even to turn
with the wind; for when the cross, surplice, and mass-
book were urged, you yielded to them, and swore canonical obedience to the bishops, your fathers, and did preach
that the common prayer-book, and the ceremonies, and the
government of archbishops, &c., was the government of
Christ, with many other things, which now you deny.
Because the tide is turned, you are turned; and when
the tide turns again, you may guess where we shall have
you, seeing ye can face about as ye were.[5]

4. If you had had the truth on your side, and the
Spirit of God to direct you, you might with ease and
speed have given a sufficient answer to the questions the
parliament gave you to answer;[6] and seeing you have sat
so long, and done so little, it doth not appear to us, that
God will ever use you, unless it be for a rod.[7]

5. Because we see you are enemies to the truth, in
seeking to hinder printing, and preaching of many truths
of God; and that under a pretence of suppressing errors.

---

[5] [Baxter says, "Almost all those
afterwards called presbyterians were
before conformists;" and "that those
who were the honour of parliament,
were previously conformists."—Life,
i. 33, 35.]

[6] [See before, p. 266, note 7.]

[7] [The slowness of the proceedings
of the assembly was a frequent matter of complaint. Thus Baillie:—
"Their longsomeness is woful at this
time, when their church and kingdom
lie under a most lamentable anarchy
and confusion. They see the hurt of
their length, but cannot get it helped:
for being to establish a new platform
of worship and discipline to their nation for all time to come, they think
they cannot be answerable if, solidly

and at leisure, they do not examine
every point thereof." — Hanbury's
Hist. Mem. ii. 218, note. The scurrilous journals of the time did not let
this pass unnoticed. " The synod
does little, and good reason, so long
as they have four shillings a day for
sitting." " There is a monstrous
beast to be seen at Westminster, that
can devour three or four churches, as
many lectures, beside four shillings a
day for journeywork. His name is
Ass in the head, and LY in the tail.
He hath been brooding three years,
but brought forth nothing. And he
would roost there for ever."—Mercu-
rius Morbicus, or News from Westminster and other parts, pp. 2, 4.
4to. 1647.]

6. Are they not guilty of murder, who did seek to those in authority to destroy them that differ from them, root and branch, and speak to have them hanged at their doors, and upon the beams of the houses where they dwell? Wherein appears your envy, hatred, and malice, and that you are the persons that go in sheep's clothing, but inwardly are ravening wolves.

7. Are they not hypocrites in pleading and urging persons to go forth and fight for the protestant religion, and to contribute largely to it, yet petitioned the parliament to be exempted, both in person and purse, from any part of the charge; thus laying heavy burdens upon others, but will move none themselves? Is not this horrible hypocrisy, as Matt. xxiii. 4, 23?

8. We know no warrant that you, nor any men else, have to impose upon us any thing in matters of religion, whether we will or no, as you do; therefore we judge you to be, as you are, usurpers and tyrants, and not the lambs of Christ.

9. Neither are they any of the ministers of Jesus Christ, unless the pope be a true minister of Christ; because their ministry came from him, as appears by Mason's Book of Ordination,[8] and Yates' Model of Divinity,[9] and yourselves confess.

[8] ["The Validity of the Ordination of the Ministers of the Reformed Churches beyond the Seas, maintained against the Romanists, by Francis Mason. With a brief declaration premised thereunto of the several forms of government received in those churches, by John Duree. Oxford. 1641."]

[9] Page 257. ["We deny not that we are ministers by Rome, but we affirm, we are not the ministers of Rome; and they may as truly be instruments of our ministry as of our baptism. For, as Ezek. xvi. 20, the Jews did beget children unto God, but consecrate them unto Molech: so papists may beget both a people and pastor for God; but till they separate they are both consecrated unto antichrist. And here let all take notice how separatists gnaw this bone, and suck in nothing but the blood of their own jaws."—A Model of Divinity

TOLERATION.]   T

Therefore we dare not submit to you. Do but consider
Rev. ix. 3, and xii. 2, and xvi. 13; 2 Cor. xi. 13, 14, 15,
and x. If the government of Christ were a presbyterial
government, we cannot in conscience submit to the presbytery set up in England.

1. Because their priesthood is false and antichristian.

2. Because by covenant we are sworn to oppose it, it
being a branch of the hierarchy and popery.[1]

3. Because the church whereof they are ministers, is no
church of Christ, much less a reformed church; for the
church of Christ consists of living stones, visible saints.
But in the church of England, there be many dead stones,
who are visible swearers, drunkards, persecutors.

1 Pet. ii. 5; 1 Cor. i. 2.

4. If they were true ministers and members of a true
church, we could not submit to them, we being not members of that congregation they are; for no true church nor
minister hath any power over any one member of another
church or congregation.

Also for the matter of things they impose upon us, we
find it not so written in the word of God, therefore we
slight it; for we are resolved not to presume above what
is written in the holy scriptures, and therefore we cannot
submit to you nor to your faith. Also, you have not
studied a religion for us out of the word of God; but
have borrowed us one out of Scotland, as some say;[2]

catechistically composed. Wherein is delivered, the matter and method of religion, &c. By John Yates, B.D. London: 1622. 4to.]

[1] [On Feb. 2nd, 1644, all persons above the age of eighteen were ordered to swear, " with their hands lifted up to the most high God," to the solemn league and covenant, previously sworn to by the parliament and the assembly of divines. In this they promise to " endeavour the extirpation of popery, and prelacy, that is, church government by archbishops, bishops, &c., and all other ecclesiastical officers depending on that hierarchy."—Neal, ii. 222, 219.]

[2] [Commissioners were sent from Scotland to the assembly for the purpose of effecting an uniformity in religion, in their confession of faith, form of church government, directory

as wicked king Ahaz brought a pattern of the altar from
Damascus to Jerusalem, which is unjustifiable by the
word of God.

THE CONCLUSION.

Mr. Presbyter, your principles are large and dangerous,
who can tell what you will judge tolerable? Such as
cannot dance after your pipe, and rule in your way,
you judge heretics, and they must appear before your
dreadful tribunal, to receive your reproof, which is sharp
and terrible, and strikes at our liberties, estates, and lives.
Your care is to destroy, which is contrary to the word
of the Lord, which saith, *they shall not kill nor hurt in my* Is. xi. 9.
holy hill. Is your church this holy hill, seeing it is so
corporal?

Your argument is authority; what you say must be
an oracle of all men, to be deferred to without opposition
or contradiction. What is contrary to you is heresy, *ipso
facto*, to be punished with fagot and flaming fire. Have
you not been one hundred and twenty days a heating the
furnace for good men, whom you call heretics? Your
definitions must stand: what you approve, is catholic;

for worship and catechising. The
Directory, before its imposition, was
sent into Scotland for the approbation
of the general assembly. Baillie, one
of the commissioners, thus delivered
himself in a speech to the assembly,
on its establishment. "That in place
of episcopacy, a Scotch presbytery
should be concluded in an English
assembly, and ordained in an English
parliament ...... that the practice of
the church of Scotland, set down in a
most wholesome, pious, and prudent
directory, should come in the place of
a liturgy in all the three dominions :
such stories lately told would have
been counted fancies, dreams, mere
impossibilities."—Neal, ii. 274. Price,
Hist. of Noncon. ii. 293, note.]

what you condemn, is heresy.   How have you laboured
for to have power to go to the old trade of persecution!—
how have your teeth been set on edge! But, see, you
are disappointed, and can do nothing; it is but a folly
to stir further.

You want still to use a sword; who sees not but if you
had it, you would have wounded yourselves and others?
It is better that the sword be in the hands of the advo-
cates of Christians, honest and faithful Fairfax and Cromwell, &c., who know how to use it for the safety of the
kingdom, and to relieve the innocent, and help the Lord
against the mighty; whom God hath, and will, wonder-
fully bless, and make successful.   God is with them, and
for them, and they are for all honest men, of what judgment soever; all your reproaches and plots against them
shall vanish and come to nothing.[3]   Therefore sit still
quietly, and be humbled, for your folly in calling persecution discipline and just deserved censure; and in calling
your priesthood and presbytery a holy order, and yet are
but the pope's priesthood.   And we had as good be under
the pope, as under your presbyterian check.

What, are you worthy of the name of Christians, of
ministers of the gospel, and yet seek only your own
things?   You would all be tolerated, and would have
none tolerated but yourselves; you would suffer none
to live quietly, and comfortable, but those of your way.
Is this to do as you would be done by? and would you

---

[3] ["There doth not appear more
love to God, to his people, and to
this nation, than in the officers of the
army. They deserve the greatest
honour and trust among men that
have suffered, been wounded, and
shed their blood for this nation, have
freely offered for God's sake, and for
our sakes, their lives and estates to
save ours. I pray you, give us leave
to own and speak well of them who
have saved our estates and lives."—
Richardson's Cause of the Poor
pleaded, p. 15. edit. 1653.]

be a company of cruel taskmasters over others?[4] Oh,
that you would be ashamed of such baseness! And if
you have any interest with those in authority, improve it
that all other men may live as quietly and comfortably as
yourselves. Then shall you love your enemies, and do
good to them that hate you, &c.; or else, how can we
look upon you to be reformed, much less to be reformers.

[4] [The Lancashire ministers could thus stigmatize toleration. It would be " putting a cup of poison into the hand of a child ; a letting loose of madmen with firebrands in their hands: .... a toleration of soul-murder (the greatest murder of all), and for the establishing whereof, damned souls in hell would accuse men on earth. Neither would it be to provide for tender consciences, but to 'take away all conscience. If evil will be suffered, it will not suffer good ; if error be not forcibly kept under, it will be superior."—Price, ii. p. 332.]

F I N I S.

AN

HUMBLE PETITION

AND

REPRESENTATION,

BY

THE ANABAPTISTS.

1660.

THE

HUMBLE PETITION

AND

REPRESENTATION

OF THE

Sufferings of several Peaceable, and Innocent Subjects,
called by the Name of

ANABAPTISTS,

Inhabitants in the County of *Kent,* and now Prisoners in
the Gaol of *Maidstone,* for the Testimony of
a good Conscience.

Together with their Free and Faithful Acknowledgement
of the King's Authority and Dignity in Civil things,
over all manner of Persons, Ecclesiastical and Civil,
within his Majesties Dominions.

With their *Reasons,* meriting the King's Protection in their
Civil and Spiritual Rights, equal with other his Majesties
Obedient Subjects.

Humbly Offered to the King's Majesty, and the Consideration
of our Fellow Brethren and Subjects. Well
worthy General Observation.

Act. xvii. [26.] *He hath made of one Bloud all Nations of men, &c.*
Job iv. 7. *Remember, I pray thee, who ever perished being Innocent? or where were the
Upright destroyed?*
Job xxxiv. 28. *So that they have caused the Voice of the Poor to come unto him, and he hath
heard the Cry of the Afflicted.*
Rom xiv. 3. *Let not him that Eateth, despise him that Eateth not, and let not him which
Eateth not, condemn him that eateth; for God hath received him.*

London, Printed for *Thomas Smith,* at the *Elephant* and *Castle,*
near Temple-Bar, 1660.

INTRODUCTORY NOTICE.

CHARLES the Second was restored to his ancestral throne on the 29th May, 1660. Persecution of the baptists preceded him; it followed in his train. Under the pretence of searching for concealed arms, many outrages had been committed. The anticipated restoration was rejoiced in as promising a favourable opportunity for their extirpation, and in many counties they had to submit to the vilest indignities.[1]

The baptists embraced an early opportunity of laying their grievances before the king. On the 26th July, the messengers of the "good and peaceable people in Lincolnshire," were presented to his majesty. They informed him of their sufferings; "being commanded thereto by the Lord, we have met often together, to acquaint each other, what God hath done, doth daily, and will do for our souls; and what therefore we ought to do towards him, each other, and all men. From which assemblings, O king! we have been discharged by some in magistratical capacity in these parts; although therein, we bless God, none hath ever found us with multitude or with tumult. But being taught of God

---

[1] Crosby, ii. 28, 31.

to obey him in the things by him commanded, rather than man, though in the place of magistracy, when commanding things contrary; we therefore durst not receive that discharge. Wherefore some of us have been silenced from making mention of the name of the Lord, as formerly, by being entangled in bonds, pretendedly imposed upon us for this good behaviour. Since thus entangled, O king! we have been much abused as we pass in the streets, and as we sit in our houses; being threatened to be hanged, if but heard praying to the Lord in our families, and disturbed in our so waiting upon God, by uncivil beating at our doors, and sounding of horns; yea, we have been stoned when going to our meetings, the windows of the place where we have been met, struck down with stones; yea, taken as evil doers, and imprisoned, when peaceably met together to worship the Most High, in the use of his most precious ordinances." Even the courts of justice augmented their sorrows, by the abuse there lavished upon them. They were threatened with the severe fines imposed by the Elizabethan law of uniformity, for non-attendance at the parish church. Thirty-five signed this appeal to the royal clemency and justice, on their own behalf and for many others. The king gave them fair words, and expressed his anxiety that none should trouble them for their consciences in things pertaining to religion. To this narrative was subjoined their Confession of Faith, which had been agreed upon in the previous month of March.[2]

On the same day the London baptists united in the

---

[2] Crosby, ii. 19—32. Kennet's Register, &c. p. 211.

presentation of " An Humble Apology." They complained
of the unjust aspersions and calumnies of their adversaries;
the groundless and injurious reports taken up against them
by the press, in the pulpit, and in common discourse,
whereby their inoffensive conversation was defamed. They
were charged with "disobedience to magistracy and civil
government." Thus necessitated, they now renew the
vindications and proofs of fidelity, which in former times
they had in the most public manner declared. In conclusion, they say, " We do hope and desire that none of us
upon the re-establishment of the present government, shall
now be adjudged criminal by our present governors; but
that we may, notwithstanding, reap the benefit of that
favour that hath been declared and tendered by the king's
majesty, and be protected from all injury and violence
whatsoever, equally with others his majesty's subjects, in
the quiet and peaceable enjoyment of our religious and
civil rights and liberties, we desiring and endeavouring to
behave ourselves in all good conscience towards God and
man, remembering that rule of our Lord, that we are to
render unto Cæsar the things which are Cæsar's, and to
God the things which are God's; and that we, as well as
our rulers, must certainly at the great day be accountable
to the just and righteous Judge of all the earth, for all our
doings."[3]

Persecution was not stayed. Perfidy ruled in the counsels of the sovereign. In August (1660), the congregations
in North Wales, collected and taught by Mr. Vavasor
Powell, were ordered to be broken up. That excellent

[3] Kennet, p. 211. The Humble Apology, &c. p. 19, 4to. 1660.

man was called a seditious sectarist, and his people " restless
and rebellious spirits, frequently meeting in private houses,
neglecting the public places of the worship of God."[4]   In
the month of September, the House of Lords gave directions to suppress the Northamptonshire churches, and to prevent throughout the county their assembling for worship.
In November, John Bunyan was apprehended while preaching, and thrown into Bedford jail.   There he found two
other ministers, with above sixty dissenting brethren.[5]
These severities were exercised, while yet " fair words "
were issuing from the lips of the sovereign.   In October, he
put forth a further declaration, promising satisfaction to
tender consciences, and renewing his Breda declaration,
that no man should be called in question, or disquieted for
differences of opinion in religion.[6]

The churches in Kent, consisting chiefly of general
baptists, had also to bear the weight of the oppressor's
hand.   Many members of the flourishing communities of
Chatham, Dover, and Canterbury, received the reward of
their adherence to the truth, in wearisome imprisonments
and destitution.   From some of these, confined in the gaol
at Maidstone, issued the following petition.   Mr. Jeffrey
and Mr. Reeve were fellow-elders of the church assembling
at Bradbourne, near Sevenoaks ; Mr. G. Hammon and Mr.
Blackmore, co-pastors of the church at Biddenden.[7]   To
this course they seem to have been encouraged by a royal
proclamation, (January 10, 1660—1,) " that if any should be

---

[4] Kennet, p. 241.

[5] Kennet, p. 247.   Crosby, ii. 92.
Ivimey, i. 299.

[6] Neal, iii. 61.

[7] Taylor's History of Gen. Baptists,
i. pp. 281, 283.

so hardy as to seize the persons of any without warrant, that then they should be left open to the law, to be proceeded against, and receive according to their demerit."[8] Unjustly detained, they hoped by this appeal to move the royal compassion. Their hopes were illusory ; neither honour nor truth influenced the mind or the ministry of the king. Greater severities were yet in store for them ; and they had painfully to learn the lesson, *put not your trust in princes,* Ps. cxlvi. 3. *nor in the son of man, in whom there is no help.*

Other opportunities will occur for delineating the characters of these sufferers for conscience' sake. The petitioners were men eminent for their gifts, and their success in planting churches of Christ. Two of them, Mr. Jeffrey and Mr. Hammon, have left us several works of interest and value. When they recovered their liberty, is uncertain ; but the churches in which they ministered, continued to prosper, and the hand of the Lord was with them while bearing the cross.[9]

The present reprint is from a copy of the original edition in the Bodleian Library, to which access has been granted by the kindness of the librarian, Dr. Bandinel.

[8] Crosby, ii. 162.   [9] Taylor, i. 285, &c.

TO

HIS MAJESTY,

CHARLES THE SECOND,

KING of England, Scotland, France, and Ireland ; and the
Dominions thereunto belonging.

May it please your MAJESTY,

FORASMUCH as by authority derived from yourself,
several of us your subjects, inhabitants in the county
of Kent, are now imprisoned; it therefore much concerns
thee, O king, to hear what account we give of our present
distressed condition.

Thou hast already seen our Confession of Faith, wherein
our peaceable resolutions were declared.[1] We have not
violated any part thereof that should cause that liberty
promised from Breda,[2] to be withdrawn. And now for

---

[1] [See Introductory Notice. Grantham's Christianismus Primitivus. B.
ii. ch. 5, p. 61. The articles relating
to liberty of conscience and magistracy, may be seen in the Addenda, Note
C.]

[2] [The king, previous to his restoration, addressed to the convention parliament a letter from Breda, in which
he promised "liberty to tender consciences, and that no man shall be disquieted or called in question for differences of opinion in matters of religion,
which do not disturb the peace of the
kingdom. And we shall be ready to
consent to such an act of parliament
as, upon mature deliberation, shall be
offered to us, for the full granting that
indulgence." This promise he renewed
after his return, in a declaration dated
October 25th, 1660. Kennet, p. 108.
Neal's Hist. of Puritans, iii. pp. 33,
60.]

HUMBLE PETITION.]

U

our principles, that most particularly relate to magistrates and government, we have with all clearness laid them here before thee, humbly beseeching they may be read patiently; and what we say, weighed in the balance of the sanctuary; and then judge how worthy we are of either bonds or imprisonment. And this we the more earnestly desire, because not only our own lives are in danger, but also an irresistible destruction cometh on our wives and little ones, by that violence which is now exercised on us. Disdain not our plainness of speaking, seeing the great God accepts of the like.

And now, O king, that all thy proceedings both towards us and all men, may be such as may be pleasing unto the eternal God, in whose hands your and our breath is, and who ere long will judge both quick and dead, according to their works, is the prayer of thy faithful subjects and servants,

The Prisoners in the Gaol of Maidstone,

for the testimony of a good conscience.

A FREE AND FAITHFUL ACKNOWLEDGMENT OF THE KING'S AUTHORITY AND DIGNITY IN CIVIL THINGS, OVER ALL MANNER OF PERSONS, ECCLESIASTICAL AND CIVIL, WITHIN HIS MAJESTY'S DOMINIONS, ETC.

Acts xvii.26. GOD, *that hath made of one blood all nations of men, for to dwell on all the face of the earth, and hath determined the times before appointed, and the bounds of their habitation;* hath made this land the place of our nativity and abode, by which we have an interest in common with others, thy subjects, in this nation; so that none can deprive us of that which is our propriety and native birth-right, without violating the laws of God and nature. Yet, may it please thee, O king, as if that law of *doing unto others as we would* [Luke vi. 31.] *be done unto*, had never been written, neither any bounds set unto the wills of men: we, thy imprisoned subjects, have (some of us) had our houses broken open in the dead of the night, without producing any authority from thee, or any inferior minister under thee;[3] our goods and cattle taken away from some others, and yet detained from us; our bodies, some taken from our own dwellings, and others from our peaceable meetings, and made prisoners; and this done unto many of us some days before thy proclamation was published; which proceedings do bring great distress and ruin to ourselves and families. For such is our mean condition in this world, that almost all of us have our outward subsistence, through the blessing of God, on our daily labours. Also some amongst us that were employed in the public service at Chatham, and at sea, being yet unpaid. The bread which our families have eaten this ten or twelve months, hath been taken up upon credit. And all of us being detained from our employments, the cries of our families, who suffer hunger, become great.

And now, O king, that the oppressed may be relieved, and justice and judgment executed amongst men, and the creation of God kept from being a chaos of confusion, the God of order hath ordained government, and setteth up magistrates, to execute such power as is given from himself, for the ends aforesaid. And this we have always asserted

---

[3] [These illegal proceedings were forbidden by a proclamation, issued a week or fortnight before the presentation of this petition. Kennet gives the date of the proclamation as the 17th of January; Crosby, the 10th. It was, however, entirely disregarded. Crosby, ii. 162, 164. Kennet's Reg. p. 361.]

in our discourses and writings; as appears in our Declaration
of Faith, printed about three months before thy coming
over, and re-printed and presented to thyself above four
months sinc e.

And as for thyself, O king, we do believe, and do freely
acknowledge, that the authority and dignity that thou now
hast, in being chief governor over this kingdom and its
dominions, is given thee of God; whose the kingdoms of
Dan. iv. 25. the world are, *and he giveth them unto whomsoever he will.*
Ps.lxxv.6,7. And *promotion cometh neither from the east, nor from the west,*
nor from the south; but God is the Judge, he putteth down one,
and setteth up another. So saith the New Testament, *the*
Rom. xiii. 1. *powers that be are ordained of God.* And seeing the Lord
Mat.xxii.21. Jesus hath commanded us his servants, *to give unto Cæsar*
the things that are Cæsar's, therefore shall we pay custom
and tribute unto thee; and in all temporal causes and things,
shall we yield cheerful obedience, not only to thyself as
supreme, but also to all inferior magistrates sent by thee.
[Rom. xiii.
5,4.] And this we do, *not only for wrath, but also for conscience,*
sake, knowing that God hath given thee power to punish
any that shall do that unto another which he would not
have done unto himself; and in so doing, thou wilt be a
minister of God to us for good, a revenger to execute wrath
upon him that doeth evil.

And whereas it is alleged against us as a crime, that we
cannot acknowledge any authority that God hath given
thee, in spiritual things or causes; yet, if thou wouldst
condescend to the reading, and serious considering our
ensuing reasons, it is possible we may be justified by thee,
as in this matter we are in the sight of God, whose word,
not only in this, but in all other causes, we desire to make
our rule. We therefore beseech thee to consider, O king!
if thou hast any power to be a lord over our faith, or by
outward force to impose any thing in the worship of God,

on our consciences, it is given unto thee as thou art a
magistrate, or as thou art a Christian; but that thou hast no
such power given unto thee of God, as thou art a magistrate,
appears:—

1. Because if magistrates, as such, have such an authority,
then all magistrates in all nations have the same power.
Then, if we lived in Turkey, we must receive the Koran,
and be a worshipper of Mahomet; if in Spain, be a papist;
in England, sometimes a papist, as in Henry the Eighth's
days, a protestant in Edward the Sixth's, a papist
again in Queen Mary's, and a protestant again in Queen
Elizabeth's. And so for ever, as the authority changes
religion, must we do the same. But God forbid.

2. Because the apostles themselves, that gave forth those
commandments that are written in scripture, to be obedient
to magistrates, refused to be obedient to their rulers when
they were commanded to forbear that which they judged
part of the worship of God; and said, *Whether it be* Acts iv. 9;
right in the sight of God, to hearken unto you more than unto v. 29.
God, judge ye.

3. All the scriptures of the New Testament that enjoin
obedience unto magistrates, were written when the Romans
had the empire of the world; whose emperors were for
the most part, if not all, heathenish idolaters, for the first
three hundred years, until Constantine's time. It therefore
cannot be supposed, that any of these texts of scripture that
call for obedience to magistrates, intend an obedience in
matters of faith or worship; for then the Christians that
lived under those emperors, must needs have denied
Christ, and worshipped the Roman gods, as some of the
emperors commanded.

And now, O king, that no man as he is a Christian, hath
power to be a lord over another's faith, or by outward force
to impose any thing in the worship of God, is as clear:—

1. Because the Lord Jesus himself, nor his disciples, would never by any outward force compel men to receive them or their doctrine. For when the disciples of Christ, supposing they might use violence as under the law, would have commanded fire to come from heaven, as Elias did, to consume them that would not receive them, Christ turned [Luke ix. 55, 56.] and rebuked them, saying, *Ye know not what spirit ye are of, for the Son of man is not come to destroy men's lives, but to save them.*

2. If any men under heaven have had any such power in the days of the gospel, the apostles and elders in the primitive times must needs have had it, but this they disowned. The apostle Paul in 2 Cor. i. 24, saith thus, *Not for that we have dominion over your faith, but are helpers of your joy ; for by faith ye stand.* Yea, the Lord Jesus, when [Matt. xx. 25, 26.] they strove for domination, forbade it, saying ; *Ye know that the princes of the gentiles exercise dominion over them, and they that are great do exercise authority upon them, but it shall not be so amongst you.* Even so saith Peter, speaking to [1 Pet. v. 2, 3.] the elders ; *Feed the flock of God which is among you, taking the oversight thereof, not by constraint, but willingly ; not for filthy lucre, but of a ready mind ; neither as being lords over God's heritage, but being examples to the flock.* And in truth, the apostles and disciples were not to use any external force to carry on their master's work, but only by showing the terrors of the Lord, were to persuade men. And in case of resistance, to shake the dust from their feet, as a witness against their opposers.

[Mat. xiii. [24 — 30, 36 — 43.] 3. It is very plain that the Lord Jesus himself, in his parable of the tares and wheat, forbids any force to be exercised upon false worshippers, as such. For by the tares, which he forbids the pulling up, cannot be intended the transgressors of the second table, such as thieves, murderers, &c. ; because all confess with one consent, that the

magistrate's authority reaches such.   But those that Christ
Jesus would have remain amongst his wheat, in the field
of the world, are the children of the wicked one, through
idolatry and will-worship.   This will further appear, if the
28th, 29th, and 30th verses, be compared with the 38th and
39th of the same chapter.   And the reason the Lord Jesus
gives, why both tares and wheat must grow together,—O
king, that it were engraven with the point of a diamond, and
often laid before thee!—is, lest in gathering up the tares,
the wheat also be rooted up with them.

How sad is it to remember, how in all ages since Christ,
very strange mistakes have been on this account.   The
Lord of life himself was put to death, for supposed blasphemy and wickedness, and accused for being an enemy to
Cæsar.   And this [was] done unto him by a people that
had the law of God amongst them, and were famous in the
world for their earthly wisdom and knowledge.   Stephen
was stoned, and James the apostle killed with the sword;
supposed to be tares, or the children of the wicked one,
when they were the precious wheat of God.   The Christians that suffered in the ten persecutions, were they not
accused of being pestilent fellows, movers of sedition,
turners of the world upside down, enemies to Cæsar, when
the contrary was most true ?   And they will be found to
be the faithful martyrs of Jesus.   So in later times, many
of those that have been put to death for heresy and blasphemy, are by this age acknowledged to be the saints of
God.

O king ! that our words might be acceptable to thee,
consider that neither thyself nor councillors, have the spirit
of infallibility.   If the apostles, that had an extraordinary
spirit of discerning, must not pluck up the tares, lest they
root up the wheat also, how can any prince on earth undertake a work so dangerous ?   It is possible many of those

Margin notes:
Matt. xxvi.
65.
John xix. 12.

Acts vi. 13,
14; [vii. 59;]
xii. 2.

Acts xxiv. 5,
12; xvii. 6,7.

that are accounted false worshippers and heretics in this day, may, at the time when God shall judge the world in righteousness, be found the servants of the Most High God. Remember, we pray thee, that those that lived in the days of the Lord Jesus, accused their fathers for being guilty of the blood of the prophets; saying, *If we had been in the days of our fathers, we would not have been partakers with them in the blood of the prophets;* yet themselves killed the Lord of life. The Romish church also saith, "if we had lived in the days of the heathen emperors, we would not have been partakers with them in the blood of the Christians;" yet put to death many as righteous as they were. And now many of thy subjects in this nation are ready to say, "if we had lived in the days of Queen Mary, we would not have been guilty with our fathers in the blood of those good men that then suffered;" yet such a spirit of persecution is now risen up, as (if not restrained) will terminate in the blood of many good men, and so bring down the wrath of God upon this generation, and there will be no remedy.

Matt. xxiii. 29, 30.

4. To inflict temporal punishments, upon any of us thy subjects, for not conforming to thy decrees that restrain us from the worship that we know to be of God; is it not a breach of that royal law, that commands thee, that *whatsoever ye would that men should do to you, do ye even so to them; for this is the law and the prophets?* And we would in all humility offer to thy consideration, if thy soul were in our souls' stead, wouldst thou be satisfied with the same measure as is now dealt unto us, when neither the God of heaven, nor our own consciences, doth condemn us of any evil intended against thy person or authority? Nor can the greatest of our enemies, make any due proof of any combination or plotting, with any upon the face of the earth, for the disturbance of the public peace. And this we can with boldness say, because we know our own innocency.

Matt. vii. 12.

But whereas it is objected, that the kings of Israel and Judah, under the old testament, had power in spiritual causes, and did punish blasphemy and idolatry, which are crimes of the highest nature against God; we confess they had such power, which was given to them in plain precepts, written in the law of Moses. But the gospel that we live under is another dispensation, in which the Lord Jesus is the only law-giver: who doth not, as Moses, proceed against the transgressors of his precepts, by external force and power, to the destroying them in their bodies and estates in this life; but in long-suffering waits on men, not willing [1 Thess. i. 9; 2 Peter iii. 9; Acts xvii. 31.] they should perish, but rather that they should repent and be saved. And when any continue in disobedience to the gospel, his punishment is eternal in the world to come. The apostle Paul testifies of himself, *That he was a blas-* [1 Tim. i. 13.] *phemer and persecutor.* And if the mind of God had been that he should have suffered death in that condition, how should he have had repentance given him, and been such a glorious instrument in the church, as afterward he was?

Furthermore, it is too well known that the Jews are the greatest blasphemers against our Lord Jesus Christ that are on the earth, yet it is not the mind of the Lord they should be destroyed from the face of the earth; for how then should the scripture be fulfilled, wherein God hath promised to call them, and make them the most glorious nation in the world? Oh! how can they be converted, if they be not permitted where the gospel is preached? We speak not this in favour of any blasphemy, for our souls abhor it, but because we would have the lives of men as precious in thy eyes, O king, as they are in the eyes of the righteous and most holy God.

5. As it is in nowise lawful from the word of God, for Christian magistrates to destroy, and root out the contrary-minded in religious matters, although idolaters; so such

proceedings may many times prove inconsistent with the very being of nations; for suppose any nation were wholly heathenish idolaters, and the word of God coming in amongst them, should convert the chief magistrates, and a twentieth part of the nation more: must he, with that twentieth part, destroy all the other nineteen, if they will not be converted, but continue in their heathenish idolatry? It cannot possibly be supposed to be warrantable.

From all this that we have said, thou, O king, mayest see, that not without grounds do we deny the taking the oath of thy supremacy, which calls for obedience, as well in spiritual and ecclesiastical things and causes, as temporal. Not but that we can freely acknowledge thee to be supreme governor of all persons, as well ecclesiastical as temporal, but still in temporal causes and things. We do also as freely renounce all foreign jurisdictions and powers whatsoever, that any on the earth may pretend to have over any of thy dominions or subjects. And whereas, some have said that no more is required in the oath, considered together with the proviso in the statute of the 5 Elizabeth, and the queen's admonition: yet we humbly conceive there is; because the queen, both in the proviso and admonition, challenges such a power as was challenged by her father, king Henry the 8th,[4] which was to burn his subjects at the stake for their dissenting from him in religious matters, as by his practice appeared. And the queen

---

[4] [" Provided also, that the oath expressed in the said act made in the said first year (1 Eliz. c. 1), shall be taken and expounded in such form as is set forth in an admonition annexed to the queen's majesty's injunctions, published in the first year of her majesty's reign; that is to say, to confess and acknowledge in her majesty, her heirs and successors, none other authority than that was challenged, and lately used, by the noble king Henry the eighth, and king Edward the sixth." Statutes at Large, 5 Eliz. c. 1, p. 157, vol. 6.]

herself exercised the same authority, in putting some to
death for their conscience in religion.[5]

And whereas many of us that are now prisoners cannot
take the oath of allegiance, because we cannot swear at all,
the Lord Christ having forbidden, in the fifth of Matthew,
33rd verse, compared with James v. 12, not only vain
oaths, but also such swearing as was delivered of old time,
and lawful under the law, as in our consciences we are
persuaded, and therefore before now, under former powers,
have denied to swear; yet God is our witness, who is the
searcher of all hearts, we deny not this oath because we
would not yield due subjection and obedience to thee and
thy authority. For this we say, in the presence of him
that shall judge the quick and dead, We do, without any
deceit, promise to live peaceably under thy government,
and in case any thing should be by thee commanded in
spiritual matters, wherein we cannot obey, we shall not then
take up any carnal or temporal weapon against thee or thy
authority, but patiently suffer such punishment as shall be
inflicted on us for our consciences.

And now may it please thee, O king, that these engagements, which we humbly tender unto thee, may be accepted
of by thee, and not destruction brought on us and our
families for not taking of an oath; when the engagements
before recited, taken before some justice of the peace in a
solemn manner, with calling God to witness to the truth
of what we say, without doubt answer the end of the law
that enjoins the oath of allegiance, and may be as much
security from us to thee, as if we took many oaths.[6] Why

[5] [Peters and Terwoort in 1575.
See Introduction.]

[6] ["John Tombes saith, That those
baptists of Maidstone have offered an
engagement taken before some justices
of the peace in a solemn manner, with
calling to God to witness to the truth
of what they say, and that they do
offer to swear and take an oath."
Sam. Fisher's Supplementum Subla-

should the very rigour of the law be exercised on us? Yea, but that we fear we are too tedious unto thee, we could make it clear, that the late dealing of thy inferior ministers hath been such towards us, as neither law nor custom hath prescribed. And now having faithfully laid our condition and principles, so far as they relate to magistrates or government, before thee, we therefore beseech thee, O king, that liberty may be given us to worship our God, and such bowels of compassion be in thee, as to give us such speedy relief as may be agreeable to the mind of God: Psalm cxlvi. *which made heaven and earth, which executeth judgment for* 6, 7. *the oppressed, which giveth food to the hungry. The Lord looseth the prisoners.*

Signed by us in the name of the Baptists, now prisoners in the gaol at Maidstone,

WILLIAM JEFFERY,   JOHN REVE,
GEORGE HAMMON,   JAMES BLACKMORE.

Dated the 25th day of the 11th month, commonly called January, [1660—1.]

tum, &c. p. 835. Works, fol. 1679. As two of those who signed this petition were engaged a few months after in the preparation of the piece entitled, " Signs for Sion," &c. it is probable that they were released on taking the above engagement.]

FINIS.

A PLEA

FOR

TOLERATION.

1661.

A

PLEA FOR TOLERATION

OF

OPINIONS AND PERSUASIONS

IN

MATTERS OF RELIGION,

DIFFERING FROM THE

CHURCH OF ENGLAND.

Grounded upon good Authority of Scripture, and the
practice of the Primitive Times.

Shewing the unreasonableness of prescribing to other
mens Faith, and the evil of persecuting
differing Opinions.

Humbly presented to the King's most excellent Majesty, by
Iohn Sturgion, a Member of the Baptized People.

Acts v. 38, 39. *And now I say unto you, Refrain from these men, and let them alone, for
if this counsel (or this work) be of men, it will come to nought; but if it be of God, ye
cannot overthrow it, lest haply ye be found, even to fight against God.*

London, Printed by *S. Dover*, for *Francis Smith*, at the *Elephant*
and *Castle*, near *Temple-Bar*, 1661.

INTRODUCTORY NOTICE.

"JANUARY 2nd, Wednesday, 1660—1. Whitehall Council Board. Whereas divers factious persons, under pretence of the liberty indulged by his majesty's late gracious declaration, in reference unto tender consciences, do meet in great numbers and at unusual times, whereby it may be justly apprehended, that many of them enter into plots and conspiracies to disturb the peace of the kingdom: It was thereupon ordered by his majesty in council, that Mr. Solicitor-general should forthwith prepare a proclamation, commanding all such persons going under the notion of anabaptists, quakers, and other sectaries, henceforward not to meet, under pretence of serving God, at unusual hours, nor in great numbers; and particularly that none of them go out of the precincts of his or their habitation, to any spiritual exercise, or serving of God after their own way, but that they do the same in their own parish. And if any shall be found to offend therein, the next justices of the peace are to cause them, and every of them, to be proceeded against, according to the laws provided against riotous and unlawful assemblies." [1]

[1] Kennet's Register, p. 352.

The proclamation was issued eight days after the above order in council, the day following the arrest of Thomas Venner, whose insurrection gave an ostensible reason for its necessity. It must be remarked, that numerous acts of persecution were daily committed upon the baptists and quakers throughout the kingdom; that repeated representations were being made to the sovereign of the illegal proceedings and injustice to which they were subjected; that the declaration of Breda, and its subsequent acknowledgment, hampered the king's ministry in its persecuting purposes; and that there was needed some insurrectionary movement, to justify the refusal of further liberty to the sectaries, and give free scope to the base and wicked cruelties, with which they were universally treated. This justification was found in the mad attempt of Thomas Venner and his accomplices.

Suspicion, however, arises, that the intentions of the rebels were known to the government; and, from the perfidious character of the sovereign and his advisers, that the fifth-monarchists were either driven or led into it by some secret intrigue. Or why should this proclamation be determined upon five days before the outbreak, making this to be the reason for its promulgation? It was on Sunday night, January 7th, that Venner and his disciples broke forth into open rebellion. Their meeting was late. Urged by curiosity, it is said, the landlord peeped through the chinks of the door. He saw them arming, and proceeded immediately to acquaint some officers who were at hand. The duke of York, the lord mayor, and several soldiers, were quickly on the spot; but, owing to the darkness, the insurgents escaped. After wandering in the neighbourhood of London for a few days, pursued ineffectually, because languidly, by General Monk, on Wednesday, divided into two bands, the rebels entered the city, but were immediately over-powered by the soldiery. In the struggle, five or six of Venner's party were slain. It is obvious, that the government was prepared for this event, and that they had officers and soldiers there, ready to act on the first manifestation of a rebellious intent.

Scarcely were Venner and his associates secured, than the previously prepared proclamation was issued, in oppo-sition to all the king's assurances of protection to the peaceable, in the enjoyment of the rights of conscience, and to the manifest injury of the innocent who were thus wittingly confounded with the guilty. Similar pro-clamations were issued in Scotland and Ireland, within a fortnight. It is probable, that the Council hoped to have drawn others into a similar act of rebellion, and to have called forth a wider display of disaffection, to justify the severe measures contemplated. This oppor-tunity for further severity was not afforded them. On the very day of the appearance of the edict, the London baptists, with Mr. W. Kiffin and Mr. Henry Denne at their head, presented an "Humble Apology," with a "Protestation against the late wicked and most horrid treasonable insurrection, and rebellion, acted in the city of London." They complain of the reproaches they had to endure, of the impious opinions and designs imputed to them; and declare, that far from participating in the

x 2

sentiments and treasonable practices of the rebels, "to the best of our information, they were all, except one, assertors of infant baptism, and never had communion with us in our assemblies; nor hath there been any correspondence nor converse between us; but, contrariwise, in their meetings they have inveighed bitterly against us, as worshippers of the beast, because of our constant declaring against their conceited, wild interpretations of dark prophecies, and enthusiastical impulses, and professed and practised our duty of subjection to the civil magistracy." [2] Of their rebellious intentions they declare that they were entirely ignorant, and that many of them did all they could to repress the insurrection on its outburst. They conclude, that if their " constant and continued opposition unto the impious tenets and practices of these persons, both in our doctrine and lives, will not be esteemed a pregnant and cogent evidence of our unspotted innocence from their treason and rebellion, and satisfy every man that our souls never entered into their secrets, we can only appeal to the all-seeing God, the Judge of all the earth, to vindicate us in his righteous judgment." [3]

Six days after, (Jan. 16th) the baptists of Lincolnshire laid their " Second Humble Address" at the foot of the throne. Distressed, yet faithful subjects, they sought " to spread their innocency and sorrow of heart" before their sovereign. They assure him that they were pure and clean from any wicked practices against him or his

---

[2] The Humble Apology of some commonly called Anabaptists, &c. p. 8. 4to. 1660.
[3] Humble Apology, &c. p. 9.

government, and that they had faithfully observed their promises, made when his "princely favour" permitted them on a former occasion to enter into his presence. They appeal to him: "Shall the righteous suffer with the wicked? God forbid. Must your peaceable subjects be judged rioters, whilst many unpeaceable ones, such as swearers and drunkards, are freed from that judgment?" They therefore request that a righteous distinction may be made in the administration of punishment, "lest the cries of the innocent and their ruined families come up before the Lord, whilst your prisons are filled with such as whose prayers have come up to the throne of grace on your majesty's behalf." They conclude by intimating that conscience will constrain them still to meet together for the worship of God, however it may be forbidden, although it cost them "the loss of all they have and are." From so great a loss they would not shrink, but, by divine strength, bear it meekly and patiently.[4]

These appeals were useless. Persecution was determined upon. Mr. Hanserd Knollys, and many other godly and peaceable persons, were haled out of their houses, and committed to prison. Mr. Vavasor Powell's house was violently entered, he himself seized, and, with many others, kept prisoners for about nine weeks.[5] During the eighteen weeks after Venner's insurrection, and preceding the king's coronation, great numbers were immured in close dungeons. About four hundred were crowded into Newgate alone, and the other city prisons

[4] Second Humble Address of those who are called Anabaptists, in the county of Lincoln, &c. A broad sheet, 1660.   [5] Crosby, ii. 91,

were similarly filled. At the coronation a general pardon was proclaimed, and these sufferers for "conscience' cause" were temporarily released. In the following month of May, the persecution was revived, by the parliament directing a bill to be prepared for the suppression of the baptists and quakers.[6]

Mr. Sturgion's pamphlet was published at the end of the month of March. Why he preferred to stand separated from his brethren on this occasion, can only be conjectured. Not improbably the reason may be found in a remarkable document, preserved by the historian Clarendon, and regarded by Crosby as authentic. Neal, indeed, doubts its genuineness, and seems to regard it "as an artifice to get a little money out of the poor king's purse."[7] A consideration of the document itself would have corrected the first objection, and the letter accompanying it sufficiently explains its object and occasion. It is only in connexion with this paper that we know any thing of Mr. Sturgion beyond the "Plea for Toleration" now reprinted. Some consideration must therefore be given to it.

It can awaken no surprise that there were many baptists who regarded the course of Cromwell with dislike. Strange it would be, had perfect unanimity prevailed in communities, where freedom of judgment was their glory and pride. Openly, on several occasions, they had stood in opposition to the public policy of the Protector. For their fidelity to republican principles, all

---

[6] Kennet, Reg. p. 448. Crosby, ii. 93.   [7] Neal, ii. 695.

the officers of his own regiment were summarily dismissed, among other pretences, "for that they were anabaptists." [8]   This state of feeling was adapted to encourage the intrigues of any parties, who, for selfish or unworthy ends, desired to ingratiate themselves with the exiled prince, and, it may be, lay a foundation for a claim of remuneration for services thus rendered.   It was at the beginning of the year 1658, or perhaps some months earlier, that the writer of the letter to Charles which accompanied the address, frankly tells us, that seeing the perplexities and embroiled state of the various parties in the country, and the strong dislike many evinced towards the Protector, "he presently conceived hopes of being able, in a short time, to put in practice those thoughts of loyalty" to his majesty, which he had long entertained.   The absolute authority acquired by Cromwell as Protector, and the "rage and just indignation" with which the assumption of that title was received, gave him "a fit opportunity of giving birth" to his designs.   He therefore went among the baptists. He sought and found admittance to their consultations. With some, whom he calls "Levellers," he had many private interviews, encountered their prejudices with success, and sought to engage them "to their obedience" to his majesty.

That he might irrecoverably commit them, he urged them to send an humble address to their sovereign: he succeeded in his efforts.   True, the parties with whose fidelity to the protectorate he had thus tampered were

[8] Neal, iii. 381.

not of "great families or great estates," but they had
great influence among the people: "a desperate game
at chess has been recovered after the loss of the nobility,
only by playing the pawns well." For this service he
humbly desired the "advance of two thousand pounds,"
to establish and complete the design he had begun.
That he had miscalculated the desires and character of
the men whom he sought to attach to Charles, is evident
from the address itself. For while they warmly, even
virulently, declaim against the Protector, and lament
most sorrowfully the afflictions that had been endured
through years of war, turmoil, and change, they offer
certain proposals or terms, on which they would be willing to yield to his authority. 1. That the parliament
of 1640 should be re-assembled, and all its acts confirmed. 2. That the treaty of the Isle of Wight should
be ratified by the king. 3. That no popish, nor tyrannical hierarchy—episcopal or presbyterian—should be
erected, and liberty of worship be allowed to all. 4.
That tithes should be abolished, and some other way found
to support "that which is called the national ministry,"
to which dissenters should not be compelled to contribute. 5. That an amnesty for all crimes, treasons,
and offences, committed since the beginning of the war,
should be passed. To this address the names of nine
persons, otherwise unknown to us, with that of Mr.
Sturgion, are subscribed.[9]

It is evident, that these parties had no idea of be-
traying, or of yielding up to regal hands, the liberties

[9] Crosby, i. App. 72—93.

of their country. Well would it have been, had those who effected the restoration, been alike jealous and wary in opening the way for Charles's return. Mr. Sturgion probably cherished the hope that his part in this affair, might tend to fix the royal attention upon his " Plea for Toleration," and lead to some favourable result towards the numerous sufferers, who had to mourn bitterly the faithlessness of the king to all his solemn and reiterated promises.

The present reprint is from a copy in the library of the British Museum.

A

PLEA FOR TOLERATION

OF OPINIONS AND PERSUASIONS IN MATTERS OF RELI-
GION, DIFFERING FROM THE CHURCH OF ENGLAND.

MAY IT PLEASE YOUR MAJESTY,—

I have had strong impulses upon my mind for some
days to present this paper to your majesty, and I humbly
hope it will not be made to suffer much under an evil
resentment, upon its presentation to your hand, because it
bears a testimony about it of the author's good affections to
your royal self; for my witness is on high, that I did not
write this paper because I love you not, because I honour
you not, because I own you not, in your royal capacity of
magistracy and civil power. God knoweth that you have
not any subject more christianly real or cordial unto you,
and I humbly beg that your majesty would be pleased so
far to deny yourself, as to read it with patience, and to
judge of it as you shall see cause.

I beseech your majesty to consider, That it is one of the
sovereign and high concernments of your soul, to understand, and to be acquainted with the counsels and mind of
God, and to find time to search throughly into those
worthy mysteries, which the blessed angels, those great
princes of heaven, judge it nowise beneath them to pry 1 Pet. i. 12.

into. And when they, who are gods by institution, shall narrowly and with delight contemplate the real excellency of his glory, who is a God by nature, they must needs be transformed into his likeness, according to that most observable passage of the great apostle, *but we all, with open face beholding, as in a glass, the glory of the Lord, are changed into the same image.* And when the gods on earth shall be changed into the same image with the God of heaven, no doubt but blessedness is coming on apace upon the world.

2 Cor. iii. 18;

[Exod. xxii. 28 ; Psalm lxxxii. 6 ; John x. 34, 35.]

Now if your majesty be pleased to look into the excellent proceedings of the King of kings, and Lord of lords, towards men, he doth not take away his favour, nor withdraw his grace from all men, because some abuse it, and render themselves so fearfully wicked, as not only to sin against the law of commandments, but against that glorious gospel of grace, sealed and confirmed by the blood of [the] ever blessed Jesus. Nor will he punish the innocent for the guilty, but *the soul that sins shall die.* The father shall not answer for the son, nor the son for the father, but every soul shall bear the burden of his own sin. Oh! that your princely mind might be illuminated, or enlightened by this heavenly instance, that your majesty's actions to all your subjects, from the peer to the poorest, may be guided by that rule which God himself hath been pleased to lay before you!

Ezek. xviii. 20.

I shall humbly take leave to remind your majesty of the liberty of tender consciences, which your majesty declared to indulge in your declaration from Breda ;[1] for which many thousands did, in all humility, bless the Most High God, who put it into your majesty's heart to declare your resolution to provide in that particular, That such as did

[1 See before, page 297.]

not disturb the peace of the kingdom, might worship God according to their light; and that no man should be molested or disquieted for differing opinions in matters of religion, who could not join in the public service of worship.[2] Yet in regard of some rebellious persons in the city of London, who pretended to the like liberty of worshipping God apart from the parochial assembly, who made insurrections and committed murder under groundless pretences of fighting for the kingdom of Christ; hereupon, your majesty, by proclamation, hath forbid all meetings whatsoever, in private houses, or houses built, or purchased for the use of prayer, and other ordinances of God's worship, whereby the innocent suffer for the guilty. And many of your majesty's loyal and obedient subjects are questioned, and publicly suspected, to their great prejudice in their reputations, the consequence whereof is very mischievous to them and their families.[3]

I cannot imagine how your majesty can be unsatisfied as to the innocency of the baptized people and others, who have not only disclaimed the wicked rebellion of the said persons, but they have pressed their innocency from the very thought, or imagination of any such wickedness.[4] If your majesty please to consider that in case three or four of your domestic servants should have committed, or done some unworthy act, whereby they had incurred your just displeasure, upon which your majesty should have discharged all your servants from any further attendance in your royal court, although they never had any thing to do with the offenders, or their ways; it may be supposed that the innocent would have thought this a very severe act. I

---

[2] [Clarendon, Hist. of Rebell. iii. 990, ed. 1819.]

[3] [See Introductory Notice, p. 313, 315.]

[4] The Apology of the baptized people of London, the Lincolnshire two addresses, the Kentish petition, and many more to that purpose.

shall humbly leave your majesty to make the application.

But if it be said, the law is against that indulgence formerly granted unto us by your majesty, as was hinted in the answer to the petition of the congregations in London, given at your majesty's most honourable privy council, to the said petitioners,[5] and therefore no longer to be continued unto us, unless the next parliament, to whom we are referred, provide for the same :

Upon which answer some make this observation, that seeing the discontinuance of your majesty's gracious indulgence, proceedeth from the aspect of some old law, then we should have felt the influence thereof, although Venner and his disciples had never been born.   Moreover, if there be any such law, it was in being before your majesty sent that dove, with the olive-branch of liberty of conscience, viz. your Declaration that granted us toleration ; for no law was made against our meetings by that parliament, which your majesty termed, the healing and blessed parliament.[6]

Now if your majesty saw reason to suspend the execu-

[5] [This must have been the Humble Apology presented to the council the day after Venner's arrest. The whole of the London baptists united in this petition, which was signed by their principal ministers. Kennet's Register, &c. p. 358. Crosby, ii. 35. Mr. Sturgion's account of the council's reply is the only report of the interview that we have met with.]

[6] [At the close of the convention parliament, the speaker of the commons thus addressed the restored sovereign, " Royal sir, you have denied us nothing we have asked this parliament, indeed you have outdone your parliament by doing much more for us than we could agree amongst ourselves to ask, and therefore must needs be a happy parliament. This is a healing parliament, a reconciling, peacemaking parliament, a blessed parliament, a parliament *propter excellentiam*, that may truly be called *parliamentissimum parliamentum !* " The king replied, " Many former parliaments have had particular denominations from what they have done : they have been styled learned and unlearned, and sometimes have had worse epithets. I pray, let us all resolve that this be for ever called the healing and the blessed parliament ! " Kennet's Register, &c. pp. 336, 339.]

tion of those laws, they being hurtful and pernicious to
men of tender consciences; then there is the same reason
for your majesty to suspend them still, out of tenderness
to all such as have in no wise abused your clemency and
grace, to them vouchsafed in that particular.

And whoever have [moved], or shall move your majesty,
to continue your proclamation against meetings to worship
God, or to take occasion by those laws, to grieve and afflict
poor men and women, who have opinions different from
those of the church of England, (for such endeavours are
not wanting by them that know not what spirit they are
of;) this is matter of astonishment and wonder, if your
majesty consider it, how far such men are from improving
your excellent proclamations against swearing, debauchery,
and drunkenness, or being in taverns after nine of the
clock at night.[7]   Oh! how little notice is taken of these
proclamations, or of the laws to which they direct, either
by the swearing, debauched persons themselves, or by your
majesty's subordinate ministers!   And how few, if any,
have been prosecuted upon those two proclamations, and
what multitudes upon the other!   And this is much to be
lamented, that men may with less danger meet at taverns,
ale-houses, and other places of debauchery, to drink above
measure, or swear, game, rant and tear, as if there were
neither heaven nor hell, God nor magistrates, but if a few
poor men and women, meet together in the fear of the

---

[7] [On the 30th May, 1660, a proclamation was issued against vicious,
debauched, and profane persons, and
by a subsequent proclamation in August, this was directed to be read in
all churches and chapels in England
and Wales. These are the two proclamations referred to by our author.
The very great increase of crime and
debauchery throughout the country
called forth three years afterwards
another proclamation, requiring the
clergy to read the first, once every
month, for the space of half a year.
The vices of the sovereign and the
court, with the generally low character
of the clergy, were doubtless an edifying commentary on the text thus
afforded them.   Kennet's Register,
pp. 167, 230.]

Lord, having mutual faith, and oneness of heart, to pray unto Almighty God—a part of whose petition is, that God

1 Tim. ii. 2. would bless and guide your majesty, *and all that are in authority, that we may lead a quiet and peaceable life, in all godliness and honesty,*—at such meetings many are offended.

And may it further please your majesty, to consider your afflicted and innocent subjects, how they have been haled from their peaceable habitations, and thrust into prisons, almost in all counties in England, and many are still detained to the utter undoing of themselves and families.[8] And most of them are poor men, whose livelihood, under God, depends upon the labour of their hands. So that they lie under more than an ordinary calamity, there being so many thrust into little rooms together, that they are an annoyance each to other, especially in the city of London, where the lord mayor crowds them very close together, that it hath been observed, the keepers have complained they have had too many guests. And whilst they suffer there, some of their wives and tender babes want bread at home.[9]

And how long this will be the portion of some, I know not, unless your majesty extend the like grace to other prisoners, as your majesty did most princely to them at Westminster, in giving order to discharge them, they acknowledging by subscription, your majesty to be the

---

[8] [" Such is the portion of many of us, to be taken out of our houses, and from our employments, beaten and abused in the streets by the rude multitude, haled before the justices and other officers, and then having nothing to charge us with, they put us to the oath, and upon refusal, though Christ hath prohibited swearing at all, especially any promissory oath, are we sent to prison, to the impoverishing and ruin of us, our lives, and children." To the king of these nations, by several societies called anabaptists, &c. A sheet, 1660.]

[9] [See Crosby's History of English Baptists, vol. ii. 149—172, for an account of these sufferings.]

supreme magistrate of this kingdom, and of all others of your majesty's kingdoms and dominions, without pressing the oath of allegiance; which some are not free to take,[1] by reason Christ saith, Matt. v. 34, *Swear not at all;* and, in St. James v. 12, *Above all things, my brethren, swear not.* They, mistaking these two places, understand that Christians should not swear in any case; and therefore out of mere fear, lest they should offend against a divine law, have fallen under the penalty of that human law, which requireth us to swear our allegiance to your majesty. Oh, that your majesty's clemency might interpose, that their weakness on the one hand, and the severity of the law on the other, might not ruin many hundred families!

But to return to that for which I am in travail, viz., that we may worship God, according to our light and measure of understanding, unto which we have attained; without being restrained from the exercise thereof, by the magistrate, or by having any thing imposed upon us, as articles of faith, or rules of worship. In the behalf of which, I humbly tender these six reasons following.

Reason 1. First, be pleased, royal Sir, to consider, that such imposing of the magistrates, is contrary to the nature of the gospel; because it is one of the glories of the Christian religion, that it was so pious, excellent, powerful, and persuasive, that it came in upon its own piety and wisdom; with no other force, but a torrent of arguments, and demonstration of the Spirit, beating down all strong holds, and every high thought and imagination that exalted [2 Cor. x. [4,] 5.]

---

[1] [Of this class of baptists were those who early in the year 1661 presented, "To the king of these nations," their humble representations, quoted in a previous note, " where, in short, they declare their innocency, sufferings, desires, and resolutions." It is signed by twenty-six persons, for themselves and the congregations to which they respectively belonged. One of them, Samuel Hodgkin, replied to a piece published by Mr. Jeremiah Ives, in favour of taking the oaths of allegiance and supremacy.]

itself against the same. But towards the persons of men, it was always full of meekness and charity, compliance, and toleration, and bearing one with another, restoring persons overtaken with an error, with the spirit of meekness. The consideration is as prudent, and the proposition as just, as the precept is charitable, and the precedent most pious and holy.

Gal. vi. 1.

That precept which it chiefly preaches in order to all blessedness, is, meekness, mercy, and charity, whereby it should preserve itself, and promote its own interest. For, indeed, nothing will do it so well, nothing doth so excellently insinuate itself into the understanding and affections of men, as when the principles, actions, and persuasions of a people are in every part suitable. And it would be a mighty disparagement to so glorious an institution, that in its principles it should be so merciful and humane, and in the promotion and propagation of it so inhuman and dishonourable to Christ. It may serve the Turk to support his Alkoran [thus], but it will much dishonour Christianity, to offer to support it by that which good men believe to be a distinctive cognizance of the Mahometan religion from the excellency and piety of Christianity; whose sense and spirit is excellently described by St. Paul, *The servant of the Lord must not strive; but be gentle unto all men; in meekness instructing those that oppose themselves.*

2 Tim. ii. 24. 25.

If, then, any man will smite those that are his opposites in opinion, he must quit the title of being God's servant for his pains. Nor can a distinction of persons, ecclesiastical and secular, give advantage for an escape; for even the secular power, if it be Christian, must not be a striker of others for the matters of their faith, for God alone is judge of erring persons, as that learned doctor, Jeremiah Taylor, now bishop of Down, saith in the thirteenth page of his epistle dedicatory, to that famous book, entitled, The Liberty of Prophesy. [2]

Reason 2. The second reason against restraining or using force in matters of religion, is, because Christ, who is the only Lawgiver to his church, gives this precept for the regulation of the conversation of his disciples, *Whatso-* Matt. vii. 12. *ever ye would have men do unto you, do ye even so unto them ;* than which there is no law more reasonable, nor more just. It cannot be supposed, that kings sitting in the throne of government, or place of trust and rule, are exempted from the observation of this commandment; which, if so, then, if the magistrates be of this persuasion, that Christ died for all men, and the people believe as Calvin did, that he died for the elect only; what can the magistrates do in this case? For if they make a law in favour of the people's judgment, then they wrong themselves, which I suppose they will not do. If a law be made in favour of their own opinion against the people's, then, besides the injury which is done to the people, they break that royal law before mentioned, and thereby become guilty before God.

Reason 3. The third reason against restraining, or

[2] [A Discourse of the Liberty of Prophesying, by Jer. Taylor, D.D., chaplain to his majesty, ed. 1647. 4to. " No man or company of men can judge or punish our thoughts, or secret purposes, while they so remain, and yet it will be unequal to say, that he who owns this doctrine preaches it lawful for men to think or purpose what they will. And so it is in matters of doubtful disputation (such as are the distinguishing articles of most of the sects of Christendom.) So it is in matters intellectual (which are not cognoscible by a secular power ;) in matters spiritual (which are to be discerned by spiritual authority, which cannot make corporal inflictions); and in questions indeterminate, (which are doubtfully propounded or obscurely, and therefore may be *in utramque partem,* disputed or believed); for God alone must be the judge of these matters, who alone is master of our souls, and hath a dominion over human understanding, and he that says this, that indifferency is persuaded, because God alone is judge of erring persons."]

Y 2

using force in matters of religion, is taken from the unreasonableness of such proceedings. For what is more
unreasonable, than to deny men the use of their reason, in
[the] choice of their religion? For if scripture, tradition,
councils, and fathers, be the evidence in a question; yet
reason is the judge. That is, we being the persons that
are to be persuaded, we must see that we be persuaded
reasonably, and it is against reason to assent to a lesser
evidence, when a greater is propounded. But every man
for himself is to take cognizance, if he be able to judge;
but if he be not, then he is not bound under the tie of
necessity to know it, nor will God punish him for not
knowing it. And not only the unreasonableness, but the
impiety of using force in this case, may be further seen,
if it be considered, that there is nothing, under God, hath
power over the understanding of a man. God, commanding us to believe his revelations, persuades and satisfies the
understanding, by his commanding and revealing it; for
there is no greater probation in the world that a proposition is true, than because God hath commanded it to be
believed. But then it must certainly be made [to] appear
to us, that God hath so commanded it. But no man hath
any efficacy or authority on the understanding of another,
but by proposal and persuasion, and then a man is bound
to assent according to the operation of the argument, and
strength of the persuasion. Neither indeed can he assent
sooner, nor otherwise, though he would never so fain.

He, therefore, that in this case useth force or punishment, punisheth a man for keeping a good conscience, or
forceth him into a bad. He both punishes sincerity, and
persuades hypocrisy. He persecutes a truth, and drives
into an error. He teacheth a man to dissemble, to be
safe; but never to be honest, nor acceptable to God.
Learned Doctor Taylor's argument for toleration is very

excellent, in his epistle to his Liberty of Prophesying, in page 14. "This very thing," saith he, "being one of the arguments I use to persuade permissions, lest compulsion introduce hypocrisy, and make sincerity troublesome and unsafe."[3]

Reason 4. The fourth reason which I humbly offer to consideration, against persecution for conscience, or the civil magistrate using force in the matters of religion, is, because it came in through [the] corruptions of the times, so that it is so far from being of divine sanction, that it is earthly and sensual. For the proof of this I shall only transcribe a passage out of that worthy author, Doctor Taylor, in his aforesaid epistle to his Liberty of Prophesying,[4] which is as followeth: "But besides that against this I have laid prejudice enough from the dictates of holy scripture, it is observable that this with its appendant degrees, I mean restraint of prophesying, imposing upon other men's understanding, being masters of their consciences, and lording it over their faith, came in with the retinue and train of antichrist; that is, they came as other abuses and corruptions of the church did, by reason of the iniquity of times, and the cooling of the first heats of Christianity, and the increase of interest, and the abatements of Christian simplicity, when the church's fortune grew better, and her sons grew worse, and some of her fathers worst of all; for in the first three hundred years there was no sign of persecuting any man for his opinion, though at that time there were very horrid opinions commenced, and such which were exemplary and parallel

---

[3] ["For I earnestly contend that another man's opinion shall be no rule to mine, and that my opinion shall be no snare and prejudice to myself, that men use one another so cha- ritably and so gently, that no error or violence tempt men to hypocrisy, this very thing," &c.]

[4] Pages 18, 19.

enough to determine this question; for they then were assaulted by new sects which destroyed the common principles of nature, of Christianity, of innocence and public society; and they who used all the means, Christian and spiritual, for their disimprovement and conviction, thought not of using corporal force, otherwise than by blaming such proceedings. And therefore I do not [only] urge their not doing it, as an argument of the unlawfulness of such proceeding, but their defying it, and speaking against such practices, as unreasonable and destructive of Christianity."

For which the learned doctor cites all these fathers; Tertullian, St. Cyprian, Lactantius, St. Hilary, Minucius Felix, Sulpicius Severus, St. Chrysostom, St. Hierom, St. Austin, Damascene, Theophylact, Socrates Scholasticus, and St. Bernard. And he further saith, "That all wise princes, till they were overborne with faction, or solicited by peevish persons, gave toleration to differing sects, whose opinions did not disturb the public interest." And in page 20, " Till four hundred years after Christ, no catholic persons, or very few, did provoke the secular arm, or implore its aid." [5] So far he. From which it is evident, that the magistrate's imposing in matters of religion, is an evil, from which I pray God deliver your majesty.

Reason 5. The fifth reason is taken from the principles and practices of some great princes, who did both give and persuade toleration. King James, your majesty's royal grandfather, " in his letters to the states of the United

---

[5] [" — against the heretics, save only that Arius behaved himself so seditiously and tumultuarily, that the Nicene fathers procured a temporary degree for his relegation, but it was soon taken off, and God left to be his judge, who indeed did it to some purpose, when he was trusted with it, and the matter wholly left to him."]

Provinces, dated the 6th of March, 1613," amongst other things, "thus wrote, Et districtè imperetis ut pacem colant se invicem tolerando in istâ opinionum ac sententiarum discrepantiâ : eoque justiùs videmur vobis hoc ipsum suadere debere quòd neutram comperimus adeò deviam, ut non possint et cum fidei Christianæ veritate, et cum animarum salute, consistere :[6] (Englished for common benefit.)—That you charge them to maintain peace by bearing one with another in such difference of opinions and judgments; therefore it seemeth more right, that you should be thus persuaded, seeing neither of the judgments is found so dangerous, but that it may stand with the true faith of a Christian, and the salvation of souls.[7]

" The like counsel in the divisions of Germany at the first Reformation, was thought reasonable by the Emperor Ferdinand, and his excellent son Maximilian. [For] they had observed that violence did exasperate, was unblessed, unsuccessful, and unreasonable; and therefore they made decrees of toleration, and appointed tempers and expedients to be drawn out by discreet persons ; and George Cassander was designed to this great work, and did something towards it. And Emanuel Philibert, Duke of Savoy, respecting of his war undertaken for religion against the Piedmontans, promised them toleration, and was as good as his word. As much is done by the nobility of Polonia."[8] And Theodoricus the sage, king of the Goths, assuaging the vehemency of the Arians against the orthodox, " No belief,"

[6] [Lib. of Prophesying, p. 23, Epist. Dedic.]

[7] There were very sharp contentions about religion amongst the Holland ministers at that time. King James adviseth the magistrate to moderate them, not to kill nor punish them, for they may both be saved. [These contentions were about the *five points*, and ultimately led to the assembling of the synod of Dort. These opinions, says James, " we do not perceive so absurd as not to consist with the truth of the Christian faith, as well as with the salvation of men's souls." Brandt, Hist. of Reformation in the Netherlands, ii. 124, fol. edit. 1721.]

[8] [Lib. of Proph. pp. 23, 24.]

saith he, "is carried on by blows." Nor is that excellent
saying of King Edward VI. to be forgotten; he being
solicited to put a heretic to death, made this wise answer;
Will you have me send her to hell in her sins?[9]   But to
conclude this, the French king, although he be the second
son of the church of Rome, gives toleration to different
persuasions in matters of religion; for the Huguenots have
their churches, and places of meeting for to worship God
in, according as they are persuaded, by order from their
king; and the world is witness how prosperous they have
been, since they have left fighting for religion among
themselves.

Reason 6.   The sixth and last reason I have taken from
the ill success that always attends such proceedings.   For
whoever uses force upon the body to change the mind, or to
make men believe something they are not persuaded of, or
to disbelieve something they have received for truth, or
to leave off worshipping God in that way which they think
is most agreeable to his will; they will have no better
success than that man had, that clapt his shoulder to the
ground to stop the earthquake.   And the experiences
which Christendom hath had in this last age, are sufficient
instances.   When France fought amongst themselves, the
catholics against the Huguenots, the spilling of their own
blood was argument enough, of the imprudence of that way
of promoting religion; and that all the blood shed in open
arms, and private massacres, could not prevent their
further growth, nor extinguish that light that sprung up
amongst that people; and the name of the Huguenots
is not only in France still, but they and their religion
tolerated.[1]

" But the great instance is in the differing temper,

<hr>

[9] [See before, p. 37.]   [1] [Lib. of Proph. p. 21, Epist. Ded.]

government, and success, which Margaret of Parma and the Duke of Alva had. The clemency of the first had almost extinguished the flame; but when she was removed, Duke Alva succeeded, and managed the matter of religion with fire and sword; he made the flame so great, that his religion, and his prince too, have [both] been [almost] quite turned out" of a great part "of the country."[2]

And we are not without example nearer home in Queen Mary's days. What force and violence were then used, to make the people believe as the queen and her bishops believed! Some were burnt to death, some destroyed in prisons, and many that escaped with life, were undone in their estates and livelihood. And all this was so unsuccessful, as to the suppressing their further growth, that it did quite the contrary, for the more they were oppressed, the more they grew.

I shall only add a passage out of learned Bishop Taylor, in his Epistle to his Liberty of Prophesying.[3] "But it is," saith he, "observed by Socrates, that when the first persecution was made against them," that is, such as differed in opinion from the bishop, "at Rome, by Pope Innocent the First; at the same instant, the Goths invaded Italy, and became lords of all; it being just in God to bring a persecution upon them for true belief, who with an incompetent authority, and insufficient grounds, do persecute an error less material, in persons agreeing with them, in the profession of the same common faith."

The next thing I humbly offer to your princely consideration is the divine bond upon our hearts, to worship God according to our light; and the crying sin we must commit if we shall resist our own understanding, and refuse to

---

[2] [Lib. of Proph. pp. 21, 22, Epist. Ded.]   [3] Page 25.

obey the command of God upon our conscience, to assemble
Heb. x. 25. ourselves together for his worship; and that we ought to
esteem our duty to God, much dearer than our estates,
liberty, or lives.

And our souls are fully persuaded, that it is our duty to
meet together, and speak often one to another; to exhort
each other daily, to take heed of sin, and to follow after
virtue, and to press after the mark of our high calling of
God, in Christ Jesus our Lord; and to provoke to love and
good works, and if any be overtaken in a fault, to restore
them in the spirit of meekness; and to relieve the poor, and
to support the weak, that by bearing one another's burthens
we may fulfil the law of Christ; and to walk so inoffensively
in our conversation, as to give no just occasion, neither to
your majesty as supreme magistrate, nor to any of your
ministers under you, nor to any of the people or neighbours
about us; but to observe that excellent law of Christ,
Matt. vii. 12. *whatsoever ye would that men should do unto you, do ye even
so to them.* And if any shall persecute us for our profession's
sake, to bear it with patience, and not to return evil for
evil, nor reviling for reviling; but contrariwise, to do them
Matt. v. 44. good for evil, and to pray for them, that their eyes may be
opened, and that God may not lay their sin, in this case,
to their charge.

Now if your majesty will but consider, what it is which
the baptized people and divers others have made such
earnest suit to your majesty for; it is not for titles of
honour, nor for places of great profit, either in a civil or
ecclesiastical capacity, but this only is their request, and
humble desire: that we may serve the Lord without
molestation in that faith and order which we have learned
1 Pet. ii. 17. in the holy scripture; giving *honour to* our *king,* to whom
honour belongs; fear to whom fear; tribute to whom
tribute. In every thing, as far as we have abilities, to

render to God the things that are God's, and to the magi- Rom. xiii. 7.
strate the things that are his.

We likewise judge it our duty to be always willing and
ready to give an answer to every man that shall ask us; a
reason of our hope that is in us, with meekness and fear.
Now if any who judge themselves to be spiritual guides,
will but take the pains to endeavour our conviction, if
they think we err, or at least to hear what we have to
say, why we dissent from the public worship; we doubt
not but through the grace of God, we shall be able to
give such an account of our faith and practice, [as may
show] that we do not deserve those epithets some are
pleased to give us.

I shall only transcribe one passage out of that ingenious
doctor, Dr. Jeremiah Taylor, which I find in sect. 18, number 34. of his Liberty of Prophesying.[4] He, speaking of
the anabaptists, saith, " That since there is no direct
impiety in the opinion, nor any that is apparently consequent to it, and they with so much probability do, or may,
pretend to true persuasion, they are, with all means
Christian, fair, and humane, to be redargued, or instructed;
but if they cannot be persuaded, they must be left to
God, who knoweth every degree of every man's understanding, all his weaknesses and strengths, what impress
each argument maketh upon his spirit, and how irresistible
every reason is; and he alone judges his innocency and
sincerity. And for that question, I think there is so
much to be pretended against that which I believe to be
the truth, that there is much more truth than evidence
on our side; and therefore we may be confident, as for
our own particulars, but not too forward peremptorily to
prescribe to others, much less, to damn, or to kill, or to

---

[4] Page 245.

persecute them, that only in this particular disagree."
So far he.

I shall conclude with this humble petition, that seeing
your majesty hath been most earnestly supplicated, by
many petitions, addresses, and papers, to continue your
former indulgence : Oh ! that your majesty would be graciously pleased to do something in it, that may recommend
your name to be embalmed by them for perpetuity; through
the remembrance of your just, righteous, and merciful
actions, in breaking every yoke of oppression, and to the
easing of the conscience of every man professing Jesus
Christ, from all unrighteous impositions. And as this
will administer peace, joy, and comfort to many of your
suffering subjects, so it will bring most excellent consolation unto your majesty's soul, when the heavens shall
be no more. And as your majesty desires to be found
on the right hand of the great Judge in that his day; so
in this your day remember and consider, that magistracy
and power of government are no institutions of God,
either to fill the purses, or to furnish the tables, or to
lift up the minds, or in any kind to gratify the flesh of
those in whom they are invested; but rather to serve,
to accommodate, and bless the societies and communities
of men on earth, unto which they respectively relate,
according to that worthy item, which the queen of Sheba
1 Kings x. 9. gave unto Solomon, *Because the Lord loved Israel for
ever ; therefore made he thee king, to do judgment and justice.*

The same Lord and mighty God so overshadow your
majesty with his power and good Spirit, that the concep-
tions of your heart may be holiness to him ; wealth, and
peace, and gladness of heart to the people of these great and
famous kingdoms, the government whereof God hath been
pleased to intrust with you ; to your royal self, honour and

safety, and length of days, with the peace and joy of a good conscience on earth, and a far more exceeding eternal weight of glory in the heavens.

So prayeth,

Your humble and dutiful subject,

JOHN STURGION.

THE END.

SION'S GROANS

FOR HER

DISTRESSED,

OR

SOBER ENDEAVOURS TO PREVENT INNOCENT BLOOD,

&c.

1661.

INTRODUCTORY NOTICE.

THE circumstances which preceded the publication of the ensuing excellent treatise, have been sufficiently related in the notices prefacing the two previous tracts. The names of Mr. Jeffery and Mr. Hammon are found subscribed to the petition from Maidstone gaol, and in addition to their signatures to the preface of the present piece, there are the names of five others who do not appear to have been fellow-sufferers with them on that occasion. Several of the arguments already adduced in the Maidstone petition are here again employed, but much amplified; while, with greater vigour and cogency of reasoning, they urge anew their objections to the magistrate's claim of right to impose any thing in the worship of God, and enforce their righteous demand for spiritual and mental liberty.

Mr. Monck was a general baptist minister. He assiduously laboured to sow the seed of divine truth in Buckinghamshire and its vicinity. He is also regarded as the author of the "Orthodox Creed," which, in the year 1678, the general baptists of the counties of Bucks, Hereford, Bedford, and Oxford, published. In this some approximation was attempted and made towards a more Calvinistic expression of their faith. A small piece entitled, A Cure for the Cankering Error of the New Eutychians, issued from his pen in 1673.[1]

Mr. Wright was pastor of the church at Maidstone, a zealous preacher of the gospel, and a faithful sufferer in the cause of nonconformity. He received his education at one of the universities, and was united with Mr. Grantham as a messenger to deliver the petition of the Lincolnshire baptists to the king in the year 1660. He was a man of great piety and learning, a serious and diligent preacher. He spent no less than twenty years in prison for conscience' sake.[2]

Ravensthorpe, in Northamptonshire, was the chief scene of the labours of "that eminent servant of Christ," Mr. Francis Stanley. Here for many years he superintended a church in conjunction with Mr. Benjamin Morley, and was most instrumental in promoting the increase and order of the communities around him. He has left us a little work of some excellence, containing rules, motives, and encouragements for the due exercise of discipline in the churches. Its title is, "Christianity indeed, or the well disciplined Christian the delight of Christ," &c.[3]

At a meeting of elders and brethren at Stamford, in 1656, Mr. Reynolds and another minister were appointed to proceed as messengers of the churches into the west,

---

[1] Taylor's Hist. of Gen. Baptists, i. 300, 360.   [2] Ivimey, Hist. of Eng. Baptists, ii. 238.   [3] Taylor, i. 160, 233, 321.

for the work of the ministry. They were to be supported by the mutual contributions of the churches
forming the assembly. Of the nature of this service
no account exists, nor of Mr. Reynolds in connexion
with it, until we find him uniting with the above servants
of Christ, in the publication of this treatise.[4]

Of the last whose name appears in the following pages,
Mr. Francis Smith, another opportunity will hereafter
occur, for a reference to his many eminent services to
the cause of truth, both as a printer and preacher, in
presenting the reader with a reprint of the useful works
he has bequeathed to posterity.

We are indebted to the historian Crosby for the
ensuing piece, from whose pages it is reprinted; all efforts
have failed in discovering an original copy of it. On his
accuracy the fullest dependence may be placed.

[4] Ibid. p. 159.

EPISTLE TO THE READER.

COURTEOUS READER,

WITH burthened hearts, as once the two disciples travelling into Emmaus, spoke to Christ, a supposed stranger, so [Luke xxiv. 13.] speak we unto thee. Art thou a stranger in our island, and hast not known the things that have come to pass in these our days; while the father hath been divided against the [Matt. x. 55, 56.] son, and the son against the father, three against two, and two against three? Even a man's foes [are] they of his own household. So great have been our divisions, like Reuben, that no sooner light hath been by God's grace manifested to the begetting children of the free-woman, but presently they are persecuted by the children of the bond-woman.

And how unpleasing this is to Jesus Christ, and how unlike his golden rule, that saith, *And all things whatsoever ye* [Matt. vii. 12.] *would that men should do to you, do ye even so to them; for this is the law and the prophets.* We say, how unpleasing this is to him, judge upon thy serious perusal of this following treatise; which we commend to thy perusal in thy most retired consideration, when thou canst read with thy thoughts least cumbered with other business. Our design in what we beg may be perused, is [the] general good, in setting at liberty that which God made free, even the conscience.

Thou canst not be ignorant of the great controversy that now is on foot, as to uniformity in worship, to impose by violence where they cannot persuade, under the seeming pretence of scripture-warrant and antiquity; the contrary to which is asserted in the words of truth and soberness, by scripture, reason, and practice of primitive times.

And lest violence and oppressing of conscience should run up to that height, till it terminate in the blood of some who are dear, and their blood precious in the eyes of the God of all the earth; therefore have we committed this unto the view of all men, as part of the work of our generation, in singleness of heart. And remain lovers and prayers for all men, that we might live a peaceable and a quiet life in all godliness and honesty. Farewell.

THOMAS MONCK.   FRANCIS STANLEY.
JOSEPH WRIGHT.   WILLIAM REYNOLDS.
GEORGE HAMMON.   FRANCIS SMITH.
WILLIAM JEFFERY.

The 8th day of the 3rd month, [*May*] 1661.

SION'S GROANS,

ETC.

As all the holy scriptures, say they, have been *written* [Rom. xv. 4. *aforetime for our learning* and *admonition, upon whom the ends* [1 Cor. x. 11.] *of the world are come ;* so that particular book of the Revelation is of such excellent worth, that *blessed is he that read-* [Rev. i. 3.] *eth, and they that hear the words of this prophecy, and keep those things that are written therein, for the time is at hand.* In which book, in no less than three several texts, it is [Rev. xiv. 8; xvii.2; xviii.] testified, that the nations of the world and inhabiters of the [3.] earth, with their kings, would drink the wine of the fornication of that abominable harlot, that sitteth upon peoples, and multitudes, and nations, and tongues ; and by her sorceries deceiveth all nations until they become drunk, and altogether incapable, in that condition, to receive the pure waters of life, tendered to them in the plain way of the gospel of our Lord Jesus.

This, with grief of heart, we see too visible. For the doctrine and traditions of Rome, who is mystery, Babylon, and since her apostasy the mother of harlots—for *the woman* Rev.xvii.18. *which thou sawest, is that great city, which reigneth over the kings of the earth,*—have so corrupted the earth, and clouded the understandings of the sons of men, that the great and most important truths of God cannot be received or believed. The reason why the nations are so generally beguiled in the concernments of their souls, is, because the greatest part being carnal and unregenerate persons, they are naturally inclined to such ways of worship, as are accompanied with external pomp and glory. And therefore, the Spirit of the Lord testifies, that the great harlot Rev. xvii. 4. filleth her abominations, and filthy fornications, in a golden cup. Like the physician that gilds his bitter pill, that his patient may the better swallow it.

Thus doth the Romish church and her followers, who, to make their carnal ordinances find the better reception, deliver them to the inhabitants of the earth, by such as are honourable amongst men, in worldly sanctuaries, most magnificently built and adorned, endowed with lordly revenues, accompanied with music, and voices, and pontifical vestments ; yea, many superstitions and customs merely earthly and sensual, if not worse. Which, we say, so pleaseth the earthly and unregenerate man, that he is ready to say, this is the best religion, which is of most esteem in the nations, and accompanied with all earthly glory and Matt. vii. 14. delights. Altogether forgetting, that *strait is the gate, and narrow is the way that leads to life, and few there be that find* Luke xvi. 15. *it.* And *that which is highly esteemed among men, is abomination in the sight of God.*

And if it had been the mind of the Lord Jesus that the gospel should have been recommended unto the world, and accompanied with these ceremonies and formalities that are practised in the worship of the nations, or were used among the Jews, it is very strange we should not have one word for it [in] all the scriptures of the New Testament, when Heb. iii. 2, 5, Christ was as faithful over his house, as Moses was over 6. Deut. xviii his, and is to be heard in all things, as Moses himself com- 18, 19. manded.

And there will be little encouragement to touch with the Gentile nations in their superstitious ceremonies, when it shall be considered that the rites and ceremonies of the Mosaical law, being once the appointment of God, did far exceed in glory what the shallow inventions of the Romish, or any of the national churches, are able to produce, yet [are] wholly taken away. Which the author [of the epistle] to the Hebrews notably proves: saying, *Then* [Heb. ix.1—3.] *verily the first covenant had also ordinances of divine service, and a worldly sanctuary. For there was a tabernacle made; the first, wherein was the candlestick, and the table, and the shewbread; which is called the sanctuary. And after the second veil, the tabernacle, which is called the Holiest of all.*

They had also their high priest, and offerings, and linen ornaments, belonging to this covenant. But, saith our author, *If that first covenant had been faultless, then no place* Heb. viii. 7. *had been sought for the second. And he taketh away the* Heb. x. 9. *first, that he might establish the second.* And now under the second covenant, which is the gospel, the Romish bishop, or any man upon earth, cannot be our high priest. For *we have such an high priest, who is set on the right hand of the* [Heb. viii.1, 2.] *throne of the majesty in the heavens, a minister of the sanctuary, and of the [true] tabernacle, which the Lord pitcheth, and not man.*

And under this second covenant, God hath not promised his presence to any temple built with wood and stone, as of old. For now *the Most High dwelleth not in temples made* Acts vii. 48. *with hands,* as the superstitious clergy would persuade us; but *where two or three are gathered together in the name* [Matt. xviii. 20.] of Christ, *there is he in the midst of them,* although it be in a house, by a river's side, on a mountain, or in a wilderness. Such little respect hath he to place.

As little respect hath God to persons, because of any honour or esteem they may have in the world, either for 1 Cor. i. 26, birth or natural endowments. But such as usually are fool-&c. ish, weak, and base in the eyes of the world, doth he make use of in the work of the gospel; that so the learned doctors, and masters of art, may not have wherewithal to boast.

Which despised way of the gospel, we well know, becomes a stumbling-block to the Gentile nations; as in the first delivery of it, it did unto the Jews, who would not receive the Lord of life, nor his doctrine, because not accompanied with that earthly glory which their corrupt hearts affected; and rather would retain that exploded dispensation of the law which God had departed from, than they would receive the glorious gospel by those hands the wisdom of God thought fit to tender it. For which obstinacy, as the apostle Paul saith, *the wrath of God is come upon them to the uttermost,* even to the laying waste their temple and cities, the great slaughter of their persons, and captivating their posterity, as at this day.

1 Thess. ii. 16.

Let, therefore, the Gentile nations fear; but more especially this nation. For some such spirit seems to appear amongst those that would retain their empty and dead forms of worship, which God hath showed his displeasure against, and [that] have no footing in the whole book of God, rather than they will receive the pure way of God, without the mixture of human inventions and traditions.

But the bare rejection of truth, and embracing of error, is not all the evil that the nations generally are engaged in by the church of Rome and her followers. But for to complete and fill up the measure of their iniquities, like Nebuchadnezzar, nothing less must be inflicted on the servants of the most high God, that cannot bow down to the golden image of their inventions, than the fiery furnace of persecution, many times unto death itself.

And this the people of the Lord must endure, it being as certainly their portion to be persecuted, as it is the practice of the false churches to persecute; who build their superstructures of will-worship on no other foundations but violence and cruelty. Else what mean these imprisonments, banishments, wars, and massacres, which have been made in Europe for religion? What troubles and desolations in Germany; civil commotions in France; cruelties exercised in the Netherlands, by that darling of the Romish church, the duke of Alva, and others! What massacres in France, Piedmont, and Ireland, to carry on the business of religion, for the satisfaction of a blood-thirsty and insatiable clergy; when the disciples of the Lord Jesus were to use no other violence against those that rejected them, than to shake the dust from their feet, which would be a witness Matt. x. 14 against them at the tribunal of Jesus, not Cæsar's! 15; Acts xiii. 51.

Yea, this popish principle of propagating religion by the sword, hath reached the poor Americans, many hundred thousands of them having been destroyed because they would not be proselytes; no other cause being to be given. For it cannot be supposed, those remote and simple people had so much as known the Spaniard, much less done any injury to him. Our own nation hath also felt the rage of this fury, both before, and in the reign of queen Mary. And the wise may judge, whether the bishops' endeavours to impose their liturgy in Scotland, with their cruelties in England, did not contribute much to our late unhappy troubles.

But certainly, if the Romish and national clergy were guided by the Spirit of God, the authority of Scripture, or force of argument, to support their forms of worship, they would not then impose them by external force; when by such proceedings they render themselves altogether unlike the Lord Jesus, the Prince of peace, who came *not to* [Luke ix. 56. *destroy men's lives, but to save them.*

But on the contrary, it will evince to all that have their eyes open, how like they are to that woman, which is *drunken with the blood of saints, and with the blood of the* Rev. xvii. 6. *martyrs of Jesus;* in whom will be *found the blood of* Rev. xviii. 24.

prophets, and of saints, and of all that were slain upon the earth. Although as our Lord and Master hath foretold, [John xvi. 2.] in killing others, she may think she doth God service.

Lest, therefore, those unchristian principles of persecution for conscience which troubleth the world, should take root in this nation, to the stirring up men's minds to shed the blood of the innocent, the guilt whereof is able to sink the most flourishing kingdoms into an ocean of misery and calamity, we have here following written some arguments, which we humbly offer to all men, to prove how contrary to the gospel of our Lord Jesus, and to good reason, it is for any magistrate, by outward force, to impose any thing in the worship of God, on the consciences of those whom they govern. But that liberty ought to be given to all such as disturb not the civil peace, though of different persuasions in religious matters.

In which discourse we neither desire, nor design, to diminish any of that power which God hath given to the king's majesty that now reigneth; whom we own to be chief magistrate and governor of these nations, over all persons, as well ecclesiastical as temporal. And to all his commands that do not oppose the scriptures of truth, shall we yield active obedience, not only for wrath, but also for conscience' sake. And if any thing otherwise shall be required, we shall be passive, and suffer what may be inflicted on us for our consciences. For, whatever hath been suggested by evil men, yet, that magistracy and government is an ordinance of God, hath been frequently asserted in our discourses and writings,[1] and is by us believed, as fully as the apostle Paul in the thirteenth of the Romans hath taught. And all that we desire, which is

---

[1] See the Confession of Faith, printed in March, 1659 [1660], and since reprinted and presented to his majesty. [Crosby, ii. App. p. 76—90. Grantham's Christianismus Prim. B. ii. c. v. p. 62.]

dearer to us than our lives, is, that our spirits and consciences may be left free to serve the eternal God. Which ought to be granted us, seeing, as the same apostle saith in these cases, We shall *every one of us give an account of him-* Rom.xiv.12. *self to God.*

But to our arguments. The first of which shall be that which some of us made use of to the king's majesty from Maidstone, which we have not yet seen weakened.[2]

Let it, therefore, be considered, if any magistrate under heaven, in the days of the gospel, hath power by outward force to impose any thing in the worship and service of God on the conscience, it is given him as he is a magistrate only, or as a Christian so considered. But that no such power is given by God to any magistrate, appears—

1. Because if magistrates, as such, have such an authority, then all magistrates in all nations have the same power. Then, if we lived in Turkey, must we receive the Alcoran, and be worshippers of Mahomet. If in Spain, be papists; in England, sometimes papists, as in Henry the Eighth's days; protestants in Edward the Sixth's; papists again in Queen Mary's; and protestants again in Queen Elizabeth's. And so for ever, as the authority changes religion, we must do the same. But God forbid, for nothing is more absurd.

2. Seeing in the days of the gospel, the Lord Jesus is [Deut. xviii. 15—18.] that great prophet, which, as Moses said, is to be heard in all things; and, as himself testifieth, hath *all power in heaven* Matt.xxviii *and earth given unto him;* then, if magistrates have power 18. to impose any thing by outward force upon the conscience, it must be committed unto them from the Lord Jesus, and written in the scriptures of the New Testament. Or else how doth it appear? Let no man *think of men above that* 1 Cor. iv. 6.

[2] [See before, p. 298.]

which is written. But the whole stream of the New Testament scriptures runs clear in another channel. And there is no colour for any such imposition. As further appears—

3. Because the apostles themselves, that gave forth those commands which are written in scripture, to be obedient to magistrates, refused to be obedient to their rulers, when they were commanded to forbear that which they judged part of the worship of God. And said, *Whether it be right in the sight of God, to hearken unto you more than unto God, judge ye.*

Acts iv. 19, 20.

4. All the scriptures of the New Testament, that enjoin obedience unto magistrates, were written when the Romans had the empire of the world; whose emperors were for the most part, if not all, heathenish idolaters for the first three hundred years, until Constantine's time. It, therefore, cannot be supposed, that any of those texts of scripture that call for obedience to magistrates, intend an obedience in matters of faith. For then the Christians that lived under these emperors must needs have denied Christ, and worshipped the Roman gods, as some of the emperors commanded.[3]

5. If magistrates, as such, have power from God in the days of the gospel to command in spiritual matters, and to punish those that obey not, then must Christians surely be actually obedient, *not only for wrath, but also for conscience'*

[Rom. xiii. 5. 2.]

---

[3] As Dioclesian, Euseb. b. viii. c. 3. Under this emperor took place the tenth of the general persecutions suffered by the Christians of the primitive age. Their sacred books were burnt: their churches destroyed, and themselves deprived of their public employments and their property. Their only security was in submission to the edicts commanding divine worship to be paid to the pagan gods. The attempt to extirpate utterly the Christian name failed, and in despair at his ill success, Dioclesian abdicated the imperial crown. Magdeburg. Centur. Cent. iv. pp. 16, 909, tom. i. ed. 1624.]

sake, because else they should *resist the ordinance of God.*
But if this were true, the way to heaven would be so far
from being strait and narrow, that any might be a disciple
of Christ, without taking up the cross and following him. Luke xiv. 27.
Yea, all sufferings and persecutions should wholly be at an
end, and they that undergo them should utterly be condemned. For it is not to be supposed there could be persecutions, if all the commands of the magistrate in spiritual
causes were actually to be obeyed. It, therefore, reasonably follows, that no magistrate, as such, hath power from
God to compel in spiritual causes. But on the contrary,
for saints to endure persecutions and sufferings, rather than Rev. vii. 14,
actually obey, is abundantly by the Lord foretold, re- 15; James i.
warded, and justified, as by the scriptures of the New Testa- 22; 2 Tim. ii.
ment appears.   11, 12.

But if it be objected, that neither the magistrate is to
command, nor the subjects actually to obey any thing but
what is according to the mind of God, it is answered: that
all magistrates suppose whatever they impose to be so; but
the question is, who is to determine? For if the magistrate,
or any other man, or men, have power from God to judge
and determine what is lawful for men to obey, then no room
is left for them to dispute the lawfulness of any of his
commands, it being their duty to obey whatever is commanded; and so as it hath been said before, the cross of
Christ ceases. But if *every one shall give an account for* Rom. xiv. 12,
himself to God, then it reasonably follows, that every man
must judge for himself in matters spiritual. And there- Josh. xxiv.
fore for the magistrate to compel, cannot be warrantable by 15.
scripture or reason.

Again: that the power to judge and determine in spiritual matters is not in a magistrate, as such, Gallio, the
Roman deputy of Achaia, well understood, when *the Jews* Acts xviii.
made insurrection with one accord against Paul, and brought 12, &c.

him to the judgment-seat, saying, This fellow persuadeth men to worship God contrary to the law. Which almost ever since hath been the great cry by all sorts of the national clergy, whose turns it hath been to have the magistrate on their sides, against all others that have differed from them. But Gallio said, *If it were a matter of wrong, or wicked lewdness, O ye Jews, reason would that I should bear with you: but if it be a question of words, and names, and of your law, look ye to it, for I will be no judge of such matters. And he drave them from the judgment-seat.*[4] Which worthy example, if magistrates would be persuaded to follow, by judging and punishing only civil injuries and wrongs, and leaving spiritual differences to be decided, and judged, and punished by Jesus Christ according to the gospel; they would then find themselves and [their] governments quickly free from many inconveniences that now they are involved in, about deciding religious controversies with external force and power.

And now, that no magistrate, although a Christian, hath power to be a lord over another's faith, or by outward force to impose any thing in the worship of God, is also very clear.

1. Because the Lord Jesus himself would never by any outward force compel men to receive him or his doctrine. Luke ix. 54, &c. For when his disciples, supposing they might use violence, as under the law, would have commanded fire to come down from heaven, as Elias did, to consume them that would not receive him, Christ *turned and rebuked them,* saying, *Ye know not what spirit ye are of; for the Son of man is not come to destroy men's lives, but to save them.* And most remarkable doth it appear, that it is not the intent of the Lord Jesus that judgment should be executed on those that

---

[4] But in that he suffered Sosthenes to be beaten he did not well, it being a civil injury.

reject his words, to the punishing them in their bodies and estates in this life, as under the law, from his own sayings, which speak thus : *If any man hear my words, and believe* John xii. 47, *not, I judge him not : for I came not to judge the world, but* 48. *to save the world. He that rejecteth me, and receiveth not my words, hath one that judgeth him ; the word that I have spoken, the same shall judge him at the last day.*

And the apostles also, were so far from propagating the gospel by outward violence and force, that all their proceedings were by entreaty and persuasion; and in case of resistance, to shake the dust from their feet as a witness Matt. x. 14; against their opposers. Acts xiii. 51.

Nor will it avail to say, because the magistrate exercises authority in civil and temporal things, which the Lord Christ would not,[5] that therefore in spiritual things they may do the same; unless it may be supposed [to be] the magistrate's right to have supremacy over the world to come, in all heavenly and eternal things, because God hath given him power over the world that now is, in earthly and temporal things. Which may be conjectured upon as good ground from what is written, as that a magistrate under the gospel dispensation hath more power in spiritual causes, than the Lord Christ or his apostles would exercise. Especially, seeing there is not the least warrant for any such power from Christ or the apostles, from any thing that is written in the scriptures of the New Testament. And *to* [Isa.viii.20.] *the law, and to the testimony; if they speak not according to this word, it is because there is no light in them.*

2. If any men, as Christians, under heaven, have had any such power in the days of the gospel, the apostles and elders in the primitive times must needs have had it. But this they utterly disclaimed. As Paul, *Not for that we* 2 Cor. i. 24.]

---

[5] As the dividing inheritances, &c.

SION'S GROANS.   A A

have dominion over your faith, but are helpers of your joy: for by faith ye stand. Yea, the Lord Jesus, when they strove for domination, forbade it, saying, *Ye know that the princes of the gentiles exercise dominion over them, and they that are great, do exercise authority upon them; but it shall not be so amongst you.* Even so saith Peter, speaking to the elders, *Feed the flock of God which is amongst you, taking the oversight thereof, not by constraint, but willingly ; not for filthy lucre, but of a ready mind ; neither as being lords over God's heritage, but being examples to the flock.*

Matt. xx. 25, 26.

1 Pet. v. 2,3,

Why, therefore, the Christian religion should be built and supported by violence and cruelty, when the foundation was laid, and the work carried on all the apostles' days, and some hundreds of years after, by a quite contrary means, is a question would be resolved by those, whose strongest argument for the support of their religion is, TAKE HIM, JAILOR. For such is the difference between the way which the apostles and primitive saints took in carrying on the work of the gospel, and approving themselves to be the ministers of God, and the way now used by the national clergy; than which nothing is more unlike. They being ambassadors for the Prince of peace, did in his stead beseech and pray the disobedient to be reconciled to God ; never stirring up the nations to ruin and destroy, by external violence, those that opposed them in their ministry. But as the apostle Paul saith, *Being reviled, we bless; being persecuted, we suffer it ; being defamed, we entreat. Giving no offence in any thing, that the ministry be not blamed. But in all things approving ourselves as the ministers of God, in much patience, in afflictions, in necessities, in distresses, in stripes, in imprisonments, in tumults, in labours, in watchings, in fastings; by pureness, by knowledge, by long-suffering, by kindness, by the Holy Ghost, by love unfeigned, &c.*

2 Cor. v. 20.

1 Cor. iv. 12, 13.

2 Cor. vi. 3, &c.

O ye rulers of the world, and inhabitants of the earth!

this was the way the Lord of all things, with his disciples, and followers, took to plant and establish the doctrine of the gospel in the hearts and affections of the sons of men. Be ye not therefore unlike those whom you say you follow, by imposing your doctrines and traditions by the violence of penal laws and edicts, to the imprisoning, banishing, and spoiling the goods of the conscientious; causing them, as the saints of old, to be *destitute, afflicted, and tormented,* Heb. xi. 36, although for their innocency and uprightness, *the world is not worthy of them.* &c.

3 It is very plain, that the Lord Jesus himself, in his Matt. xiii. parable of the tares and wheat, forbids any outward force 24—30, 36— or violence to be exercised upon false worshippers and 43. heretics as such. For by the tares, which he forbids the pulling up, cannot be intended the transgressors of the second table, such as thieves, murderers, or any that should do that civil injury or wrong unto another, which he would not have done unto himself. For all confess, with one consent, that the magistrate's authority reaches such.[6] Neither can it be intended that *the children of the wicked one,* in any sense, that visibly appear to be so, should be tolerated in the church; for that destroys the power of excommunication. That which unavoidably then follows is, that although men are *tares,* or *the children of the wicked one,* by erring in the worship of God, yet should they not be plucked up, but tolerated in the field of the world, until the harvest shall come at *the end of this world;* when the angels who are to be the reapers, and can infallibly distinguish between the tares and the wheat, which no magistrate now can, shall gather the tares in bundles, *and cast them into a furnace of fire; there shall be wailing and gnashing of teeth.*

[6] [" The magistrate's office......and aim must be the suppression of crimes, or of those actions which malignantly affect society." Warburton's Alliance, p. 36.]

A A 2

Which scripture so eminently concludes for a toleration, that the greatest enemies to true liberty have been at a great loss, when they have endeavoured to make it speak some other thing. As that expositor is, who says,[7] "It seems to him, not to note the duty of the civil magistrate, but the event of God's providence, that God would permit the cohabitation of the wicked in the world with the just; not that magistrates or ministers should permit them, and not by civil punishment or ecclesiastical, remove them out of the church or the world."

But if men did not fight against truth, they would not so evidently contradict their own sayings. For who can believe that it should be the mind of God to permit the cohabitation of the wicked in the world with the just, as aforesaid, and yet the magistrate should not permit them, but remove them by civil punishment out of the world? Hath the magistrate power to remove those out of the world, that God would have permitted to live? How soon may a magistrate, if guided by such doctrine, bring the 2Kingsxxiv. blood of the innocent upon himself and nation? And inno-4. cent blood the Lord will not pardon.

It therefore highly concerns all magistrates, before they persecute any for matters of faith or worship, to see they have a better warrant for so doing, than the word of men; Rom. ii. 16. which will not secure them at that day, *when God shall judge the secrets of men by Jesus Christ, according to the gospel.* Which will be found to be the book that shall be Rev. xx. 12. opened, when *the dead, both small and great, shall stand before God,* to be judged by what is written therein, *accord-* [John xii. *ing to their works.*[8] As the Lord Jesus saith, *The word* 48.] [Matt. xiii. *that I have spoken, the same shall judge you at the last day.* 30.]

---

[7] I. T. Supplement, p. 29.
[8] So many as have lived where the word of the gospel comes.

And this is his word, to let both tares and wheat grow together in the field of the world, until the harvest.

4. It can in nowise be safe for magistrates, in the days of the gospel, to persecute and destroy those that are contrary-minded in religious matters, because of their fallibility. And that is the very reason why the Lord Jesus, in the forementioned parable, forbids the gathering up the tares, lest Matt. xiii. 29. the wheat be rooted up along with them. That magistrates may err in spiritual and religious matters, woful experience hath taught the world in all ages. The Lord of life himself was put to death, for supposed blasphemy and wickedness, and accused for being an enemy to Cæsar. Which great mistake was committed through ignorance, as Peter saith, *And* Acts iii. 17. *now, brethren, I wot that through ignorance ye did it, as did also your rulers.* And at this day, what mistakes are continued in magistrates about religion ! Some being Calvinists, as in Holland and Geneva ; in Europe, more Lutherans ; but the greatest part, papists. And each of these condemneth, and many times persecuteth the other for heresy, or superstition.

Unavoidably, therefore, it follows, that some of these must err. But we need not go far for the proof of this in one and the same person, who receives that at one time for truth, which at another time must be persecuted for error. This appeared notably in king Henry VIII. who persecuted the protestants to death, and wrote against Luther, for which the pope gave him the title of Defender of the Faith.[9]

[9] [" When Martin Luther had uttered the abominations of the pope and his clergy, with God's word, and divers books were come into England, our Cardinal (Wolsey) thought to find a remedy against that well enough, and sent to Rome for this vain title, Defender of the Faith, which the vicar of Croydon preached, that the king's grace would not lose for all London, and twenty miles round about it. Neither is it marvel, for it had cost more than London and forty miles about it is able to make, I think, at this hour ; beside the effusion of innocent blood that was offered unto the

And yet a while after he received some of Luther's doctrines, and rejected the supremacy and authority of the pope, and served the papists as he did the protestants.

Nor will magistrates be the more free from mistakes, by relying on the authority of synods, popes, or general councils, because such eminent contradictions and oppositions have appeared amongst each of them, that nothing is more uncertain than their conclusions.[1]   As for general councils, whose authority is in the greatest estimation of the three, it is plain, they are so far from being infallible, that their decrees have been not only directly opposite to plain texts of scripture, and the practice of the primitive church, but also against each other.   Which appeared first in the council of Constance, in the thirteenth session; where it was decreed, that the Lord's supper should be given but in one kind, when nothing is more plain than that the Lord Jesus instituted it; the apostle afterwards delivered it to the Corinthians, and the primitive church received it, with both the bread and the cup.[2]

Matt. xxvi. 26, 27.
1 Cor. xi. 24, 25.

So for the council of Trent, to decree that the service in the church should be performed in Latin,[3] how contrary is it to the doctrine of Paul, who said, *In the church he had rather speak five words with understanding, that he might teach others, than ten thousand words in an unknown tongue.* So also have they clashed one with another.   The council of Trent allowing picturing of God the Father, the council

1 Cor. xiv. 19.

---

idol, and daily is offered thereto." Tyndale's Pract. of Prelates, Works, i. 483.]

[1] As Jer. Taylor, now bishop of Down, in his Liberty of Proph. Sect. vi. at large proves. [Edit. Lond. 4to. 1647.]

[2] [" In the preface of the decree,

Christ's institution and the practice of the primitive church is expressed— *licet Christus in utraque specie, et licet ecclesia primitiva,* &c.—and then with a *non obstante,* communion in one kind is established."   Lib. of Prophesying, Sect. vi. No. 2, p. 156.]

[3] [Ibid.]

of Nice altogether disallowing it.[4]   And in the great
Arian controversy, which was no circumstantial business,
how many councils and conventions, were both for and
against it.

As little reliance can be put on any supposed infallibility the pope may have, there having been two or three
at one time, each raging against the other with their censures and decrees.[5]   And notorious it is what dissension
there was amongst the popes and cardinals about pope
Formosus; who, being first bishop of Pontignac, was de-
graded by pope John VIII., and made to take an oath to
lead a secular life all his days.   Yet, by pope Martin, that
succeeded John, was Formosus released from his oath,
restored to his bishoprick, and afterwards came to be pope,
and so continued five years, making several decrees.   But
Stephen VI. coming to the popedom, abrogates the decrees
of Formosus, takes up his body, cuts off two of his fingers,
throws them into the river Tiber, and then buries him in
a layman's sepulchre.

Next to Stephen, succeeds Romanus; who, on the other
hand, repeals the acts and decrees of his predecessor
Stephen, against Formosus.   And pope John X. in a
synod at Ravenna, ratifies all the decrees and doings of
Formosus.   Yet, after all this, comes pope Sergius, digs
up again Formosus, cuts off his head and three more of his
fingers, and throws his body into the Tiber, and likewise

---

[4] [Ibid. Sect. vi. No. 2, p. 156.]

[5] Benedict. Silvester III. Gregory
VI. [Benedict. IX. is said to have
obtained the papacy by magical arts,
his oppressive and cruel conduct led
to his deposition by the Roman people. By large bribes Silvester obtained the papal chair, which he
occupied for forty-nine days only, his
rival overthrowing his authority by
force.   Again pope Benedict completed the infamy of his character by
selling the papal crown to Gregory,
whose skill had been of essential service to him, and gave himself up to
luxury and debauchery.   Magdeburg.
Centur. Cent. xi. p. 279, 280, tom.
iii.]

deposed all such as had been consecrated by him. All
which schisms and dissensions make it plain to the world,
that there is nothing of infallibility in the popes.[6]

And for national conventions and synods, they are so
far from any show of infallibility, that the same complexion
and temper the nation is of, wherein they are called, and
have their promotions, you shall be sure to find them of;
because they have their dependency on the authority that
calls them together. So that although the last national
synod in this nation would have established presbytery,
because then that was most like to take, yet it is very
questionable, if now a convention were called, whether it
will be much talked of amongst them.

Then this must be concluded from all : that seeing
magistrates themselves, general councils, popes, or national
synods, may err in judging and determining the most
weighty controversies in religion ; there can be, therefore,
no security for a magistrate that he doth well in persecuting,
or putting to death, the contrary-minded in religious matters;
seeing, through mistake, he may as soon persecute, or put
to death, the true followers of the Lord Jesus as any other.
Yea, in [all] likelihood, much sooner, because they, in conscience towards God, cannot receive the inventions and
traditions of men in the worship of God, but must be a
witness for the eternal God against them. For which they
are accounted, as the saints of old, pestilent fellows, movers
of sedition, turners of the world upside down, enemies to
Cæsar, and upon this account persecuted. When the
greatest part of men being unregenerate, and having no
other spirit in them but what is of the world, there is
therefore no reason why the world should persecute and
hate his own.

Acts xxiv
5 ; xvii. 6,
7.

5. For magistrates to inflict temporal punishments upon

---

[6] Fox's Acts and Mon. p. 188, [vol. 1, edit. 1641.]

any of their subjects, for not conforming to their decrees that enjoin any spiritual worship or service, is undoubtedly a breach of that royal law, which says, *Whatsoever ye would* Matt.vii. 12. *that men should do to you, do you even so to them, for this is the law and the prophets.* And it is a sure and standing rule, by which all men, if they would deal ingenuously by themselves, might measure the justice of their proceedings towards others. For who, that was not a desperate enemy to himself, would put out another man's eye, if he were [Lev. xxiv. 20 ; Matt. v. 38.] sure his own should be put out as soon as he had done, as he was to be served by the judicial law? Neither would those that are forward to persecute be very zealous in their proceedings, if they were sure that those whom they persecute should have power on their sides, to mete the same mea- [Matt.vii.2.] sure unto them.

And this is worthy of observation, that this rule of doing as we would be done unto, can be received and pleaded by all sorts of men, whilst they are under affliction and persecution; but who remembers it, when they have power to afflict and persecute others? The papists themselves, when out of power, in this and other nations, can plead against persecution for their conscience, as they did in the reign of queen Elizabeth,[7] procuring the letters of the emperor, and other princes to intercede for some places to be allowed where they might worship by themselves. But in this they desired more than themselves would allow to

---

[7] Cambden's Annals of Eliz. p. 20. [Hoc tempore quum Imperator et Catholici Principes crebris literis intercederent, ut clementer cum episcopis abdicatis ageretur, et templa in urbibus seorsim pontificiis permitterentur, respondit. . . . Templa in quibus sua divina officia seorsim celebrent, salva republica, et illæso honore atque conscientia, concedere non posse. Nihil aliud esset, quam religionem ex religione serere, mentes bonorum varie distrahere, factiosorum studia alere, religionem atque rempublicam conturbare, et divina humanaque commiscere. Camdeni Annales, p. 52, tom. i. ed. 1717.]

others when in power. So many of the protestants, where
the magistrate is different from them in religion,[8] can be well
pleased with a toleration.   And Martin Luther, in his
sermon of the good Shepherd, Englished by W. G. in the
year 1581, speaking of the kingdom of Christ, saith, "It
is not governed at all by any force or power, but by outward preaching alone, that is by the gospel."[9]

Why, therefore, cannot the protestants, who would seem
to have an honourable esteem of this man, be of the same
spirit.   And the papists be as much for liberty in prosperity as in adversity, seeing the Lord Jesus hath not
directed at one time, to the use of force and violence, in
the work of the gospel; and at another time, if the civil
sword be not to be procured, then to use arguments and
persuasions.   No, at all times the rule which his disciples
must take notice of, says, *Whatsoever ye would that men
should do to you, do you even so to them.*   For *with what
measure ye mete, it shall be measured to you again.*

And because Mystery, Babylon, hath not regarded
these sayings, but exerciseth all manner of cruelties and
deaths upon such as cannot believe as she believes and
practices; therefore God will find a way to retaliate upon
her all the blood of his servants.   And *in the cup which she
hath filled,* shall it be filled *to her double.   How much she
hath glorified herself, and lived deliciously, so much torment
and sorrow give her ; for she saith in her heart, I sit a queen,
and am no widow, and shall see no sorrow.   Therefore shall her
plagues come in one day, death, and mourning, and famine,*

Matt. vii. 12.

Matt. vii. 1, 2.

Rev. xviii. 6, &c.

---

[8] As in France.

[9] ["Not having met with the translation referred to, the original old
German is subjoined:—" Und das es
nit regiert wirt mit ainiger gwalt, son-
der durch die müntliche predig, das
ist durchs Euangelium."   Ain Sermon D. Martini Luthers auff das
Euangelion Johañ. x.   Von dem
guten hyrten. Durch jn überlesen
MDxxiii.]

and she shall be utterly burnt with fire, for strong is the Lord who judgeth her. *And the kings of the earth, who have committed fornication, and lived deliciously with her, shall bewail and lament for her.* And her merchants, which are the great men of the earth, who traffic with her in things costly, delicate, and of esteem in the world, *and in slaves and souls of men ;* or, as by the margin it may be read, *bodies and souls of men,* these also shall *mourn over her : for no man buyeth their merchandize any more.* And thus the fierceness of God's wrath will overtake her, to the sinking of her like a millstone into the bottom of the sea, because the great weight of innocent blood lieth upon her. For in her will be *found the blood of prophets, and of saints, and of all that were slain upon the earth.*

He that therefore would not partake with her in any of her plagues, let him flee from her, and partake not with her in any of her sins ; one of the greatest being the persecution of men for keeping a good conscience. For except the great God should cease to be what he is, if men repent not of their deeds, there will be as certainly punishment as there is sin. And it will not be the arm of flesh that will be able to support this strumpet, although many kingdoms should engage in her quarrel ; neither shall the wisdom and prudence of great statesmen be able to keep off her judgments ; for if men should cease to do any thing against her, yet God will make the very elements to fight against her, and will contend with her by famine and pestilence, yea, and sword too, although she fears it not ; for God will [Rev. xvii. 16.] stir up the ten kings to do his will upon her, and by his great works, and judgments, that he will manifest in the earth, will he gain himself a name, and great honour, and glory. Even so. Amen.

As it is no wise lawful from the word of God for Christian magistrates, in the days of the gospel, to destroy and root out the contrary-minded in religious matters, though idolaters, so such proceedings may sometimes prove inconsistent with the very being of nations. For suppose any nation were wholly heathenish idolaters, and the word of God coming in amongst them, should convert the chief magistrate, and one-twentieth part of the nation more, must he then, with that twentieth part, destroy all the other nineteen, if they will not be converted, but continue in their heathenish idolatry? It cannot possibly be supposed to be warrantable.

And this reason holds good, likewise, against the rooting up and destroying heretics out of the world; because if the church proceeds against any of her members to excommunication, the church's deportment towards him so cast out, is to be the same as towards an heathen. So saith Matt. xviii. 17. Christ himself, *If he neglect to hear the church, let him be unto thee as an heathen man, and a publican;* who, for the aforesaid reason, is not to be destroyed because he is so. And moreover, seeing the Lord, who is abundantly merciful, many times gives repentance, not only to the unbelieving idolater, but also to the excommunicated person; he therefore that destroys the body of such an one, doth, as in him lieth, destroy the soul also. For the Lord, you [Matt. xx. 1—6.] see, brings into his vineyard some at the third hour, some at the sixth, some at the ninth, and others at the eleventh. He, therefore, that shall destroy any at the third, or sixth hour of the life, hinders his conversion, that possibly may be called at the ninth or eleventh hour, and so may be charged with bringing eternal loss and damage to him whom he destroys.

OBJECTION. But whereas the example of the kings of Israel and Judah is made the greatest pillar to support the magistrates' proceedings under the gospel, in persecuting and punishing the contrary-minded in religious matters,

or such as shall be adjudged guilty of blasphemy or idolatry; therefore, the second canon of the English church
tells us, "Whosoever shall affirm that the king's majesty
hath not the same authority in causes ecclesiastical, that
the godly kings had amongst the Jews, shall be excommunicated." But if magistrates would defer persecuting any
man for religion, until the clergy had proved this unto
them, it would be happy for the most conscientious under
them, and themselves too.

ANSWER. But in answer, we deny not but the kings of the
Jews had power to punish idolaters and blasphemers, and
some other transgressors of the then law of God: which
power was given them of God, and written in plain precepts,
in the Mosaical law. But who tells them that magistrates
under the gospel dispensation hath such power? Hath the
Lord Jesus said any such thing? Or if he have, where is
it written? Nay, where is it written from the beginning
of Genesis to the end of the Revelations, that magistrates
under the gospel should have the same power in religious
causes, as those under the law? If the judicial law be a
rule for magistrates under the gospel to walk by, then
why must it be mangled in pieces, and just so much
taken of it as suits their interest, and all the rest rejected?
Is it left to magistrates now, or was it ever left to the
Jewish kings, to take what part of it they please to be a
rule to them, and reject all the rest?

And it is eminently remarkable, how this plea is by the
clergy themselves, that most contend for it, made altogether
invalid; for by it they will stir up the civil magistrate to
punish those that dissent from them about the doctrine and
worship, under the notion of a blasphemer or heretic; and
against such this law must be held authentic. But he that [Exod. xxi.
15, 16, 17;
smiteth, or curseth his father or mother, or stealeth a man, Lev. xx. 10;
Exod. xxxi.
or him that committeth adultery, or breaketh the sabbath, 14.]

who were all [of] them sure to be put to death by the same judicial law; yet in these cases they will not tell the magistrate it is any rule; but it is to be rejected, because here they cannot much make it reach their supposed heretics, who they are more jealous of than any of the afore-mentioned offenders.

But, besides, it is observable, that the kings of the Jews, all the time they kept to the law of God, had advantages to give righteous judgment in spiritual causes, which magistrates under the gospel have not. For they had that standing oracle of God amongst them, the Urim and Thummim, together with extraordinary prophets, which in all difficult cases they had recourse unto, and would infallibly direct them to judge according to the mind of God. But when these kings became wicked, and lost the benefit of the above-said oracle, and extraordinary prophets: then, although they had the written law amongst them, did they run headlong into such gross mistakes, that the true prophets of the Lord were sure to be persecuted. And those prophets which would prophesy smooth things unto them, were cherished, although many times, by hearkening unto them, they lost their kingdoms, lives, and it is to be feared, souls and all.

[1 Kings xviii. 17; xxii. 27.] How grossly did Ahab mistake, when he accounted Elijah the troubler of Israel; and caused poor Micaiah to be imprisoned, and fed with bread and water of affliction, because he would not help to deceive him, as his four Jer. xxxviii. 4—6. hundred time-serving prophets had done? [1] So Jeremiah was accused for seeking the hurt of his nation, and not the welfare, and must be put in a miry dungeon, because he in plainness delivered the mind of the Lord to the king,

---

[1] Four hundred false prophets must eat bread at Jezebel's table, when Micaiah must have bread and water of affliction.

his princes and people.[2] How, therefore, can the gentile rulers assure themselves they do any better than these rulers did, if they shall persecute the contrary-minded in religious matters; seeing they have neither an infallible oracle to inquire at, nor extraordinary prophet, nor yet such written precepts, as the Jews under the Mosaical law had; that did not only direct them what offenders should be punished, but also what the particular punishment to every several offence should be?

Furthermore, it is very plain, that the gospel which we live under, is clearly another dispensation, far different in all its ordinances and administrations from the law, under which the Lord Jesus is the only. Lawgiver, who doth not, as Moses, proceed against the transgressors of his precepts by external force and power, to the destroying them in their bodies and estates in this life; but in long- 1 Thess. v. 9; suffering waits on men, not willing they should perish, but 2 Pet. iii. 9. Acts xvii.31. rather that they should repent and be saved. And when any continue in disobedience to the gospel, his punishment is eternal in the world to come. Therefore, as the apostle [1 Cor. iv. 5.] Paul saith: *Judge nothing before the time, until the Lord come; who will bring to light hidden things of darkness, and will make manifest the counsels of the hearts; and then shall every man have praise of God.* The same apostle testifieth of himself, that he was *a blasphemer and a persecutor;* and 1 Tim. i. 13. if the mind of God had been, that he should have suffered death in that condition, how should he have had repentance given him, and been such a glorious instrument in the church, as afterwards he was?

And it is too well known, that the Jews are the great blasphemers against our Lord Jesus Christ, that are on earth. Yet it is not the mind of the Lord, they should be destroyed from the face of the earth. For how then

---

[2] As it hath been in our day.

should the scripture be fulfilled, wherein God hath promised to call them, and make them the most glorious
nation on the earth? Or how can they be converted, if
they be not permitted, where the gospel is preached?
We speak not this in favour of any blasphemy, for our
souls abhor it; but because all men that have power in
their hands, might be as tender of the lives of men, as the
most righteous and holy God is; who would have men be
imitators of himself, in mercy and goodness towards others,
[Matt. v. and *maketh his sun to rise on the evil and on the good, and*
45.]   *sendeth rain on the just and on the unjust.*

If it shall still be objected, that it is inconsistent with
the safety and well-being of any nation, to allow or tolerate
any more ways of worship than one: we answer, experience hath taught the contrary to several countries of
Europe: as France, and the United Provinces, and several countries of Germany. Besides, those that say they
are the servants of God, should conclude that to be most
for the safety and well-being of their countries, which
is most agreeable to his heavenly will, declared in his
word.

It was the ruin of Jeroboam, and almost all the kings of
Israel that succeeded him, that they would rather act by
corrupt principles of state policy than by the word which
God had spoken. And although God had rent ten tribes
from Rehoboam, and given them to him, yet he wanted
faith to believe his new kingdom could any ways be secured to him, or kept from going back to the lineage of
David, unless he devised some new way of worship, to
keep the people in their own land. And for his so doing,
he thought he had much reason of state. For what prince
now will conclude it good policy, to permit his people to
go up yearly into his enemy's chief city to worship; but
will conclude it to be a notable way to alienate the affec-

tions of his subjects from him, to his great prejudice and detriment? Thus Jeroboam reasons, as by his words appears. Take them at length.

And Jeroboam said in his heart, Now shall the kingdom 1 Kings xii. 26—28. *return to the house of David: if this people go up to do sacrifice in the house of the Lord at Jerusalem, then shall the heart of this people turn again unto their land, even unto Rehoboam, king of Judah, and they shall kill me. Whereupon the king took counsel, and made two calves of gold, and said to them, It is too much for you to go up to Jerusalem: behold thy gods, O Israel, which brought thee out of the land of Egypt.* Which policy of his procured this event, which God denounced against him, saying, *I will bring evil upon* 1 Kings xiv 10, 11. *the house of Jeroboam, and will cut off from Jeroboam him that pisseth against the wall, and him that is shut up and left in Israel, and will take away the remnant of the house of Jeroboam, as a man taketh away dung, till it be all gone.* And for the sin wherein he made Israel to sin, is he branded to all posterity.

But, on the other hand, had he permitted the people to go up to Jerusalem to worship, and kept the appointments of God, though seemingly against his present interest; then had the promise of God been made good unto him, which the prophet Ahijah declared long before he came to the kingdom, saying, *And it shall be, if thou wilt hearken* 1 Kings xi. 38. *unto all that I command thee, and wilt walk in my ways, and do that is right in my sight, to keep my statutes and commandments, as David my servant did; that I will be with thee, and build thee a sure house, as I built for David, and will give Israel unto thee.* Which things were written for the example of such, as should come after. *Be wise now, therefore, O ye kings; be instructed, ye judges of the earth. Serve* Ps. ii. 10—12. *the Lord with fear, and rejoice with trembling. Kiss the Son, lest he be angry, and ye perish from the way, when his wrath*

SION'S GROANS.]   B B

is kindled but a little.   Blessed are all they that put their trust in him.

We shall take leave to mind and keep in memory the liberty of tender consciences, which the king's majesty declared from Breda.   And shall yet live in hope and expectation to be partakers of the benefit thereof ; being reasonably persuaded, that the same principle that led his majesty to assert such Christian liberty, still remains with him, to the allowing and protecting his peaceable subjects in their religious concernments.   Humbly praying, that God may order his heart, and the hearts of his great council, to proclaim liberty by a law, and the opening of the prisons to them that are bound.

That these desires may not seem novel, or suggested by us in the day of our distress, we have herewith inserted the testimony of the ancients ; which we have collected out of Dr. Jer. Taylor's " Liberty of Prophesying;" which we pray may be impartially considered.

It is observable, that restraining of liberty, " imposing upon other men's understanding, being masters of their consciences, and lording it over their faith, came in with the retinue and train of antichrist.   That is, they came as other abuses and corruptions of the church did, by reason of the iniquity of the times, and cooling of the first heats of Christianity, and the increase of interest, and the abatement of Christian simplicity: when the church's fortune became better, and her sons grew worse, and some of her fathers worst of all.   For in the first three hundred years, there was no sign of persecuting any man for his opinion, though at that time there were very horrid opinions commenced.   For they then were assaulted by new sects, which destroyed the common principles of nature, of Christianity, of innocence, and public society.   And they who used all the means, Christian and spiritual, for their disprovement and conviction, thought not of using corporal force, otherwise than by blaming such proceedings." [3]

" To which I add, that all wise princes, till they were overborne with faction, or solicited by peevish persons, gave toleration to differing sects, [whose opinions] did not disturb the public interest." [4]

" And the experience which Christendom hath had in this last age, is argument enough, that toleration of differing opinions is so far from disturbing the public peace, or destroying the interest of princes and commonwealths, that it does advantage to the public. It secures peace, because there is not so much as the pretence of religion left to persons to contend for it, being already indulged to them. When the French fought against the Huguenots, the spilling of her own blood was argument enough, of the imprudence of that way of promoting religion. But since she hath given permission to them, the world is witness, how prosperous she hath been ever since." [5]

" Indeed, there is great reason for princes to give toleration to disagreeing persons, whose opinions by fair means cannot be altered. For if the persons be confident, they will serve God according to their pretensions; and if they be publicly prohibited, they will privately convene." [6]

" And it is also a part of Christian religion, that the liberty of men's consciences should be preserved in all things, where God hath not set a limit or made a restraint; that the soul of man should be free, and acknowledge no master but Jesus Christ; that matters spiritual should not be restrained by punishments corporal; and that the same meekness and charity should be preserved in the promotion of Christianity, that gave it foundation and

[3] [Pages 18, 19. Epist. Ded. 4to. Lond. 1647.]
[4] [Page 19.]
[5] [Page 21.]
[6] [Page 22.]

B B 2

increment, and firmness, in the first publication; that conclusions should not be more dogmatical than the virtual resolution and efficacy of the premises; and that the persons should not more certainly be condemned, than their opinions confuted; and lastly, that the infirmities of men, and difficulties of things, should be both put in balance, to make abatement in the definitive sentence against men's persons." [7]

" And therefore the best of men, and most glorious of princes, were always ready to give toleration, but never to make executions, for matters disputable: as Eusebius, in his second book of the life of Constantine, reports." [8]

Also, king James, writing to the states of the United Provinces, [in his letters] dated the 6th of March, 1613, among other things, saith; "that you charge them to maintain peace, by bearing one with another, in such differences of opinions and judgments." [9] . . . "The like counsel in the divisions of Germany, at the first reformation, was thought reasonable by the emperor Ferdinando, and his excellent son Maximilian. For they had observed that violence did exasperate, was unblessed, unsuccessful, and unreasonable; and therefore they made decrees of toleration, and appointed tempers and expedients to be drawn up by discreet persons. And Emanuel Philibert, duke of Savoy, repenting of his war, undertaken for religion against the Piedmontani, promised them toleration, and was as good as his word. As much is done by the nobility of Polonia. So that the best princes and best bishops gave toleration and impunities." [1]

Also in Rome itself, " till the time of Justinian the

[7] [Page 215.]   [8] [Page 22.]   istâ opinionum ac sententiarum dis-
[9] [" ...... ac districtè imperetis ut   crepantiâ," p. 23.]
pacem colant se invicem tolerando in   [1] [Pages 23, 24.]

emperor, A.D. 525, the catholics and Novatians had churches indifferently permitted." [2]

" And the popes were the first preachers of force and violence in matters of religion; and yet it came not so far as death. But the first that preached that doctrine was Dominic, the founder of the begging order of friars, the friars preachers; in memory of which the inquisition is intrusted only to the friars of his order." [3]

" In England, although the pope had as great power here as any where, yet there were no executions for matter of opinion, until Henry the Fourth, who, because he usurped the crown, was willing by all means to endear the clergy, by destroying their enemies, that so he might be sure of them to all his purposes. And, indeed, it may become them well enough, who are wiser in their generations than the children of light. It may possibly serve the policies of evil persons, but never the pure and chaste designs of Christianity." [4]

" By this time, I hope it will not be thought reasonable to say, he that teacheth mercy to erring persons, teacheth indifferency in religion; unless so many fathers, and so many churches, and the best of emperors, and all the world, till they were abased by tyranny, popery, and faction, did teach indifferency. For I have shown that Christianity does not punish corporally persons erring spiritually, but indeed popery does; . . . and hath done ever since they were taught it by their St. Dominic." [5]

" And yet after all this, I have something more to exempt myself from the clamour of this objection. For let all errors be as much and as zealously suppressed as may be, but let it be done by such means as are proper

---

[2] [Page 25.]
[3] [Page 26.]
[4] [Page 27.]
[5] [Page 28.]

instruments of their suppression, by preaching and disputation, so that neither of them breed disturbance, by
charity and sweetness, by holiness of life, assiduity of
exhortation, by the word of God and prayer. For these
ways are most natural, most prudent, most peaceable, and
effectual. Only let not men be hasty in calling every dis-
liked opinion by the name of heresy : and when they have
resolved that they will call it so, let them use the erring
person like a brother; not beat him like a dog, nor convince him with a gibbet, nor vex him out of his understanding and persuasion." [6]

" Why are we so zealous against those we call heretics,
and yet great friends with drunkards, and fornicators, and
swearers, and intemperate, and idle persons? I am certain
that a drunkard is as contrary to God, and lives as contrary
to the laws of Christianity, as a heretic. And I am also
sure that I know what drunkenness is ; but I am not sure,
that such an opinion is heresy," &c.[7] Thus far Dr. Taylor, now Bishop of Down.

Now whereas we have given publicly an account of the
former ages, in their carriages and behaviours towards persons differing in judgment in religious things; we take the
leave humbly to desire, and beg the same privilege, as was
granted unto the Waderdopers, by the prince and state of
the Netherlands:[8] which was to admit a public dispute,
between the ministers and the persons aforesaid, in the
presence of the prince. Which we humbly conceive is but
a reasonable request.

[6] [Pages 28, 29.]
[7] [Page 38.]
[8] [Two of these disputations took
place in the Netherlands in the years
1578 and 1596. The first at Emb-
den, the last at Leeuwarden. They
were afterwards published under the
title, De Protocollis, with a disputation which had taken place at Frank-
enthal, in the palatinate, in the year
1571. Schyn's Plenior Deductio
Hist. Mennonitarum, p. 223.]

ADDENDA.

ADDENDA.

A.

NOTE ON THE FAMILY OF LOVE.

Pages 113, 147, 164.

THE Family of Love had its origin in the fancies of Henry
Nicholas, a Westphalian, who about the year 1556 began to
propagate his sentiments in Amsterdam, where for a long time he
abode. (Hoornbeek, Summa Controv. lib. vi. p. 393.) His followers were early discovered in England, the chief of whom was
Christopher Vitells, a joiner by trade. By him the sect was
propagated in Essex and Cambridgeshire. In the latter county
they "did very much increase, and united themselves into a kind
of church, with officers. And the chief elders of the *lovely
fraternity*, some of them were weavers, some basket-makers, some
musicians, some bottle-makers, and such other like ; which by
travelling from place to place did get their livings ;.....running and
frisking from place to place, (they) stayed not any where long, save
where they light upon some simple husbandman, whose wealth was
greater than his wit." (Strype's Annals, II. i. 487, ii. 285.) In
the year 1575, an Apology was presented by them to the parliament, which contains, "A brief rehearsal of the belief of the
good-willing in England, which are named the Family of Love."
In this they deny the many accusations made against them,
" standing," they say, " bound to love the same God of life, with
all our heart, soul, and might, and our neighbour as ourselves."
Still it would appear they allowed of going to mass, if any of the

fraternity should happen to dwell in a place where the magistrate
commanded it, notwithstanding they "utterly detested all superstitious papistry." (Strype, Annals, II. i. 557, 561.) In 1577
many of the works of Nicholas were published in this country,
especially " The choice letters of H. N. which he by the Holy
Spirit of love hath set forth," &c.   His most famous book was
called *Evangelium Regni ;* in which he declares, " That the day
of the Lord (by him preached) is the appearance of our Lord Jesus
Christ in the resurrection from the dead...Further, he saith, he is
the angel of the Lord, or messenger before him, for to prepare his
way, and to publish an everlasting *evangelie*...He maketh the day
of publishing his *evangelie* to be the last coming of Christ in judgment with thousands of saints.   The day of the *love* is the last
coming of Christ...God raised him up from the death, anointed
him with his godly being, named himself with him, godded him
with himself."   These sentiments found vigorous opponents in
Mr. W. Wilkinson, and J. Knewstubs; the former of whom is
accused by one of the Family, as having " out of a malicious mind
perverted the sense and true mind of the author, and framed sundry of them into errors."   (Strype, Annals, II. ii. 149, 287, 301.)
John Rogers, in " The displaying of an horrible sect of gross and
wicked heretics, calling themselves the Family of Love," tells us,
that H. N. had in 1578 as many as 1000 followers in England.
This number is probably underrated, for in the following year the
privy council took measures to hinder their further progress.
For this purpose a form of abjuration was prepared and tendered
to them ; " Whosoever teacheth, that the dead which are fallen
asleep in the Lord, rise up in this day of his judgment, and appear
unto us in godly glory, which shall henceforth live in us everlastingly with Christ, and reign upon the earth, is a detestable
heretic.   Whosoever teacheth, that to be born of the virgin Mary
out of the seed of David, after the flesh, is to be expounded of the
pure doctrine out of the seed of love, is a detestable heretic.   Whosoever teacheth, that Jesus Christ is come unto us according to his
promise, to the end that all they which love God and his righteousness, and Christ and perfect being, might presently enter into true

rest, which God has prepared from the beginning for his elect, and inherit the everlasting life, is a detestable heretic." This was accompanied by a proclamation, that all suspected persons should be severely dealt with, and if any books were found upon them, imprisoned, their books and writings destroyed and burnt. (Documentary Annals, i. 392, 396.) At the same time, the Convocation, by letters patent from the Privy Council, were directed to take the matter into consideration. (Strype's Grindal. p. 383.) The sect continued, however, to propagate its sentiments, and to find converts, among whom were two daughters of one Warwick. To these two "maidens," H. N. dedicated an epistle, which was, in 1608, replied to by H. Ainsworth. In the year 1604, the Familists presented a petition to king James I. in which they " utterly disclaim and detest all the absurd and self-conceited opinions, and disobedient and erroneous sorts of the anabaptists, Brown, Penry, puritans, and all other proud-minded sects and heresies." They complain of the slanderous accusations made against them, and for which, though unproved, many of them were cast into prison, to their "great hindrance and discredit." From this "hard dealing" they pray to be delivered, offering to give every satisfaction to his majesty, by consultation or examination of their writings, by learned men skilled in the same. (Fuller's Ch. Hist. iii. 205.) They continued, however, under the ban of the law, until they were finally absorbed among the numerous parties of the Commonwealth.

The following extracts from the writings of Henry Nicholas, will give a far better idea of the nature of his sentiments, and his unintelligible manner of stating them, than any general description can possibly do. His "Evangelium Regni" thus commences ;— " H. Nicholas, through the grace and mercy of God, through the Holy Spirit of the love of Jesus Christ : raised up by the highest God from the death, according to the providence of God, and his promises : anointed with the Holy Ghost, in the old age of the holy understanding of Jesus Christ ; godded with God in the Spirit of his love,—elected to be a minister of the gracious word, which is now in the last times raised up by God, according to his promises

in the most holy service of God, under the obedience of his love."
(Fuller, iii. 519.) In a work entitled " An Introduction to the
Holy Understanding of the glass of righteousnes; set forth by
H. N." is the following development of his doctrine:—" C. 5,
No. 28. Behold this same holy being of God is indeed the right
food of the soul and bread of life, and is descended unto us from
heaven for a life to the man ; and was heretofore broken and distributed to the people of Israel and to the disciples of Christ to
feed on in their souls....33. Behold that same bread or body of
Christ is the Word that became flesh, and it dwelt among them....
34. *And the same is the New Testament* which God in those days
made and appointed with his people....Unto all that believed was
the resurrection from the dead, and everlasting life, witnessed and
promised through Jesus Christ. In sure and firm hope whereof
the upright believers have rested in the Lord Jesus Christ, till the
appearing of his coming, *which is now, in the day of the Love, revealed out of the heavenly Being.* With which Jesus Christ the
former believers of Christ, who were fallen asleep, rested or died
in him are *now manifested in glory.*" (Keble's Hooker, vol. i.
note, pp. 148, 149.) His Epistle, sent unto the two daughters of
Warwick, thus begins : " The wisdom of the Father through the
love of Christ in the power of the Holy Ghost, in the second birth
out of the new life of the heavenly being, be unto every one which
with an impartial heart seeketh the godliness in Jesus Christ to a
hearty salvation." In the course of his reply, Ainsworth gives us
the following from his other works : " The God of heaven, as the
Father himself is come down, and he bringeth in the service of his
love, himself with his Christ and his Holy Ghost, and with all that
which with him is God's : unto his obedient man, H. N. and
godding the same with him, he hath manned him with the same,
and his will is, that now in the last time, through his service of
love, all people or generations of men, which are good-willing to his
righteousness, should assemble them unto him, and his godded
man....to the end that they all should become of one being with
him and his godded man, and so be all named gods." (Ainsworth's
Refutation, 1608, pp. 9, 16.) Very much more of this rhapsody,

if not blasphemy, might be quoted. Hooker has perhaps well stated the principles of Nicholas, in whose works, he says, "that 'Christ' doth not signify any one person, but a quality whereof many are partakers: that to be 'raised,' is nothing else but to be regenerated, or indued with the said quality; and that when separation of them which have it, from them which have it not, is here made, this is judgment." (Hanbury's Hooker, i. 29.) It is evident that the Familists had nothing in common with the baptists, with whom they were often unfairly associated by opponents.

B.

Page 156.

The views of Mr. John Robinson appear to be here referred to, who, in his work, "Of Religious Communion, Private and Public," &c. writes as follows :—"I come to the thing I aim at in this whole discourse, which is, that we who profess a separation from the English national, provincial, diocesan, and parochial church and churches, in the whole formal state and order thereof, may, notwithstanding, lawfully communicate in private prayer, and other the like holy exercises, not performed in their church communion, nor by their church power and ministry, with the godly amongst them, though remaining; of infirmity members of the same church or churches, except some other extraordinary bar come in the way between them and us."

" As we are, then, to join ourselves with them wherein God hath joined us, so are we wherein he severeth us to sequester and sever ourselves. . . . . . If the parish assemblies, gathered by compulsion of all the parishioners promiscuously, be of God, then is our fellowship, only of persons sanctified, at least outwardly, joining themselves by voluntary profession under the government and ministry of an eldership ; conceiving prayers and thanksgivings according to the church's present occasions, by the teachings of the Spirit, and so administering the sacraments according to the simplicity of the gospel, not of God, nor from heaven. If on the contrary, ours be of God and of his Christ, then is theirs of antichrist." Pp. 2, 17. See also Hanbury's Historical Memorials, i. 259, 260.

C.

FROM THE CONFESSION OF FAITH PUBLISHED IN 1611.

Page 179.

Of the Incarnation of Christ.

VIII. That JESUS CHRIST, the Son of God, the second person, or subsistence in the Trinity, in the fulness of time was manifested in the flesh, being the seed of David, and of the Israelites, according to the flesh, the son of Mary the virgin, made of her substance, by the power of the Holy Ghost overshadowing her; and being thus true man, was like unto us in all things, sin only excepted, being one person in two distinct natures, TRUE GOD, and TRUE MAN.

Of Magistracy.

XXIV. That MAGISTRACY is a holy ordinance of God, that every soul ought to be subject to it, not for fear only, but for conscience' sake. Magistrates are the ministers of God for our wealth, they bear not the sword for nought. They are the ministers of God, to take vengeance on them that do evil. That it is a fearful sin to speak evil of them that are in dignity, and to despise government. We ought to pay tribute, custom, and all other duties. That we are to pray for them, for God would have them saved, and come to the knowledge of his truth. And therefore they may be members of the church of Christ, retaining their magistracy; for no ordinance of God debarreth any from being a member of Christ's church. They bear the sword of God, which sword, in all lawful administrations, is to be defended and supported by the servants of God that are under their government, with their lives, and all that they have, according as in the first institution of that holy ordinance. And whosoever holds otherwise, must hold, if they understand themselves, that they are the ministers of the devil, and therefore not to be prayed for, nor approved, in any of their administrations; seeing all things they do, as punishing offenders, and defending their countries, state, and persons, by the sword is unlawful. That it is lawful in a just cause for the deciding of strife, to take an oath by the name of the Lord. Crosby, Hist. of English Baptists, vol. ii. Appendix, pp. 4, 8, 9.

C.*

Page 297.

Art. 24. That it is the will and mind of God, in these gospel times, that all men should have the free liberty of their own conscience in matters of religion or worship, without the least oppression or persecution, as simply upon that account; and that for any in authority, otherwise to act, we confidently believe is expressly contrary to the mind of Christ, who requires that *whatsoever men would that others should do unto them, they should even so do unto others*, Matt. vii. 12, and that the tares and the wheat should grow together in the field, which is the world, until the harvest, which is the end of the world. Matt. xiii. 29, 30, 38, 39.

Art. 25. We believe that there ought to be civil magistrates in all nations, *for the punishment of evil-doers, and for the praise of*

C C

them that do well, 1 Peter ii. 14, and that all wicked lewdness and fleshly filthiness, contrary to just and wholesome (civil) laws, ought to be punished according to the nature of the offences ; and this without respect of any persons, or religion, or profession whatsoever, and that we, and all men, are obliged by gospel rules, *to be subject to the higher powers, to obey magistrates,* Titus iii. 1, *and to submit to every ordinance of man for the Lords sake,* as saith Peter ii. 13.   But in case the civil power do, or shall at any time impose things about matters of religion, which we, through conscience to God, cannot obey, then we, with Peter also, do say, that we ought in such cases *to obey God rather than men,* Acts v. 29.   And accordingly do hereby declare our whole and holy intent and purpose, That through the help of grace we will not yield, and in such cases actually obey them ; yet humbly purposing, in the Lord's strength, patiently to suffer whatsoever shall be inflicted upon us for our conscionable forbearance.   Crosby, vol. ii.   Appendix, pp. 87, 88.

INDEX.

Act of Six Articles, li. repealed, lxii.

Act of Uniformity, 18.

Adam, God's purpose not to condemn without remedy, 171. not created unchangeable, 173. his posterity the same power to evil, but not to good, 173.

Ainsworth, Henry, 387.

Albigenses, crusade against them, 252, n. 6.

Allegiance, of subjects to an excommunicated king, absolved by the pope, 115. oath of, 135.

Allen, cardinal, on Council Lateran, 208, n. 1.

Alphonso di Castro, preaches against persecution, cxx.

Alva, duke of, his persecutions, 77, n. 6. 337.

Anabaptists, condemned in the Articles, xlv. cxiii. Cranmer in commission to search for, l. put to death, lxxii. falsely so called, 101, 231. opinions on magistracy, &c. 179. unjustly charged, 179. order in Council against, 313.

Annates abolished, xxi.

Anne Boleyn, her marriage to Henry, legitimated by Cranmer, xxx. countenances the reformers, xxxvii. beheaded, xl.

Antichrist, denies the coming of Christ in the flesh, 44. persecutes the apostolic church, 45. sits in temple of God, 58. shall be destroyed, 80. is Rome, 159. seeks the power of compelling conscience, 230.

Anti-papal principles in England, xxii.

Apostles, and others appointed to go about to preach the gospel, 133. obeyed not magistrates in things of God, 301. did not propagate the gospel by force, 361.

Arianism, approved by councils of Ephesus and Seleucia, 207, 367.

Army of the commonwealth, its services, 238, 244, 284.

Articles of faith settled, xliv. lxvii. had especial reference to the baptists, cxiii.

Assembly of Divines, questions to, 255, 266. questioned by parliament, 266, n. 7. what claim to the title of "divines," 267. impose the Directory, 268, 277. cannot hinder errors, 275. teach that they are the church, 276. are the only lawgivers, 276. pretend uniformity in religion, 278. maintain tithes, 278. licensers of the press, 279. their slow proceedings, 280.

Augustine, on the incarnation, cviii. on scripture, 202.

Baptism, its true nature, xcviii. necessary after repentance, 158. of church of England from Rome, 159. of bells, 160. of church of England, not true, 162. water, washing, and words, not sufficient, 162. who may baptize, 164, 168. of infants, unscriptural, 169. as administered in 1646, 238.

Baptists, sought for by Cranmer, l. exposed to death, as heretics, lxx. their rise, lxxiii. their opinions, lxxiv. xci. xcviii. cxiii. cxxv. desire liberty of conscience, lxxviii. assailed by Calvin, lxxviii. reject secular authority in the church, lxxxi. their character by Cardinal Hosius, lxxxiii. an example of their persecutions, lxxxiv. their appearance in England, lxxxv. proclamations against, lxxxvii. xci. xciv. martyred, lxxxix. xciii. stigmatized and persecuted by the reformers, xcv. called Pelagians, xcvii. cix. cxxiii. exempted from pardon, cviii. a congregation discovered in Essex and Kent, cix. cxxii. sufferings in James's reign, 185, 190, 211. complaints disregarded, 187. their numbers, 187. desire not liberty from *civil* laws, 192, 338. despise not learning, 214. their loyalty, 230, 338, 356. confession of 1644 on liberty of conscience, 244. suffer for preaching, by ordinance of Long Parliament, 263. inveighed against by Baillie, 267, n. 8. persecuted under Charles II. 291, 293, 294, 299, 313, 317, 328. of Lincolnshire, petition Charles II. 291, 325. of London, address the king, 292, 326. confession of 1660, 292, 297, 300, 391. views on magistracy, lxxix. 298, 300. refuse oath of supremacy, why, 306, 326. apology and protestation against Venner's rebellion, 315, 326. of Lincolnshire, their second address, 316. many disapprove of Cromwell's protectorate,

xxxiv. solicits help from protestant princes and reformers, xxxvii. sets up a spiritual power, xliii. 142. his desire to settle the nation's belief, xliii. xliv. his attempt at sovereignty over conscience, liii. on the progress made in reformation, lvi. sends an embassy to Smalcalde, xc. obtains title of Defender of the Faith, 365.

Herbert, a notable speech preserved by, xiv.

Heresy, statutes against it, amended, xxxi. great numbers persecuted for, xxxvi. adjudged by scripture by royal command, xxxvii. punished with death by reformers, lxx. made treason, c. not destroyed by fire and sword, 22. saints in all ages put to death for, 303.

Heretics burnt by Henry VIII. and Mary, 55. at instigation of their bishops, 55.

High commission, court of, 134.

Hilary, condemns persecution, 218.

Hitton, Thomas, burnt, xxxvi.

H. N. founder of Family of Love, 385.

Hodgkin, Samuel, replies to Jeremiah Ives, on oaths, 329, n. 1.

Holy Spirit, the interpreter of scripture, 197. given to all that fear God, 199. for the most part, given to the poor and unlearned, 200.

Homilies, book of, lx.

Hooker, calls Rome, "a limb of the visible church," 46, n. 2.

Hooper, John, lxii. lxviii. cxix.

Hosius, cardinal, president of Council of Trent, his character of the baptists, lxxxiii. quoted, 204.

House of Commons, limits papal immunities, xiii. complains of grievances, xxi. remonstrates against the clergy, xxiii. xxiv. summoned and addressed by the king, xxviii. confirms the submission of the clergy, xxxii. memorable session of, in 1620, 186.

Huguenots, enjoy liberty of conscience, 336.

"Humble Supplication for Toleration," quoted, 223, n. 9.

Huss, John, burnt for heresy, 253.

Hutchinson, Roger, cv. cvii. cxxvi.

Hypocrisy, produced by compulsion of conscience, 139, 261, 332.

Idolaters, not to be put to death, 305.

Images, "representers of virtue," xlv. forbidden and destroyed, 65.

Incarnation of Christ, Joan Boucher's views on, civ. cvii. baptists' sentiments on, 179, 390.

Infant-baptism, said to be necessary to remission of sins, xlv. exorcism employed in, lxiv. denial of it, heretical, lxx. maintained by Philpot, cxxiv. unscriptural, 169. variations in those maintaining it, 170. asserters of it engaged in Venner's rebellion, 316.

Infants, not condemned for Adam's transgression, 171.

Innocent, pope, at Council of Lateran, 207.

"Institution of a Christian man," published, xlvii.

Israel, kings of, interfered in religion, 91. their example no authority in the Christian church, 99, 124, 226, 372. proportion between the gospel and, 123. Christ king of, 125, 126. kingdom of gospel not the same as the kingdom of, 126. compelled men to serve the Lord, answered, 272, 305. had Urim and Thummim to guide them, 374. ruined by state-policy, 376.

Ives, Jeremiah, 329, n. 1.

Jacob, Henry, 237.

James I., calls Rome, "our mother church," 46, n. 2. the profligacy of his reign, 67, n. 5. 70. his prerogative advanced by Cowell and Blackwood, 71, n. 1. not a blood-thirsty man, 97. entreated not to persecute, 97. confesses God only can change the mind, 97. quoted, 6, 99, 109, 124. says the church is not planted by bloodshed, 100. on the two witnesses, 128. n. 2. his reception on coming to the crown, 131. his explanation of oath of allegiance, 137. his intolerance, 137, n. 9. testimonies against persecution from his writings, 140, 190, 216, 227, 231, 334, 380. assembles parliament in 1620, 186. his speech, 186. on the laws of Moses, their non-obligation, 228.

Jeffrey, William, 294, 295, 308, 345, 350.

Jeroboam, king of Israel, ruined by state-policy, 376.

Jerome, condemns persecution, 220.

Jerome of Prague, burnt for heresy, 253.

Jessey, Henry, 237.

Jesuits, maintain the pope's deposing power, 115. n. 2. instigate the murder of Henry IV. 138, n. 3. seek to establish religion by blood, 225.

Jewel, bishop, countenances punishing heresy with death, lxxii.

Jews, if persecuted cannot be converted, 28. persecuted in Spain and Portugal, 30. expelled by Ferdinand and Isabella, 31, n. 4. kept back from God's word by persecution, 47. their unbelief removed, if liberty of conscience be allowed them, 71, n. 9. conversion to be waited for, 120. not to be put to death as blasphemers, 123, 305, 375. resist the truth, 205.

John Palsgrave, against oppression of conscience, 69, n. 7.

Johnson, Francis, quoted 29, n. 2. regards Rome as a true church, 73.

John VIII. pope, 367.

John X. pope, 367.

Jurisdiction of bishops, suspended by the king, xxxviii. restored on their entreaty, xxxix.

D D

ERRATA.

Page lxxv.   In note 5, line 2, ... for *cœlo*, read *cœlo.*

,,   ,,   4, ... for *cœlorum*, read *cœlorum.*

lxxix. note 3, last line but two, for *presently*, read *subsequently.*

297, note 1, ... for *Note C.*, read *Note C.**

308, note .... for *Signs for Sion*, read *Sion's Grouns.*

364, note 7, add, [A Supplement to the Serious Consideration of the Oath
of the King's Supremacy, &c., by John Tombes, B.D.,
London, 1660, 4to. pp. 41.]

LONDON:
J. HADDON, PRINTER, CASTLE STREET, FINSBURY.

A
BIOGRAPHICAL SKETCH
OF
EDWARD BEAN UNDERHILL
(1813-1901)

BY

JOHN FRANKLIN JONES

A
BIOGRAPHICAL SKETCH
OF
EDWARD BEAN UNDERHILL
(1813-1901)

Edward Bean Underhill—Baptist, missionary statesman, historian—was born at Oxford, England October 4, 1813. He was reared under the influence of the New Road Baptist Church, Oxford, during tenure of its pastor, James Hinton. Schooled in Hinton's school, Underhill was converted at age sixteen and united with the New Road church in 1831 (*DEB*).

He married Sophia Collingwood, the daughter of Samuel Collingwood, a printer of Oxford, and worked in the grocery business in Oxford for fifteen years. He moved to Avening, Gloucestershire to study Baptist history (*DEB*).

Underhill was appointed joint secretary of the Baptist Missionary Society in 1849 along with Brederick Trestrial. He devoted the first five years in that position to restoring Baptist confidence in the agency and to rebuilding its finances (*DEB*). He was sole secretary of BMS 1869-1876 (B)

He spent October 1854 to 1856 revitalizing the work in India, the primary field of BMS. His work there resulted in initiating greater self-sufficiency among the churches (*DEB*).

He visited the West Indies (1859-60) and later published his conclusions in *The West Indies: their Social and Religious Condition* (1862). He advocated relief for the former slaves in Jamaica and wrote a letter indicating same to Edward Cardwell, Secretary of State for the Colonies. The publication in Jamaica of that letter fomented protest meetings, called "Underhill meetings" and was associated with an unrest climaxing in the Morant Bay uprising, which was brutally suppressed by Governor Eyre (*DEB*).

Underhill retired from the BMS in 1876 but served as honorary secretary till his death. He also
served as treasurer of the Bible Translation Society (after 1876); treasurer of Regent's Park College; and was elected president of the Baptist Union (1873). He was awarded an honorary LL.D. by Rochester University in 1870 (*DEB*).

Underhill's interest in Baptist history spawned the Hanserd Knollys Society in 1845, and he became its first secretary. In that society, he edited seven of the ten volumes on early Baptist texts published by the Society and published biographies of James Phillippo, Alfred Saker, John Wenger, Edward Steane, and other missionary texts (*DEB*).

Underhill edited and authored several books. He edited *The Bloudy Tenent of Persecution for Cause of Conscience Discussed and Mr. Cotton's Letter Examined and Answered by Roger Williams* (1848). His edition of *Confessions of Faith and other Public Documents illustrative of the History of the Baptist Churches of England in the Seventeenth Century* (1854) contains the reprints of seven Baptist Confessions dating from 1611 to 1688, Collins Baptist Catechism, and several letters/documents from the early history of the Baptists in England (CCEL).

Underhill authored *The West Indies: Their Social and Religious Condition* (1861, 1862, 1970); *Dr. Underhill's Letter: A Letter Addressed to the Rt Honourable E Cardwell, with Illustrative Documents on the Condition of Jamaica and an explanatory statement* (1866); *Life of James Mursell Phillippo, Missionary in Jamaica* (1887); *The Tragedy of Morant Bay: A Narrative of the Disturbances in the Island of Jamaica in 1865* (1865; 1895, reprint; 1971; reprint, 1997);

and *Tracts on Liberty of Conscience and Persecution, 1614-1661, with an Historical Introduction* (1846, 1966) (B).

With John Turland Brown, he wrote *Emancipation in the West Indies. Two Addresses by EB Underhill and JT Brown, the Deputation from the Baptist Missionary Society to the West Indies* (1861). With Richard F. Burton, he authored *Alfred Saker, Missionary to Africa: A Biography* (1884) (B).

He died in London, May 11, 1901 (*DEB*).

BIBLIOGRAPHY

Dictionary of Evangelical Biography, 1730-1860. S.v. "Underhill, Edward Bean," by Brian Stanley.

http://www.books.ai/8th/U.htm. Accessed June 15, 2006. (Cited as B).

http://www.ccel.org/ccel/schaff/creeds1.x.vi.html. Accessed July 4, 2006. (Cited as CCEL).

BY JOHN FRANKLIN JONES
CORDOVA, TENNESSEE
JULY 2006

THE BAPTIST STANDARD BEARER, INC.

a non-profit, tax-exempt corporation
committed to the Publication & Preservation
of the Baptist Heritage.

———◆◈◆———

CURRENT TITLES AVAILABLE IN
THE BAPTIST *DISTINCTIVES* SERIES

CARSON, ALEXANDER   Ecclesiastical Polity of the New Testament. (Dublin: William Carson, 1856).

BOOTH, ABRAHAM   A Defense of the Baptists. A Declaration and Vindication of Three Historically Distinctive Baptist Principles. Compiled and Set Forth in the Republication of Three Books. Revised edition. (Paris, AR: The Baptist Standard Bearer, Inc., 2006).

BOOTH, ABRAHAM   Paedobaptism Examined on the Principles, Concessions, and Reasonings of the Most Learned Paedobaptists. With Replies to the Arguments and Objections of Dr. Williams and Mr. Peter Edwards. 3 volumes. (London: Ebenezer Palmer, 1829).

CARROLL, B. H.   *Ecclesia* - The Church. With an Appendix. (Louisville: Baptist Book Concern, 1903).

CHRISTIAN, JOHN T.   Immersion, The Act of Christian Baptism. (Louisville: Baptist Book Concern, 1891).

FROST, J. M.   Pedobaptism: Is It From Heaven Or Of Men? (Philadelphia: American Baptist Publication Society, 1875).

FULLER, RICHARD   Baptism, and the Terms of Communion; An Argument. (Charleston, SC: Southern Baptist Publication Society, 1854).

GRAVES, J. R.   Tri-Lemma: or, Death By Three Horns. The Presbyterian General Assembly Not Able To Decide This Question: "Is Baptism In The Romish Church Valid?" 1st Edition.

	(Nashville: Southwestern Publishing House, 1861).
MELL, P.H.	Baptism In Its Mode and Subjects. (Charleston, SC: Southern Baptist Publications Society, 1853).
JETER, JEREMIAH B.	Baptist Principles Reset. Consisting of Articles on Distinctive Baptist Principles by Various Authors. With an Appendix. (Richmond: The Religious Herald Co., 1902).
PENDLETON, J.M.	Distinctive Principles of Baptists. (Philadelphia: American Baptist Publication Society, 1882).
THOMAS, JESSE B.	The Church and the Kingdom. A New Testament Study. (Louisville: Baptist Book Concern, 1914).
WALLER, JOHN L.	Open Communion Shown to be Unscriptural & Deleterious. With an introductory essay by Dr. D. R. Campbell and an Appendix. (Louisville: Baptist Book Concern, 1859).

For a complete list of current authors/titles, visit our internet site at:
www.standardbearer.org
or write us at:

The Baptist Standard Bearer, Inc.

NUMBER ONE IRON OAKS DRIVE • PARIS, ARKANSAS 72855

TEL # 479-963-3831   *FAX # 479-963-8083*
EMAIL: Baptist@centurytel.net   http://www.standardbearer.org

Thou hast given a standard to them that fear thee; that it may be displayed because of the truth. — Psalm 60:4

www.ingramcontent.com/pod-product-compliance
Lightning Source LLC
Chambersburg PA
CBHW020329270326
41926CB00007B/104